# Datsun Pick-up Automotive Repair Manual

## by J H Haynes

Member of the Guild of Motoring Writers

## and Peter Ward

**Models covered**

**USA:**
Datsun pick-up, 620 Series. 97.3 cu in (1595 cc) ohc
Datsun pick-up, 620 Series. 108 cu in (1770 cc) ohc
Datsun pick-up, 620 Series. 119.1 cu in (1952 cc) ohc

**UK:**
Datsun 1 ton pick-up. 1483 cc (90.5 cu in) ohv

**Other territories:**
Datsun pick-up, 620 Series. 1299 cc (79.3 cu in) ohv

*Covers standard and long bed models, plus Double pick-up and King Cab (deluxe) versions.*

**ISBN O 85696 643 6**

© **Haynes North America, Inc.**   1976, 1981, 1984, 1986

With permission from J. H. Haynes & Co. Ltd.

ABCDE
FG

2

Printed in the USA        *(1X5 - 277)*

**Haynes Publishing Group**
Sparkford Nr Yeovil
Somerset BA22 7JJ England

**Haynes North America, Inc**
861 Lawrence Drive
Newbury Park
California 91320 USA

# Acknowledgements

Thanks are due to the Nissan Motor Company Limited of Japan for The provision of technical information and certain illustrations. Castrol Limited supplied lubrication data.

*Car mechanics* magazine supplied many of the photographs used in the bodywork repair Section of Chapter 12.

Tor View Garage, Glastonbury, Somerset very kindly loaned us the Datsun pick-up featured in many of the photographs throughout this manual, Peter Knowles was particularly helpful.

Lastly, thanks to all of those at Sparkford who helped in the production of this manual. Particularly, Brian Horsfall and Les Brazier, who carried out the mechanical work and took the photographs respectively; Ted Frenchum who planned the layout of each page and Rod Grainger the editor.

# Introduction to the Datsun 620 Pick-up

This manual covers the Datsun 620 pick-up and its variants.

This pick-up is available in a long or standard, wheelbase form: the difference being in the pick-up bed length. The body is bolted to a ladder type chassis; the crossmembers being welded to the two longitudinal members. From mid 1976 onwards a 'King Cab' (deluxe) version of the pick-up is available for certain markets. This uses the long wheelbase chassis, the standard wheelbase bed, and an extended version of the standard cab. The extended cab has over 11 cubic feet of storage space behind the twin reclining seats.

A double pick-up, which is virtually a passenger car with a small cargo bed at the rear, is also manufactured for some markets. This model utilizes an integral body frame built on passenger car principles.

Apart from being left or right-hand drive, all Datsun pick-up models are practically identical for all markets when viewed from the outside or the driver's seat. However, vehicles manufactured for the USA have a wider range of accessories available, and later models have a sophisticated emission control system to limit the polutants emitted to the atmosphere.

Models manufactured for the USA have an overhead camshaft, Datsun L-series engine which is also used in several Datsun passenger cars. For 1973 this engine was of 1595 cc (97.3 cu in) capacity, was increased to 1770 cc (108 cu in) for 1974 and then increased again to 1952 cc (119.1 cu in) for 1975/1979. The UK model of the Datsun pick-up (introduced in 1976) uses the Datsun J-series overhead valve engine which is very similar to the British Leyland (BLMC) A-series engine. A 1483 cc (90.5 cu in) engine is used for the British version, but some models for other markets use a 1299 cc (79.3 cu in) engine.

On all models drive to the rear axle is through a two-piece propeller shaft from a floorshift four or five forward speed synchromesh transmission. Certain models are available with a column-shift arrangement, and a three speed automatic transmission can be supplied for USA models. Clutch and brake systems are both hydraulically operated.

On 1977 through 1979 models, most specifications and procedures given for the 1976 model can be used. Refer to Chapter 13 for differences.

# About this manual

*Its aims*

The aim of this book is to help you get the best value from your vehicle. It can do so in two ways. First it can help you decide what work must be done (even should you choose to get it done by a garage), the routine maintenance, and the diagnosis and of course action when random faults occur. However, it is hoped that you will also use the second and fuller purpose by tackling the work yourself. On the simpler jobs it may even be quicker than booking the vehicle into a garage and going there twice, to leave and collect it. Perhaps most important, much money can be saved by avoiding the costs a garage must charge to cover their labour and overheads.

The book has drawings and descriptions to show the function of the various components so that their layout can be understood. Then the tasks are described and photographed in a step-by-step sequence so that even a novice can cope with complicated work. Such a person is the very one to buy a vehicle needing repair yet be unable to afford garage costs.

The jobs are described assuming only normal tools are available, and not special tools. But a reasonable outfit of tools will be a worthwhile investment. Many special workshop tools produced by the makers merely speed the work, and in these cases guidance is given as how to do the job without them, the oft quoted example being the use of a large hose clip to compress the piston rings for insertion in the cylinder. But on a very few occasions the special tool is essential to prevent damage to components, then its use is described. Though it might be possible to borrow the tool, such work may have to be entrusted to the official agent.

The manufacturer's official workshop manuals are written for their trained staff, and so assume special knowledge; detail is left out. This book is written for the owner, and so goes into detail.

*Using the manual*

The book is devided into twelve Chapters. Each Chapter is devided into numbered Sections which are headed in **bold type** between horizontal lines. Each Section consists of serially numbered paragraphs.

There are two types of illustration: (1) Figures which are numbered according to Chapter and sequence of occurrence in that Chapter. (2) Photographs which have a reference number on their caption. All photographs apply to the Chapter in which they occur so that the reference figure pinpoint the pertinent Section and paragraph number.

Procedures, once described in the test, are not normally repeated. If it is necessary to refer to another Chapter the reference will be given.

When the left or right side of the vehicle is mentioned it is as if looking forward from the rear.

Great effort has been made to ensure that this book is complete and up-to-date. However, it should be noted that manufacturers continually modify their vehicles even in retrospect.

Whilst every care is taken to ensure that the information in this manual is correct no liability can be accepted by the authors or publishers for loss, damage or injury caused by any errors in, or omissions from, the information given.

# Contents

Datsun 620 (Li'l Hustler) Pick-up - North American specification

Datsun 1-ton (620 Series) Pick-up - UK specification

# Buying spare parts
# and vehicle identification numbers

## Buying spare parts

Replacement parts are available from many sources, which generally fall into one of two categories – authorized dealer parts departments and independent retail auto parts stores. Our advice concerning these parts is as follows:

*Retail auto parts stores*: Good auto parts stores will stock frequently needed components which wear out relatively fast, such as clutch components, exhaust systems, brake parts, tune-up parts, etc. These stores often supply new or reconditioned parts on an exchange basis, which can save a considerable amount of money. Discount auto parts stores are often very good places to buy materials and parts needed for general vehicle maintenance such as oil, grease, filters, spark plugs, belts, touch-up paint, bulbs, etc. They also usually sell tools and general accessories, have convenient hours, charge lower prices and can often be found not far from home.

*Authorized dealer parts department*: This is the best source for parts which are unique to the vehicle and not generally available elsewhere (such as major engine parts, transmission parts, trim pieces, etc.).

*Warranty information*: If the vehicle is still covered under warranty, be sure that any replacement parts purchased – regardless of the source – do not invalidate the warranty!

To be sure of obtaining the correct parts, have engine and chassis numbers available and, if possible, take the old parts along for positive identification.

## Vehicle identification numbers

Modifications are a continuing and unpublished process in vehicle manufacture quite apart from major model changes. Spare parts manuals and lists are compiled on a numerical basis, the individual vehicle numbers being essential to correct identification of the component required.

The illustration shows the position of various identification plates and labels; in addition, a *vehicle loading plate* is attached to the inside of the passenger door on UK models (photo).

The *engine number* is stamped on the right side of the engine cylinder block and is prefixed by the engine type number.

The *chassis number* is stamped on the front upper face of the left side member for right–hand drive models, or on the right side member for left–hand drive models. It is prefixed by the vehicle type number.

The *manual transmission number* is stamped on the top of the clutch bellhousing, the automatic transmission number is stamped on the right side of the transmission case.

The *steering gearbox number* is stamped on the top cover plate.

The *rear axle model and unit number* will be found on the rear of the differential cover.

The *front axle number* is stamped on the front face of the left and right lower suspension arms.

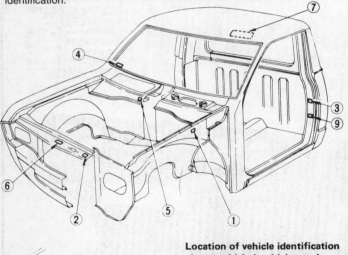

**Location of vehicle identification plates and labels which may be installed**

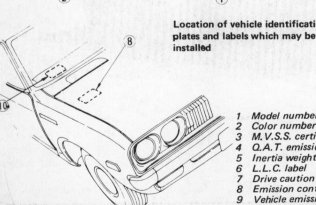

1   Model number plate
2   Color number label
3   M.V.S.S. certificate label
4   Q.A.T. emission level sticker (California)
5   Inertia weight label
6   L.L.C. label
7   Drive caution label (on sun visor, California)
8   Emission control system label
9   Vehicle emission control information label
10   Auto-choke instruction label (in glove box)

**NISSAN MOTOR COMPANY TOKYO**

| | |
|---|---|
| VEHICLE TYPE | 620 PICK UP |
| ENGINE TYPE | J 15   ENGINE POWER   73 HP (DIN) |
| CHASSIS NUMBER | 3-72 05- |
| NUMBER OF AXLES | 2 |
| MAX. AXLE WEIGHTS FRONT | 690 KG |
| REAR | 1560 KG |
| MAX. GROSS WEIGHT | 2210 KG |
| MAX. TRAIN WEIGHT | |

**Vehicle ordering plate for UK models**

# Routine maintenance

Maintenance is essential for ensuring safety, and desirable for the purpose of getting the best in terms of performance and economy from the vehicle. Over the years the need for periodic lubrication - oiling, greasing and so on - has been drastically reduced if not totally eliminated. This has unfortunately tended to lead some owners to think that because no such action is required, the items either no longer exist or will last for ever. This is a serious delusion. It follows therefore that the largest initial element of maintenance is visual examination. This may lead to repairs or renewal.

### Jacking and towing

Before carrying out any servicing or repair operations, make sure that you know where to position the jack and axle stands. It is most important to use only the specified points in order to prevent accidents and damage to the vehicle itself.

If the vehicle breaks down or becomes bogged down, a front mounted towing hook is provided to which a tow rope may be attached. No rear hook is provided but a tow rope can be attached to the rear suspension leaf spring shackle.

On vehicles equipped with automatic transmission, the towing speed should not exceed 20 mph (30 km/h) nor the towing distance 6 miles (10 km) otherwise the transmission may be damaged due to lack of lubrication. If towing distances are excessive, disconnect the propeller shaft from the rear axle pinion flange and tie the shaft up out of the way.

### Spare wheel

The spare wheel is mounted in a larger assembly beneath the rear cargo bed. To lower it, insert the crankhandle and turn it counter-clockwise; installation is the reverse of this procedure.

### Maintenance schedule

In the following Sections the 'essential for safety' items are shown in **bold type**. These **must** be attended to at the regular frequencies shown in order to avoid the possibility of accidents and loss of life. Other neglect results in unreliability, increased running costs, more rapid wear and more rapid depreciation of the vehicle in general.

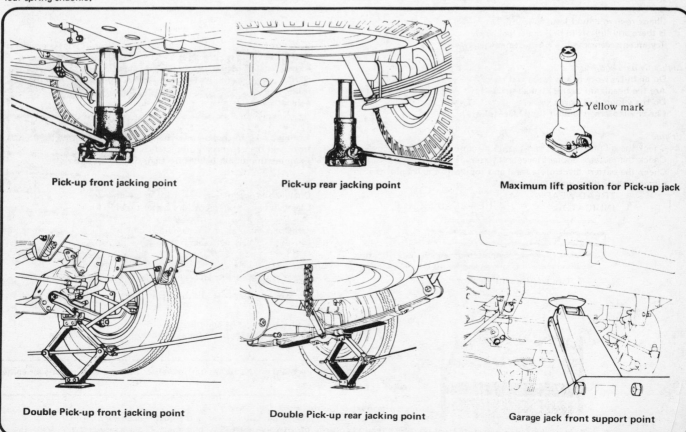

Pick-up front jacking point

Pick-up rear jacking point

Yellow mark

Maximum lift position for Pick-up jack

Double Pick-up front jacking point

Double Pick-up rear jacking point

Garage jack front support point

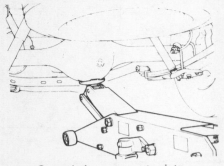

Garage jack rear support points

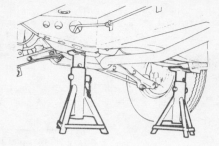

Axle stand front support points

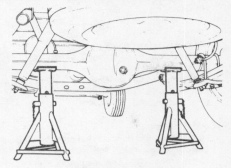

Axle stand rear support points

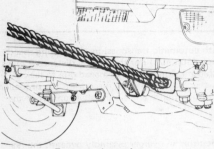

Front towing point

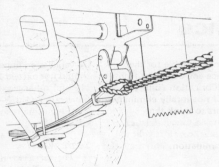

Rear towing point

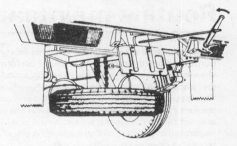

Spare wheel removal

---

**Every 250 miles (400 km) travelled or weekly - whichever comes first**

*Steering*
Check the tire pressure.
Examine tires for wear or damage.
Is steering smooth and accurate?

*Brakes*
Check reservoir fluid level (photo).
Is there any fall-off in braking efficiency?
Try an emergency stop - is adjustment necessary?

*Lights, wipers and horns*
Do all bulbs work at the front and rear?
Are the headlamp beams aligned properly?
Do the wipers and horns work?
Check windscreen washer fluid level (photo).

*Engine*
Check the oil pan oil level and top-up if required (photo).
Check the radiator coolant level and top-up if required.
Check the battery electrolyte level and top-up to the level of the plates with distilled water as needed.

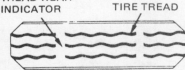

TREAD WEAR INDICATOR          TIRE TREAD

Tire tread wear indicator

Checking battery electrolyte level

---

**Every 3000 miles (5000 km) travelled, or 3 months, whichever comes first**

*Steering*
Examine all steering linkage rods, joints and bushes for signs of wear or damage.
Check tightness of steering box mounting bolts.
Check the steering box oil level.

*Brakes*
Examine brake shoes to determine the amount of friction material left. Renew if necessary.
Examine all hydraulic pipes, cylinders and unions for signs of chafing, or corrosion, dents or any other form of deterioration or leaks.
Adjust brakes.

*Suspension*
Examine all nuts, bolts and shackles securing the suspension units, front and rear. Tighten if necessary.
Examine the rubber bushes for signs of wear and play.

*Engine*
Change oil (photo).
Clean air cleaner element (dry paper type).

*Transmission (manual and automatic)*
Check oil level and top-up if necessary (photo).

*Clutch*
Check fluid reservoir level and top up if necessary (photo).
Check pedal travel.

*Body*
Lubricate all locks and hinges.
Check that water drain holes at bottom of doors are clear.

---

**Every 6000 miles (10000 km) travelled, or 6 months, whichever comes first**

*Engine*
Check fan belt tension and adjust if necessary.
Check valve clearances and adjust if necessary.

Renew oil filter (photo).
Clean and adjust distributor contact breaker points (except California 1976).
Clean and adjust spark plugs.
Check condition of distributor cap, rotor and leads.
Lubricate distributor.
Lubricate carburetor.linkate.
Check dwell angle/ignition timing.
Check idle speed.

*Steering/suspension*
Rotate roadwheels and rebalance if necessary.
Lubricate suspension and steering grease points (photo).
Check front wheel bearing play.

*Rear axle*
Check oil level and top-up if necessary (photo).

*Body*
Check tightness of body mounting points.

## Every 12000 miles (20000 km) travelled, or 12 months, whichever comes first

*Engine*
Arrange for your Datsun dealer to check the operation of the emission control system(s) (as applicable).
Replace distributor contact breaker points.
Replace spark plugs.

*Transmission*
Check security of propeller shaft bolts.

*Steering/suspension*
Lubricate steering idler arm.
Lubricate front wheel bearings.
Check wheel alignment.
Check vehicle trim height.

*Brakes*
Renew brake fluid.

## Every 24000 miles (40000 km) travelled, or 24 months, whichever comes first

*Engine*
Flush cooling system and renew antifreeze mixture.
Renew air cleaner element.
Replace fuel filter.

*Transmission*
Change oil in manual transmission (photo).
Check for wear in propeller shaft points.

*Rear axle*
Change oil.

## Every 48000 miles (20000 km) travelled, or 48 months, whichever comes first

*Brakes*
Renew all the hoses and seals in the braking system.

Checking brake fluid reservoir level

Windscreen washer reservoir

Topping-up engine oil - typical

Engine oil pan drain plug - typical

Filler/level plug on manual transmission

Clutch master cylinder

Using a chain wrench to remove an oil filter - typical

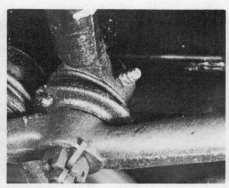

Steering linkage grease nipple

Rear axle filler/level and drain plugs

Transmission drain plug

**Additionally the following items should be attended to as time can be spared**

*Cleaning*

Examination of components requires that they be cleaned. The same applies to the body of the car, inside and out, in order that deterioration due to rust or unknown damage may be detected. Certain parts of the body frame, if rusted badly, can result in the vehicle being declared unsafe and it will not pass the annual test for roadworthiness.

*Exhaust system*

An exhaust system must be leak proof, and the noise level below a certain minimum. Excessive leaks may cause carbon monoxide fumes to enter the passenger compartment. Excessive noise constitutes a public nuisance. Both these faults may cause the vehicle to be kept off the road. Repair or replace defective sections when symptoms are apparent.

# Recommended lubricants and fluids

| Component | Type | Castrol product |
|---|---|---|
| Engine (1) ... ... ... ... ... | Multigrade engine oil ... ... ... | Castrol GTX * |
| Manual transmission (2) ... ... ... | SAE 90EP gear oil ... ... ... | Castrol Hypoy * |
| Automatic transmission (2) ... ... | Dexron ... ... ... | Castrol TQ Dexron ® |
| Rear axle (differential) (3) ... ... ... | SAE 90EP gear oil ... ... ... | Castrol Hypoy B * |
| Steering gearbox ... ... ... ... | SAE 90EP gear oil ... ... ... | Castrol Hypoy * |
| Wheel bearings (4) ... ... ... ... | General purpose lithium based grease ... | Castrol LM Grease |
| Chassis lubrication ... ... ... ... ... | General purpose lithium based grease ... | Castrol LM Grease |
| Brake and clutch master cylinders (5) ... | DOT 3 (MVSS 116) or SAE J1703C ... | Castrol Girling Universal Brake and Clutch Fluid |
| Cooling system (6) ... ... ... | Ethylene glycol based antifreeze ... ... | Castrol Antifreeze |

*These oils are for use in temperate climates. Where the vehicle is operated in very high or very low temperatures, consult your Datsun dealer for a suitable alternative. In addition, engine oil or light lubricating oil (eg: Castrol Everyman Oil) may be used to lubricate hinges, pivot pins, carburetor linkage, lock mechanisms, etc. General purpose grease should be used for exposed items such as tailgate catches and spare wheel hanger assembly.*

# Chapter 1: Part A Overhead camshaft engines

## Contents

1A

## Specifications

### Engine application
| | | |
|---|---|---|
| 1973 models ... ... ... ... ... ... ... ... | L16 |
| 1974 models ... ... ... ... ... ... ... ... | L18 |
| 1975/76 models ... ... ... ... ... ... ... | L20B |

### Engine (general)
Engine type ... ... ... ... ... ... ... ... Four cylinder, in-line overhead camshaft (ohc)

| | L16 | L18 | L20B |
|---|---|---|---|
| Displacement ... ... ... ... ... ... ... | 97.3 cu.in (1595 cc) | 108.0 cu.in (1770 cc) | 119.1 cu.in (1952 cc) |
| Bore ... ... ... ... ... ... ... | 3.27 in (83.0 mm) | 3.35 in (85.0 mm) | 3.35 in (85.0 mm) |
| Stroke ... ... ... ... ... ... ... | 2.90 in (73.7 mm) | 3.07 in (78.0 mm) | 3.39 in (86.0 mm) |
| Compression ratio ... ... ... ... ... | 8.5 : 1 | 8.5 : 1 | 8.5 : 1 |

Firing order ... ... ... ... ... ... ... 1 - 3 - 4 - 2 (No 1 cylinder nearest radiator)
Oil pressure (warm) @ 2000 rpm ... ... ... ... 50 to 57 lb f/sq. in (3.5 to 4.0 kg f/sq. cm)
Oil capacity ... ... ... ... ... ... ... 9 US pt/7½ Imp. pt (4.3 litres)
Oil type ... ... ... ... ... ... ... ... See lubrication chart

Cylinder location and distributor rotation

### Crankshaft
Journal diameter ... ... ... ... ... ... ... 2.3599 to 2.3604 in (59.942 to 59.955 mm)
Max. taper or out-of-round ... ... ... ... ... 0.0004 in (0.01 mm)
Crankshaft end-play ... ... ... ... ... ... 0.0020 to 0.0071 in (0.05 to 0.18 mm)
Max. crankshaft end-play ... ... ... ... ... 0.0118 in (0.3 mm)
Crankpin diameter ... ... ... ... ... ... 1.966 to 1.967 in (49.961 to 49.974 mm)

Max. taper or out-of-round ... ... ... ... ... ... ...     0.0004 in (0.01 mm)
Main bearing thickness (standard) ... ... ... ... ... ...     0.0719 to 0.0722 in (1.827 to 1.835 mm)
Main bearing clearance ... ... ... ... ... ... ...     0.0008 to 0.0024 in (0.020 to 0.062 mm)
Max. main bearing clearance ... ... ... ... ... ...     0.0047 in (0.12 mm)
Max. permissible crankshaft bend ... ... ... ... ...     0.0020 in (0.05 mm)

## Camshaft

Journal diameter ... ... ... ... ... ... ...     1.8877 to 1.8883 in (47.949 to 47.962 mm)
Bearing inner diameter ... ... ... ... ... ... ...     1.8898 to 1.8904 in (48.000 to 48.016 mm)
Journal to bearing clearance ... ... ... ... ... ...     0.0015 to 0.0026 in (0.038 to 0.067 mm)
Max. permissible camshaft bend ... ... ... ... ...     0.0007 in (0.02 mm)
Camshaft end-play ... ... ... ... ... ... ...     0.0032 to 0.0150 in (0.08 to 0.38 mm)
Camshaft lobe lift:
   Inlet ... ... ... ... ... ... ... ... ...     0.276 in (7.0 mm)
   Exhaust ... ... ... ... ... ... ... ...     0.276 in (7.0 mm)

## Pistons

|  | L16 | L18 and L20B |
|---|---|---|
| Piston dia (standard) | 3.2671 to 3.2691 in (82.985 to 83.035 mm) | 3.3451 to 3.3470 in (84.965 to 85.015 mm) |
| Piston dia. (oversize 0.0197 in/0.50 mm) | 3.2860 to 3.2880 in (83.465 to 83.515 mm) | 3.3648 to 3.3667 in (85 465 to 85.515 mm) |
| Piston dia. (oversize 0.0394 in/1.00 mm) | 3.3057 to 3.3077 in (83.965 to 84.015 mm) | 3.3844 to 3.3864 in (85.965 to 86.015 mm) |
| Piston to bore clearance | 0.0010 to 0.0018 in (0.025 to 0.045 mm) | |
| Piston ring groove widths: | | |
|   Top compression | 0.0787 in (2.0 mm) | 0.0799 to 0.0807 in (2.030 to 2.050 mm) |
|   Second compression | 0.0787 in (2.0 mm) | 0.0795 to 0.0803 in (2.020 to 2.040 mm) |
|   Oil control | 0.1575 in (4.0 mm) | 0.1581 to 0.1591 in (4.015 to 4.040 mm) |

## Piston rings

|  | L16 | L18 and L20B |
|---|---|---|
| Thickness: | | |
|   Top compression | 0.0788 in (1.977 mm) | 0.0778 to 0.0783 in (1.977 to 1.990 mm) |
|   Second compression | 0.0778 in (1.977 mm) | 0.0776 to 0.0783 in (1.970 to 1.990 mm) |
| Clearance in groove: | | |
|   Top compression | 0.0016 to 0.0031 in (0.040 to 0.080 mm) | 0.0016 to 0.0029 in (0.040 to 0.073 mm) |
|   Second compression | 0.0012 to 0.0028 in (0.030 to 0.070 mm) | 0.0012 to 0.0028 in (0.030 to 0.070 mm) |
| Piston ring end gap: | | |
|   Top compression | 0.0098 to 0.0157 in (0.25 to 0.040 mm) | 0.0098 to 0.0157 in (0.25 to 0.040 mm) |
|   Second compression | 0.0059 to 0.0118 in (0.15 to 0.30 mm) | 0.0118 to 0.0197 in (0.30 to 0.50 mm) |
|   Oil control | 0.0118 to 0.0354 in (0.30 to 0.90 mm) | 0.0118 to 0.0354 in (0.30 to 0.90 mm) |

## Piston pins (gudgeon pins)

Diameter ... ... ... ... ... ... ... ... ...     0.8265 to 0.8268 in (20.993 to 21.000 mm)
Length ... ... ... ... ... ... ... ... ... ...     2.8445 to 2.8740 in (72.25 to 73.00 mm)
Pin to piston clearance ... ... ... ... ... ... ...     0.0001 to 0.0006 in (0.003 to 0.015 mm)
Pin to connecting rod bushing (interference fit) ... ... ...     0.0006 to 0.0013 in (0.015 to 0.033 mm)

## Connecting rods

|  | L16 | L18 | L20B |
|---|---|---|---|
| Distance between centres of small-end and connecting rod (big-end) bearings | 5.25 in (133.0 mm) | 5.132 in (130.35 mm) | 5.748 in (146.0 mm) |
| Bearing thickness | 0.0588 to 0.0593 in (1.493 to 1.506 mm) | | |
| Side play | 0.0079 to 0.0118 in (0.20 to 0.30 mm) | | |
| Bearing clearance | 0.0010 to 0.0022 in (0.025 to 0.055 mm) | | |

## Valves

Clearance
  Cold:
    Intake ... ... ... ... ... ... ... ...     0.008 in (0.20 mm)
    Exhaust ... ... ... ... ... ... ...     0.010 in (0.25 mm)
  Warm:
    Intake ... ... ... ... ... ... ... ...     0.010 in (0.25 mm)
    Exhaust ... ... ... ... ... ... ...     0.012 in (0.30 mm)

| | L16 | L18 | L20B |
|---|---|---|---|
| Valve head diameter: | | | |
|   Intake   ...   ...   ...   ...   ...   ... | 1.6535 in (42.00 mm) | 1.650 to 1.657 in (41.9 to 42.1 mm) | 1.654 to 1.661 in (42.0 to 42.2 mm) |
|   Exhaust  ...   ...   ...   ...   ...   ... | 1.2992 in (33.00 mm) | 1.378 to 1.386 in (35.0 to 35.2 mm) | 1.378 to 1.386 in (35.0 to 35.2 mm) |

| | |
|---|---|
| Valve stem diameter: | |
|   Intake  ... ... ... ... ... ... ... ... | 0.3136 to 0.3142 in (7.965 to 7.980 mm) |
|   Exhaust  ... ... ... ... ... ... ... ... | 0.3128 to 0.3134 in (7.945 to 7.960 mm) |
| Valve length: | |
|   Intake  ... ... ... ... ... ... ... ... | 4.524 to 4.535 in (114.9 to 115.2 mm) |
|   Exhaust  ... ... ... ... ... ... ... ... | 4.555 to 4.567 in (115.7 to 116.0 mm) |

| | L16 | L18 | L20B |
|---|---|---|---|
| Valve lift: | | | |
|   Intake  ... ... ... ... ... ... ... | 0.413 in (10.5 mm) | 0.413 in (10.5 mm) | 0.413 in (10.5 mm) |
|   Exhaust  ... ... ... ... ... ... ... | 0.413 in (10.5 mm) | 0.413 in (10.5 mm) | 0.413 in (10.5 mm) |

| | |
|---|---|
| Valve spring free-length (intake and exhaust): | |
|   Inner ... ... ... ... ... ... ... ... ... | 1.766 in (44.85 mm) |
|   Outer ... ... ... ... ... ... ... ... ... | 1.968 in (49.98 mm) |

| | L16 | L18 | L20B |
|---|---|---|---|
| Valve spring coil dia: | | | |
|   Intake | | | |
|     Inner  ... ... ... ... ... ... ... | 0.862 in (21.9 mm) | 0.953 in (24.2 mm) | 0.953 in (24.2 mm) |
|     Outer  ... ... ... ... ... ... ... | 1.150 in (29.4 mm) | 1.150 in (29.4 mm) | 1.150 in (29.4 mm) |
|   Exhaust: | | | |
|     Inner  ... ... ... ... ... ... ... | 0.862 in (21.9 mm) | 0.0953 in (24.2 mm) | 0.0953 in (24.2 mm) |
|     Outer  ... ... ... ... ... ... ... | 1.150 in (29.4 mm) | 1.150 in (29.4 mm) | 1.150 in (29.4 mm) |

| | |
|---|---|
| Valve guide length  ... ... ... ... ... ... | 2.323 in (59.0 mm) |
| Valve guide height from surface of cylinder head  ... ... ... ... | 0.417 in (10.6 mm) |
| Valve guide inner diameter  ... ... ... ... ... | 0.3150 to 0.3154 in (8.000 to 8.018 mm) |
| Valve guide outer diameter  ... ... ... ... ... | 0.4733 to 0.4738 in (12.023 to 12.034 mm) |
| Valve stem to guide clearance: | |
|   Intake  ... ... ... ... ... ... ... ... | 0.0008 to 0.0021 in (0.020 to 0.53 mm) |
|   Exhaust  ... ... ... ... ... ... ... ... | 0.0016 to 0.0029 in (0.0040 to 0.0073 mm) |

| | L16 | L18 | L20B |
|---|---|---|---|
| Seat width: | | | |
|   Intake  ... ... ... ... ... ... ... | 0.0551 in 1.5 mm | 0.0551 to 0.0630 in 1.4 to 1.6 mm | 0.0551 to 0.0630 in 1.4 to 1.6 mm |
|   Exhaust  ... ... ... ... ... ... ... | 0.0512 in 1.3 mm | 0.0709 to 0.0866 in 1.8 to 2.2 mm | 0.0709 to 0.0866 in 1.8 to 2.2 mm |
|   Seat angle  ... ... ... ... ... ... | 45° | 45° 30' | 45° 30' |

| | |
|---|---|
| Valve seat interference fit: | |
|   Intake  ... ... ... ... ... ... ... ... | 0.0032 to 0.0044 in (0.081 to 0.113 mm) |
|   Exhaust  ... ... ... ... ... ... ... ... | 0.0025 to 0.0038 in (0.064 to 0.096 mm) |
| Valve guide interference fit  ... ... ... ... ... | 0.0011 to 0.0019 in (0.027 to 0.049 mm) |

## Engine lubrication (L16, L18, L20B)

| | Standard tolerance | Wear limit |
|---|---|---|
| Oil pump: | | |
|   Rotor side clearance (outer to inner rotor)  ... ... ... ... | 0.0016 to 0.0032 in (0.04 to 0.08 mm) | 0.0079 in (0.20 mm) |
|   Maximum rotor tip clearance  ... ... ... ... | 0.0047 in (0.12 mm) | 0.0079 in (0.20 mm) |
|   Outer rotor to body clearance  ... ... ... ... ... | 0.0059 to 0.0083 in (0.15 to 0.21 mm) | 0.0197 in (0.5 mm) |
|   Rotor to bottom cover clearance  ... ... ... ... ... | 0.0012 to 0.0051 in (0.03 to 0.13 mm) | 0.0079 in (0.20 mm) |
| Oil pressure regulator valve: | | |
|   Oil pressure at idling  ... ... ... ... ... ... | 11 to 40 lb f/sq. in (0.8 to 2.8 kg f/sq. cm) | |
| Regulator valve spring: | | |
|   Free length  ... ... ... ... ... ... ... ... | 2.067 in (52.5 mm) | |
| Regulator valve opening pressure  ... ... ... ... ... | 50 to 71 lb f/sq. in (3.5 to 5.0 kg f/sq. cm) | |
| Oil pressure warning light illuminates at  ... ... ... ... | 5.7 to 8.5 lb f/sq in (0.4 to 0.6 kg f/sq. cm) | |

## Torque wrench settings

| | lb f ft | kg f m |
|---|---|---|
| Cylinder head bolts  ... ... ... ... ... ... ... ... | 60 | 8.3 |
| Connecting rod big-end nuts  ... ... ... ... ... | 40 | 5.5 |
| Flywheel bolts  ... ... ... ... ... ... ... ... | 110 | 15.2 |
| Main bearing cap bolts  ... ... ... ... ... ... | 40 | 5.5 |
| Camshaft sprocket bolt  ... ... ... ... ... ... | 85 | 11.8 |

| | | | | | | | | | | | |
|---|---|---|---|---|---|---|---|---|---|---|---|
| Sump drain plug | ... | ... | ... | ... | ... | ... | ... | ... | ... | 20 | 2.8 |
| Rocker pivot locknuts | ... | | ... | ... | ... | ... | ... | ... | ... | 40 | 5.5 |
| Carburettor mounting nuts | ... | ... | ... | ... | ... | ... | ... | ... | 40 | 5.5 |
| Crankshaft pulley bolt | ... | ... | ... | ... | ... | ... | ... | ... | ... | 100 | 13.8 |
| Clutch housing to engine bolts | | ... | ... | ... | ... | ... | ... | ... | 35 | 4.8 |
| Torque connector housing to engine bolts | ... | | ... | ... | ... | ... | 35 | 4.8 |
| Driveplate to torque connector | ... | ... | ... | ... | ... | ... | 35 | 4.8 |
| Clutch to flywheel bolts | ... | | ... | ... | ... | ... | ... | ... | 20 | 2.8 |
| Cylinder block reinforcement plate | ... | ... | ... | ... | ... | ... | 24 | 3.3 |
| Engine front mounting to bracket | ... | ... | ... | ... | ... | ... | 20 | 2.8 |
| Engine front mounting bracket to crankcase | | ... | ... | ... | ... | 20 | 2.8 |
| Rear mounting crossmember to bodyframe | ... | | ... | ... | ... | ... | 20 | 2.8 |
| Oil pump bolts | ... | ... | ... | ... | ... | ... | ... | ... | ... | 9.4 | 1.3 |
| Oil pump cover bolt | ... | ... | ... | ... | ... | ... | ... | ... | 6.1 | 0.85 |
| Oil pump regulator valve cap nut | ... | ... | ... | ... | ... | ... | 33 | 4.6 |

## 1  General description

The engine is of the four cylinder in-line type, with valve operation by means of an overhead camshaft.

The cast iron cylinder block contains the four bores and acts as a rigid support for the five bearing crankshaft. The machined cylinder bores are surrounded by water jackets to dissipate heat and control operating temperatures.

A disposable oil filter is located on the right-hand side of the cylinder block and supplies clean oil to the main gallery and various oilways. The main bearings are lubricated from oil holes, which run parallel with the cylinder bores. The forged steel crankshaft is suitably drilled for directing lubricating oil so ensuring full bearing lubrication.

To lubricate the connecting rod small end, drillings are located in the big-ends of the rods so that the oil is squirted upwards.

Crankshaft endfloat is controlled by thrust washers located at the centre main bearings.

The pistons are of a special aluminium casting with struts to control thermal expansion. There are two compression and one oil control ring. The piston (gudgeon) pin is a hollow steel shaft which is fully floating in the piston, and a press fit in the connecting rod little end. The pistons are attached to the crankshaft via forged steel connecting rods.

The cylinder head is of aluminium and incorporates wedge type combustion chambers. A special aluminium bronze valve seat is used for the inlet valve whilst a steel exhaust valve seat is fitted.

Located on the top of the cylinder head is the cast iron camshaft which is supported in four aluminium alloy brackets. The camshaft bearings are lubricated from drillings which lead from the main oil gallery in the cylinder head.

The supply of oil to each cam lobe is through an oil hole drilled in the base circle of each lobe. The actual oil supply is to the front oil gallery from the 3rd camshaft bearing. These holes on the base circle of the lobe supply oil to the cam pad surface of the rocker arm and to the valve tip end.

Two valves per cylinder are mounted at a slight angle in the cylinder head and are actuated by a pivot type rocker arm in direct contact with the cam mechanism. Double springs are fitted to each valve.

The camshaft is driven by a double row roller chain from the front of the crankshaft. Chain tension is controlled by a tensioner which is operated by oil and spring pressure. The rubber shoe type tensioner controls vibration and tension of the chain.

The operations described in this part of the Chapter apply to all ohc engine capacities and any differences in procedure are shown. Reference of engine application, and variations between the different power units.

## 2  Major operations possible with engine installed

1  The following operations can be carried out when the engine is still installed in the vehicle.

(a) Removal and installation of the camshaft: This will require keeping the tension on the timing chain using a hooked piece of wire as the crankshaft sprocket is being removed. Once the sprocket is removed, maintain the tension (using a long wooden wedge if desired to offset the force of the chain tensioner) or the chain may become disconnected from the crankshaft pulley and if this happens, complete retiming will have to be carried out (Section 37).

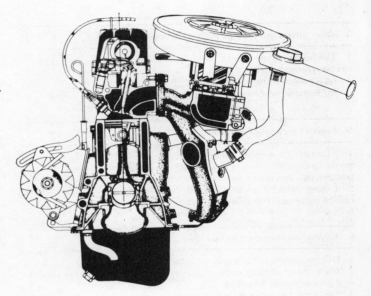

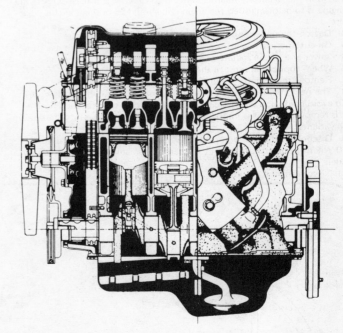

**Fig. 1.1. Sectional views of typical L-series ohc engine**

(b) *Removal and installation of the cylinder head:* The remarks made in the preceding paragraph regarding the timing chain apply.

(c) *Renewal of the engine mountings:* The weight of the engine will have to be taken on a hoist or a jack and an insulating block placed under the oil pan before this work can be carried out. (See Section 24).

(d) *Removal and installation of the timing cover:* This work may be required to renew a faulty timing cover oil seal, or to renew one or more of the timing gear or chain components. First remove the radiator. Unscrew the crankshaft pulley wheel bolt but be sure to jam the flywheel starter ring gear to prevent the crankshaft turning.

Take care not to break the oil pan gasket at its joint with the timing cover. If it does break, cut a fresh section from a new gasket and use plenty of gasket jointing compound when refitting.

(e) *Removal of the oil pan and piston/connecting rod assemblies:* It is possible to remove the oil pan with the engine in the vehicle but certain steering linkages will first have to be removed and the engine hoisted slightly after disconnection of the mountings, to permit removal of the oil pan from above the crossmember.

### 3  Major operations only possible with engine removed

1  The following operations can only be carried out after the engine has been removed from the vehicle:
　　(a) *Renewal of the main bearings.*
　　(b) *Removal and installation of the crankshaft.*

### 4  Engine - method of removal

1  Although the engine can be removed independently of the transmission unit, it will be found easier to remove the engine/transmission as a combined unit for later separation.

2  Lifting tackle of suitable strength will be required particularly in the case of automatic transmission, as the unit is very heavy.

### 5  Engine and transmission - removal

1  Disconnect the battery ground cable.

2  Mark the hood hinge location on the underside of the hood to assist in alignment when installing.

3  Drain the radiator coolant, referring to Chapter 2 if necessary. If the engine is to be dismantled the engine oil should be drained at this stage also.

4  Detach the upper and lower coolant hoses from the engine.

5  On automatic transmission models, detach the oil cooler hose from the lower end of the radiator.

6  Where applicable, remove the radiator shroud.

7  Remove the radiator, referring to Chapter 2 if necessary.

8  The next step is to remove the air cleaner and its connecting hoses. To avoid confusion when reconnecting, take care to label each hose as it is removed since it is impossible to give comprehensive information on all variants.

9  Disconnect the fuel pump-to-filter hose, and the fuel return hose.

10  When applicable disconnect the carbon canister hose on the engine side.

11  Disconnect the air pump air cleaner-to-pump hose.

12  Disconnect the accelerator cable at the carburettor, referring to Chapter 3 if necessary.

13  Disconnect the electrical wires to the engine and ancillary components, labelling any which could be exentrally installed incorrectly. Typically these will be:
　　(a) *Engine ground cable from the block above the alternator.*
　　(b) *Ignition coil-to-distributor HT wire.*
　　(c) *Distributor wire at the body terminal.*
　　(d) *Oil pressure switch and thermal transmitted wires.*
　　(e) *Wires to the carburetor BCDD, anti-dieseling solenoid and automatic choke heater.*
　　(f) *EGR solenoid wires.*
　　(g) *Alternator wires.*
　　(h) *Starter motor wires.*
　　(j) *Wires to the manual or automatic transmission, switches and/or solenoid.*

14  Detach the heater inlet and outlet hoses.

15  Detach the master-vac servo hose from the intake manifold (where applicable).

16  Detach the speedometer drive cable from the transmission.

17  Detach the manual or automatic transmission control lever or linkage, referring to Chapter 6, as necessary.

18  On manual transmission models remove the clutch operating cylinder and flexible hose as an assembly.

19  Disconnect the front exhaust tube from the manifold flange connection (photo).

20  Detach the centre propeller shaft bearing from the crossmember, the rear end from the companion flange and the front end from the transmission. Refer to Chapter 7 for details and alignment precautions. Plug the transmission or tie on a polythage bag to prevent oil spillage as the engine/transmission is lifted out.

21  Position the hoist over the engine compartment and attach the sling or chain to the engine lifting points. Raise the hoist so that it *just* takes the engine weight.

22  Remove the bolts from the engine mountings at the front support member (photo).

23  Position a jack beneath the transmission, with a wooden block between the jack head and transmission base. Raise the jack so that it *just* takes the transmission weight.

24  Loosen the two transmission mounting bolts.

25  On 1976 California models, loosen the two exhaust tube hanger bolts.

26  Remove two bolts at each side and detach the rear support from the sidemembers.

27  On 1976 models, remove the steering idler arm bolts and push down the cross rod.

28  Raise the engine slowly and carefully from the engine compartment, watching out for any items which may foul the vehicle bodywork or may not have been disconnected.

29  Transfer the engine and transmission to a suitable workbench or clean floor area so that the transmission and engine ancillaries can be detached as necessary.

### 6  Engine - separation from manual transmission

1  With the engine and transmission now removed from the vehicle, unscrew and remove the bolts which connect the clutch bellhousing to the engine block.

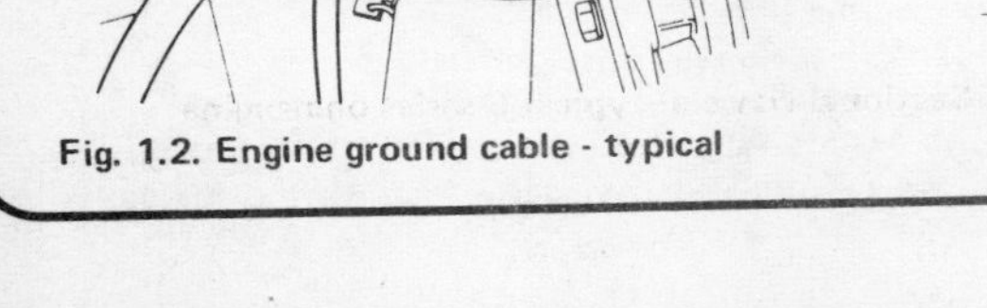

**Fig. 1.2. Engine ground cable - typical**

**Fig. 1.3. Disconnection points for carburetor wires - typical**

**Fig. 1.4. Master - Vac hose disconnection point - typical**

2   Unbolt and remove the starter motor.
3   Pull the transmission from the engine in a straight line, at the same time supporting the transmission so that its weight does not hang up on the primary shaft, even momentarily, whilst the shaft is still engaged with the clutch mechanism.
4   It is recommended that the clutch is removed also at this stage if the engine is undergoing repair. This is to prevent contamination by cleaning solvents when cleaning the engine (Section 8). Refer to Chapter 5 for further information on clutch removal (photo).

### 7   Engine - separation from automatic transmission

1   Remove the rubber plug from the lower part of the engine rear plate.
2   Unscrew and remove the bolts which secure the driveplate to the torque converter. The crankshaft will have to be turned by means of the pulley bolt so that each driveplate bolt comes into view in turn.
3   With all the driveplate bolts removed, mark the relative position of the driveplate to the torque converter. This is best ahcieved by placing a dab of coloured paint around one bolt hole in the driveplate and also on the torque converter hole top threads.
4   Remove the starter motor and the fluid filler tube support bolt.
5   Unscrew and remove the bolts which secure the torque converter housing to the engine.
6   Withdraw the automatic transmission in a straight line; expect some loss of fluid as the torque converter moves away from the driveplate.

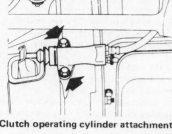

Fig. 1.5. Clutch operating cylinder attachment points

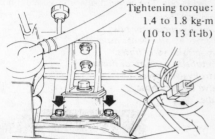

Tightening torque:
1.4 to 1.8 kg-m
(10 to 13 ft-lb)

Fig. 1.6. Disconnection points for front engine mounting

5.19 Disconnecting exhaust downpipe - typical

5.20 An engine mounting

6.4 Clutch removal

### 8   Engine dismantling - general

1   It is best to mount the engine on a dismantling stand but if one is not available, then stand the engine on a strong bench so as to be at a comfortable working height. Failing this, the engine can be stripped down on the floor.
2   During the dismantling process the greatest care should be taken to keep the exposed parts free from dirt. As an aid to achieving this, it is a sound scheme to thoroughly clean down the outside of the engine, removing all traces of oil and congealed dirt.
3   Use kerosene or a good grease solvent. The latter compound will make the job much easier, as, after the solvent has been applied and allowed to stand for a time, a vigorous jet of water will wash off the solvent and all the grease and filth. If the dirt is thick and deeply embedded, work the solvent into it with a wire brush.
4   Finally wipe down the exterior of the engine with a rag and only then, when it is quite clean should the dismantling process begin. As the engine is stripped, clean each part in a bath of kerosene.
5   Never immerse parts with oilways in kerosene, (eg; the crankshaft) but to clean, wipe down carefully with a kerosene dampened rag. Oilways can be cleaned out with wire. If an air-line is present all parts can be blown dry and the oilways blown through as an added precaution.
6   Re-use of old engine gaskets is false economy and can give rise to oil and water leaks, if nothing worse. To avoid the possibility of trouble after the engine has been reassembled always use new gaskets throughout.
7   Do not throw the old gaskets away as it sometimes happens that an immediate replacement cannot be found and the old gasket is then very useful as a template for making up a replacement. Hang up the old gaskets as they are removed on a suitable hook or nail.

8   To strip the engine it is best to work from the top down. The oil pan provides a firm base on which the engine can be supported in an upright position. When the oil pan stage where the oil pan must be removed is reached, the engine can be turned on its side and all other work carried out with it in this position.
9   Wherever possible install nuts, bolts and washers fingertight from wherever they were removed. This helps avoid later loss and muddle. If they cannot be installed then lay them out in such a fashion that it is clear from where they came.

### 9   Ancillary components - removal

1   If you are stripping the engine completely or preparing to install a reconditioned unit, all the ancillaries must be removed first. If you are going to obtain a reconditioned 'short' motor (block, crankshaft, pistons and connecting rods) then obviously the cam box, cylinder head and associated parts will need retention for installing to the new engine. It is advisable to check just what you will get with a reconditioned unit as changes are made from time to time.
2   Remove the fan assembly, noting that the shallow recess of the fan boss faces the radiator.
3   Remove the right-hand engine mounting bracket.
4   Unscrew and remove the oil filter and discard it. (photo). The use of a chain wrench or similar tool wrench or similar tool will probably be required to remove the filter.
5   Unscrew and remove the oil pressure switch.
6   Withdraw the engine oil dipstick.
7   Unscrew the crankshaft pulley bolt. To prevent the engine turning during this operation, jam the flywheel starter ring gear by passing a

sharp cold chisel or large screwdriver through the starter motor aperture in the engine rear plate.

8   Withdraw the crankshaft pulley. The insertion of two tire levers behind the pulley will usually extract the pulley but if it is exceptionally tight, use an extractor but take care not to distort the rims of the pulley.

9   Disconnect the HT leads from the spark plugs then remove the distributor cap complete with leads.

10 Unscrew and remove the spark plugs.

11 The next step is to detach the fuel, water, air and suction hoses. These vary considerably on the different engines and the only satisfactory way of doing the job is to attach identity labels so that installation can be readily carried out. The connections will typically be:

(a) Crankcase PCV hoses.
(b) Fuel pump-to-carburetor hose.
(c) Rocker cover-to-air cleaner hose.
(d) Intake manifold water hoses.
(e) Vacuum tube to carburetor hoses.
(f) Air control valve hoses.
(g) EGR valve vacuum hose.
(h) EGR tube.

(j) Anti-backfire valve hose.

12 Having removed the hoses, the associated emission control or engine ancillary items can be removed. Typically these will be:

(a) EGR valve, tube and passage (Fig. 1.9 and 1.10).
(b) Fuel pump.
(c) Air pump and idler pulley.
(d) PCV valve.
(e) Dashpot bracket.
(f) Check valve.
(g) Air control valve (Fig. 1.11).

13 Remove the thermostat housing.

14 Unbolt and remove the manifold assemblies complete with carburetor.

15 Remove the engine left-hand mounting bracket.

16 Remove the water pump.

17 Unscrew and remove the distributor clamp plate bolt from the crankcase and withdraw the distributor from its recess. Refer to Chapter 4 for further information.

18 Remove the rocker cover (photo).

19 The engine should now be stripped of its ancillary components, and dismantling proper may be carried out as described in Section 10 onwards.

1A

9.4 Oil filter removal

9.18 Interior of rocker cover showing baffle

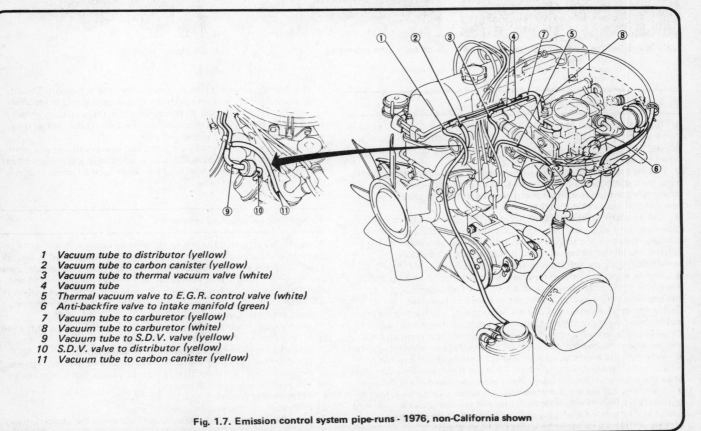

1   Vacuum tube to distributor (yellow)
2   Vacuum tube to carbon canister (yellow)
3   Vacuum tube to thermal vacuum valve (white)
4   Vacuum tube
5   Thermal vacuum valve to E.G.R. control valve (white)
6   Anti-backfire valve to intake manifold (green)
7   Vacuum tube to carburetor (yellow)
8   Vacuum tube to carburetor (white)
9   Vacuum tube to S.D.V. valve (yellow)
10  S.D.V. valve to distributor (yellow)
11  Vacuum tube to carbon canister (yellow)

Fig. 1.7. Emission control system pipe-runs - 1976, non-California shown

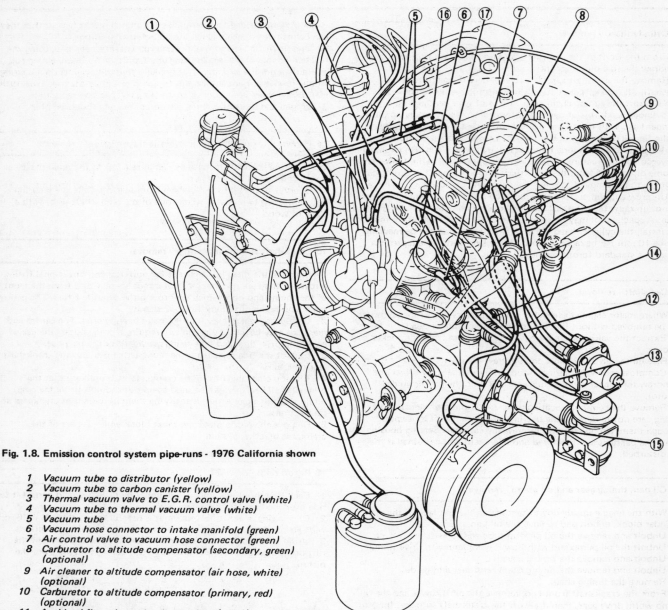

**Fig. 1.8. Emission control system pipe-runs - 1976 California shown**

1   *Vacuum tube to distributor (yellow)*
2   *Vacuum tube to carbon canister (yellow)*
3   *Thermal vacuum valve to E.G.R. control valve (white)*
4   *Vacuum tube to thermal vacuum valve (white)*
5   *Vacuum tube*
6   *Vacuum hose connector to intake manifold (green)*
7   *Air control valve to vacuum hose connector (green)*
8   *Carburetor to altitude compensator (secondary, green)*
    *(optional)*
9   *Air cleaner to altitude compensator (air hose, white)*
    *(optional)*
10  *Carburetor to altitude compensator (primary, red)*
    *(optional)*
11  *Anti-backfire valve to intake manifold (green)*
12  *B.C.D.D. to control valve (white)*
13  *Vacuum hose connector to E.A.R. control valve (green)*
14  *B.C.D.D. control valve to intake manifold (green)*
15  *Control valve to air pump air cleaner*
16  *Vacuum tube to carburetor (yellow)*
17  *Vacuum tube to carburetor (white)*

**Fig. 1.9. EGR valve removal -
1974 model shown**

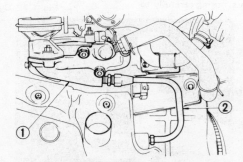

**Fig. 1.10. EGR tube and passage removal -
1976 model shown**

1  *EGR passage*      2  *EGR tube*

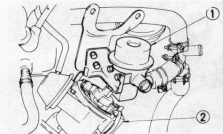

**Fig. 1.11. Air control valve (California 1976)
location**

1  *Air control valve*      2  *Distributor*

## 10 Cylinder head - removal

1 From the front of the camshaft, remove the centre bolt and withdraw the fuel pump eccentric cam.
2 Remove the camshaft sprocket complete with chain from the camshaft. Slip the sprocket out of the loop of the timing chain and then support the timing chain with a piece of wire pending removal of the cylinder head. It is of particular importance when removing the cylinder head with the engine in the vehicle that tension is maintained on the timing chain so that it does not become disengaged from the crankshaft sprocket. A long tapering wooden wedge can also be inserted to overcome the pressure of the chaintensioner. Should the timing chain become disengaged from the crankshaft sprocket, then the timing cover will have to be removed to re-set the chain and sprockets.
3 Unscrew and remove the cylinder head bolts in the sequence shown. **Do not unscrew the camshaft bearing housing bolts by mistake** (Fig. 1.12). Note: A special tool may be required (tool no ST10120000) to remove and install the cylinder head bolts. Alternatively, one can be made up from a 10 mm AF hexagon wrench (Allen key) suitably adapted for use with a standard torque wrench.

## 11 Camshaft - removal

1 Where major engine overhaul is not being carried out, the camshaft can be removed without first withdrawing the cylinder head.
2 Extract the valve rocker springs by lifting them from the rocker arm grooves.
3 Release the pivot locknuts and unscrew the pivots.
4 Compress each valve spring in turn using a large screwdriver and withdraw the rocker arms, taking care to retain the rocker guides (photo).
5 Remove the camshaft locating plate and withdraw the camshaft, taking care not to damage the bearings as the camshaft lobes pass through them. **On no account unscrew the camshaft bearing housing bolts.** The bearings are line-bored and alignment will be ruined if they are disturbed.

## 12 Oil pan, timing gear and oil pump - removal

1 With the engine upside-down standing on the top face of the cylinder block, unbolt and remove the oil pan.
2 Unbolt and remove the oil pick-up tube and screen.
3 Unbolt the oil pump and withdraw it complete with drive spindle.
4 Unbolt and remove the timing cover.
5 Unbolt and remove the timing chain tensioner and guide.
6 Remove the timing chain.
7 From the crankshaft front end, remove the oil thrower and the oil pump worm drive gear, then draw off the crankshaft sprocket (photo).

## 13 Piston/Connecting rod assemblies - removal

1 Examine the big-end bearing caps and connecting rods. They should be match-marked from 1 to 4 from the front of the engine. If they are not, dot punch the caps and rods at adjacent points, noting carefully to

which side of the engine the numbers or punch marks face so that they can be installed in their same original relative positions.
2 Unbolt No. 1 big-end (connecting rod bearings) cap and, using the wooden handle of a hammer, carefully tap the piston/connecting rod assembly from the cylinder. It is unlikely that the original shell bearings will be used again but should this be the case, retain them in exact order, identifying them in respect of connecting rod and cap sections.
3 Ectract the remaining three piston/connecting rod assemblies.

## 14 Flywheel (or driveplate - automatic transmission) - removal

1 Mark the position of the flywheel in relation to the crankshaft flange and unbolt the flywheel.
   In order to prevent the flywheel from turning while the securing bolts are being unscrewed, wedge one of the crankshaft webs with a piece of wood.

## 15 Crankshaft and main bearings - removal

1 Examine the main bearing caps for numbers and directional fitting arrows. If they are not marked, dot punch them 1 to 5 from the front of the engine and note which way round the caps are fitted. The centre main bearing incorporates thrust washers.
2 Unbolt and remove each of the main bearing caps. The centre and rear caps may be very tight and will require tapping out or the use of an extractor, a threaded hole being provided for the purpose.
3 Extract the side seals from the rear bearing cap also the crankshaft rear oil seal.
4 Lift the crankshaft from the crankcase. It is unlikely that the original shell bearings will be used again but should this be the case, retain them in exact order, identifying them in respect of crankcase and cap sections.
5 Remove the baffle plate and mesh block which is part of the crankcase breather system.

## 16 Piston rings - removal

1 Each ring should be sprung open only just sufficient to permit it to ride over the lands of the piston body.
2 Once a ring is out of its groove, it is helpful to cut three ¼ in (6 mm) wide strips of tin and slip them under the ring at equidistant points.
3 Using a twisting motion this method of removal will prevent the ring dropping into an empty groove as it is being removed from the piston.

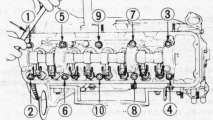

**Fig. 1.12. Cylinder head bolt loosening sequence**

11.4 Removing rocker arms

12.7 Removing crankshaft sprocket

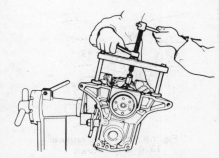

**Fig. 1.13. Using an extractor to remove the rear main bearing cap**

## 17 Piston pin (gudgeon pin) - removal

1   The piston pins are a finger pressure fit (at room temperature) in the pistons but are an interference fit in the connecting rod small end.
2   It is recommended that the removal of the piston pins is left to a service station having a suitable press.
3   Where such facilities are available to the home mechanic, the body of the piston must be supported on a suitably shaped distance piece into which the piston pin may be ejected. Ensure that each piston pin remains with its correct piston.

## 18 Lubrication system - description

Oil is drawn from the engine oil pan through an oil strainer by a trochoid-type oil pump. This is driven by a spindle which in turn is driven from the crankshaft. The upper end of the spindle drives the distributor. Oil is passed under pressure through a replaceable canister type oil filter and onto the main oil gallery. It is then distributed to all the crankshaft bearings, chain tensioner and timing chain. The oil that is supplied to the crankshaft is fed to the connecting rod big-end bearings via drilled passages in the crankshaft. The connection rod little ends and underside cylinder walls are lubricated from jets of oil issuing from little holes in the connection rods.

Oil from the centre of the main gallery passes up to a further gallery in the cylinder head. This distributes oil to the valve mechanism, and to the top of the timing chain. Drillings pass oil from the gallery to the camshaft bearings. Oil that is supplied to number 2 and 3 camshaft bearings is passed to the rocker arm, valve and cam lobe by two drillings inside the camshaft and small drillings in the cam circle of each arm.

The oil pressure relief valve is located in the oil pump cover, and is designed to control the pressure in the system to a maximum of 71 lbf/in$^2$ (5 kgf/cm$^2$).

## 19 Crankcase emission control system

The closed type of crankcase emission control system installed to models covered by this manual draws air from the air cleaner and passes it through a mesh type flame trap to a hose connected to the rocker cover.

The air is then passed through the inside of the engine and back to the intake manifold via a hose and regulating valve. This means that fumes in the crankcase are drawn into the combustion chambers, burnt and passed to the exhaust system.

When the vehicle is being driven at full throttle conditions, the inlet manifold depression is not sufficient to draw all fumes through the regulating valve and into the intake manifold. Under these operating conditions the crankcase ventilation flow is reversed with the fumes drawing into the air cleaner instead of the intake manifold.

To prevent engine oil being drawn into the intake manifold, a baffle plate and filter gauze pack is positioned in the crankcase.

Maintenance of the system simply involves inspection of the system, and renewal of any suspect parts. Check the condition of the rocker cover to air cleaner hose and the crankcase to intake manifold hose. Check for blockage, deterioration or collapse; should either be evident, new hoses must be installed.

Inspect the seals on the engine oil filler cap and dipstick. If their condition has deteriorated renew the seals.

Operation of the ventilation regulation valve may be checked by running the engine at a steady idle speed and disconnecting the hose from the regulation valve. Listen for a hissing noise from the valve once the hose has been detached. Now position a finger over the inlet valve, and a strong depression should be felt immediately as the finger is placed over the valve.

Should the valve prove to be inoperative, it must be renewed as it is not practical to dismantle and clean it.

Other symptoms showing a faulty or inoperative valve are:
*(a) Engine will not run smoothly at idle speed.*
*(b) Smoky exhaust.*
*(c) Engine idle speed rises and falls, but engine does not stop.*
*(d) Power loss at speeds above idle.*

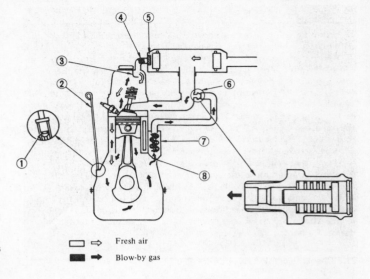

**Fig. 1.14. Crankcase emission control system - typical**

| | | | |
|---|---|---|---|
| 1 | O-ring | 5 | Filter |
| 2 | Dipstick | 6 | PCV valve |
| 3 | Baffle | 7 | Steel net |
| 4 | Flame trap | 8 | Baffle |

## 20 Examination and renovation - general

With the engine stripped, and all components thoroughly cleaned, it is now time to examine everything for wear and damage.

Parts and assemblies should be checked and, where possible, renovated or otherwise renewed as described in the following Sections.

## 21 Crankshaft and main bearings - examination and renovation

1   Examine the crankpin and main journal surfaces for signs of scoring or scratches. Check the ovality of the crankpins at different positions with a micrometer. If out of round by more than the specified amount, the crankpin will have to be reground. It will also have to be reground if there are any scores or scratches present. Also check the journals in the same fashion.
2   If it is necessary to regrind the crankshaft and fit new bearings your local Datsun garage or engineering works will be able to decide how much metal to grind off and the size of new bearing shells, required.
3   Full details of crankshaft regrinding tolerances and bearing undersizes are given in Specifications.
4   The main bearing clearances may be established by using a strip of Plastigage between the crankshaft journals and the main bearing/shell caps. Tighten the bearing cap bolts to a torque of between 33 and 40 lb/ft (4.6 and 5.5 kgfm). Remove the cap and compare the flattened Plastigage strip with the index provided. The clearance should be compared with the tolerances in the Specifications.
5   Temporarily install the crankshaft to the crankcase having positioned the other halves of the shell main bearings in their locations. Install the centre main bearing cap only, complete with shell bearing and tighten the securing bolts to between 33 and 40 lff ft (4.6 and 5.5 kgf m) torque. Using a feeler gauge, check the end-play by pushing and pulling the crankshaft. Where the end-play is outside the specified tolerance, the centre bearing shells will have to be renewed (photo).
6   Finally examine the clutch pilot bearing (bush) which is located in the centre of the flywheel mounting flange at the rear end of the crankshaft. If it is worn, renew it by tapping a thread in it and screwing in a bolt. Carefully press in the new bush so that its endface will lie below the crankshaft flange surface by between 0.18 and 0.20 in (4.5 and 5.0 mm). Lubrication of the bush is not required.

21.5 Checking crankshaft endfloat

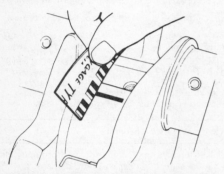

Fig. 1.15. Measuring main bearing clearance

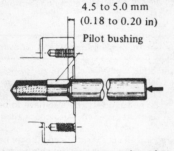

4.5 to 5.0 mm
(0.18 to 0.20 in)

Pilot bushing

Fig. 1.16. Clutch pilot bearing (bush) installation

## 22 Connecting rods and connecting rod (big-end) bearings - examination and renovation

1   Big-end bearing failure is indicated by a knocking from within the crankcase and a slight drop in oil pressure.

2   Examine the bearing surfaces for pitting and scoring. Renew the shells in accordance with the sizes specified in Specifications. Where the crankshaft has been reground, the correct undersize shell bearings will be supplied by the repairer.

3   Should there be any suspision that a connecting rod is bent or twisted or the small end bush no longer provides an interference fit for the gudgeon pin then the complete connecting rod assembly should be exchanged for a reconditioned one but ensure that the comparative weight of the two rods is equal within 0.25 oz (7 gr).

4   Measurement of the big-end bearing clearances may be carried out in a similar manner to that described for the main bearings in the previous Section. The running clearances are given in Specifications.

5   Finally check the big-end thrust clearance which should be between 0.008 and 0.012 in (0.2 and 0.3 mm) with a maximum wear limit of 0.024 in (0.6 mm).

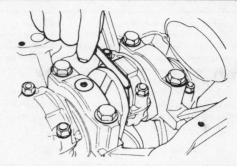

Fig. 1.17. Checking connecting rod (big-end) bearing side thrust clearance

## 23 Cylinder bores - examination and renovation

1   The cylinder bores must be examined for taper, ovality, scoring and scratches. Start by carefully examining the top of the cylinder bores. If they are at all worn, a very slight ridge will be found on the thrust side. This marks the top of the piston ring travel. The owner will have a good indication of the bore wear prior to dismantling the engine, or removing the cylinder head. Excessive oil consumption accompanied by blue smoke from the exhaust is a sure sign of worn cylinder bores and piston rings.

2   Measure the bore diameter just under the ridge with a micrometer and compare it with the diameter at the bottom of the bore, which is not subject to wear. If the difference between the two measurements is more than 0.008 in (0.2 mm) then it will be necessary to install special pistons and rings, or to have the cylinders rebored and install oversize pistons.

3   The standard clearance between a piston and the cylinder walls is between 0.0010 and 0.0018 in (0.025 and 0.045 mm). The easiest way to check this is to insert the piston into its bore with a feeler blade 0.0016 in (0.04 mm) in thickness inserted between it and the cylinder wall. Attach the feeler blade to a spring balance and note the force required to extract the blade while pulling vertically upwards. This should be between 0.4 and 3.3 lb (0.2 and 1.5 kg). The ambient temperature during this test should be around 68°F (20°C).

4   Where less than specified force is required to withdraw the feeler blade, then remedial action must be taken. Oversize pistons are available as listed in Specifications.

5   These are accurately machined to just below the indicated measurements so as to provide correct running clearances in bores bored out to the exact oversize dimensions.

6   If the bores are slightly worn but not so badly worn as ro justify reboring them, then special oil control rings and pistons can be installed, which will restore compression and stop the engine burning oil. Several different types are available and the manufacturer's instructions concerning their installation must be followed closely.

7   If new pistons are being installed and the bores have not been reground, it is essential to slightly roughen the hard glaze on the sides of the bores with fine glass paper so that the new piston rings will have a chance to bed in properly.

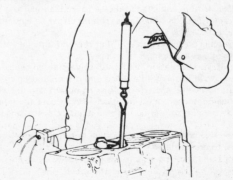

Fig. 1.18. Measuring piston clearance in cylinder

1A

## 24 Crankcase, cylinder block and mountings - examination and renovation

1    Examination of the cylinder block and crankcase should be carried out in conjunction with examination of the cylinder bores. Obviously if any faults or damage are visible, it will be a waste of money having the block rebored.

2    Check for cracks especially between the cylinder bores. Repair of cast iron is a specialized job and it may be more economical to purchase a new assembly or one in good condition from a car breaker.

3    Examine stud and bolt holes for stripped threads. New spiral type thread inserts can often be used to overcome this problem but the manufacturer's fitting instructions must be stricly observed.

4    Probe all oil and water passages with a piece of wire to ensure freedom from obstruction.

5    Now is the time to examine the engine mountings. Although the mountings can be renewed with the engine still in position in the vehicle by taking its weight on a hoist, now is the best opportunity to check for perished rubber or deformation, and to purchase or order new ones.

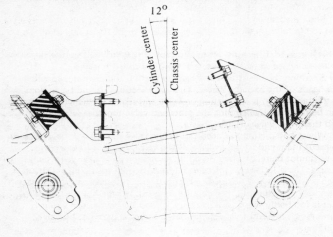

FRONT

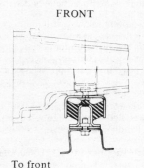

To front

REAR

**Fig. 1.19. Sectional views of engine/transmission mountings for 1973/74 models**

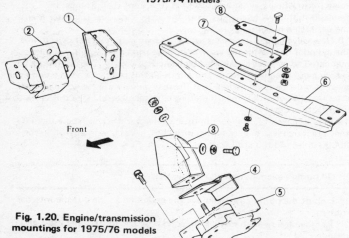

Front

**Fig. 1.20. Engine/transmission mountings for 1975/76 models**

1  Bracket (rh)       5  Insulator (lh)
2  Insulator (rh)     6  Rear support
3  Bracket (lh)       7  Rear insulator
4  Heat shield        8  Exhaust tube hanger
                         (California 1976 only)

## 25 Pistons and piston rings - examination and renovation

1    Where new pistons have been supplied to match the rebore diameter, new sets of piston rings will also be provided but it is worthwhile checking the ring clearances, as described in the following paragraphs.

2    If the original pistons are being used, carefully remove the piston rings as described in Section 16.

3    Clean the grooves and rings free from carbon, taking care not to scratch the aluminium surfaces of the pistons.

4    If new rings are being fitted to old pistons (cylinders not rebored) then order the top compression ring to be stepped to prevent it impinging on the 'wear ring' which will almost certainly have been formed at the top of the cylinder bore.

5    Before installing the rings to the pistons, push each ring in turn down its cylinder bore (use an inverted piston to do this to keep the ring square) and then measure the ring end gap. The gaps must be given in the Specifications according to engine type and should be measured with a feeler blade.

6    The piston rings should now be tested in their respective grooves for side clearance. The clearances must be as listed in the Specifications.

7    Piston ring end gaps can be increased by rubbing them carefully with carborundum stone.

8    Where necessary, a piston ring which is slightly tight in its groove may be rubbed down holding it perfectly squarely on a carborundum or a sheet of fine emery cloth laid on a piece of plate glass. Excessive tightness can only be rectified by having the grooves machined out.

9    The piston pin should be a push fit into the piston at room temperature. If it appears slack, then both the piston and piston pin should be renewed.

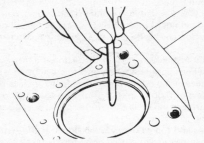

**Fig. 1.21. Checking piston ring end gap**

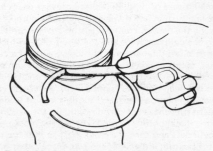

**Fig. 1.22. Checking piston ring side clearance**

## 26 Camshaft and camshaft bearings - examination and renovation

1 Carefully examine the camshaft bearings for wear. If the bearings are obviously worn or pitted then they must be renewed. This is an operation for your local Datsun dealer or local engineering works as it demands the use of specialized equipment. The bearings are removed with a special drift after which new bearings are pressed in, and line-bored, care being taken to ensure the oil holes in the bearings line-up with those in the pedestal brackets.

2 The camshaft itself should show no signs of wear, but, if very slight scoring on the cams is noticed, the score marks can be removed by very gently rubbing down with very fine emery cloth. The greatest care should be taken to keep the cam profiles smooth.

3 Check the camshaft sprocket for hooked teeth or distortion and renew if evident.

4 When installed, the camshaft end-play must be between 0.003 and 0.015 in (0.08 and 0.38 mm). If above the maximum, the locating plate must be renewed.

## 27 Timing chain, gears and tensioner - examination and renovation

1 Wear in the timing chain can be compensated for by adjusting the position of the camshaft sprocket as described in the reassembly operations but if the chain is obviously very badly worn or stretched, and a high mileage has been covered, renew it.

2 Check the condition of the chain tensioner and guide, and renew them if necessary.

3 Examine the crankshaft and camshaft sprocket teeth for wear and damage, renewing as necessary.

## 28 Cylinder head and valves - servicing and decarbonising

1 With the cylinder head removed, use a blunt scraper to remove all traces of carbon and deposits from the conbustion spaces and ports. Remember that the cylinder head is aluminium alloy and can be damaged easily during the decarbonising operations. Scrape the cylinder head free from scale or old pieces of gasket or jointing compound. Clean the cylinder head by washing it in kerosene and take particular care to pull a piece of rag through the ports and cylinder head bolt holes. Any dirt remaining in these recesses may well drop onto the gasket and cylinder block mating surface as the cylinder head is lowered into position and could lead to a gasket leak after reassembly is complete.

2 With the cylinder head clean, test for distortion if a history of coolant leakage has been apparent. Carry out this test using a straight edge and feeler gauges or a piece of plate glass. If the surface shows any warping in excess of 0.0039 in (0.1 mm) then the cylinder head will have to be resurfaced which is a job for a specialist engineering company.

3 Clean the pistons and top of the cylinder bores. If the pistons are still in the block then it is essential that great care is taken to ensure that no carbon gets into the cylinder bores as this could scratch the cylinder walls or cause damage to the piston and rings. To ensure this does not happen, first turn the crankshaft so that two of the pistons are at the top of their bores. Stuff rag into the other two bores or seal them off with paper and masking tape. The waterways should also be covered with small pieces of masking tape to prevent particles of carbon entering the cooling system and damaging the water pump.

4 Before scraping the carbon from the piston crowns, press grease into the gap between the cylinder walls and the two pistons which are to be worked on. With a blunt scraper carefully scrape away the carbon from the piston crown, taking great care not to scratch the aluminium. Also scrape away the carbon from the surrounding lip of the cylinder wall. When all carbon has been removed, scrape away the grease which will be contaminated with carbon particles, taking care not to press any into the bores. To assist prevention of carbon build-up the piston crown can be polished with a metal polish. Remove the rags or masking tape from the other two cylinders and turn the crankshaft so that the two pistons which were at the bottom are now at the top. Place rag or masking tape in the cylinders which have been decarbonised and proceed as just described.

5 The valves can be removed from the cylinder head by the following method. Compress each spring in turn with a valve spring compressor until the two halves of the collets can be removed. Repease the compressor and remove the spring and spring retainer.

6 If, when the valve spring compressor is screwed down, the valve spring retaining cap refuses to free to expose the split collet, do not continue to screw down the compressor as there is a likelihood of damaging.

7 Gently tap the top of the tool directly over the cap with a light hammer. This will free the cap. To avoid the compressor jumping off the valve spring retaining cap when it is tapped, hold the compressor firmly in position with one hand.

8 Slide the rubber oil control seal off the top of each valve stem (where applicable) and then drop out each valve through the conbustion chamber.

9 **It is essential that the valves are kept in their correct sequence** unless they are so badly worn that they are to be renewed.

10 Examine the heads of the valves for pitting and burning, especially the heads of the exhaust valves. The valve seatings should be examined at the same time. If the pitting on valve and seat is very slight the marks can be removed by grinding the seats and valve together with coarse, and then fine, valve grinding paste.

11 Where bad pitting has occurred to the valve seats it will be necessary to recut them and fit new valves. If the valve seats are so worn that they cannot be recut, then it will be necessary to fit new valve seat inserts. These latter two jobs should be entrusted to the local Datsun agent or engineering works. In practice it is very seldom that the seats are so badly worn that they require renewal. Normally, it is the valve that is too badly worn for replacement, and the owner can easily purchase a new set of valves and match them to the seats by valve grinding.

12 Valve grinding is carried out as follows:

Smear a trace of coars carborundum paste on the seat face and apply a suction grinder tool to the valve head. With a semi-rotary motion, grind the valve head to its seat, lifting the valve occasionally to redistribute the grinding paste. When a dull matt even surface finish is produced on both the valve seat and the valve, wipe off the paste and repeat the process with fine carborundum paste, lifting and turning the valve to redistribute the paste as before. A light spring placed under the valve head will greatly ease this operation. When a smooth unbroken ring of light grey matt finish is produced, on both valve and valve seat faces, the grinding operation is complete.

13 Scrape away all carbon from the valve head and the valve stem. Carefully clean away every trace of grinding compound, taking great care to leave none in the ports or in the valve guides. Clean the valves and the valve seats with a kerosene soaked rag then with a clean rag, and finally, if an air-line is available, blow the valves, valve guides and valve ports clean.

14 Test each valve in its guides for wear. After a considerable mileage, the valve guide bore may wear oval. This can best be tested by inserting a new valve in the guide and moving it from side to side. If the tip of the valve stem deflects by about 0.0080 in (0.2 mm) them it must be assumed that the tolerance between the stem and guide is greater than the permitted maximum.

15 New valve guides (oversizes available) may be pressed or driven into the cylinder head after the worn ones have been removed in a similar manner. The cylinder head must be heated to 392°F (200°C) before carrying out these operations and although this can be done in a domestic oven, it must be remembered that the new guide will have to be reamed after installation and it may therefore be preferable to leave this work to your Datsun dealer.

16 Finally check the free-length of the valve springs and renew them if they are much less than specified or if they have been in operation for 30000 miles (48000 km) or more.

## 29 Oil pump - examination and renovation

1 Unbolt the pump cover, remove the gasket and slide out the internal rotors.

2 Remove the regulator valve threaded plug and extract the valve and spring.

3 Clean all components and carry out the following checks for wear using a feeler gauge:

a) Check the clearance between the outer rotor and the oil pump body. This should be between 0.0059 and 0.0083 in (0.15 and 0.21 mm) with a wear limit of 0.020 in (0.5 mm).

**1A**

b) *Check the clearance between the high points of the inner and outer rotors. This should be less than 0.005 in (0.12 mm) with a maximum of 0.008 in (0.20 mm).*

c) *Using a straight-edge, check outer to inner rotor clearance. This should be 0.0016 to 0.0032 in (0.04 to 0.08 mm) with a wear limit of 0.008 in (0.20 mm).*

d) *Using a straight-edge, check the gap between the rotor and the bottom cover face. This should be 0.0012 to 0.0051 in (0.03 to 0.13 mm) with a wear limit of 0.008 in (0.20 mm).*

4   Where any of the clearances are outside the specified tolerances, renew the oil pump complete.

## 30 Flywheel - servicing

1   Examine the clutch driven plate contact area on the flywheel for scoring or cracks. If these are severe or extensive then the flywheel should be renewed. Surface grinding is not recommended as the balance of the crankshaft/flywheel assembly will be upset.

2   If the teeth on the flywheel starter ring are badly worn, or if some are missing then it will be necessary to remove the ring and fit a new one, or preferably exchange the flywheel for a reconditioned unit.

3   Either split the ring with a cold chisel after making a cut with a hacksaw blade between the teeth, or using a soft headed hammer (not steel) to knock the ring off, striking it evenly and alternately at equally spaced points. Take great care not to damage the flywheel during this process.

4   Heat the new ring in either an electric oven to about 392°F (200°C) or immerse in a pan of boiling oil.

5   Hold the ring at this temperature for five minutes and then quickly fit it to the flywheel so the chamfered portion of the teeth faces the transmission side of the flywheel.

6   The ring should be tapped gently down onto its register and left to cool naturally when the contraction of the metal on cooling will ensure that it is a secure and permanent fit. Great care must be taken not to overheat the ring, indicated by it turning light metallic blue, as if this happens the temper of the ring will be lost.

## 31 Driveplates - servicing

1   This component, fitted instead of the flywheel in conjunction with automatic transmission should be checked for distortion and elongation of the bolt holes which secure it to the torque converter.

2   Examine the starter ring gear teeth for wear or chipping.

3   Where any of these faults are evident, renew the driveplate complete.

## 32 Oil seals - renewal

1   At the time of major overhaul, renew the timing cover oil seal and the crankshaft rear oil seal as a matter of routine.

2   Make sure that the lips of the seals face the correct way as shown.

3   Removal and installation of the timing cover oil seal should be carried out using a piece of tubing as a drift (photo).

## 33 Engine reassembly - general

1   Before commencing reassembly, gather together the necessary tools, gaskets and other small items.

2   Observe absolute cleanliness during reassembly and lubricate each component before installation with clean engine oil.

3   Do not use unnecessary force to install a part, but re-check clearances and tolerances where difficulties are encountered.

## 34 Crankshaft and main bearings - reassembly

1   Install the upper halves of the main bearing shells into the crankcase and oil them liberally. Note that the center shell incorporates the thrust washers. Shell bearings (nos. 2 and 4) are similar and interchangeable. The front and rear bearing shells are similar but they are not interchangeable as only the front bearing incorporates an oil hole for the timing chain oil spray. All upper and lower bearing halves of similar type are

interchangeable (photos).

2   If the crankcase breather baffle and mesh were removed, install them now before installing the crankshaft (photo).

3   Lower the crankshaft carefully into the crankcase (photo).

4   Install the main bearing caps complete with shells making sure they go back in their numbered sequence and also the correct way round (photo).

5   Tighten the main bearing cap bolts to the specified torque, progressively and in the sequence shown (photo).

6   Smear jointing compound on the new rear main bearing cap side seals and tap them into their recesses (photo).

7   Install the crankshaft rear oil seal tapping it into position with a piece of tubing (photo).

## 35 Flywheel (or driveplate) - installation

1   Bolt the engine rear plate to the crankcase (photo).

2   Bolt the flywheel (or driveplate - automatic transmission) to the crankshaft rear mounting flange.

3   Tighten the bolts to the specified torque (photo).

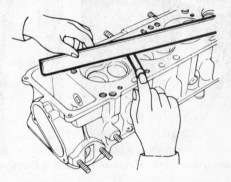

**Fig. 1.23. Checking the cylinder head for distortion**

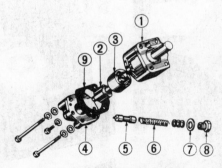

| 1 | Pump body |
| 2 | Inner rotor and shaft |
| 3 | Outer rotor |
| 4 | Pump cover |
| 5 | Regulator valve |
| 6 | Spring |
| 7 | Washer |
| 8 | Regulator cap |
| 9 | Cover gasket |

**Fig. 1.24. Oil pump components**

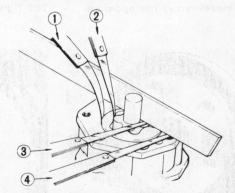

**Fig. 1.25. Checking the pump rotor clearances**

| 1 | Outer rotor top body | 3 | Side |
| 2 | Tip | 4 | Rotor to body |

32.3 Timing cover oil seal

34.1A. Oiling crankcase bearing shells

34.1B. Main bearing shell incorporating thrust washer

34.1C. Front main bearing with timing chain oil spray hole

34.2 Crankcase breather baffle

34.3 Installing crankshaft

34.4 Installing centre main bearing cap and shell

34.5 Tightening a main bearing cap bolt

34.6 Rear main bearing cap side seal

34.7 Crankshaft rear oil seal

35.1 Engine rear plate

35.3 Tightening flywheel bolts

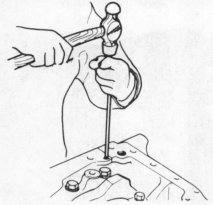

Fig. 1.26. Crankcase breather baffle and mesh

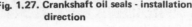

Fig. 1.27. Crankshaft oil seals - installation direction

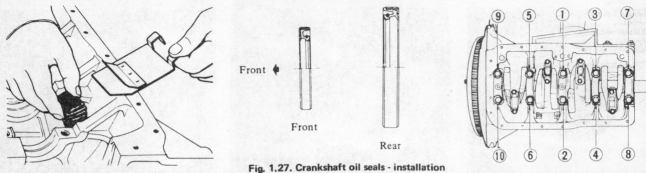

Fig. 1.28. Main bearing cap bolt tightening sequence

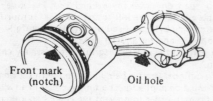

Fig. 1.29. Tapping in a new rear main bearing cap side seal

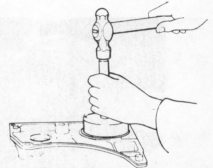

Fig. 1.30. Installing the crankshaft rear oil seal

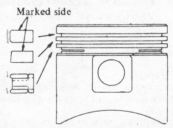

Fig. 1.32. Piston ring installation diagram

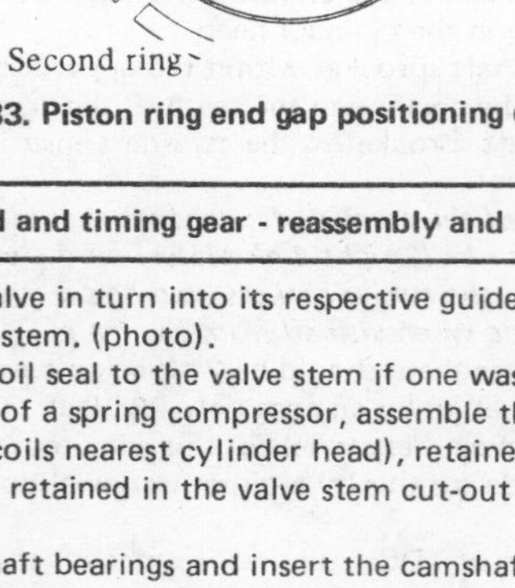

## 36 Pistons, rings and connecting rods - reassembly and installation

1    As previously recommended, the pistons will probably have been assembled to their connecting rods by the dealer supplying the new components. When correctly assembled, the notch on the piston crown (on some pistons an 'F' mark is used adjacent to the piston pin boss) must face the front of the engine while the oil hole in the connecting rod will be towards the right-hand side of the engine (photo).
2    Install the piston rings by reversing the removal procedure described in Section 16. When correctly installed, the markings on the rings must be facing upwards. The top compression ring is chromium plated while the second compression ring is tapered towards the top. The oil control ring has two rails which can be interchanged and located at the top and bottom of the groove. Stagger the piston ring gaps as shown (Fig. 1.33).
3    Install the bearing shells to the connecting rod and big-end cap (photo).
4    Compress the piston rings with a suitable compressor and, having well lubricated the rings and the cylinder bore with engine oil, tap the piston/connecting rod assembly into the cylinder (photo).
5    Engage the connecting rod with the crankpin when the crankpin is at its lowest point of rotational travel. Lubricate the exposed part of the crankpin.
6    Install the big-end cap complete with shell bearing making sure that the numbers are adjacent and in their correct sequence (photo).
7    Tighten the big-end nuts to specified torque (photo).
8    Repeat the operations to install the remaining three piston/connecting rod assemblies.

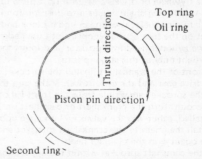

Fig. 1.33. Piston ring end gap positioning diagram

## 37 Cylinder head and timing gear - reassembly and installation

1    Insert each valve in turn into its respective guide, applying a little engine oil to the stem. (photo).
2    Install a new oil seal to the valve stem if one was originally installed and with the aid of a spring compressor, assemble the springs (outer spring has close coils nearest cylinder head), retainers and split collets. The latter can be retained in the valve stem cut-out with a dab of thick grease.
3    Oil the camshaft bearings and insert the camshaft carefully into position (photo).
4    Screw the valve rocker pivots complete with locknuts into the pivot bushes.

Fig. 1.31. Piston correctly assembled to connecting rod

36.1 Piston directional fitting mark

36.3 Installation of connecting rod bearing shell

36.4 Piston installation

36.6 Installing a connecting rod (big-end) cap and shell

36.7 Tightening a connecting rod bearing nut

**1A**

5   Install the rocker arms and guides by depressing the valve springs with a screwdriver.

6   Engage the rocker springs.

7   Install the camshaft locating plate to the camshaft so that the horizontally engraved line is visible from the front and is positioned at the top of the plate (photo).

8   Rotate the camshaft until the valve, of no 1 cylinder are fully closed (equivalent to no. 1 piston at TDC) and then turn the crankshaft (by means of the flywheel or driveplate) until no 1 piston is at TDC,

9   Bolt the two timing chain guides into position (photo).

10  Clean the mating surfaces of the cylinder block and head, and locate a new gasket on the face of the block; do not use gasket cement (photo).

11  Lower the cylinder head into position and insert the two centre bolts finger-tight only at this stage (photo).

12  To the front of the crankshaft, install the sprocket, oil pump/distributor drive gear and the oil thrower. Make sure that the timing marker on the sprocket are visible from the front (photos).

13  On no account turn the crankshaft or camshaft until the timing chain is installed, otherwise the valves will impinge upon the piston crowns. Install the chain to the crankshaft sprocket and draw the chain through the opening in the cylinder head.

14  Engage the camshaft sprocket within the upper loop of the timing chain, then engage the chain with the teeth of the crankshaft sprocket and bolt the camshaft sprocket to the camshaft ensuring that the following conditions are met:

  i)   The keyway of the crankshaft sprocket should point vertically.
  ii)  The timing marks ('bright' link plates) on the chain should align with those on the two sprockets, and be positioned on the right-hand side when viewed from the front.

On L20B type engines there should be 21 black plates between the two bright plates and on all other engines only 20 black plates between them.

Where a timing chain has stretched, this can upset the valve timing and provision is made for this by alternative dowel holes drilled in the camshaft sprocket.

With no. 1 piston at TDC (compression stroke) check whether the notch in the camshaft sprocket (with chain correctly engaged) appears to the left of the engraved line on the locating plate. If this is the case, disengage the camshaft sprocket from the chain and move the sprocket

round so that when it is re-engaged with the chain it will locate with the camshaft flange dowel in its no. 2 hole. Where this adjustment does not correct the chain slack, repeat the operation using no. 3 hole of the camshaft sprocket to engage with the flange dowel. Where no. 2 or 3 sprocket holes are used, then the no. 2 or 3 timing marks must be used to position the chain. Where this adjustment procedure still will not correct or compensate for the slackness in the timing chain, then the chain must be renewed (photos).

15  When the timing is satisfactory, tighten the camshaft sprocket bolt to the specified torque (photo).

16  Install the chain tensioner so that there is the minimum clearance between the spindle/slipper assembly and the tensioner assembly (photo).

17  Thoroughly clean the mating faces of the front cover and cylinder block.

18  Locate a new gasket on the front face of the engine, applying gasket cement to both sides of it.

19  Apply gasket cement to the front cover and cylinder block as indicated.

20  Offer up the front cover to the engine and insert the securing bolts finger tight. Take care not to damage the head gasket which is already in position (photo).

21  The top face of the front cover should be flush with the top surface of the cylinder block or certainly not more than 0.0059 in (1.5 mm) difference in level.

22  Tighten the front cover bolts to the correct torque.

23  Install the water pump (photo).

24  Oil the lips of the front cover oil seal and push the pulley onto the crankshaft. Tighten its securing bolt to the specified torque (photo).

25  Insert the remaining cylinder head bolts noting carefully the position of the longer bolts (A) and the shorter ones (B).

26  Tighten the bolts to the specified torque progressively and in the sequence shown.

Note: Where the cylinder head is being installed with the engine in the vehicle, tension must be applied to the timing chain in an upward direction at all times in order to prevent the chain becoming disengaged from the crankshaft sprocket (See Section 10).

37.1 Installing a valve

37.2a Installing valve spring retainer

37.2b Compressing a valve spring

37.3 Installing camshaft

37.6 Engaging rocker springs with the rocker arms

37.7 Installing camshaft locating plate

37.9 Installing a timing chain guide

37.10 Cylinder head gasket located on block

37.11 Lowering cylinder head into position

37.12a Installing crankshaft sprocket

37.12b Installing oil pump/distributor drive gear

37.12c Installing crankshaft oil thrower

37.14a Engaging timing chain with camshaft sprocket

37.14b Installing camshaft sprocket bolt and fuel pump eccentric

37.14c Crankshaft sprocket timing mark aligned with chain 'bright' link

37.14d Camshaft sprocket timing mark aligned with chain 'bright' link

37.15 Tighten the camshaft sprocket bolt to the specified torque

37.16 Installing timing chain tensioner

37.20 Installing front cover

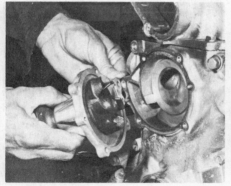
37.23 Installing water pump

37.24 Installing crankshaft pulley

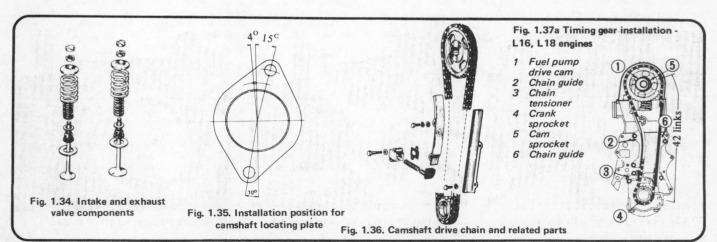

Fig. 1.34. Intake and exhaust valve components

Fig. 1.35. Installation position for camshaft locating plate

Fig. 1.36. Camshaft drive chain and related parts

Fig. 1.37a Timing gear installation - L16, L18 engines

1 Fuel pump drive cam
2 Chain guide
3 Chain tensioner
4 Crank sprocket
5 Cam sprocket
6 Chain guide

42 links

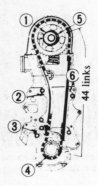

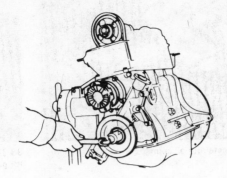

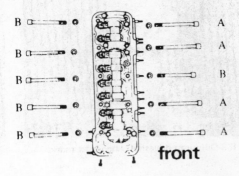

**Fig. 1.37b Timing gear installation - L20B engine**

*1   Fuel pump eccentric cam*
*2   Chain guide*
*3   Tensioner*
*4   Crankshaft sprocket*
*5   Camshaft sprocket*
*6   Chain guide*

**Fig. 1.38. Installing crankshaft pulley and bolt**

**Fig. 1.40. Locations of long and short cylinder head bolts**

*A   Long*                    *B   Short*

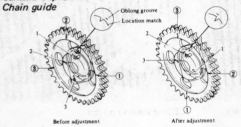

**Fig. 1.39. Camshaft sprocket adjustment positions to compensate for timing chain stretch. Numbers in circles indicate timing marks, other numbers indicate dowel positioning holes (see Section 37)**

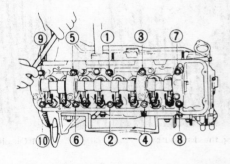

**Fig. 1.41. Cylinder head bolt tightening sequence**

## 38   Oil pump and distributor - installation

1   Set the engine so that No. 1 piston is at TDC on its compression stroke.
2   Align the punch mark on the oil pump driveshaft with the oil hole just below the driven gear (photo).
3   Use a new flange gasket and insert the oil pump into its recess so that as its driveshaft meshes with the drivegear on the crankshaft; the distributor drive tongue will take up a position as shown being at 5° to a line drawn through the centers of the bolt holes of the distributor mounting flange (when viewed from above) and having the smaller segment towards the front of the engine (photo).
4   Tighten the oil pump securing bolts.
5   Without moving the crankshaft, insert the distributor into its recess so that the large and small segments of the driveshaft engage correctly, then tighten the clamp plate bolt at its original position in the elongated hole (photo).
6   The ignition timing should be precisely checked and adjusted, as described in Chapter 4.

## 39   Oil strainer and oil pan - installation

1   Bolt the oil strainer and pick-up tube assembly to the flange of the crankcase (photo).
2   Clean the mating surfaces of the crankcase and the oil pan. Apply gasket cement at the points indicated, then smearing a film of cement to the crankcase flange, stick the oil pan gasket to the crankcase.
3   Smear the flange of the oil pan with gasket cement then bolt it to the crankcase. Do not overtighten these bolts (photo).

## 40   Valve clearances - adjustment

1   To adjust the valve clearance, turn the crankshaft until no. 1 piston

is at TDC on its compression stroke. In this position the high points of the cam lobes will be furthest from the rocker arms. Check the clearance between the heel of the cam and the rocker arm by inserting the appropriate feeler blade. The blades, should be a stiff sliding fit and to adjust the clearance, release the locknut and turn the pivot screw. The valve clearances **cold** are inlet 0.008 in (0.20 mm); exhaust 0.010 in. (0.25 mm). (photos).
2   As the firing order is 1—3—4—2 it will reduce the amount of the crankshaft rotation required if valve clearances are adjusted in accordance with the firing order. To obtain a better appreciation of the valve clearance it is recommended that the rocker arm springs are detached. Numbering from the front, the inlet valves are 2—3—6—7 and the exhaust valves 1—4—5—8.
3   When carrying out valve clearance adjustment with the engine in the car, the crankshaft can most easily be turned by engaging top gear, jacking-up and turning a rear roadwheel (manual transmission). On vehicles with automatic transmission a wrench will have to be applied to the crankshaft pulley bolt which makes the adjustment procedure somewhat more protracted. With either method, the work will be facilitated if the spark plugs are first removed.

## 41   Ancillary components - installation

1   This is essentially the reverse of the removal procedure described in Section 9. However, for L16 and L18 engines, ensure that the carburetor flange insulator is installed on the manifold so that its marking is visible from above. For L20B engines, remember to install the heat shield plate for the carburetor; note that the joint seat duct is inserted into the primary hole in the carburetor.
2   Lubricate the oil filter seal with engine oil and install hand-tight only.
3   Refer to Figs. 1.7 and 1.8 and Chapter 3 for information on pipe-runs for the emission control items.

38.2 Oil pump driveshaft alignment marks

38.3a Installing oil pump

38.3b Correct position of distributor drive tongue after installation of oil pump

38.5 Installing the distributor

39.1 Oil pick-up tube and strainer installed

39.3 Installing oil pan

40.1a Checking an inlet valve clearance

40.1b Adjusting a valve clearance

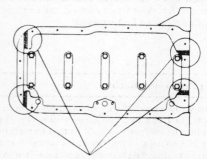
Apply sealant at these points

Fig. 1.42. Crankcase - sealant application areas

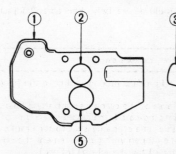
Fig. 1.43. Carburetor joint components (L20B type engine)

1   Heatshield plate        4   Joint seat
2   Primary hole            5   Secondary hole
3   Duct

## 42 Engine/transmission - installation

1    Install the clutch (where applicable) by following the procedure given in Chapter 5.

2    Reconnect the engine to the manual or automatic transmission by reversing the procedure given in Section 6 or 7.

3    Using the hoist and slings, install the engine/transmission in the vehicle by reversing the removal procedure given in Section 5.

4    When installation is complete, check and adjust the tension as described in Chapter 2, Section 11.

5    Refill the engine with the correct grade and quantity of oil (where applicable).

6    Refill the cooling system (Chapter 2).

7    Check the level in the manual or automatic transmission, and top-up if necessary.

## 43 Initial start-up after major repair

1    With the engine installed in the vehicle, make a final visual check to see that everything has been reconnected and that no loose rags or tools have been left within the engine compartment.

2    Turn the idling speed adjusting screw in about ½ turn to ensure that the engine will have a faster than usual idling speed during initial start-up and operation.

3    Start the engine. This may take a little longer than usual as the fuel pump and carburetor bowls will be empty and will require priming.

4    As soon as the engine starts, allow it to run at a fast-idle. Examine all hose and pipe connections for leaks.

5    After the engine has been run for several minutes check the tightness of the cylinder head bolts.

6    Operate the vehicle on the road until normal engine temperature is reached, then remove the rocker cover and adjust the valve clearances hot, as described in Section 40.

7    Where the majority of engine internal bearings or components (pistons rings etc) have been renewed then the operating speed should be restricted for the first 500 miles (800 km), and the engine oil changed at the end of this period.

8    Check and adjust if necessary the ignition timing (Chapter 4).

9    Check and adjust the carburetor and all exhaust emission control equipment as far as is practicable (Chapter 3).

## 44 Fault diagnosis - engine

Refer to Section 85 in Part B of this Chapter

# Chapter 1: Part B Overhead valve engine

**Contents**

**1B**

---

**Specifications**

## Engine application
Vehicle models 620U, G620U, L620, U620U, LG620, UL620,
L620T, LG620T ... ... ... ... ... ... ... ... ... ... J13
Vehicle models N620U, GN620U, NL620, GNL620, UNL620
NL620T, GNL620T ... ... ... ... ... ... ... ... J15

## Engine (general)
Engine type ... ... ... ... ... ... ... ... ... Four cylinder, in-line, overhead valve (ohv)

| | J13 | J15 |
|---|---|---|
| Displacement ... ... ... ... ... ... ... ... | 79.3 cu. in | 90.5 cu. in |
| | 1299 cc | 1483 cc |
| Bore ... ... ... ... ... ... ... ... ... | 2.87 in | 3.07 in |
| | 73 mm | 78 mm |
| Stroke ... ... ... ... ... ... ... ... | 3.06 in | 3.06 in |
| | 77.6 mm | 77.6 mm |

Firing order ... ... ... ... ... ... ... ... 1, 3, 4, 2 (No. 1 cylinder nearest radiator)
Compression ratio ... ... ... ... ... ... ... ... 8.2 : 1          8.3 : 1
Oil capacity, including filter (approximate) ... ... 8.5 US pt/7 Imp. pt (4 litres)
Oil type ... ... ... ... ... ... ... ... ... See lubrication chart

Cylinder location and
distributor rotation

## Crankshaft and main bearings
Journal diameter ... ... ... ... ... ... ... 2.0005 to 2.0010 in (50.813 to 50.825 mm)
Max. taper and out-of-round ... ... ... ... ... 0.0004 in (0.01 mm)
Crankshaft end-play ... ... ... ... ... ... ... 0.0020 to 0.0079 in (0.05 to 0.20 mm)
Max. crankshaft end-play ... ... ... ... ... ... 0.0118 in (0.3 mm)
Crankpin diameter ... ... ... ... ... ... ... 1.8756 to 1.8761 in (47.640 to 47.652 mm)
Max. taper or out-of-round ... ... ... ... ... 0.0004 in (0.01 mm)
Main bearing thickness (standard) ... ... ... ... 0.0717 to 0.0722 in (1.822 to 1.835 mm)
Main bearing clearance ... ... ... ... ... ... 0.0008 to 0.0020 in (0.02 to 0.05 mm)
Max. main bearing clearance ... ... ... ... ... 0.0039 in (0.10 mm)
Max. permissible crankshaft bend ... ... ... ... 0.0012 in (0.03 mm)

## Camshaft

| | |
|---|---|
| Camshaft end-play ... ... ... ... ... ... ... ... | 0.0020 to 0.0114 in (0.05 to 0.29 mm) |
| Camshaft lobe lift ... ... ... ... ... ... ... ... | 0.2421 in (6.15 mm) |

Journal diameter (standard size):

| | |
|---|---|
| Front ... ... ... ... ... ... ... ... ... | 1.7887 to 1.7892 in (45.434 to 45.447 mm) |
| Center ... ... ... ... ... ... ... ... | 1.7282 to 1.7287 in (43.897 to 43.910 mm) |
| Rear ... ... ... ... ... ... ... ... | 1.6228 to 1.6233 in (41.218 to 41.231 mm) |
| Max. permissible camshaft bend ... ... ... ... ... ... | 0.0012 in (0.03 mm) |

Journal to bearing clearance:

| | |
|---|---|
| Front ... ... ... ... ... ... ... ... ... | 0.0011 to 0.0020 in (0.027 to 0.050 mm) |
| Center ... ... ... ... ... ... ... ... | 0.0015 to 0.0025 in (0.038 to 0.064 mm) |
| Rear ... ... ... ... ... ... ... ... | 0.0010 to 0.0019 in (0.026 to 0.049 mm) |

Bearing inner diameter:

| | |
|---|---|
| Front ... ... ... ... ... ... ... ... ... | 1.7903 to 1.7907 in (45.474 to 45.484 mm) |
| Center ... ... ... ... ... ... ... ... | 1.7302 to 1.7307 in (43.948 to 43.961 mm) |
| Rear ... ... ... ... ... ... ... ... | 1.6243 to 1.6247 in (41.257 to 41.267 mm) |

## Pistons

| | J13 | J15 |
|---|---|---|
| Piston diameter (standard) ... ... ... ... ... | 2.8735 to 2.8755 in (72.987 to 73.037 mm) | 3.0683 to 3.0763 in (77.935 to 77.985 mm) |
| Piston diameter (oversize 0.0197 in/0.50 mm) ... ... ... | 2.8924 to 2.8944 in (73.467 to 73.517 mm) | 3.0871 to 3.0892 in (78.415 to 78.465 mm) |
| Piston diameter (oversize 0.0394 in/1.00 mm) ... ... ... | 2.9121 to 2.9140 in (73.967 to 74.017 mm) | 3.1069 to 3.1089 in (78.915 to 78.965 mm) |
| Piston diameter (oversize 0.0591 in/1.5 mm) ... ... ... | 2.9318 to 2.9337 in (74.467 to 74.517 mm) | 3.1266 to 3.1285 in (79.415 to 79.465 mm) |
| Ellipse difference (ovality) ... ... ... ... ... | 0.0028 to 0.0067 in (0.07 to 0.17 mm) | |
| Piston ring groove width: | | |
|    Top compression ... ... ... ... ... ... | 0.0787 in (2.0 mm) | |
|    Second compression ... ... ... ... ... | 0.0787 in (2.0 mm) | |
|    Oil control ... ... ... ... ... ... | 0.1575 in (4.0 mm) | |
| Piston to bore clearance ... ... ... ... ... | 0.0009 to 0.0017 in (0.023 to 0.043 mm) | 0.0010 to 0.0018 in (0.025 to 0.045 mm) |
| Piston pin hole offset ... ... ... ... ... ... ... | Zero | 0.0374 to 0.0413 in (0.95 to 1.05 mm) |
| Piston pin hole diameter ... ... ... ... ... | 0.6871 to 0.6874 in (17.453 to 17.460 mm) | 0.8268 to 0.8271 in (21.001 to 21.008 mm) |

## Piston rings

| | J13 | J15 |
|---|---|---|
| Ring thickness: | | |
|    Top compression ... ... ... ... ... ... | 0.0781 in (1.984 mm) | |
|    Second compression ... ... ... ... ... | 0.0781 in (1.984 mm) | |
| Clearance in groove: | | |
|    Top compression ... ... ... ... ... ... | 0.0014 to 0.0030 in (0.036 to 0.076 mm) | |
|    Second compression ... ... ... ... ... | 0.0014 to 0.0030 in (0.036 to 0.076 mm) | |
| Piston ring end gap | | |
|    Top compression ... ... ... ... ... ... | 0.0079 to 0.0130 in (0.20 to 0.33 mm) | 0.0079 to 0.0138 in (0.20 to 0.35 mm) |
|    Second compression ... ... ... ... ... | 0.0079 to 0.0130 in (0.20 to 0.33 mm) | 0.0055 to 0.0114 in (0.14 to 0.29 mm) |
|    Oil control ... ... ... ... ... ... | 0.0118 to 0.0354 in (0.30 to 0.90 mm) | |

## Piston pins (gudgeon pins)

| | J13 | J15 |
|---|---|---|
| Diameter ... ... ... ... ... ... ... | 0.6869 to 0.6871 in (17.447 to 17.452 mm) | 0.8265 to 0.8267 in (20.993 to 20.998 mm) |
| Length ... ... ... ... ... ... ... | 2.5681 to 2.5780 in (65.23 to 65.48 mm) | 2.6142 to 2.6240 in (66.40 to 66.55 mm) |
| Pin to piston clearance ... ... ... ... ... | 0.00004 to 0.00051 in (0.001 to 0.013 mm) | 0.00012 to 0.00059 in (0.003 to 0.015 mm) |
| Pin to connecting rod bushing (interference fit) ... ... ... | Bolt clamp | 0.0006 to 0.0013 in (0.015 to 0.033 mm) |

## Connecting rods

| | J13 | J15 |
|---|---|---|
| Distance between centres of small end and connecting rod (big-end bearings) ... ... ... ... ... ... ... | 5.617 in (142.67 mm) | 5.506 in (139.85 mm) |
| Bearing thickness ... ... ... ... ... | 0.0720 to 0.0724 in (1.83 to 1.84 mm) | |
| Side play ... ... ... ... ... ... ... | 0.0079 to 0.0118 in (0.20 to 0.30 mm) | |
| Bearing clearance ... ... ... ... ... | 0.0004 to 0.0020 in (0.011 to 0.052 mm) | |

## Valves

| | J13 | J15 |
|---|---|---|
| Valve clearance (hot) intake and exhaust ... ... ... ... ... | | 0.0138 in (0.35 mm) |
| **Valve head diameter:** | | |
| Intake ... ... ... ... ... ... ... ... ... | 1.3740 in (34.9 mm) | 1.4921 in (37.9 mm) |
| Exhaust ... ... ... ... ... ... ... ... ... | 1.1811 in (30.0 mm) | 1.2598 in (32.0 mm) |
| Valve stem diameter intake and exhaust ... ... ... | | 0.3417 to 0.3422 in (8.680 to 8.693 mm) |
| **Valve length:** | | |
| Intake ... ... ... ... ... ... ... ... ... | 4.305 to 4.317 in (109.35 to 109.65 mm) | 4.305 to 4.317 in (109.35 to 109.65 mm) |
| Exhaust ... ... ... ... ... ... ... ... ... | 4.274 to 4.285 in (108.55 to 108.85 mm) | 4.305 to 4.317 in (109.35 to 109.65 mm) |
| **Valve spring free-length:** | | |
| Outer ... ... ... ... ... ... ... ... ... | | 2.047 in (52 mm) |
| Inner ... ... ... ... ... ... ... ... ... | | 1.969 in (50 mm) |
| **Valve spring coil diameter:** | | |
| Outer ... ... ... ... ... ... ... ... ... | | 0.9921 in (25.2 mm) |
| Inner ... ... ... ... ... ... ... ... ... | | 0.7244 in (18.4 mm) |
| **Valve guide length:** | | |
| Intake ... ... ... ... ... ... ... ... ... | | 1.874 in (47.6 mm) |
| Exhaust ... ... ... ... ... ... ... ... ... | | 2.205 in (56.0 mm) |
| Valve guide height from cylinder head surface ... ... ... ... | | 0.610 to 0.626 in (15.5 to 15.9 mm) |
| **Valve guide inner diameter:** | | |
| Intake ... ... ... ... ... ... ... ... ... | | 0.3438 to 0.3443 in (8.732 to 8.745 mm) |
| Exhaust ... ... ... ... ... ... ... ... ... | | 0.3443 to 0.3448 in (8.744 to 8.757 mm) |
| Valve guide outer diameter. intake and exhaust ... ... ... | | 0.5635 to 0.5640 in (14.313 to 14.326 mm) |
| **Valve guide-to-stem clearance:** | | |
| Intake ... ... ... ... ... ... ... ... ... | | 0.0015 to 0.0026 in (0.039 to 0.065 mm) |
| Exhaust ... ... ... ... ... ... ... ... ... | | 0.0020 to 0.0030 in (0.051 to 0.077 mm) |
| Valve guide interference fit ... ... ... ... ... ... | | 0.0005 to 0.0018 in (0.013 to 0.045 mm) |
| Valve seat width intake and exhaust ... ... ... ... ... | | 0.0630 to 0.0669 in (1.6 to 1.7 mm) |
| Valve seat angle intake and exhaust ... ... ... ... ... | | 45° |
| Valve seat interference fit exhaust ... ... ... ... ... | | 0.0021 to 0.0031 in (0.054 to 0.080 mm) |

## Engine lubrication (J13 & J15)

| | Standard tolerance | Wear limit |
|---|---|---|
| **Oil pump:** | | |
| Rotor side clearance (outer to inner rotor) ... ... ... ... | 0.0016 to 0.0031 in (0.04 to 0.08 mm) | 0.008 in (0.2 mm) |
| Maximum rotor tip clearance ... ... ... ... ... ... | 0.0047 in (0.12 mm) | 0.008 in (0.2 mm) |
| Outer rotor to body clearance ... ... ... ... ... | 0.0059 to 0.0083 in (0.15 to 0.21 mm) | 0.020 in (0.5 mm) |
| Maximum rotor to bottom cover clearance ... ... ... ... | 0.0016 in (0.04 mm) | 0.008 in (0.2 mm) |
| **Oil pressure regulating valve:** | | |
| Oil pressure at idling ... ... ... ... ... ... | 14 to 28 lb f/sq. in (1.0 to 2.0 kg f/sq. cm) | |
| Regulating valve spring free length ... ... ... ... ... | 1.839 in (46.7 mm) | |
| Regulating valve opening pressure ... ... ... ... ... | 39.8 to 41.3 lb f/sq. in (2.8 to 2.9 kg f/sq. cm) | |
| **Oil pressure warning light** | | |
| Illuminates at ... ... ... ... ... ... ... | 2.8 to 5.7 lb f/sq. in (0.2 to 0.4 kg f/sq. cm) | |

## Torque wrench settings

| | lb f ft | kg f m |
|---|---|---|
| Cylinder head stud nut ... ... ... ... ... ... ... ... | 36 to 43 | 5.0 to 6.0 |
| Rocker shaft bracket bolt ... ... ... ... ... ... ... | 14 to 22 | 2.0 to 3.0 |
| Connecting rod big-end nuts ... ... ... ... ... ... | 20 to 25 | 2.8 to 3.5 |
| Connecting rod small end bolt (J13 engine) ... ... ... ... | 18 to 25 | 2.5 to 3.5 |
| Flywheel bolts ... ... ... ... ... ... ... ... | 29 to 36 | 4.0 to 5.0 |
| Main bearing cap bolts ... ... ... ... ... ... ... | 72 to 80 | 10 to 11 |
| Camshaft sprocket bolt ... ... ... ... ... ... ... | 29 to 36 | 4.0 to 5.0 |
| Oil pan bolts ... ... ... ... ... ... ... ... | 3.6 to 7.2 | 0.5 to 1.0 |
| Oil pump bolts ... ... ... ... ... ... ... ... | 8.7 to 13 | 1.2 to 1.8 |

1B

| | | | | | | | | | | | |
|---|---|---|---|---|---|---|---|---|---|---|---|
| Oil drain plug | ... | ... | ... | ... | ... | ... | ... | ... | ... | 14.5 to 21.7 | 2.0 to 3.0 |
| Camshaft locating plate bolts | ... | ... | ... | ... | ... | ... | ... | ... | | 3.6 to 5.8 | 0.5 to 0.8 |
| Carburetor nuts | ... | ... | ... | ... | ... | ... | ... | ... | ... | 5.8 to 8.7 | 0.8 to 1.2 |
| Manifold nuts | ... | ... | ... | ... | ... | ... | ... | ... | ... | 12 to 17 | 1.7 to 2.3 |
| Fuel pump nuts | ... | ... | ... | ... | ... | ... | ... | ... | ... | 8.7 to 13.0 | 1.2 to 1.8 |
| Crankshaft pulley bolt | ... | ... | ... | ... | ... | ... | ... | ... | 87 to 101 | 12 to 14 |
| Engine front plate bolts: | | | | | | | | | | | |
|    7/16 in bolts | ... | ... | ... | ... | ... | ... | ... | ... | ... | 3.6 to 6.5 | 0.5 to 0.9 |
|    1/2 in bolts | ... | ... | ... | ... | ... | ... | ... | ... | ... | 6.5 to 11 | 0.9 to 1.5 |
| Engine rear plate bolts: | | | | | | | | | | | |
|    9/16 in bolts | ... | ... | ... | ... | ... | ... | ... | ... | ... | 22 to 29 | 3.0 to 4.0 |
|    1/2 in bolts | ... | ... | ... | ... | ... | ... | ... | ... | ... | 6.5 to 11 | 0.9 to 1.5 |

## 45 General description

The engine is of the four cylinder, in-line type with overhead valves operated from the camshaft via pushrods and a rocker arm assembly.

The cylinder block is a deep skirt, cast-iron type with cast-in cylinders and waterways. There are three crankshaft bearings, lubrication for these being provided from drillings in the crankshaft. The center crankshaft bearing is provided with thrust washers to take up the endplay. The crankshaft itself is a special steel forging with journals which are ground and case-hardened.

Aluminium-alloy cast pistons are used with forged steel connecting rods. The piston pins (gudgeon pins) are a fully floating fit in the pistons; on J13 engines a cotter bolt is used to retain the piston pin to the connecting rod small end but J15 engines use a pree-fit assembly. Oil jets in the connecting rod big-ends are used for splash lubrication of the cylinder walls.

The cast steel cylinder head has bath tub type combustion chambers. For improved life and sealing qualities a special sintered alloy exhaust valve seat is pressed into the cylinder head.

The cast steel camshaft is chain driven from the crankshaft, and has three bearings which, together with the cam lobes, are ground and case-hardened.

The rocker shaft is made from case-hardened carbon steel, and is drilled to provide lubrication for the valve rocker arms and valve operating gear. Double valve springs are used with conventional poppet-type valves which, on some models, have a stem oil seal.

The intake and exhaust manifold are cast-iron, and are bolted to the cylinder head with gaskets inserted in between.

A dual rotor oil pump and strainer are mounted to the lower side of the crankcase and deliver oil from the oil pan (sump) through a disposable element oil filter to the main oil gallery. Further information on lubrication will be found in Section 64.

Throughout this Chapter, the operations described apply to both J-series engines unless specifically indicated as being applicable to one type only. It will be noted by many owners that the J-series engines are very similar to the BLMC A and B series engines in most of their major features.

## 46 Major operations possible with the engine installed

The following operations can be carried out with the engine still in position in the bodyframe:

1 *Removal and installation of the cylinder head assembly.*
2 *Removal and installation of the timing gear and chain.*
3 *Removal and installation of the engine mountings.*

With the front crossmember removed the following operations can also be undertaken, although it is preferable to remove the complete power unit.

4 *Removal and installation of the oil pan (sump).*
5 *Removal and installation of the oil pump.*
6 *Renewal of the main bearings.*
7 *Renewal of the big-end bearings.*
8 *Removal and installation of the piston/connecting rod assemblies.*

## 47 Major operations only possible with the engine removed

1 *Removal and installation of the crankshaft.*
2 *Removal and installation of the flywheel.*
3 *Renewal of the crankshaft rear bearing oil seal.*
4 *Removal and installation of the camshaft.*

## 48 Engine - method of removal

The engine, complete with transmission, can be lifted upward and out of the engine compartment. Removal of the engine only is very difficult due to lack of forward clearance required to clear the transmission primary shaft.

## 49 Engine/transmission - removal

1   Disconnect the lead from the battery negative (−) terminal and the

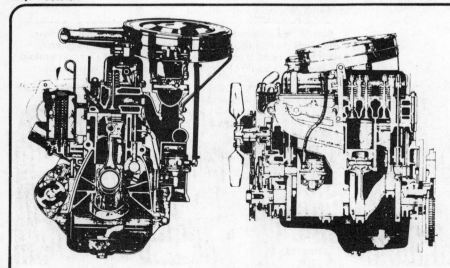

Fig. 1.44. Sectional views of typical J-series ohv engine

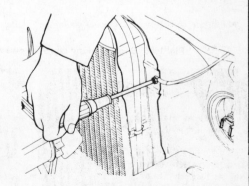

Fig. 1.45. Radiator removal. Note the body harness terminal

fusible link at its connector.

2   Mark the position of the hinge plates on the bonnet lid brackets (to facilitate installation) and then with the help of an assistant, remove the hinge bolts and lift the bonnet away.

3   Remove the air cleaner from the carburetor.

4   Drain and retain the engine coolant. If the engine is to be dismantled, drain and discard the engine oil.

5   Disconnect the radiator upper and lower hoses, then remove the radiator from the engine compartment.

6   The next step is to detach the electrical leads from the engine and ancillaries. If there is likely to be any confusion when they are reconnected, tie-on identity labels or make a sketch showing their positions. The leads vary according to the different models and engines, but will typically be:

a) *Starter motor*
b) *Alternator*
c) *HT cable at ignition coil*
d) *LT cable at distributor*
e) *Oil pressure switch lead from right-hand side of engine above starter motor (photo)*
f) *Coolant temperature switch lead from right-hand side of engine below thermostat cover (photo)*
g) *Engine ground (earth) strap from right-hand side of engine near thermostat cover*

7   Disconnect the fuel line at the fuel pump.

8   Detach the heater line from the engine side.

9   Detach the choke and accelerator wires from the carburetor (photo).

10 On column shift models, remove the cross shaft assembly from the transmission (see black arrows in Fig. 1.48). Remove the select rod from the select lever where indicated by the white arrow in Fig. 1.48. Refer to Chapter 6 for further information, if necessary.

11 On floor shift models, remove the rubber boot and shift lever. Refer to Chapter 6 for further information, if necessary.

12 Refer to the procedure given in Section 5, paragraphs 15 thru 29, except 17, 25 and 27.

---

**50 Engine - separator from manual transmission**

---

1   Refer to the procedure given in Section 6.

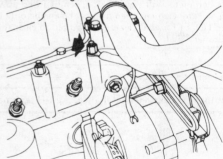

**Fig. 1.46. Engine ground strap (arrowed)**

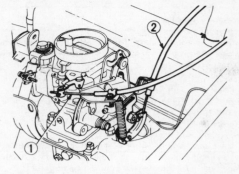

**Fig. 1.47. Choke (1) and accelerator (2) wires**

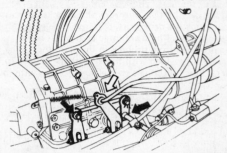

**Fig. 1.48. Column shift cross shaft and select rod removal**

1B

**Fig. 1.49. Removing floor shift lever**

---

**51 Engine dismantling - general**

---

1   Refer to the procedure given in Section 8.

---

**52 Ancillary components - removal**

---

1   Refer to the procedure given in Section 9 but note that for most applications the reference to emission control items can be ignored. Also it is preferable to remove the carburetor from the intake manifold, then remove the manifolds, from the point of view of accessibility.

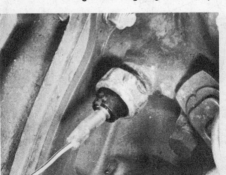

49.6e The oil pressure switch lead. The cylinder block drain plug is to the right

49.6f The coolant temperature switch lead. The engine ground strap is immediately above

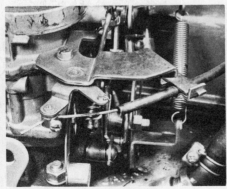

49.9 The choke wire attachment

## 53 Cylinder head - removal

1   Loosen the valve rocker shaft bracket bolts and cylinder head stud nuts in two or three progressive steps in the sequence shown in Fig. 1.52. Note the locating plate on the rear rocker shaft bracket (photo).
2   Lift off the rocker shaft as an assembly.
3   Withdraw each of the pushrods and keep them in sequences so that they can be returned to their original positions. A piece of wood with two rows of holes drilled in it and numbered will provide a very useful rack for both pushrods and valves.
4   Lift off the cylinder head. Should it be stuck, do not attempt to pry it from the engine block but tap it all round using a hardwood block or plastic faced mallet. Remove the cylinder head gasket.

## 54 Valves - removal

1   The valves can be removed from the cylinder head by the following method. Compress each spring in turn with a valve spring compressor until the two halves of the collets can be removed. Release the compressor and remove the spring and spring retainer.
2   If, when the valve spring compressor is screwed down, the valve spring retaining cap refuses to free to expose the split collect, do not continue to screw down on the compressor as there is a likelihood of damaging it.
3   Gently tap the top of the tool directly over the cap with a light hammer. This will free the cap. To avoid the compressor jumping off the valve spring retaining cap when it is tapped, hold the compressor firmly in position with one hand.
4   Slide the rubber oil control seal off the top of each valve stem and then drop out each valve through the combustion chamber.
5   It is essential that the valves are kept in their correct sequence unless they are so badly worn that they are to be renewed.

## 55 Rocker assembly - dismantling

1   Withdraw the cotter pins from each end of the rocker shaft.
2   Slide off the flat washers, wave washers, rockers, brackets, rockers and springs, keeping all of the parts in their installation order. Note that the rearmost bracket has a special set screw which secures it to the rocker shaft. This locates in the plate referred to in Section 53, paragraph 1.

## 56 Timing chain cover, timing chain and gears - removal

1   Remove the bolts from the timing chain cover, then take off the cover and gasket.
2   Remove the washer from the camshaft.
3   Remove the oil thrower disc from the crankshaft.
4   Unbolt and remove the chain tensioner.
5   Remove the camshaft and crankshaft gearwheels simultaneously complete with double roller chain. Use tire levers behind each gear, and lever them equally a little at a time. If they are stuck on their shafts, the use of a puller may be required.
6   When the gearwheels and chain are removed, extract the Woodruff keys from the crankshaft and camshaft. Note that there are two keys for the crankshaft sprocket.

## 57 Oil pan (sump), oil pump and drive gear - removal

1   Unscrew each of the oil pan retaining bolts one turn at a time to prevent distortion, then remove the oil pan and gasket.
2   Remove the bolts retaining the oil pump. Take off the oil pump and strainer assembly, and lift out the oil pump drive spindle.

## 58 Flywheel - removal

1   Fold back the lock tabs on the retaining bolt washers.
2   Loosen, then remove the crankshaft/flywheel retaining bolts. Lift away the flywheel, taking care that it is not dropped.
3   If the engine is being completely dismantled, remove the engine rear plate and gasket at this stage;

## 59 Camshaft, cam followers and engine front plate - removal

1   Remove the three bolts and washers from the camshaft retaining plate.
2   Withdraw the camshaft, rotating it as necessary. Take care that the cam lobes and journals are not damaged as they are drawn out past the cam followers and cylinder block bearings.
3   Pull out the cam followers using a magnet or suction-type valve grinding tool.
4   Remove the bolts which secure the front plate to the cylinder block, then take the front plate off.

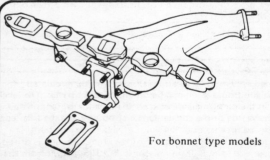

For bonnet type models

**Fig. 1.50. Intake and exhaust manifolds**

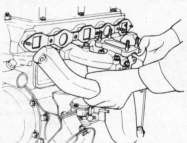

**Fig. 1.51. Removing the manifolds**

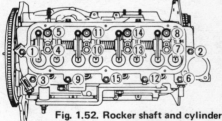

**Fig. 1.52. Rocker shaft and cylinder head nut loosening sequence**

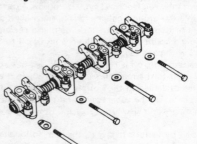

**Fig. 1.53. Rocker shaft assembly**

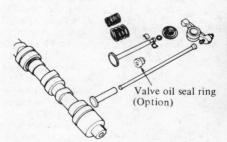

Valve oil seal ring (Option)

**Fig. 1.54. Valve operating mechanism**

53.1 The locating plate on the rear rocker shaft bracket

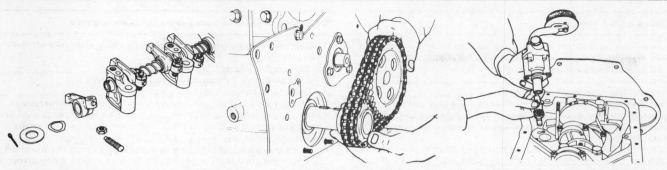

Fig. 1.55. Dismantling the rocker assembly     Fig. 1.56. Timing chain removal     Fig. 1.57. Oil pump and drive spindle removal

**1B**

### 60 Piston/connecting rod assemblies - removal

1   With the cylinder head and oil pan removed, undo the connecting rod (big-end) retaining bolts.
2   The connecting rods and pistons are lifted out from the top of the cylinder block, after the carbon or 'wear' ring at the top of the bore has been scraped away.
3   Remove the big-end caps one at a time, taking care to keep them in the right order and the correct way round. Also ensure that the shell bearings are kept with their correct connecting rods and caps unless they are to be renewed. Normally, the numbers 1 to 4 are stamped on adjacent sides of the big-end caps and connecting rods, indicating which cap is installed on which rod, and which way round the cap is installed. If no numbers or lines can be found then, with a sharp screwdriver or file, scratch mating marks across the joint from the rod to the cap. One line for connecting rod No. 1, two for connecting rod No. 2 and so on. This will ensure there is no confusion later, as it is most important that the caps go back in the correct position on the connecting rods from which they were removed.
4   If the big-end caps are difficult to remove they may be gently tapped with a soft hammer.
5   To remove the shell bearings, press the bearings opposite the groove in both the connecting rod, and the connecting rod caps and the bearings will slide out easily.
6   Withdraw the pistons and connecting rods upwards and ensure they are kept in the correct order for replacement in the same bore. Reassemble the connecting rod, caps and bearings to the rods if the bearings do not require renewal, to minimise the risk of getting the caps and rods mixed up.

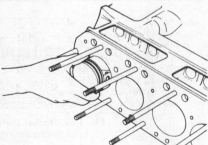

Fig. 1.58. Piston and connecting rod removal

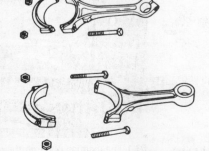

Fig. 1.59. J13 (top) and J15 (bottom) connecting rods

### 61 Main bearings and crankshaft - removal

1   Unscrew and remove the securing bolts from the main bearing caps. The caps are numbered 1 to 3 starting from the timing cover end of the engine and arrows are marked on the caps. These point towards the timing cover to ensure correct orientation of the caps when installing. If arrows are not visible, dot punch the caps on the side nearer the camshaft.
2   Withdraw the bearing caps complete with the lower halves of the shell bearings. It may be necessary to use an extractor on the rear main bearing cap - See Fig. 1.13 in Part A of this Chapter. Do not lose the thrust washers from the centre bearing cap.
3   Remove the rear oil seal.
4   Lift the crankshaft from the crankcase and then remove each of the upper halves of the shell bearings.

### 62 Piston rings - removal

1   Refer to the procedure given in Section 16 of this Chapter.

### 63 Piston pin (gudgeon pin) - removal

1   For J15 engines, refer to the procedure given in Section 17 of this Chapter.
2   For J13 engines, remove the bolt retaining the connecting rod to the piston then press the piston pin out. Ensure that each piston pin remains with its correct piston.

### 64 Lubrication system - description

A force-feed system of lubrication is fitted with oil circulated around the engine from the oil pan below the cylinder block. The level of engine oil in the oil pan is indicated by the dipstick which is fitted on the right hand side of the engine. Oil is replenished via the filler cap in the front of the rocker cover.

The oil pump is mounted at the end of the crankcase and is driven by a helical gear and spindle from the camshaft. Oil is drawn from the oil pan through a gauze screen in the oil strainer, and is sucked up the pick-up pipe and drawn into the trochoid type oil pump. From the pump it is forced under pressure along a gallery on the right hand side of the engine, and through drillings to the big-end, main and camshaft bearings. A small hole in each connecting rod allows a jet of oil to lubricate the cylinder wall with each revolution.

From the camshaft rear bearing, oil is fed through drilled passages in the cylinder block and head to the rear rocker bracket where it enters the hollow rocker shaft. Holes drilled in the hollow rocker shaft allow for lubrication of the rocker arms, the valve stems and pushrod ends. Oil from the front camshaft bearing also lubricates the timing gears and timing chain.

Oil returns to the oil pan by various passages, the cam followers being lubricated by oil returning via the pushrod drillings in the block.

A full flow cartridge type filter is fitted and oil passes through this filter before it reaches the main oil gallery. The oil is passed directly from the oil pump to the filter.

The oil pressure relief valve is located in the oil pump front cover, and is designed to control the pressure in the system to a maximum of 41 lb f/sq. in (2.9 kg f/sq. cm).

## 65 Examination and renovation - general

1   With the engine stripped, and all components thoroughly cleaned, it is now time to examine everything for wear and damage.
   Individual parts and assemblies should be checked and, where possible, renovated or otherwise renewed, as described in the following Sections.

## 66 Crankshaft and main bearings - examination and renovation

1   Refer to the procedure given in Section 21, but note the following differences:
   a)  *The torque wrench setting for the main bearing cap bolts when using Plastigage is 72 to 80 lb f ft (10 to 11 kg f m).*
   b)  *The installation depth of the clutch pilot bearing is 0.31 to 0.327 in (8.0 to 8.3 mm)*

## 67 Connecting rods and connecting rod (big-end) bearings - examination and renovation

1   Refer to the procedure given in Section 22 but note that the comparative weight of replacement connecting rods must be equal within 0.21 oz (6 gm).

## 68 Cylinder bores - examination and renovation

1   Refer to the procedure given in Section 23, but note the following differences:
   a)  *When measuring the bore diameter, the difference between the two measurements should be a maximum of 0.006 in (0.15 mm).*
   b)  *The standard clearance between a piston and the cylinder walls is between 0.0009 and 0.0017 in (0.023 and 0.0018 in (0.025 and 0.045 mm) for J15 engines.*
   c)  *The extracting force for a feeler blade 0.0016 in (0.04 mm) should be between 1.1 and 3.3 lb (0.5 and 1.5 kg).*

## 69 Crankcase, cylinder block and mountings - examination and renovation

1   Refer to the procedure given in Section 24 of this Chapter.

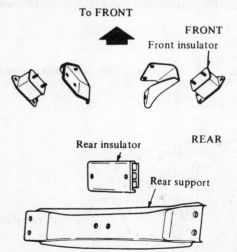

**Fig. 1.60. Front and rear engine/transmission mountings**

## 70 Pistons and piston rings - examination and renovation

1   Refer to the procedure given in Section 25 of this Chapter.

## 71 Camshaft and camshaft bearings - examination and renovation

1   The procedure is generally as described in Section 26, remembering that the camshaft bearings are in the cylinder block rather than the cylinder head.
2   Camshaft endplay should be less than 0.014 in (0.35 mm). If above the maximum, the locating plate must be renewed.

## 72 Timing chain, gears and tensioner - examination and renovation

1   Examine the teeth on both the crankshaft gear wheel and the camshaft gear wheel for wear. Each tooth forms an inverted 'V' with the gearwheel periphery, and if worn the side of each tooth under tension will be slightly concave in shape when compared with the other side of the tooth (ie; one side of the inverted 'V' will be concave when compared with the other). If any sign of wear is present the gearwheels must be renewed.
2   Examine the links of the chain for side slackness and renew the chain if any is noticeable when compared with a new chain. It is a sensible precaution to renew the chain at about 30,000 miles (48,000 km) and at a lesser mileage if the engine is stripped down for a major overhaul. The actual rollers on a very badly worn chain may be slightly grooved.
3   Examine the chain tensioner for wear, and ensure that the slipper pad and plunger move smoothly under the action of the spring. Replace as necessary.

## 73 Cylinder head and valves - servicing and decarbonising

1   Refer to the procedure given in Section 28 but note that with the cast steel cylinder head a maximum of 0.008 in (0.2 mm) of warping is permissible.

## 74 Valve operating gear - examination and renovation

1   Thoroughly clean the rocker shaft and then check the shaft for straightness by rolling it on plate glass. It is most unlikely that it will deviate from normal, but if it does, purchase a new shaft. The surface of the shaft should be free from any worn ridges caused by the rocker arms. If any wear is present, renew the shaft.
2   Check the rocker arms for wear of the rocker bushes, for wear at the rocker arm face which bears on the valve stem, and for wear of the adjusting ball ended screws. Wear in the rocker arm bush can be checked by gripping the rocker arm tip and holding the rocker arm in place on the shaft, noting if there is any lateral rocker arm shake. If shake is present, and the arm is very loose on the shaft, a new bush or rocker arm must be fitted.
3   Check the tip of the rocker arm where it bears on the valve head for cracking or serious wear on the case hardening. If none is present re-use the rocker arm. Check the lower half of the ball on the end of the rocker arm adjusting screw.
4   Check the pushrods for straightness by rolling them on the bench. Renew any that are bent.
5   Examine the bearing surface of the cam followers which lie on the camshaft. Any identation in this surface or any cracks indicate serious wear and the cam followers should be renewed. Thoroughly clean them out, removing all traces of sludge. It is most unlikely that the sides of the cam followers will prove worn, but, if they are a very loose fit in their bores, and can readily be rocked, they should be exchanged for new units. It is very unusual to find any wear, and any wear is likely to occur only at very high mileages.

## 75 Oil pump - examination and renovation

1   Refer to the procedure given in Section 29 of this Chapter.

## 76 Flywheel - servicing

1 Refer to the procedure given in Section 30 of this Chapter.

## 77 Oil seals - renewal

1 Refer to the procedure given in Section 32 of this Chapter.

## 78 Engine reassembly - general

1 Refer to the procedure given in Section 33 of this Chapter.

## 79 Engine - reassembly

1 Ensure that the oil seal groove in the crankshaft rear bearing cap is clean then press in a new seal. Repeat this operation for the groove and oil seal in the block.
2 Ensure that the seals are firmly pressed in then trim the ends flush with a sharp knife.
3 Lubricate the cam followers with engine oil then insert them into their original positions in the block.
4 Lubricate the camshaft journals and cam profiles with engine oil. Insert the camshaft carefully to avoid damage to the cams and journals.
5 Install the camshaft locating plate and tighten the bolts to the specified torque.
6 Ensure that the main bearings, bearing caps and bearing shells are clean. Position the shell halves in the block saddles and bearing caps, and stick the thrust washers to the side faces of the center bearings using a general purpose grease. Ensure that the thrust washer side oil grooves face towards the outer side of the bearing cap.
7 Lubricate the bearing shells with engine oil, ensure that the lugs on the shells are located in the bearing saddle notches then lower the crankshaft into position.
8 Ensure that the lugs on the shells are located in the steering cap notches, and that the arrow mark on the cap head is towards the timing chain end of the engine. Apply a non-setting gasket sealant to the mating faces of the rear main bearing cap then position the caps on the journals in their correct order.
9 Tighten the bearing cap bolts progressively in the order shown in Fig. 1.64 to the specified torque.
10 Check that the crankshaft rotates smoothly then check the endfloat (see Section 66).
11 Apply a non-setting gasket sealant to the rear bearing side seals and front seal. Install the seals taking care that the sealing lips are not damaged.
12 Install the engine rear plate and gasket. Tighten the bolts to the specified torque.
13 Position the flywheel on the crankshaft flange. Install the bolts and new tab washers, tightening the bolts progressively to the specified torque. Fold down the washer tabs to secure the bolts.
14 Install the piston rings to the pistons by reversing the procedure given in Section 62. Ensure that the ring end gaps are staggered as shown in Fig. 1.33, taking care that they are not in the thrust and piston pin directions. Note that the top piston ring is chromium plated while the second compression ring is tapered towards the top. The oil control ring has two rails which can be interchanged and located at the top and bottom of the groove (see Fig. 1.32).
15 The piston and connecting rod must be assembled so that the notch on the piston crown or the 'F' marking is towards the timing chain end of the engine. The connecting rods must be installed in their respective cylinders, with the connecting rod and bearing cap numbers on the same side. The oil jets in the connecting rod and big-end cap bearing shells, lubricating the bearing surfaces with engine oil.
16 Compress the piston rings with a suitable compressor and, having well lubricated the rings and the cylinder bore with engine oil, tap the piston/connecting rod assembly into the cylinder.
17 Engage the connecting rod with the crankshaft when the crankpin is at its lowest point of rotational travel. Lubricate the exposed part of the crankpin.
18 Install the big-end cap complete with shell bearing, making sure that the numbers are adjacent and in their correct sequence.

19 Tighten the nuts to the specified torque then repeat the procedure for the remaining pistons/connecting rods and bearings.
20 Install the engine front plate and gasket, and tighten the bolts to the specified torque.
21 Position the camshaft and crankshaft keys in their grooves then temporarily install both camshaft and crankshaft sprockets. Ideally the sprocket faces should be flush, but if the crankshaft sprocket is 0.020 in (0.5 mm) or more below the camshaft sprocket it is permissible to use a washer of 0.006 in (0.15 mm) under the crankshaft sprocket.
22 Remove the two sprockets then install them to the chain in the relationship shown in Fig. 1.68.
23 Install the chain and sprockets, lubricating them with engine oil. Tighten the camshaft sprocket bolt to the specified torque.
24 Install the chain tensioner, and check that the dimension 'L' (Fig. 1.69) is less than 0.591 in (15 mm). If this is not so, the tensioner slipper/spindle must be replaced.
25 Install the oil thrower to the end of the crankshaft.
26 Apply a little general purpose grease to the front cover oil seal lips, and non-setting jointing compound to the gasket surfaces. Install the cover and gasket, and tighten the retaining bolts.
27 Install the crankshaft pulley, followed by the tab washer and bolt. Prevent the crankshaft from rotating by jamming the flywheel with a sharp cold chisel or screwdriver passed through the starter motor aperture in the rear plate then tighten the bolt to the specified torque.
28 Lubricate the oil pump and drive spindle with engine oil. Position a new gasket on the oil pump then install the drive spindle. Install the pump to the block and tighten the bolts to the specified torque.
29 Install the oil pan and gasket; tighten the bolts in a crosswise order to the specified torque.

## 80 Cylinder head and rocker shaft - reassembly and installation

1 Insert each valve into its respective guide, applying a little engine oil to the stem.
2 Install a new oil seal to the valve stem and with the aid of a spring compressor, assemble the springs, retainers and split collets. The latter can be retained in the valve stem cut-out with a dab of thick grease.
3 Assemble the rocker shaft by reversing the procedure given in Section 55. The special set screw should be installed in the rear bracket to secure the shaft; if necessary it can be backed off slightly so that the oblong projection will locate in the slot of the locating plate.
4 Position a new cylinder head gasket on the block, using a non-setting sealant on the joint faces of the block and cylinder head.
5 Insert the pushrods into their original positions in the block, then position the rocker assembly so that the adjuster screws seat in the pushrod ends.
6 Tighten the cylinder head stud nuts and rocker shaft bracket bolts to their respective torque valves in the sequence shown in Fig. 1.72. This sequence should be carried out progressively and must be rechecked at a later stage after the engine has been initially warmed up.

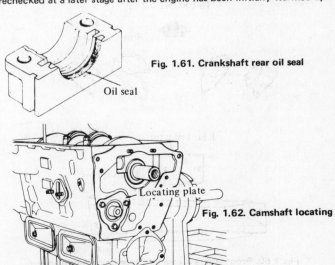

**Fig. 1.61. Crankshaft rear oil seal**

Oil seal

Locating plate

**Fig. 1.62. Camshaft locating**

**1B**

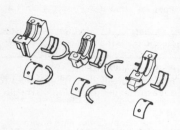

Fig. 1.63. Main bearing caps and bearings

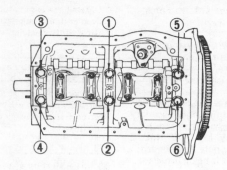

Fig. 1.64. Tightening sequence for main bearing cap bolts

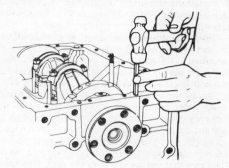

Fig. 1.65. Installing rear bearing side seal

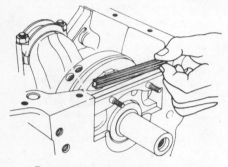

Fig. 1.66. Installing the front seal

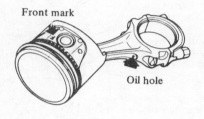

Fig. 1.67. Piston and connecting rod alignment

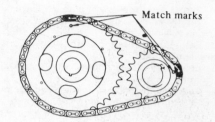

Fig. 1.68. Sprocket alignment marks

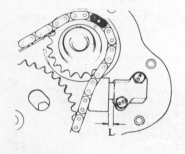

Fig. 1.69. Chain tensioner installation

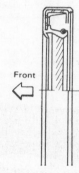

Fig. 1.70. Front cover oil seal installation

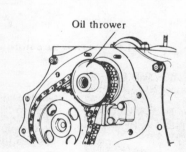

Fig. 1.71. Crankshaft oil thrower

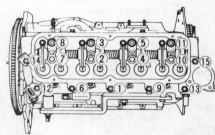

Fig. 1.72. Tightening sequence for cylinder head and rocker shaft

## 81 Valve clearance - adjustment

**Note:** The procedure given in this Section should be carried out when the engine is hot (ie; at a temperature of 176°F (80°C) or higher). If the engine is undergoing rebuild, the procedure from paragraph 2 thru 4 is applicable, using the clearances as stated. After an initial warm up run, the clearances must be rechecked after the cylinder head bolts have been retightened.

1   Remove the air cleaner and valve rocker cover.
2   Rotate the engine until no. 1 piston is at top-dead-center (tdc) on its firing stroke. At this point there should be clearance between the rockers and valve stems on no 1 cylinder exhaust valve, not cylinder intake valve, no 2 cylinder intake valve **and** no 3 cylinder exhaust valve. If it is found that there is clearance at no 2 cylinder exhaust valve, no 3 cylinder intake valve, no 4 cylinder intake valve **and** no 4 cylinder exhaust valve, the crankshaft must be rotated one turn since no 4 piston has inadvertently been set to tdc on its firing stroke.
3   With no 1 piston set as described in the previous paragraph, set the clearance on the first four valves listed (these are 1, 2, 3 and 5 in Fig. 1.73) by loosening the locknut on the adjuster screw then rotating the screw to obtain a firm sliding fit of a feeler gauge inserted between the rocker and valve stem. The correct clearance (feeler gauge thickness) is given in the specifications. Tighten the locknut on completion of each adjustment then recheck the clearance (photo).

4   Repeat the procedure for the second four valves listed in paragraph 2 (these are 4, 6, 7 and 8 in Fig. 1.73) after rotating the crankshaft one complete turn (360°).
5   On completion, install the rocker cover using a new gasket when necessary.
6   Install the air cleaner, referring to Chapter 3 as necessary.
7   Install the hose from the intake manifold (crankcase ventilation valve) to the rocker cover and secure any hoses, wires etc, in the clips (photo).

## 82 Engine - final stages of assembly after major repair

1   Install the engine side covers, tightening the bolts to the specified torque.
2   Install the water pump assembly, referring to Chapter 2 for further information, if necessary.
3   Install the thermostat and cover, referring to Chapter 3 for further information, if necessary.
4   Install the fuel pump and gasket (and heat shield, where applicable), referring to Chapter 3 for further information, if necessary.
5   Install the intake and exhaust manifolds using new gaskets, tightening the retaining bolts to the specified torque. Do not forget the engine lifting bracket and air cleaner support bracket(s).

6 Install the carburetor using a new insulating gasket with the notch facing upwards. Refer to Chapter 3 for further information, if necessary.

7 Install the alternator bracket, adjusting link, alternator, fan pulley, fan and fan belt in that order, then adjust the fanbelt tension as described in Chapter 2.

8 Install the oil filter bracket and gasket, then lubricate the oil filter seal with engine oil and install it hand-tight only.

9 Rotate the crankshaft so that number 1 piston is at tdc on its firing stroke (refer to the previous Section for further information if necessary necessary), then install the distributor driveshaft so that when engaged with the camshaft, the slot is in the position shown in Fig. 1.75. This job will be simplified if a 5/16 in (7.9 mm) diameter bolt or a wooden peg is installed in the driveshaft counterbore while it is being installed. Take care that the spindle does not drop into the oil pan (sump).

10 Install the rocker cover using a new gasket.

11 Install the spark plugs, HT cables, oil pressure switch, temperature switch and oil level dipstick.

12 Install the fuel and vacuum pipes.

## 83 Engine/transmission - installation

1 Refer to the procedure given in Section 42, but ignore any references to automatic transmission. At paragraph 3, the reference to Section 5 should be ignored, and the procedure of Section 49 should be substituted.

## 84 Initial start-up after major repair

1 Refer to the procedure given in Section 43, but note that the valve clearance adjustment procedure is given in Section 81.

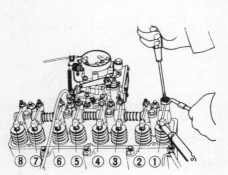

**Fig. 1.73. Valve clearance adjustment -
valve numbering sequence**

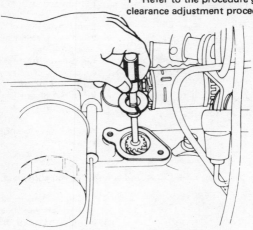

**Fig. 1.74. Installing the distributor drive**

**Fig. 1.75. The installed position of the
distributor drive spindle**

**1B**

81.3 Valve clearance adjustment

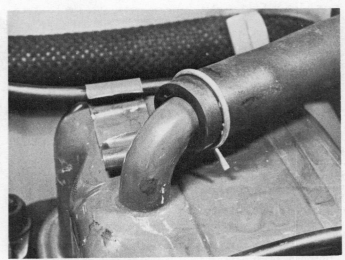

81.7 Ventilation hose connection

## 85 Fault diagnosis - engine

| Symptom | Reason/s |
| --- | --- |
| Engine will not turn over when starter switch is operated | Flat battery<br>Bad battery connections<br>Bad connections at solenoid switch and/or starter motor<br>Starter motor jammed<br>Deflective solenoid<br>Starter motor defective |
| Engine turns over normally but fails to start | No spark at plugs<br>No fuel reaching engine<br>Too much fuel reaching the engine (flooding) |
| Engine starts but runs unevenly and misfires | Igniton and/or fuel system faults<br>Incorrect valve clearances<br>Burnt out valves<br>Worn out piston rings |
| Lack of power | Ignition and/or fuel system faults<br>Incorrect valve clearances<br>Burnt out valves<br>Worn out piston rings |
| Excessive oil consumption | Oil leaks from crankshaft rear oil seal, timing cover gasket and oil seal, rocker cover gasket, oil filter gasket, oil pan gasket, oil pan plug washer<br>Worn piston rings or cylinder bores resulting in oil being burnt by engine<br>Worn valve guides and/or defective valve stem seals |
| Excessive mechanical noise from engine | Wrong valve to rocker clearances<br>Worn crankshaft bearings<br>Worn cylinders/pistons (piston slap)<br>Slack or worn timing chain and sprockets |

*NOTE: when investigating starting and uneven running faults do not be tempted into snap diagnosis. Start from the beginning of the check procedure and follow it through. It will take less time in the long run. Poor performance from an engine in terms of power and economy is not normally diagnosed quickly. In any event the ignition and fuel systems must be checked first before assuming any further investigation needs to be made.*

*On later model vehicles pay particular attention to the connections of the emission control system, and also refer to the Fault Diagnosis Section in Chapter 3.*

# Chapter 2  Cooling system

## Contents

## Specifications

**System type** ... ... ... ... ... ... ... ... ...     Pressurized with pump assistance

### Radiator
Type ... ... ... ... ... ... ... ... ...     Corrugated fin. Automatic transmission models equipped with oil cooler

Pressure cap setting ... ... ... ... ... ... ...     13 lb f/sq. in (0.9 kg f/sq. cm)

### Thermostat
Open temperature:
| | | |
|---|---|---|
| Standard ... ... ... ... ... ... ... ... ... | 180°F | (82°C) |
| Cold climates ... ... ... ... ... ... ... ... | 190°F | (88°C) |
| Hot climates ... ... ... ... ... ... ... ... | 170°F | (76.5°C) |

Fully open:
| | | |
|---|---|---|
| Standard ... ... ... ... ... ... ... ... ... | 203°F | (95°C) |
| Cold climates ... ... ... ... ... ... ... ... | 212°F | (100°C) |
| Hot climates ... ... ... ... ... ... ... ... | 194°F | (90°C) |

### Coolant capacity (J13 & J15 engines)
With heater ... ... ... ... ... ... ... ... ...     10.5 Imp. pt/12.6 US pt (6 liters)
Without heater ... ... ... ... ... ... ... ...     9.5 Imp. pt/11.4 US pt (5.4 liters)

### Coolant capacity (L16, L18 & L20B engines)
With heater ... ... ... ... ... ... ... ...     14.6 US pt/12.2 Imp. pt (6.9 liters)
Without heater ... ... ... ... ... ... ...     13.5 US pt/11.3 Imp. pt (6.4 liters)

### Antifreeze type ... ... ... ... ... ... ...     Ethylene glycol based

### Fan (J13 & J15 engines)
Type ... ... ... ... ... ... ... ... ...     Direct coupled to water pump, belt driven
Fan diameter ... ... ... ... ... ... ... ...     12.2 in (310 mm)
Number of blades ... ... ... ... ... ... ...     4

### Fan (L16, L18 & L20B engines)
1973, 74 models ... ... ... ... ... ... ... ...     Direct coupled to water pump, belt driven
1975, 76 models ... ... ... ... ... ... ... ...     Viscous coupling
Fan speed ... ... ... ... ... ... ... ...     2500 rpm max (1800 rpm max with air-conditioning)
Fan diameter ... ... ... ... ... ... ... ...     15 in (380 mm)
Number of blades ... ... ... ... ... ... ...     7 (8 with air conditioning)

## 1  General description

The cooling system comprises the radiator, top and bottom water hoses, water pump, cylinder and block water jackets, radiator cap with pressure relief valve, and flow and return heater hoses. The thermostat is located in a recess at the front of the cylinder head. The principle of the system is that cold water in the bottom of the radiator circulates upwards through the lower radiator hose to the water pump, where the pump impeller pushes the water round the cylinder block and head through the various cast-in passages to cool the cylinder bores, combustion surfaces and valve seats. When sufficient heat has been absorbed by the cooling water, the engine has reached an efficient working temperature, the water moves from the cylinder head past the now open thermostat into the top radiator hose and into the radiator header tank.

The water then travels down the radiator tubes where it is rapidly cooled by the in-rush of air, when the vehicle is in forward motion. A multi-bladed fan, mounted on the water pump pulley, assists this cooling action. The water, now cooled, reaches the bottom of the radiator and the cycle is repeated.

When the engine is cold the thermostat remains closed until the coolant reaches a pre-determined temperature (see Specifications); this assists rapid warming-up.

An electrosensitive capsule located in the cylinder head measures the water temperature.

The cooling system also provides the heat for the car interior heater and heats the inlet manifold.

On vehicles equipped with automatic transmission, the transmission fluid is cooled by a cooler attached to the base of the radiator.

On cars equipped with air conditioning systems, a condenser is placed ahead of the radiator and is bolted in conjunction with it.

On vehicles equipped with the L20B engine the radiator fan is of the fluid-coupling type and, by its limited slip characteristic, keep the fan speed down to a predetermined value which, at high engine speeds, helps to reduce power loss and noise.

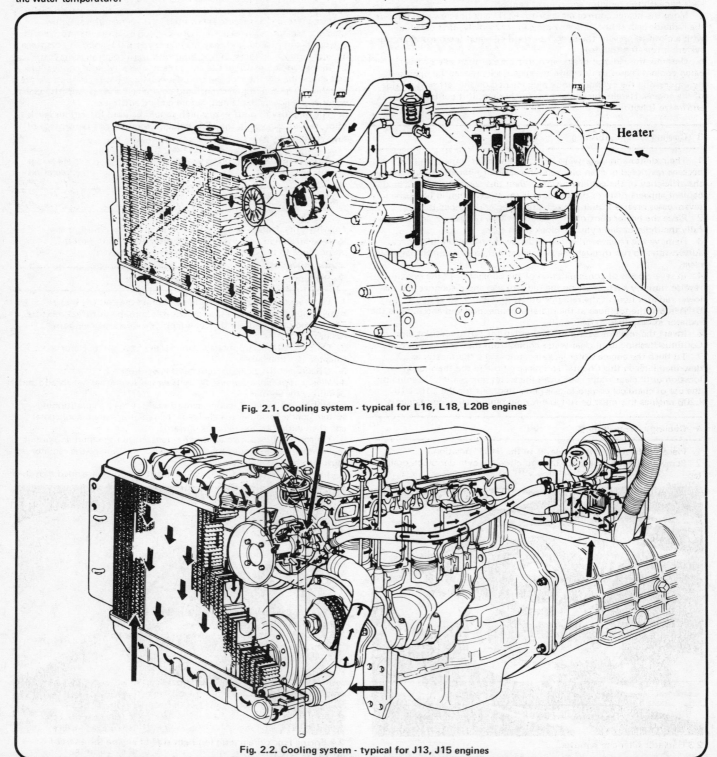

Fig. 2.1. Cooling system - typical for L16, L18, L20B engines

Fig. 2.2. Cooling system - typical for J13, J15 engines

## 2  Cooling system - draining

1   Should the system have to be left empty for any reason both the cylinder block and radiator must be completely drained, otherwise with a partly drained system corrosion of the water pump impeller seal face may occur with subsequent early failure of the pump seal and bearing.

2   Place the vehicle on level surface and have ready a container having a capacity of approximately two gallons (9 liters) which will slide beneath the radiator and oil pan (sump).

3   Move the heater control air lever to 'HOT' and unscrew and remove the radiator cap. If hot, unscrew the cap very slowly, first covering it with a cloth to prevent the danger of scalding when the pressure in the system is released (photo).

4   Unscrew the radiator drain tap at the base of the radiator then, when coolant ceases to flow into the receptacle, repeat the operation by unscrewing the cylinder block plug located on the left or right side of the engine. Retain the coolant for further use, if it contains antifreeze (photo).

## 3  Cooling system - flushing

1   The radiator and waterways in the engine after some time may become restricted or even blocked with scale or sediment which reduces the efficiency of the cooling system. When this condition occurs or the coolant appears rusty or dark in colour the system should be flushed. In severe cases reverse flushing may be required as described later.

2   Place the heater control air lever to the 'HOT' position and unscrew fully the radiator and cylinder block drain taps.

3   Remove the radiator filler cap and place a hose in the filler neck. Allow water to run through the system until it emerges quite clean and clear.

4   In severe cases of contamination of the coolant or in the system, reverse flush by first removing the radiator cap and disconnecting the lower radiator hose at the radiator outlet pipe.

5   Remove the top hose at the radiator connection end and remove the radiator as described in Section 6.

6   Invert the radiator and inser the hose in the bottom outlet pipe. Continue flushing until clear water comes from the radiator top tank.

7   To flush the engine water jackets, remove the thermostat as described later in this Chapter and place a hose in the thermostat location until clear water runs from the water pump inlet. Cleaning by the use of chemical compounds is permitted, but for the L16, L18, L20B engines this must be suitable for aluminium-alloy components.

## 4  Cooling system - filling

1   Place the heater control air lever to the 'HOT' position.

2   Screw in the radiator drain tap and close the cylinder block drain tap.

3   Pour coolant slowly into the radiator so that air can be expelled through the thermostat pin hole without being trapped in a waterway.

4   Fill to the correct level with 1¼ in. (32 mm) below the radiator filler neck and install the filler cap.

5   Run the engine at about 2000 rpm check for leaks and recheck the coolant level.

## 5  Antifreeze mixture

1   The cooling system should be filled with antifreeze solution in early autumn. The heater matrix and radiator bottom tank are particularly prone to freeze if antifreeze is not used in air temperatures below freezing. Modern antifreeze solutions of good quality will also prevent corrosion and rusting, and they may be left in the system to advantage all year around, draining and refilling with fresh solution each year.

2   Before adding antifreeze to the system, check all hose connections and check the tightness of the cylinder head bolts as such solutions are searching. The cooling system should be drained and refilled with clean water as previously explained, before adding antifreeze.

3   The quantity of antifreeze which should be used for various levels of protection is given in the table below, expressed as a percentage of the system capacity.

| Antifreeze volume | Protection to | Safe pump circulation |
|---|---|---|
| 25% | $-26°C$ ($-15°F$) | $-12°C$ ( $10°F$) |
| 30% | $-33°C$ ($-28°F$) | $-16°C$ ( $3°F$) |
| 35% | $-39°C$ ($-38°F$) | $-20°C$ ( $-4°F$) |

4   Where the cooling system contains an antifreeze solution any topping-up should be done with a solution made up in similar proportions to the original in order to avoid dilution.

## 6  Radiator - removal, inspection and installation

1   Unscrew the radiator drain plug and drain the coolant into a suitable container. Retain the coolant if it contains antifreze mixture. There is no need to drain the cylinder block when removing the radiator.

2   On L16, L18, L20B models, remove the front grille. Refer to Chapter 12, if necessary.

3   Disconnect the radiator upper and lower hoses.

4   Where applicable remove the bolts which secure the fan shroud and withdraw the shroud.

5   Unbolt the radiator, taking care to support the air conditioning system condenser mounted ahead of the radiator (where applicable) and then withdraw the radiator upwards.

6   *On cars equipped with automatic transmission* the inlet and outlet pipes which connect with the fluid cooler at the base of the radiator must also be disconnected.

7   Inspect the radiator for leaks, if evident it is recommended that the

2.3 Radiator filler cap removed

2.4 Engine block drain plug (on right side of engine for J-series) - arrowed

repair is left to a specialist or the radiator is exchanged for a reconditioned one.

8   Whenever the radiator is removed, take the opportunity of brushing all flies and accumulated dirt from the radiator fins or applying air from a tire air compressor in the reverse direction to normal airflow.

9   The radiator pressure cap should be tested by a service station and, if it leaks or its spring has weakened, it must be renewed with one of specified pressure rating.

10  Installation of the radiator is a reversal of removal. Refill the cooling system as described in Section 4.

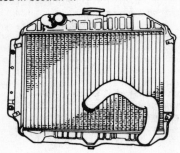

**Fig. 2.3. Radiator - typical for manual transmission models**

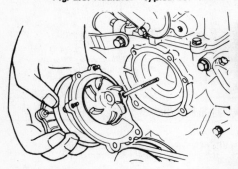

**Fig. 2.4. Removing the water pump - typical for L16, L18, L20B engines**

7.3 Removing the thermostat housing cover - typical for L16, L18, 20B engines

7.6 Correct installation of thermostat - typical for L16, L20B engines. Note the by-pass hose hole pin

## 7   Thermostat - removal, testing and installation

1   Partially drain the cooling system (about ½ gal./2.2 liters drawn off through the radiator drain plus will be sufficient).

2   Disconnect the radiator upper hose from the thermostat elbow on the left-hand side of the cylinder head.

3   Unscrew and remove the two bolts or nuts and washers, from the thermostat housing cover, and remove the cover and gasket (photo).

4   Extract the thermostat. Should it be stuck in its seat cut round its rim with a sharp pointed knife but on no account attempt to lever it out.

5   To test whether the unit is serviceable, suspend the thermostat on a piece of string in a pan of water being heated. Using a thermometer, with reference to the opening and closing temperature in Specifications, its operation may be checked. The thermostat should be renewed if it is stuck open or closed or if it fails to operate at the special temperature. The operation of the thermostat is not instantaneous and sufficient time must be allowed for the movement during test. Never install a faulty unit - leave it out if no replacement is available immediately.

6   Installation of the thermostat is the reverse of the removal procedure. Ensure the mating faces of the housing are clean. Use a new gasket with jointing compound. The word 'Top' which appears on the thermostat face must be visible from above (photo).

## 8   Water pump (L16, L18 & L20B engines) - removal and installation

1   Drain the cooling system, retaining the coolant for further use.

2   Unbolt the shroud from the radiator.

3   Loosen the alternator mounting and adjustment bolts, and push

the alternator in towards the engine so that the driving belt can be slipped off the alternator and fan pulleys.

4   Unbolt and remove the fan blade/pulley assembly from the water pump hub.

5   Unscrew evenly, and then remove, the bolts which secure the water pump to the engine front cover. If the water pump is stuck tight, do not lever it off but tap it gently with a hammer and hardwood block to break the gasket seal.

6   Where there is evidence of a leaking seal or where severe corrosion of the impeller blades has occurred, do not attempt to repair the water pump but renew it for a reconditioned exchange unit.

7   Installation is the reverse of the removal procedure, but always use a new sealing gasket and then adjust the fan belt tension, as described in Section 11. Refill the cooling system.

## 9   Water pump (J13 & J15 engines) - removal and installation

1   The procedure is as described in Section 8, except that there is no radiator shroud. Also, note that the water pump on these models can be dismantled as described in the following Section.

## 10  Water pump (J13 & J15 engines) - dismantling and reassembly

1   Remove the pump cover and gaskets by removing the countersunk screw(s).

2   Taking care that the cast iron hub is not damaged, withdraw it using a suitable puller.

3   In a similar manner, draw off the vane (impeller).

4   Pry out the locking ring with a screwdriver then press out the bearing assembly whilst supporting the pump body so that the latter cannot distort.

5   Examine the parts for damage and corrosion, and renew as necessary. Clean off any rust scale on the shaft or outer race of the bearing assembly. Inspect the mechanical seal for damage and wear.

6   Reassembly is the reverse of the removal procedure. Press off the vane (impeller), maintaining a clearance of 0.016 to 0.024 in (0.4 to 0.6 mm) between the vane tips and the pump body. Press on the hub to obtain a dimension of 3.56 to 3.57 in (90.3 to 90.7 mm) from the outer faces of the hub and pump cover.

## 11  Fanbelt - adjustment

1   In order to ensure efficient operation of the alternator and water pump, the fan drive bolt must be correctly tensioned at all times.

2   The fan belt tension is correct when there is a deflection of 0.3 to 0.47 in (8 to 12 mm) midway between the pulleys on the longest run of the belt under an applied force of 22 lb (10 kg).

3   If adjustment is required, loosen the alternator pivot and adjusting link bolts, and reposition the alternator as necessary. Tighten the bolts again afterwards.

4   If a replacement belt is installed, recheck the tension after about 200 miles (300 km) of driving.

5   Adjustment of the air pump and compressor drive bolts is achieved by repositioning the idler pulleys. The belt layout is shown in Fig. 2.7.

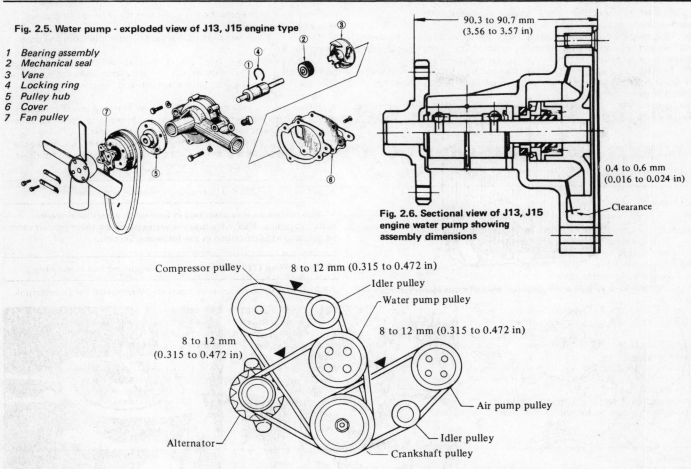

Fig. 2.5. Water pump - exploded view of J13, J15 engine type

1  Bearing assembly
2  Mechanical seal
3  Vane
4  Locking ring
5  Pulley hub
6  Cover
7  Fan pulley

90.3 to 90.7 mm
(3.56 to 3.57 in)

0.4 to 0.6 mm
(0.016 to 0.024 in)

Clearance

Fig. 2.6. Sectional view of J13, J15 engine water pump showing assembly dimensions

Compressor pulley

8 to 12 mm (0.315 to 0.472 in)

Idler pulley

Water pump pulley

8 to 12 mm (0.315 to 0.472 in)

8 to 12 mm (0.315 to 0.472 in)

Air pump pulley

Alternator

Idler pulley

Crankshaft pulley

Fig. 2.7. Layout of fan, air pump and air conditioning compressor drivebelts

## 12 Fault diagnosis - cooling system

| Symptom | Reason/s |
|---|---|
| Heat generated in cylinders not being successfully dissipated by radiator | Insufficient water in cooling system<br>Fan belt slipping (accompanied by a shrieking noise on rapid engine acceleration)<br>Radiator core blocked or radiator grille restricted<br>Bottom water hose collapsed, impeding flow<br>Thermostat not opening properly<br>Ignition advance and retard incorrectly set (accompanied by loss of power and perhaps misfiring)<br>Carburetor incorrectly adjusted (mixture too lean)<br>Exhaust system partially blocked<br>Oil level in sump too low<br>Blown cylinder head gasket (water/steam being forced down the radiator overflow pipe under pressure)<br>Engine not yet run-in<br>Brakes binding |
| Too much heat being dissipated by radiator | Thermostat jammed open<br>Incorrect grade of thermostat fitted allowing premature opening of valve<br>Thermostat missing |
| Leaks in system | Loose clips on water hoses<br>Top or bottom water hoses perished and leaking<br>Radiator core leaking<br>Thermostat gasket leaking<br>Pressure cap spring worn or seal ineffective<br>Blown cylinder head gasket (pressure in system forcing water/steam down overflow pipe)<br>Cylinder wall or head cracked |

2

# Chapter 3 Carburation; fuel, exhaust and emission control systems

*Refer to Chapter 13 for specifications and information applicable to 1977 through 1979 USA models*

## Contents

## Specifications

### Fuel pump
| | |
|---|---|
| Type ... ... ... ... ... ... ... ... ... ... | Diaphragm type, mechanically operated from camshaft eccentric |
| Fuel pressure ... ... ... ... ... ... ... ... | 3 to 3.8 lb f/sq. in (0.21 to 0.27 kg f/sq. cm) |
| Pump capacity at 1000 rpm ... ... ... ... ... ... | 1 liter/min. (2.1 US pt/1.76 Imp. pt) |

### Air cleaner
| | |
|---|---|
| Type ... ... ... ... ... ... ... ... | Viscous or dry paper element. USA models incorporate automatic inlet air temperature control device |

### Carburetor (North American)
| | |
|---|---|
| Type ... ... ... ... ... ... ... ... ... | Downdraft, twin barrel |
| 1973 models ... ... ... ... ... ... ... ... | DCH 340-8 (Manual transmission) |
| | DCH 340-9 (Automatic transmission) |
| 1974 models ... ... ... ... ... ... ... | DCH 340-12 (Manual transmission) |
| | DCH 340-13 (Automatic transmission) |
| 1975/76 models (except 1976 California) ... ... ... | DCH 340-47 (Manual transmission) |
| | DCH 340-48 (Automatic transmission) |
| 1976 California models ... ... ... ... ... ... | DCH 340-45A (Manual transmission) |
| | DCH 340-46 (Automatic transmission) |

### Carburetor specification (DCH 340-8 & -9)
| | Primary | Secondary |
|---|---|---|
| Main jet ... ... ... ... ... ... ... ... | 97.5 | 170 |
| Main air bleed ... ... ... ... ... ... ... | 65 | 60 |
| Slow jet ... ... ... ... ... ... ... ... | 48 | 90 |
| Slow air bleed ... ... ... ... ... ... ... | 145 | 100 |
| Slow economizer, in (mm) ... ... ... ... ... ... | 0.071 (1.8) | |
| Power jet ... ... ... ... ... ... ... | 53 | |
| Fuel level, in (mm) ... ... ... ... ... ... | 0.906 (23) | |
| CO emission: | | |
|   Manual transmission ... ... ... ... ... ... | 1.5 $\pm$ 0.5% at 5°/800 rpm (retard side) | |
|   Automatic transmission ... ... ... ... ... | 1.5 $\pm$ 0.5% at 5°/650 rpm (retard side) in D range | |
| Valve stem/float seat gap ... ... ... ... ... | 0.059 in (1.5 mm) | |
| Fast idle gap: | | |
|   Manual transmission ... ... ... ... ... | 0.035 to 0.039 in (0.9 to 1.0 mm) | |
|   Automatic transmission ... ... ... ... ... | 0.044 to 0.048 in (1.12 to 1.22 mm) | |

| | |
|---|---|
| Vacuum break gap ... ... ... ... ... ... ... ... | 0.067 in (1.7 mm) |
| Choke unloader gap ... ... ... ... ... ... ... ... | 0.173 in (4,4 mm) |
| Bimetal setting ... ... ... ... ... ... ... ... | 17° (center of index marks) |
| Bimetal resistance ... ... ... ... ... ... ... ... | 9.8 to 10.2 ohm at 70°F (21°C) |
| Primary/secondary throttle valve interlock opening ... ... | 0.291 in (7.4 mm) |
| Dashpot adjustment ... ... ... ... ... ... ... | 1600/1800 rpm |
| B.C.D.D. set pressure (at standard sea-level conditions): | |
| Manual transmission ... ... ... ... ... ... | $-19.7 \pm 0.79$ in Hg ($-500 \pm 20$ mm Hg) |
| Automatic transmission ... ... ... ... ... ... | $-18.9 \pm 0.79$ in Hg ($-480 \pm 20$ mm Hg) |

## Carburetor specifications (DCH 340-12 & -13)
*Carburetor details are as listed for the DCH 340-8 and -9 models, except as given below:*

| | |
|---|---|
| Main jet (primary) ... ... ... ... ... ... ... ... | 100 |
| Main air bleed (primary) ... ... ... ... ... ... ... | 60 |
| Slow jet (primary) ... ... ... ... ... ... ... ... | 45 |
| Power jet ... ... ... ... ... ... ... ... ... | 41 |
| CO emission: | |
| Manual transmission ... ... ... ... ... ... ... | 1.5% at 12°/800 rpm |
| Automatic transmission ... ... ... ... ... ... ... | 1.5% at 12°/650 rpm in D range |
| Bimetal setting ... ... ... ... ... ... ... ... | 22° (center of index marks) |

## Carburetor specifications (DCH 340-47 & -48)

| | Primary | Secondary |
|---|---|---|
| Main jet ... ... ... ... ... ... ... ... ... | 99 | 160 |
| Main air bleed ... ... ... ... ... ... ... ... | 70 | 60 |
| Slow jet ... ... ... ... ... ... ... ... ... | 48 | 80 |
| Power valve ... ... ... ... ... ... ... ... | 43 | |
| Fuel level ('H'), in (mm) ... ... ... ... ... ... | 0.906 (23) | |
| CO emission: | | |
| Manual transmission ... ... ... ... ... ... | $2 \pm 1$% at 12°/750 rpm | |
| Automatic transmission ... ... ... ... ... ... | $2 \pm 1$% at 12°/650 rpm in D range | |
| Float setting (see text): | | |
| H ... ... ... ... ... ... ... ... ... | 0.283 in (7.2 mm) | |
| h ... ... ... ... ... ... ... ... ... | 0.051 to 0.067 in (1.3 to 1.7 mm) | |
| Fast idle gap: | | |
| Manual transmission ... ... ... ... ... ... | 0.040 to 0.048 in (1.01 to 1.21 mm) | |
| Automatic transmission ... ... ... ... ... ... | 0.049 to 0.052 in (1.01 to 1.21 mm) | |
| Vacuum break gap (1975 models) ... ... ... ... | 0.065 in (1.65 mm) | |
| Vacuum break gap (1976 models) ... ... ... ... | 0.056 in (1.42 mm) | |
| Choke unloader gap ... ... ... ... ... ... ... | 0.096 in (2.45 mm) | |
| Bimetal setting ... ... ... ... ... ... ... ... | Center of index mark | |
| Bimetal resistance ... ... ... ... ... ... ... | 3.7 to 8.9 ohms at 70°F (21°C) | |
| Primary/secondary throttle valve interlock opening ... ... | 0.291 in (7.38 mm) | |
| Dashpot adjustment: | | |
| Manual transmission ... ... ... ... ... ... ... | 1900/2100 rpm | |
| Automatic transmission ... ... ... ... ... ... | 1650/1850 rpm | |
| B.C.D.D. set pressure (at standard sea-level conditions): | | |
| Manual transmission ... ... ... ... ... ... ... | $-20.7$ to $-21.1$ in Hg ($-525$ to $-535$ mm Hg) | |
| Automatic transmission ... ... ... ... ... ... | $-19.9$ to $-20.3$ in Hg ($-505$ to $-515$ mm Hg) | |

## Carburetor specifications (DCH 340-45A)
*Carburetor details are as listed for the 1976 DCH 340-47 model (manual transmission), except as given below:*

| | |
|---|---|
| CO emission ... ... ... ... ... ... ... ... ... | $2 \pm 1$% at 10°/750 rpm |

## Carburettor specifications (DCH 340-46)
*Carburettor details are as listed for the DCH 340-48 model (automatic transmission), except as given below:*

| | |
|---|---|
| Main jet (primary) ... ... ... ... ... ... ... ... | 101 |
| Slow jet (secondary) ... ... ... ... ... ... ... | 80 |
| Power valve ... ... ... ... ... ... ... ... | 40 |
| CO emission ... ... ... ... ... ... ... ... | 0.3% at 12°/650 rpm in 'D' range |
| Vacuum break gap ... ... ... ... ... ... ... | 0.059 in (1.5 mm) |

## Engine idle speed (North American models)

| | |
|---|---|
| 1973/74 models ... ... ... ... ... ... ... ... | 800 rpm (manual transmission) |
| | 650 rpm (automatic transmission, in 'D' range) |
| 1975/76 models ... ... ... ... ... ... ... ... | 750 rpm (manual transmission) |
| | 650 rpm (automatic transmission in 'D' range) |
| Fast idle speed ... ... ... ... ... ... ... ... | 1900 to 2100 rpm (manual transmission) |
| | 2300 to 2500 rpm (automatic transmission) |

## Carburetor (J13 & J15 engined models)

| | |
|---|---|
| Type ... ... ... ... ... ... ... ... ... | Downdraft, twin barrel |
| N62OU, GN620U body numbers ... ... ... ... ... | 214282 - 124 |
| NL620, GNL620, UNL620, NL620T, GNL620T body numbers ... ... | 214282 - 132 |

| | | |
|---|---|---|
| 620U, G620U, U620U body numbers ... ... ... ... ... | 214260 - 122 | |
| L620, LG620, UL620, L620T, LG620T body numbers ... ... ... | 214260 - 132 | |

## Carburetor specifications (214282 - 124 & -132)

| | Primary | Secondary |
|---|---|---|
| Main jet ... ... ... ... ... ... ... ... ... ... ... | 100 | 150 |
| Main air bleed ... ... ... ... ... ... ... ... ... ... | 60 | 60 |
| Slow jet ... ... ... ... ... ... ... ... ... ... ... | 46 | 70 |
| First slow air bleed ... ... ... ... ... ... ... ... | 100 | — |
| Second slow air bleed ... ... ... ... ... ... ... ... | 200 | 220 |
| Power jet ... ... ... ... ... ... ... ... ... ... | 45 | |
| Float lever distance from upper surface of body ... ... ... | 0.846 in (21.5 mm) | |
| Throttle valve closed angle ... ... ... ... ... ... ... | 10° | 20° |
| Secondary throttle valve opening angle ... ... ... ... | 50° | |
| Choke valve closed angle ... ... ... ... ... ... ... | 10° | |

## Carburetor specifications (214260 - 122 & -132)

| | Primary | Secondary |
|---|---|---|
| Main jet ... ... ... ... ... ... ... ... ... ... ... | 88 | 145 |
| Main air bleed ... ... ... ... ... ... ... ... ... ... | 60 | 80 |
| Slow jet ... ... ... ... ... ... ... ... ... ... ... | 48 | 70 |
| First slow air bleed ... ... ... ... ... ... ... ... | 100 | — |
| Second slow air bleed ... ... ... ... ... ... ... ... | 240 | 190 |
| Power jet ... ... ... ... ... ... ... ... ... ... | 50 | |
| Float lever distance from upper surface of body ... ... ... | 0.846 in (21.5 mm) | |
| Throttle valve closed angle ... ... ... ... ... ... ... | 7° | 20° |
| Secondary throttle valve opening angle ... ... ... ... | 53° | |
| Choke valve closed angle ... ... ... ... ... ... ... | 10° | |

## Engine idle speed (all models) ... ... ... ... ... ... ...

600 rpm

## Fuel tank capacity

| | |
|---|---|
| Pick-up ... ... ... ... ... ... ... ... ... ... ... | 11.9 US gal/9.9 Imp. gal (45 liters) |
| Double pick-up ... ... ... ... ... ... ... ... ... | 10.6 US gal/8.8 Imp. gal (40 liters) |

## Fuel octane requirement

| | |
|---|---|
| 1976 California models ... ... ... ... ... ... ... ... | Unleaded gasoline |
| Other models ... ... ... ... ... ... ... ... ... | Unleaded or low-lead gasoline, 91RON (2-star UK rating) |

## Torque wrench settings

| | lb f ft | kg f m |
|---|---|---|
| Carburetor nuts ... ... ... ... ... ... ... ... ... | 3.6 to 7.2 | 0.5 to 1.0 |
| B.C.D.D. ... ... ... ... ... ... ... ... ... | 1.45 to 2.9 | 0.2 to 0.4 |
| Anti-dieseling solenoid ... ... ... ... ... ... ... | 15 to 29 | 2.1 to 4.0 |
| Accelerator pedal stop bolt ... ... ... ... ... ... | 2.7 to 3.2 | 0.38 to 0.45 |
| Fuel tank drain plug ... ... ... ... ... ... ... ... | 36 to 43 | 5.0 to 6.0 |
| Fuel tank securing bolt ... ... ... ... ... ... ... | 8.0 to 5.8 | 0.8 to 1.1 |
| Reservoir tank securing bolt ... ... ... ... ... ... | 2.3 to 3.2 | 0.32 to 0.44 |
| Exhaust manifold to front tube nut ... ... ... ... ... | 14 to 18 | 1.9 to 2.5 |
| U-bolt nut ... ... ... ... ... ... ... ... ... | 14 to 15 | 1.9 to 2.1 |
| Mounting bracket bolt ... ... ... ... ... ... ... | 7 to 9 | 1.0 to 1.2 |
| Front tube mounting bracket bolt (1976 California) ... ... | 14 to 15 | 1.9 to 2.1 |
| Catalytic converter-to-tube bolts (1976 California models) ... ... | 23 to 31 | 3.2 to 4.3 |

## 1  General description

All models are equipped with a rear mounted fuel tank, a mechanically operated fuel pump and a carburetor with the necessary pipe lines. The type of carburetor depends upon the engine type and vehicle model (see Specifications).

Emission control systems vary considerably according to the engine type, vehicle model and operating territory. The system components are dealt with in the appropriate Sections towards the end of this Chapter.

## 2  Automatic temperature control air cleaner

1  This type of air cleaner is installed on models which have a full emission control system.

2  The air cleaner incorporates a sensor and valve device which 'mixes' the air being drawn into the carburetor to maintain the air temperature at a predetermined level thus preventing icing of the carburetor, reduction of exhaust emission and reduced condensation within the rocker cover.

3  Hot air is drawn from the interior of a deflector plate attached to the exhaust manifold.

4  When the engine is operating under full load, a vacuum diaphragm

connected to the intake manifold opens the control valve fully to exclude hot air and override the sensor 'mixing' device.

5  Renewal of the paper type element is carried out by unscrewing the wing nut, springing back the clips (where applicable), and removing the air cleaner lid (still with all connecting hoses attached).

6  If the air cleaner assembly is to be removed complete, then disconnect the following, as applicable:

a) Main air inlet hose.
b) Hot air inlet hose.
c) Sensor to inlet manifold vacuum hose.
d) Sensor to vacuum capsule hose.
e) Idle compensator to inlet manifold hose.
f) Air pump to air cleaner hose.
g) Flame trap to air cleaner hose.
h) Carburetor to air cleaner.
j) Air cleaner to rocker cover blow-by hose.

7  Unbolt the air cleaner from its supports.

8  In the event of a fault developing which may be reflected in poor idling, increased fume emission or carburetor icing, or the formation of condensation within the rocker cover, carry out the following checks:

9  Inspect all air cleaner hose connections for security and correct location.

10  Run the engine until normal operating temperature is reached and then allow the engine to idle for a few minutes with the bonnet closed. Switch off the engine and, with the aid of a mirror, inspect the position

of the air control valve within the air cleaner intake nozzle. The valve should be closed against exhaust manifold heated air. Conversely, with the engine cold and under bonnet temperature below 100°F (38°C), the valve should be open to exhaust manifold heated air.

11 Where these tests prove the sensor unit to be faulty, flatten the retaining clips and disconnect the hoses by pulling them from their nozzles. Note the relative positions of the two hoses.

12 Remove the sensor but leave the gasket which is bonded to the air cleaner body.

13 An idle compensator is installed in the base of the air cleaner assembly and its purpose is to direct air into the intake manifold to compensate for abnormal enrichment which can occur at high ambient temperature when idling. 1973 and 1974 models have a single dimetal compensator; 1975 and 1976 models have a dual bimetal compensator.

14 The single bimetal compensator opens at a temperature of 149 to 167°F (65 to 75°C). The valves of the dual bimetal compensator operate at different temperatures: No. 1 opens at a temperature of 140 to 158°F (60 to 70°C) and No. 2 opens at a temperature of 158 to 194°F (70 to 90°C).

15 A faulty idle compensator may be suspected if idling becomes erratic.

16 To test the compensator valve, ensure that the ambient temperature is below the opening level and blow and suck through the connecting hose. Any escape of air will mean that the compensator must be renewed.

17 Access to the compensator is obtained after removing the air cleaner cover.

18 Installation of the air cleaner element and component parts is the reverse of the removal procedure.

## 3  Alternative type air cleaners

1  For some markets, a dry paper element air cleaner is installed. This requires no maintenance other than periodic cleaning with a compressed air blast or replacement.

2  A viscous paper element is installed for some markets, the only maintenance being replacement at the intervals given in the Routine Maintenance Section at the beginning of the manual.

3  For most applications a summer/winter lever is incorporated to enable the intake air to be drawn from the engine compartment (summer setting) or from a heat stove around the exhaust manifold (winter setting) (photo).

4  To remove an air cleaner element, unscrew the wing nut, spring back the cover clips (where applicable) and lift off the cover. Note the flexible pipe to the heat stove, this should be detached if the cover is to be completely removed.

5  Lift off the air cleaner element, taking care that dirt does not fall into the carburetor.

6  If the air cleaner base is to be removed, undo the clamp screw and remove the screws from the support brackets. Note the ventilation hose from the engine side cover to the air cleaner base (photo).

## 4  Fuel line filter - renewal

1  The filter is of cartridge, disposable type and should be renewed at

intervals not greater than 12000 miles (20000 km).

2  The condition of the element can be seen through its transparent bowl (photo).

3  The filter is located adjacent to the mechanical fuel pump, and is removed and replaced simply by disconnecting the hoses from it and then pulling it from its retaining clip.

4  It is recommended that the filter fuel lines are not disconnected when there is a high level of fuel in the tank. In any event, the supply hose from the tank should be raised and plugged immediately it is removed from the fuel filter.

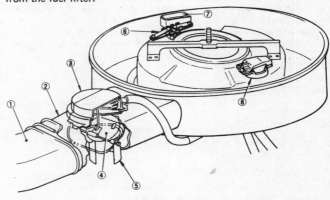

**Fig. 3.1. Automatic temperature control air cleaner**

1  Fresh air duct (except Canada)  
2  Air inlet  
3  Vacuum motor assembly  
4  Air control valve  
5  Hot air pipe  
6  Idle compensator  
7  Blow-by gas filter  
8  Temperature sensor

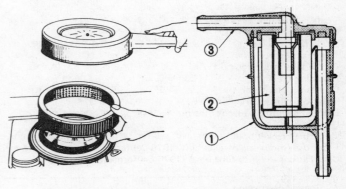

**Fig. 3.2. Air cleaner element renewal - typical**

**Fig. 3.3. Fuel line filter - sectional view**

1  Body  
2  Filter element  
3  Cover

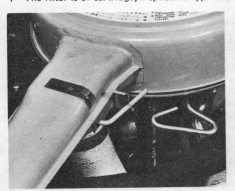

3.3 Summer/winter setting lever on air cleaner

3.6 Air cleaner clamp screw and ventilation hose

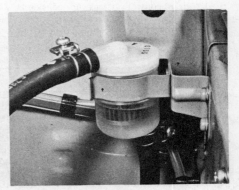

4.2 The fuel line filter

## 5   Fuel pump - description and testing

The fuel pump is actuated by the movement of its rocker arm on a camshaft eccentric. This movement is transferred to a flexible diaphragm which draws the fuel from the tank and pumps it under pressure to the carburetor float chamber. Inlet and outlet valves are incorporated to control the flow of fuel irrespective of engine speed.

Presuming that the fuel lines and unions are in good condition and that there are no leaks anywhere, check the performance of the fuel pump in the following manner: Disconnect the fuel pipe at the carburetor inlet union, and the high tension lead to the coil, and with a suitable container or a large rag in position to catch the ejected fuel, turn the engine over on the starter motor solenoid. A good spurt of fuel should emerge from the end of the pipe every second revolution.

## 6   Fuel pump - removal and installation

1   Disconnect the hoses from the pump inlet and outlet nozzles. It is recommended that the fuel lines are not disconnected when the fuel tank is fairly full and in any event the supply pipe from the tank should be raised above the level of fuel in the tank and plugged as soon as it is removed from the pump.
2   Unscrew and remove the securing nuts from the fuel pump flange and remove the pump. Note the sequence of gaskets and spacer. Note that on some models a heat shield is installed.
3   Installation is the reverse of the removal procedure.

## 7   Fuel pump - dismantling, inspection and reassembly

1   Remove the five cover securing screws; remove the cover and the gasket.
2   Scratch a mark across the edges of the upper and lower body flanges so that they can be replaced in the same relative positions.
3   Unscrew and remove the screws from the body flange.
4   Unscrew and remove the inlet and outlet elbows.
5   Unscrew and remove the two screws from the valve retainer and remove the two valves.
6   Unhook the diaphragm pushrod from the fork at the end of the rocker arm by depressing the diaphragm against the action of its spring and then tilting the diaphragm/rod assembly until the bottom of the rod can be felt to touch the inside of the pump body.
7   Take care not to damage the oil seal as the diaphragm and pushrod are released.
8   If necessary, the rocker arm pivot pin can be driven out with a small drift.
9   Examine all components for wear or cracks and the diaphragm for porosity or deterioration and renew as appropriate.
10   Reassembly is a reversal of dismantling but use new gaskets and other components from the appropriate repair kit.
11   Grease the rocker arm and pivot before assembly.
12   When the reassembly is complete, place a finger over the inlet port and depress the rocker arm fully. A strong suction noise should be heard which indicates that the pump is operating correctly.

## 8   Carburetor (L16, L18 and L20B engines) - description

The carburetor is of the downdraft dual-barrel type. The primary throttle valve is mechanically operated while the secondary one is vacuum operated by a diaphragm unit which is actuated by the vacuum in the carburetor venturi.

An electrically assisted, bimetal-type automatic choke is incorporated. This incorporates a butterfly valve which closes one of the venturi tubes and is so synchronized with the primary valve plate that the latter opens sufficiently to provide a rich mixture and an increased slow-running speed for easy starting.

For idling and slow running, the fuel passes through the slow running jet, the primary slow air bleed and the secondary slow air bleed. The fuel is finally ejected from the bypass and the idle holes. An anti-dieseling (run-on) solenoid valve is incorporated to ensure that the fuel supply is cut-off when the ignition is switched off, thus preventing the engine from running-on.

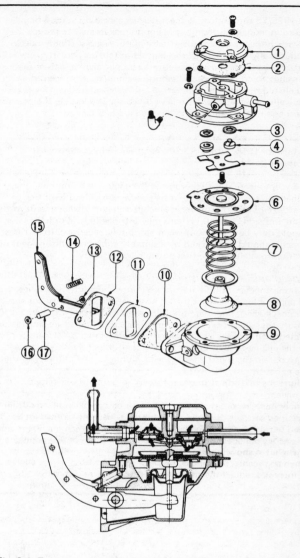

**Fig. 3.4. Fuel pump - sectional and exploded views**

| | |
|---|---|
| 1   Fuel pump cover | 10   Packing |
| 2   Cover gasket | 11   Spacer |
| 3   Valve gasket | 12   Packing |
| 4   Valve assembly | 13   Rocker arm side spacer |
| 5   Valve retainer | 14   Rocker arm spring |
| 6   Diaphragm assembly | 15   Rocker arm assembly |
| 7   Diaphragm spring | 16   Rocker arm side spacer |
| 8   Lower body seal | 17   Rocker arm pin |
| 9   Lower body | |

The accelerator pump is synchronized with the throttle valve. During periods of heavy acceleration, the pump which is of simple piston and valve construction, provides an additional metered quantity of fuel to enrich the normal mixture.

The secondary system provides a mixture for normal motoring conditions by means of a main jet and air bleed. On 1975/76 carburetors an additional high speed circuit is incorporated. It consists of a richer jet, enricher air bleed and richer nozzle, and allows additional fuel to be drawn into the secondary bore as the air velocity through that bore increases.

A boost controlled deceleration device (BCDD) is incorporated to reduce the hydrocarbons emitted which tend to occur in excess during engine over-run, when the combustion chamber fuel/air mixture is too lean to permit complete combustion. The BCDD system comprises a vacuum control solenoid valve, and a speed detecting switch and amplifier (manual transmission) or inhibitor switch (automatic transmission).

On 1975/76 carburetors, and earlier types used on automatic transmission models, a dashpot system is incorporated to reduce the rate at which the primary throttle valve closes when suddenly released. This reduces any tendency for the engine to stall, particularly when cold.

Carburetors used on 1976 California models may have an altitude compensator to correct an otherwise too rich mixture which can occur at high altitudes. The float chamber is fed with fuel pumped by the mechanically operated pump on the crankcase. The level in the chamber is critical and must at all times be maintained as specified.

## 9  Carburetor (L16, L18 and L20B engines) - adjustments with carburetor installed

**Note:** Except where it is necessary for the engine to be running, the adjustment given in this Section may also be carried out with the carburetor removed. It must be appreciated that any adjustments to the fuel (and emission control) systems may infringe federal or local laws, and should only be carried out when absolutely necessary. In all cases, adjustments should be checked by a suitably equipped Datsun agent or carburation specialist at the first possible opportunity.

### Idle speed and mixture using a CO meter

1  Run the engine until the normal operating temperature is relieved. Where applicable, disconnect the air hose between the 3-way connector and air check valve; plug the hose to prevent dust from entering.
2  Ensure that all carburetor and emission control pipes are satisfactorily connected then race the engine two or three times to 2000 rpm (approx). Allow the engine to idle for one minute then adjust the throttle speed screw to obtain the specified idle speed. Connect the CO meter to the vehicle exhaust.
3  Adjust the idle adjust (mixture) screw to obtain the specified CO percentage.
4  If necessary, repeat the procedure of paragraphs 2 and 3 to obtain the specified settings. If the idle mixture (CO percentage) cannot be adjusted within the limits of the idle limiter cap, the cap may be removed and the screw adjusted, provided that on completion of any adjustment it is installed as shown in Fig. 3.8.
5  When applicable, reconnect the air check valve hose. If the engine speed increases, adjust the throttle speed screw as necessary.

### Idle speed and mixture without using a CO meter

6  Repeat the procedure given in paragraph 1 and 2, but ignore the reference to the CO meter.
7  Rotate the idle adjust (mixture) screw until the most satisfactory idling is obtained, adjusting the idle speed screw, as necessary.
8  Rotate the idle adjust (mixture) screw clockwise until the engine speed drops by 60 to 70 rpm (manual transmission) or 15 to 25 rpm (automatic transmission) below the specified rpm. If the idle mixture cannot be adjusted within the limits of the idle limiter cap, the cap may be removed and the screw adjusted, provided that on completion it is installed as shown in Fig. 3.8.
9  Where applicable, reconnect the air check valve hose. If the engine speed increases, adjust the throttle speed screw as necessary.

### Fast idle

10  During normal tune-up operations it is possible to adjust the fast idle screw to obtain the specified rpm.

### Vacuum break (air cleaner removed)

11  This arrangement opens the choke valve plate after the engine has been started to provide the correct fuel/air ratio of the mixture under the prevailing engine operating conditions.
12  The correct setting should be checked and any adjustment carried out in the following manner. Close the choke valve plate completely with the fingers and retain the valve plate in this position using a rubber band connected between the choke piston lever and carburetor body.
13  With a pair of pliers, grip the end of the vacuum diaphragm capsule operating rod and withdraw it as far as it will go without straining it. Now bend the connecting rod (if necessary) to provide a clearance between the edge of the choke valve plate and the carburetor body as given in the Specifications.

### Choke unloader (air cleaner removed)

14  Close the choke valve plate completely with the fingers and retain the valve plate in this position using a rubber band connected between the choke piston lever and carburetor body.
15  Pull the throttle lever until it is fully open and bend the unloader tongue (if necessary) to provide a clearance between the choke valve and carburetor body as given in the Specifications.

**3**

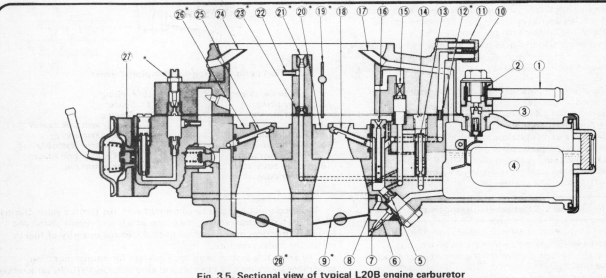

Fig. 3.5. Sectional view of typical L20B engine carburetor
Those used on other models are very similar
* Do not remove these parts

| | | |
|---|---|---|
| 1  Fuel inlet | 9*  Primary throttle valve | 15  Primary slow air bleed | 22  Richer nozzle |
| 2  Fuel filter | 10  Primary altitude compensator | 16  Primary main air bleed | 23*  Richer jet |
| 3  Needle | Pipe (California only) | 17  Primary air vent pipe | 24  Secondary air vent pipe |
| 4  Float | 11  Secondary altitude compensator | 18  Primary main nozzle | 25  Secondary main nozzle |
| 5  Primary main jet | pipe (California only) | 19  Choke valve | 26*  Secondary small venturi |
| 6  Idle adjust screw | 12*  Safe orifice | 20*  Primary small venturi | 27  BCDD |
| 7  Idle hole | 13  Primary slow jet | 21*  High-speed enricher air bleed | 28*  Secondary throttle valve |
| 8  Primary bypass hole | 14  Plug | | |

## Automatic choke

16 The normal position of the automatic choke bimetal cover is for the mark on the cover to be opposite to the centre mark of the choke housing index. Where there is a tendency to overchoke on starting up, turn the cover in a clockwise direction by not more than one division.

## Dashpot adjustment

17 Run the engine to normal operating temperature and check that the slow-running adjustment is correct.

18 Release the dashpot locknut and then adjust the position of the dashpot so that it just touches the stop plate when the engine is running at the specified speed, with the throttle linkage held open with the hand.

19 Retighten the locknut without moving the dashpot.

20 Raise the engine speed to about 2000 rpm and suddenly release the accelerator. The engine speed should be reduced to 1000 rpm in approximately three seconds otherwise the adjustment has been incorrectly carried out or the dashpot is faulty.

## Anti-dieseling solenoid valve

21 This cannot be adjusted, but in cases where the engine does not stop when the ignition is switched off a faulty solenoid is indicated and a replacement should be installed.

be as given in the Specifications.

27 If the pressure indicated on the gauge is higher than that specified, turn the adjusting screw on the valve in an anticlockwise direction; if lower, turn the screw clockwise. Repeat the testing procedure after any adjustment is made.

## Float level

28 Although the fuel level can be seen with the carburetor installed, any adjustment requires its removal. Refer to Section 10, paragraph 24.

## 10 Carburetor (L16, L18 and L20B engines) - removal, servicing and installation

**Note:** The procedure given in this Section is basically applicable to early carburetors. The slight differences on later models can be seen from the exploded illustrations.

1 Remove the air cleaner (see Section 2).

2 Disconnect the fuel and vacuum pipes from the carburetor. also the leads to the automatic choke and anti-dieseling solenoid valve.

3 Disconnect the throttle linkage from the carburetor.

4 Unscrew the four securing nuts and remove the carburetor from the intake manifold.

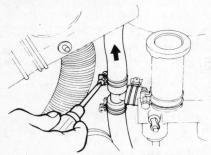

Fig. 3.6. Removing the air check valve hose

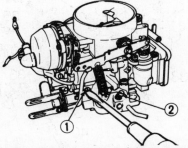

Fig. 3.7. Throttle idle speed (1) adjuster screw and idle mixture (2) adjuster screw - typical

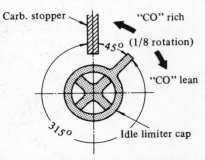

Fig. 3.8. Limiter cap correctly installed

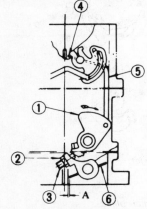

Fig. 3.9. Fast idle adjustment

1  Fast idle cam           4  Choke valve
2  Locknut                 5  Choke connecting rod
3  Fast idle adjuster screw 6  Throttle valve

A — Fast idle gap (see Specifications)

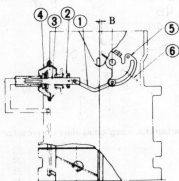
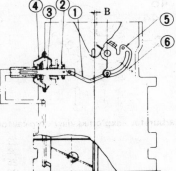

Fig. 3.10. Vacuum break adjustment

1  Choke piston rod   4  Diaphragm unit cover
2  Spring             5  Choke piston lever
3  Piston             6  Choke valve

B — Vacuum break gap (see Specifications)

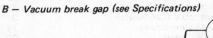

Fig. 3.11. Choke setting

1  Cover      3  Alignment
2  Housing       mark

## Boost controlled deceleration device (BCDD) - adjustment

22 It is very unusual for this operation to be required but if new components have been installed or performance is suspect proceed in the following manner.

23 A tachometer and Bourdon tube vacuum gauge will be required.

24 Run the engine until normal operating temperature is reached and then connect the vacuum gauge directly to the intake manifold. Connect the tachometer in accordance with the maker's instructions.

25 Disconnect the BCDD solenoid valve.

26 Raise the engine speed to between 3000 and 3500 rpm and then suddenly release the throttle. The manifold vacuum pressure will gradually decrease to indicate the BCDD operating pressure which should

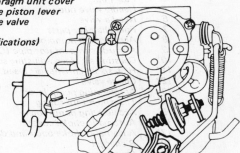

Fig. 3.12. Dashpot installation - typical

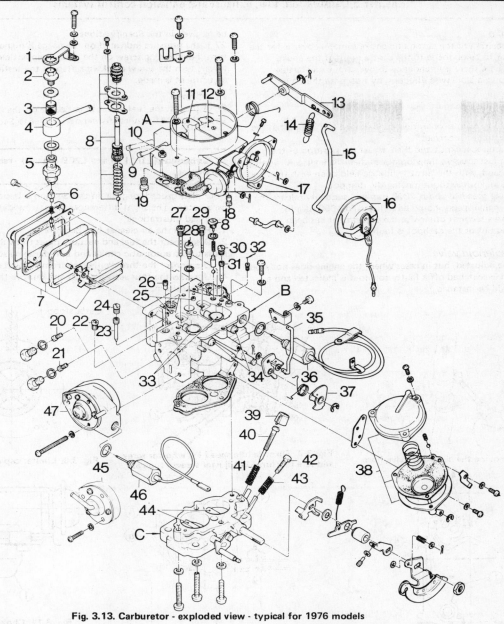

**Fig. 3.13. Carburetor - exploded view - typical for 1976 models**

| | | | | |
|---|---|---|---|---|
| A | Choke chamber | 23 | Secondary slow jet |
| B | Center body | 24 | Plug |
| C | Throttle chamber | 25* | Safe orifice |
| 1 | Lock lever | 26 | Coasting jet |
| 2 | Filter screw | 27 | Secondary main air bleed |
| 3 | Fuel filter | 28 | Power valve |
| 4 | Fuel inlet | 29 | Primary main air bleed |
| 5 | Needle valve body | 30 | Plug |
| 6 | Needle valve | 31 | Primary slow jet |
| 7 | Fuel chamber parts | 32 | No. 2 primary slow air bleed |
| 8 | Accelerating pump parts | 33* | Primary and secondary small venturi |
| 9 | Altitude compensator pipe (California) | 34* | Venturi stopper screw |
| 10* | Coasting air bleed adjusting screw | 35 | Choke connecting rod |
| 11* | High speed enricher air bleed | 36 | Anti-dieseling solenoid valve |
| 12* | Choke valve | 37 | Fast idle cam |
| 13 | Accelerating pump lever | 38 | Diaphragm chamber parts |
| 14 | Throttle return spring | 39 | Idle limiter cap |
| 15 | Accelerating pump rod | 40 | Idle adjust (mixture) screw |
| 16 | Automatic choke cover | 41 | Spring |
| 17* | Automatic choke body and diaphragm chamber | 42 | Throttle adjust screw |
| 18* | Richer jet | 43 | Spring |
| 19* | Coasting air bleed 1 | 44* | Primary and secondary throttle valve |
| 20 | Primary main jet | 45 | BCDD (California) |
| 21 | Secondary main jet | 46 | Vacuum control solenoid valve |
| 22 | Secondary slow air bleed | 47 | BCDD (non-California) |

* Do not remove these parts.

5 Clean any dirt from the external surfaces of the unit with solvent or fuel.

6 From the primary side of the carburetor, remove the throttle return spring, pump lever and rod, and the cam link rod.

7 Remove the automatic choke cover (three screws).

8 Remove the choke chamber (four screws) and detach the throttle return spring from the secondary side of the carburetor.

9 Remove the float chamber (four screws).

10 Remove the diaphragm chamber and gasket, the fast idle cam, the cam spring and the lever.

11 Remove the hollow bolt, banjo union, filter and stop plate.

12 Dismantle the accelerator pump and outlet valve taking care not to lose the ball and wieght.

13 Remove the venturis, main air bleeds and emulsion tubes from the primary and secondary sides of the carburetor.

14 Remove the slow jet and slow air bleed, primary and secondary main jets.

15 If necessary, the fuel level gauge lever and float can be removed from the float chamber.

16 Remove the power valve.

17 Remove the return plate, sleeve, fast idle lever, spring hanger and throttle lever.

18 Unscrew the anti-dieseling valve by unscrewing it from the carburetor body.

19 The BCDD unit can be removed after unscrewing the securing screws (Fig. 3.18).

20 Clean and examine all components for wear. If the throttle plates or spindles or bushes are worn, it is recommended that the carburetor is renewed completely.

21 Obtain a repair kit which will contain all the necessary gaskets and other items requiring renewal.

22 Only clean jets by blowing through them with air from a tire pump; never probe them with wire. It is worth checking their calibrations against those listed in Specifications in case a previous owner has substituted jets of incorrect size for the standard jets.

23 Reassembly is the reverse of the dismantling procedure, but the following special procedures and adjustments must be carried out.

### Float level adjustment (also see Section 9)

24 The fuel level, when viewed through the sight glass of the float chamber should be 0.91 in (23 mm) below the chamber top flange. Where the level is incorrect, invert the float chamber and bend the float arm as necessary to provide the dimension 'H' (see Specifications and Fig. 3.19). Now check that the stroke of the float arm (h) is also as given in the Specifications. If necessary, bend the stop to achieve this.

### Fast idle adjustment

25 When the automatic choke is fully closed for cold starting, the fast idle cam opens the throttle by a predetermined amount to give the specified fast idle speed.

26 If the carburetor has been completely dismantled or new components have been fitted, set the fast idle screw on the second step of the cam and adjust the screw so that the gap 'A' between the edge of the throttle valve plate and the carburetor is as given in the Specifications (see Fig. 3.9). Use a twist drill or rod of suitable diameter to carry out the measuring. A further minor adjustment can be made to the fast idle screw when the carburetor is installed and the engine is running under cold start conditions.

### Interlock opening of throttle valves

27 Check that when the primary throttle plate is opened 50°, the throttle valve adjust plate is contacting the return plate at point 'A' (Fig. 3.20). Open the throttle plate further and check that the locking arm is detached from the secondary throttle arm, allowing the secondary system to function. Bend the connecting lever, if necessary, to obtain the specified throttle valve interlock opening, measured between the edge of the throttle valve and the throttle chamber inner wall.

### Vacuum break adjustment

28 Refer to the previous Section.

### Choke unloader adjustment

29 Refer to the previous Section.

### Installation

30 Installation of the carburetor is the reverse of the removal procedure. Adjust the linkage, as described in Section 16.

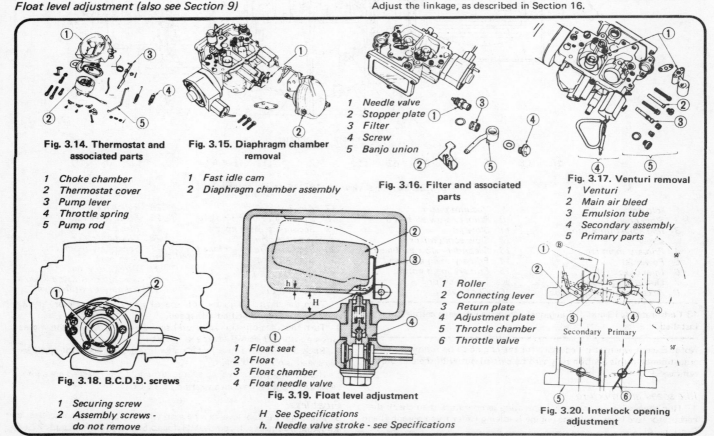

**Fig. 3.14. Thermostat and associated parts**

1 Choke chamber
2 Thermostat cover
3 Pump lever
4 Throttle spring
5 Pump rod

**Fig. 3.15. Diaphragm chamber removal**

1 Fast idle cam
2 Diaphragm chamber assembly

1 Needle valve
2 Stopper plate
3 Filter
4 Screw
5 Banjo union

**Fig. 3.16. Filter and associated parts**

**Fig. 3.17. Venturi removal**

1 Venturi
2 Main air bleed
3 Emulsion tube
4 Secondary assembly
5 Primary parts

**Fig. 3.18. B.C.D.D. screws**

1 Securing screw
2 Assembly screws - do not remove

1 Float seat
2 Float
3 Float chamber
4 Float needle valve

**Fig. 3.19. Float level adjustment**

H  See Specifications
h.  Needle valve stroke - see Specifications

1 Roller
2 Connecting lever
3 Return plate
4 Adjustment plate
5 Throttle chamber
6 Throttle valve

Secondary   Primary

**Fig. 3.20. Interlock opening adjustment**

## 11 Altitude compensator (1976 California models)

1 Any malfunction of the compensator can only be rectified by installing a replacement unit. Ensure that the colored hoses connect with the appropriate colored port markings.

2 To check for a faulty unit, attach a length of tubing to the inlet and outlet hoses and suck and blow as appropriate. If there is no restriction during these operations then either the inlet, or outlet, valve will have failed.

## 12 Carburetor (J13 and J15 engines) - description

1 The carburetor is of the downdraft dual-barrel type. It is basically similar to that used on the L16 engine models (see Section 8), with the following differences:

   *a) A manually operated choke is installed instead of the bimetal type automatic choke.*

   *b) The secondary throttle is operated through a linkage to the primary throttle instead of depending on the venturi vacuum and a diaphragm unit. In order to prevent over rich mixtures during hard acceleration, an auxiliary valve is installed upstream of the secondary throttle valve; this opens when there is sufficient airflow through the secondary venturi and closes under the action of a counterweight at low airflows.*

   *c) No anti-dieseling solenoid is installed.*

   *d) No BCDD is installed.*

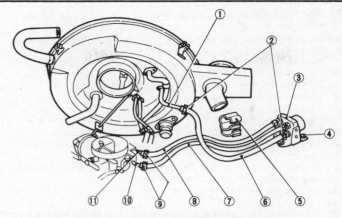

**Fig. 3.21. Altitude compensator connections**

| | | | |
|---|---|---|---|
| 1 | Altutude compensator connector | 7 | Carburetor to altitude compensator hose (green) |
| 2 | Hose clamps | 8 | Carburetor to altitude compensator hose (red) |
| 3 | Altitude compensator | 9 | Hose clamps |
| 4 | Screws with washer | 10 | Altitude compensator pipe, secondary |
| 5 | Hose clip | | |
| 6 | Air cleaner to altitude compensator hose (white) | 11 | Altitude compensator pipe, primary |

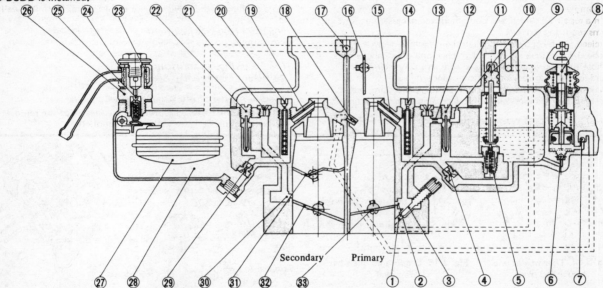

**Fig. 3.22. Sectional view of J13, J15 engine carburetor**

| 1 | Idle port | 9 | Vacuum piston | 17 | Air vent | 25 | Ball valve |
|---|---|---|---|---|---|---|---|
| 2 | Slow port | 10 | Primary slow air bleed | 18 | Accelerator pump nozzle | 26 | Float valve seat |
| 3 | Idle adjust (mixture) screw | 11 | Slow jet | 19 | Secondary main nozzle (small venturi) | 27 | Float |
| 4 | Primary main jet | 12 | Slow economizer | 20 | Secondary main air bleed | 28 | Float chamber |
| 5 | Power jet | 13 | Secondary slow air bleed | 21 | Step air bleed | 29 | Secondary main jet |
| 6 | Inlet check valve | 14 | Primary main air bleed | 22 | Step jet | 30 | Step port |
| 7 | Outlet check valve | 15 | Primary main nozzle (small venturi) | 23 | Filter | 31 | Auxiliary valve |
| 8 | Accelerator pump piston | 16 | Choke valve | 24 | Fuel union | 32 | Secondary throttle valve |
| | | | | | | 33 | Primary throttle valve |

## 13 Carburetor (J13 and J15 engines) - adjustments with carburetor installed

**Note:** Except where it is necessary for the engine to be running, the adjustments in this Section may also be carried out with the carburetor removed.

### Idle speed and mixture

1 Run the engine up to normal operating temperature then check the carburetor fuel level while the engine is idleing (refer to paragraph 6 and Section 14).

2 Turn the throttle adjuster (idle speed) screw on the primary throttle arm to obtain the specified idle speed.

3 Turn the idle adjusting (mixture) screw in, or out, until the engine runs smoothly at its highest speed (photo).

4 Back off the throttle adjuster screw if necessary until the specified idle speed is obtained again.

5 If a CO analyzer is available, adjust the idle mixture and speed if necessary to obtain a concentration of 3% CO.

### Float level

6 Although the fuel level can be seen with the carburetor installed, any adjustment requires its removal. Refer to Section 14, paragraph 27.

### Accelerator pump injection quantity

7   Ensure that the carburetor fuel level is correct then remove the air cleaner. Attach a small diameter flexible tube to the accelerator pump outlet nozzle.

8   Open the throttle valve fully and collect all the discharged fuel, then repeat the operation a further nine times.

9   Check that the average amount of fuel injected is in accordance with the following table:

| Engine | Outer hole in pump arm | Inner hole in pump arm |
|--------|------------------------|------------------------|
| J13 | 0.42 cc | 0.6 cc |
| J15 | 0.54 cc | 0.72 cc |

**Fig. 3.23. Carburetor adjustments**

*1   Idle adjuster (mixture) screw*
*2   Throttle adjuster (idle speed) screw*

### 14 Carburetor (J13 and J15 engines) - removal, servicing and installation

1   Remove the air cleaner.

2   Disconnect the fuel and vacuum pipes from the carburetor.

3   Disconnect the throttle and choke leads from the carburetor.

4   Unscrew the four securing nuts and remove the carburetor from the manifold.

5   Clean any dirt from the external surfaces of the carburetor with solvent or fuel.

6   Remove the clip at the accelerator pump arm then detach the pump connecting rod from the primary throttle lever.

7   Disconnect the starting lever connecting rod from the starting lever.

8   Disconnect the accelerator pump plunger lever then take out the pump piston.

9   Take out the clip, filter and inlet ball valve.

10   Remove the three bolts securing the air horn to the body. Remove the choke wire holder, air horn, clamp and associated parts. Do not remove the power jet and choke valve parts from the air horn, and take care not

to damage them.

11   Remove the three bolts retaining the body and flange. Note that two of the bolts are installed from the body side and one from the flange side.

12   Remove the jets and air bleed, installed on the upper surface of the body.

13   Remove the pump passage plug and take out the pump weight and pump outlet ball valve. Do not attempt to remove the pump nozzle.

14   Take out the two screws and remove the small venturi. Take care that the valve tip of the power jet valve is not damaged.

15   Remove the main passage plug at the base of the body and remove the main jet.

16   Remove the gauge level glass, cover and seals (three screws). Remove the float and collar from the pin, noting any other parts which are removed.

17   Remove the bolt, inlet and float valve seat.

18   Remove the idle adjusting (mixture) screw.

19   Remove the nut from the primary throttle shaft, then take off the throttle lever, throttle arm and starting lever.

20   Remove the plug from the primary slow port.

21   Remove the secondary throttle lever set screw and detach the throttle lever and spring.

22   Remove the plug from the secondary step port.

23   Do not attempt to remove the throttle valves, shafts or auxiliary valve from the flange. If wear exists in these parts, a new flange assembly must be obtained.

24   Clean and examine all components for wear, and obtain a repair kit or replacement parts as necessary.

25   Only clean jets by blowing them through with air from a tire pump; never probe them with wire. It is worth checking thier calibrations against those listed in the Specifications in case a previous owner has substituted jets of incorrect size for the standard jets.

26   Reassembly is the reverse of the removal procedure, but the following special procedures or adjustments must be carried out.

### Float level adjustment

27   The fuel level is governed by the position of the float lever, and when the carburetor is installed the level should correspond to the fuel level line in the float chamber. The float lever should be adjusted to give the specified dimension between the float lever and the upper body. Bend the float stopper, if necessary, to give a dimension 'H' of 0.039 in (1 mm) - see Fig. 3.32; this alters the gap between the float lever and valve stem to provide a satisfactory range of travel for the ball valve (photo).

### Idle speed and mixture screws

28   To provide a basic setting which will permit the engine to be started when the carburetor is installed, screw in the idle adjusting (mixture) screw carefully until it *just* seats, then back it off 2 7/8 turns (J13) or 2 turns (J15). Screw in the throttle adjuster (idle speed) screw two to three turns.

### Interlock opening of throttle valves

29   Check that when the primary throttle valve is opened 53° (J13) or 50° (J15), the connecting link contacts the right-hand end of the groove in the primary throttle arm (A in Fig. 3.35). To obtain the specified angle, use a twist drill or rod of suitable diameter between the edge of the throttle valve plate and the inner wall of the throttle chamber. This is dimension G1 in Fig. 3.36 and should be 0.271 in (6.89 mm) for

13.3 Idle mixture screw adjustment (air cleaner removed for clarity)

14.2 The fuel line connection to the carburetor

14.27 Carburetor fuel level correctly set

J15 or 0.254 in (6.45 mm) for J13 models. Bend the connecting link to adjust if necessary. Start interlock opening
30 Close the choke valve pulley then, without altering the setting made in paragraph 29, check for a throttle plate opening angle of 17°. This can be measured by using a twist drill or rod of suitable diameter between the edge of the throttle valve plate and the inner ball of the throttle chamber. The gauge size is 0.041 in (1.03 mm) for J13 or 0.052 in (1.33 mm) for J15 models - dimension G2 in Fig. 3.36. Bend the choke connecting rod if necessary to obtain this dimension.

*Installation*
31 Installation of the carburetor is the reverse of the removal procedure. Adjust the linkage as described in Section 15 and 16.

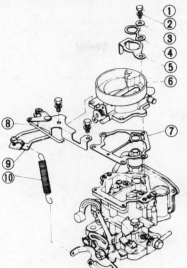

1  Screw
2  Spring washer
3  Plain washer
4  Union bolt clamp
5  Fuel union clamp
6  Air horn
7  Body gasket
8  Choke lever rod
9  Choke wire holder
10  Throttle return spring

**Fig. 3.26. Removing the air horn**

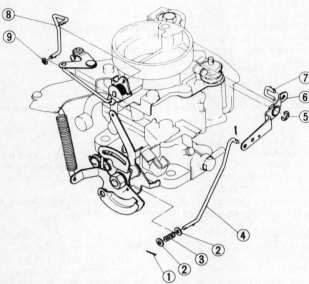

**Fig. 3.24. Dismantling the carburetor linkage**

1  Cotter pin
2  Plain washer
3  Rod spring
4  Pump rod
5  E-ring
6  Pump lever
7  Pump rod
8  Starting lever connecting rod
9  E-ring

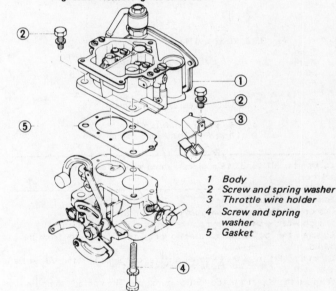

1  Body
2  Screw and spring washer
3  Throttle wire holder
4  Screw and spring washer
5  Gasket

**Fig. 3.27. Removing the body**

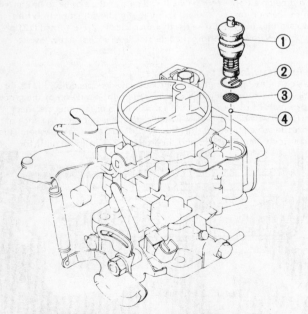

**Fig. 3.25. Removing the accelerator pump**

1  Accelerator pump piston
2  Clip
3  Filter
4  Inlet valve

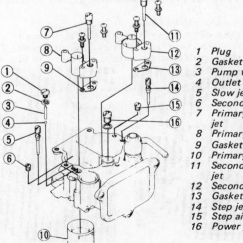

1  Plug
2  Gasket
3  Pump weight
4  Outlet valve
5  Slow jet
6  Secondary slow air bleed jet
7  Primary main air bleed jet
8  Primary small venturi
9  Gasket
10  Primary large venturi
11  Secondary main air bleed jet
12  Secondary small venturi
13  Gasket
14  Step jet
15  Step air bleed jet
16  Power jet

**Fig. 3.28. Removing the jets and associated parts**

3

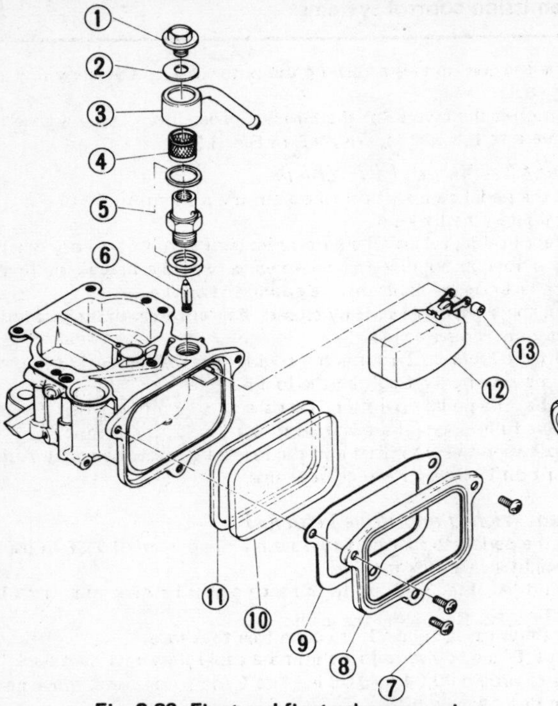

Fig. 3.29. Float and float valve removal

| 1 | Screw | 8 | Level gauge cover |
|---|-------|---|-------------------|
| 2 | Washer | 9 | Gasket |
| 3 | Inlet | 10 | Level gauge |
| 4 | Filter | 11 | Seal |
| 5 | Float valve seat | 12 | Float |
| 6 | Float valve | 13 | Collar |
| 7 | Screw | | |

Fig. 3.30. Dismantling the primary linkage

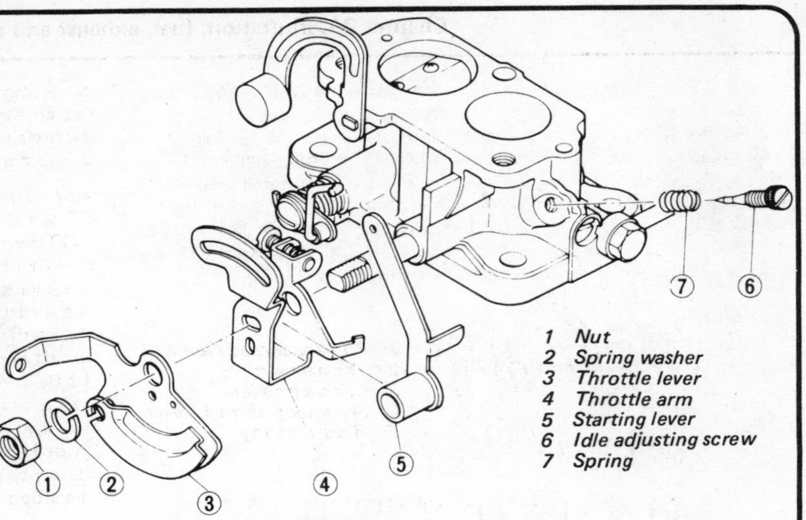

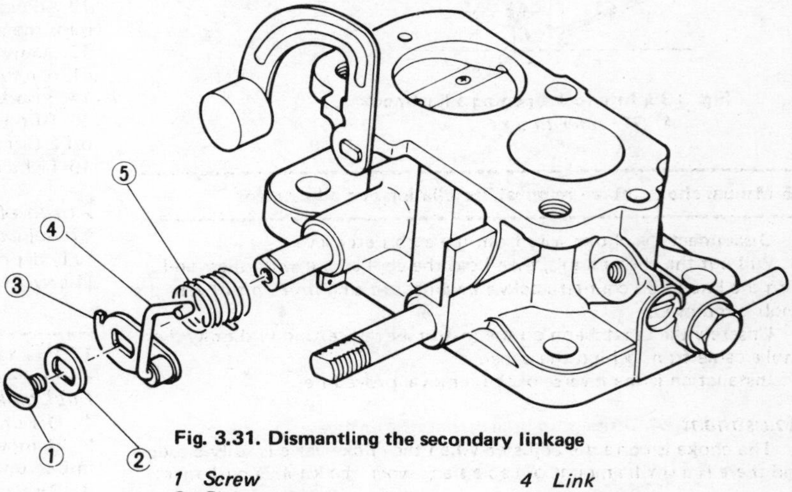

| 1 | Nut |
|---|-----|
| 2 | Spring washer |
| 3 | Throttle lever |
| 4 | Throttle arm |
| 5 | Starting lever |
| 6 | Idle adjusting screw |
| 7 | Spring |

Fig. 3.31. Dismantling the secondary linkage

| 1 | Screw | 4 | Link |
|---|-------|---|------|
| 2 | Plain washer | 5 | Spring |
| 3 | Throttle lever | | |

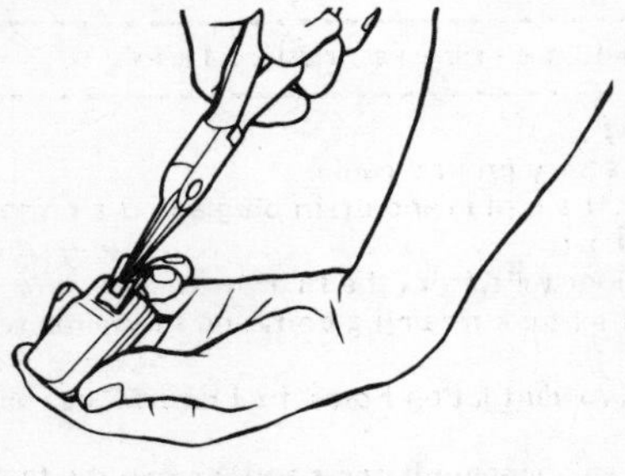

Fig. 3.33. Float lever adjustment

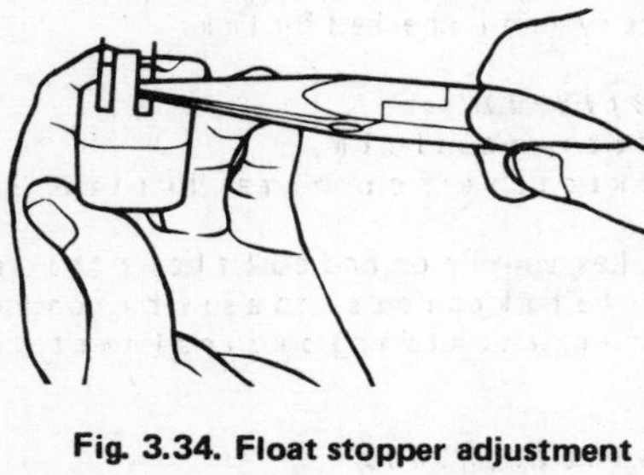

Fig. 3.34. Float stopper adjustment

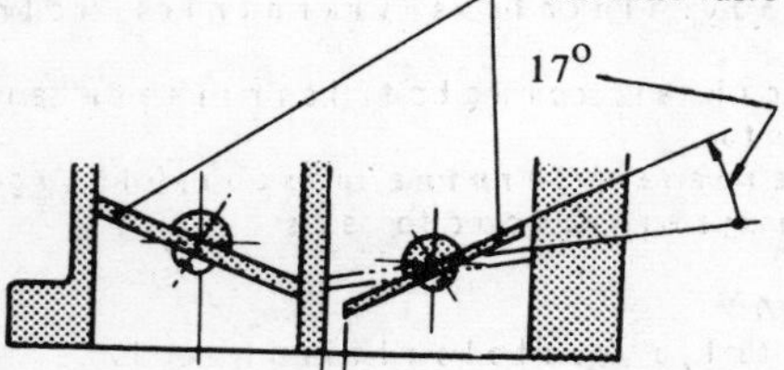

Throttle valve

$17^{\circ}$

$G_2$

Fig. 3.36. Starting interlock opening

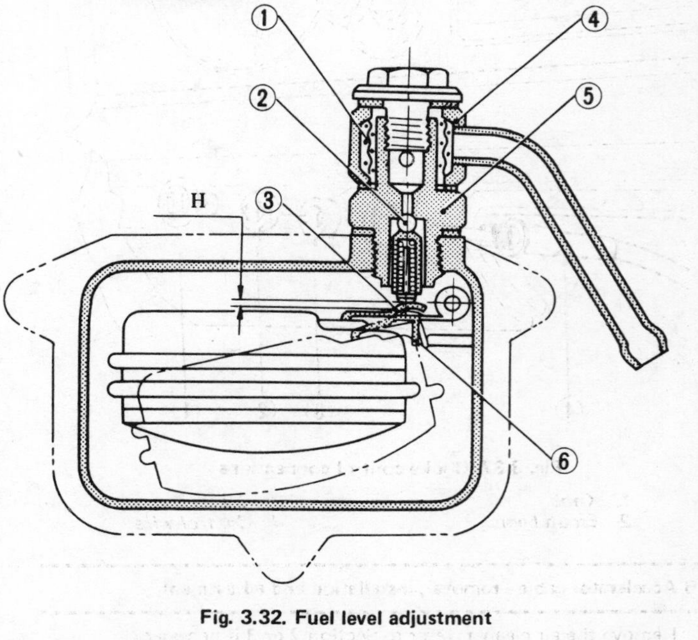

Fig. 3.32. Fuel level adjustment

| 1 | Filter | 4 | Fuel inlet union |
|---|--------|---|------------------|
| 2 | Ball valve | 5 | Valve seat |
| 3 | Float lever | 6 | Float stopper |

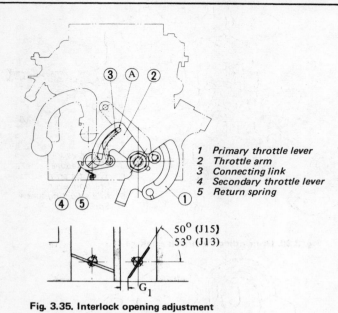

**Fig. 3.35. Interlock opening adjustment**
A, G1 - refer to text

1 Primary throttle lever
2 Throttle arm
3 Connecting link
4 Secondary throttle lever
5 Return spring

50° (J15)
53° (J13)

## 15 Manual choke cable - removal, installation and adjustment

1 Disconnect the choke wire from the carburetor lever.
2 Pull out the choke knob, then hold the choke wire with pliers and turn the knob 90° counterclockwise whilst pressing it in. In this way the knob is removed.
3 Unscrew the escutcheon on the instrument panel and withdraw the choke cable from behind the panel.
4 Installation is the reverse of the removal procedure.

### Adjustment
5 The choke is correctly adjusted when the choke valve is fully closed and there is a small amount of cable slack when the knob is pushed in.

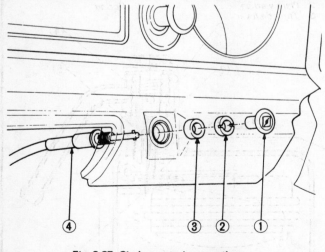

**Fig. 3.37. Choke control connections**

1 Knob          3 Spacer
2 Escutcheon    4 Control wire

## 16 Accelerator cable - removal, installation and adjustment

1 Remove the air cleaner; refer to Section 2 or 3 if necessary.
2 Disconnect the cable at the carburetor end.
3 Loosen the locknut and detach the outer case from the holder bracket.
4 Remove the spring clip and disconnect the cable from the accelerator pedal arm.

5 Remove the two screws attaching the outer case to the body and detach the cable.
6 Installation is the reverse of the removal procedure. Apply a general purpose grease to the part marked MG in Fig. 3.39.

### Adjustment (left-hand drive vehicles)
7 Adjust the pedal stopper bolt to obtain the dimension 'E' in Fig. 3.39 then tighten the locknut.
8 Where applicable, release the automatic choke (not necessary when the engine is hot) by opening the choke valve with the fingers, pulling the throttle lever up by hand then releasing the choke.
9 Position the throttle valve fully closed then position the adjust nut to just eliminate cable slackness.
10 Back off the locknut 2½ turns to provide approximately 1/8 (3 mm) free pedal movement then tighten the locknut.
11 Check that the pedal operation is satisfactory and that when the throttle valve fully opens there is 0.08 to 0.16 in (2 to 4 mm) clearance between the floor mat and the reverse side of the pedal. Adjust the stopper bolt if necessary to achieve this.

### Adjustment (right-hand drive vehicles)
12 Adjust the pedal stopper bolt to obtain a dimension of 2.36 in (60 mm) then tighten the locknut.
13 Screw nut 'A' (Fig. 3.40) up to the accelerator bracket then back it off one turn.
14 Ensure that nuts 'B' and 'C' are both free to rotate.
15 Turn nut 'B' clockwise to just eliminate cable slackness then back it off 2 turns to provide 0.04 to 0.08 in (1 to 2 mm) free pedal movement.
16 Tighten nuts 'A' and 'C'.

### Automatic transmission kick-down switch
17 Adjust the switch so that it operates when the accelerator pedal is fully depressed. Ensure that the stopper locknut is tightened afterwards.

## 17 Fuel tank and fuel lines - removal and installation

### Fuel tanks (pick-up)
1 Disconnect the battery ground cable.
2 Remove the tank drain plug and drain plug and drain the contents into a suitable container.
3 Disconnect the filler tube from the filler hose.
4 Remove the six fuel tank retaining bolts and lower the tank to the ground.
5 Disconnect the two ventilation hoses, fuel return hose and fuel outlet hose from the tank.
6 Disconnect the tank gauge unit wires and remove the tank completely.
7 Installation is the reverse of the removal procedure, following which it is essential that the system is checked for leaks.

### Fuel tank (double pick-up)
8 Disconnect the battery ground cable.
9 Remove the inspection cover from the rear floor then disconnect the gauge unit wires.
10 Disconnect the filler, ventilation and outlet hoses, then remove the drain plug and drain the tank contents into a suitable container.
11 Remove the four fuel tank retaining bolts and lower the tank in the ground.

### Reservoir tank (where applicable)
12 Disconnect the battery ground cable.
13 Disconnect the two ventilation hoses, evaporation hose and breather hose.
14 Remove the reservoir tank securing bolts then remove the tank complete with protector.
15 Installation is the reverse of the removal procedure, following which it is essential that the system is checked for leaks.

### Fuel tank gauge unit
16 Remove the fuel tank, as described earlier in this Section.
17 The gauge unit is a bayonet type and can now be removed by turning it counter-clockwise with a screwdriver.
18 Installation is the reverse of the removal procedure. Ensure that the 'O' ring is in position then align the projection of the gauge unit with the notch in the fuel tank and tighten it securely.

**3**

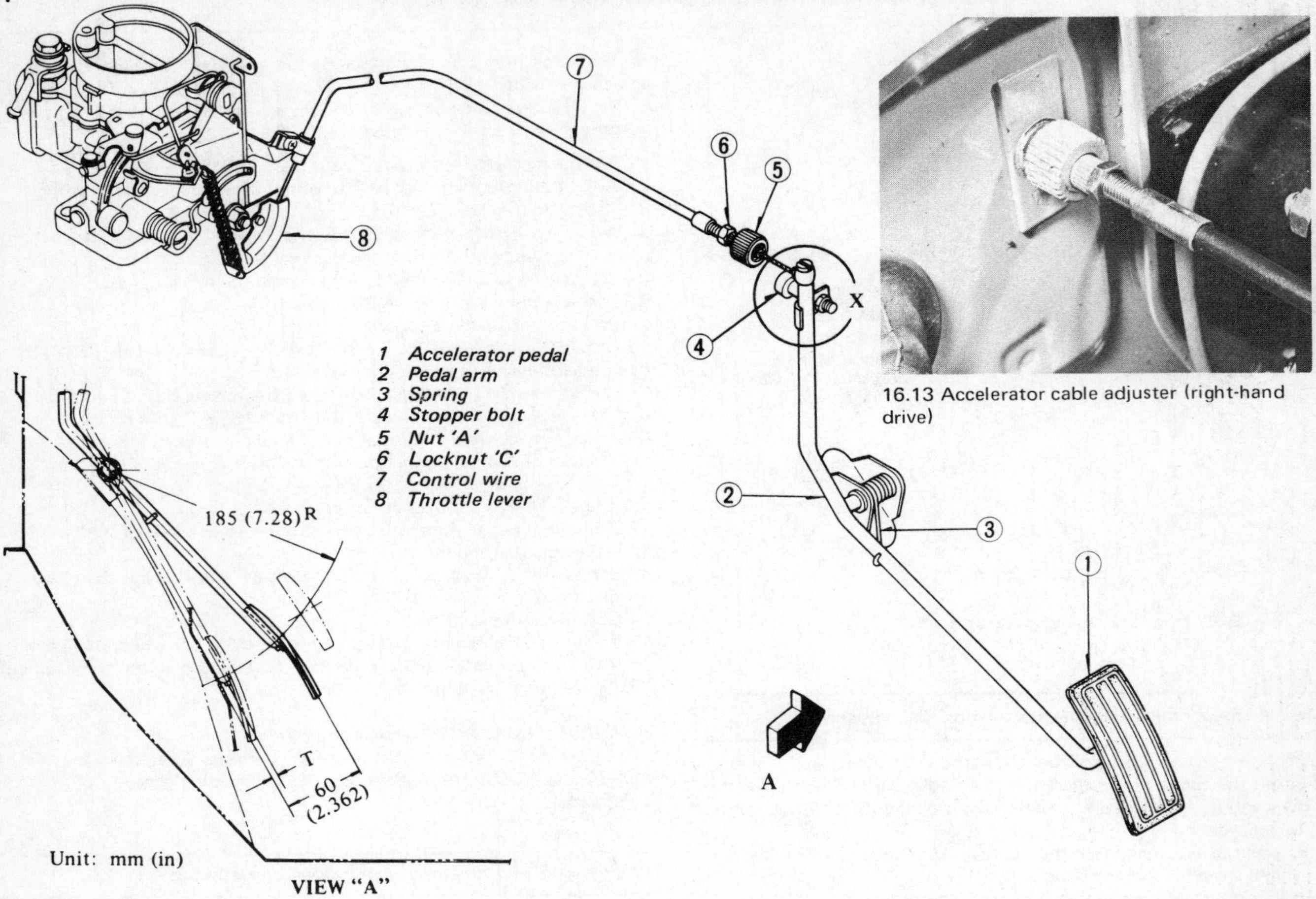

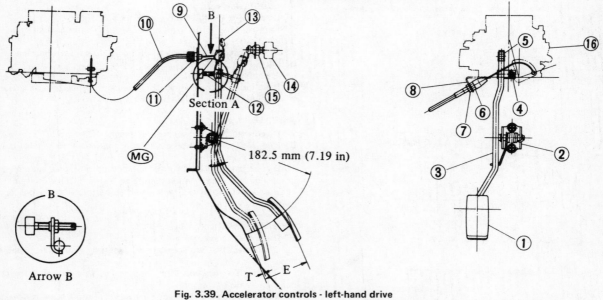

1  Accelerator pedal
2  Pedal arm
3  Spring
4  Stopper bolt
5  Nut 'A'
6  Locknut 'C'
7  Control wire
8  Throttle lever

185 (7.28) R

T
60
(2.362)

Unit: mm (in)

VIEW "A"

16.13 Accelerator cable adjuster (right-hand drive)

Fig. 3.38. Accelerator controls - right-hand drive

A

B

Arrow B

MG

Section A

182.5 mm (7.19 in)

T    E

Fig. 3.39. Accelerator controls - left-hand drive

1  Accelerator pedal
2  Pedal bracket and return spring
3  Pedal arm
4  Pedal stopper locknut

5  Spring clamp
6  Locknut
7  Adjust nut
8  Wire holder
9  Accelerator wire (inner)

10  Accelerator wire (outer)
11  Ring nut
12  Pedal stopper bolt
13  Kickdown switch striker (automatic transmission models only)

14  Kickdown switch (automatic transmission models only)
15  Switch stopper nut
16  Carburetor

E — 3.07 in (78 mm)
T — 0.08 to 0.16 in (2 to 4 mm)

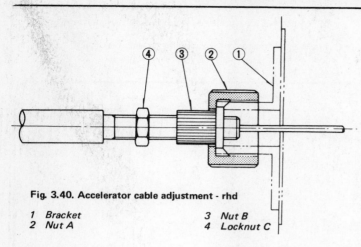

**Fig. 3.40. Accelerator cable adjustment - rhd**

| | |
|---|---|
| 1 Bracket | 3 Nut B |
| 2 Nut A | 4 Locknut C |

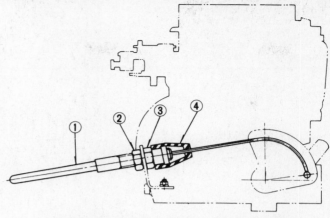

**Fig. 3.41. Accelerator cable adjustment - lhd (typical)**

| | |
|---|---|
| 1 Control wire | 3 Locknut |
| 2 Adjust nut | 4 Dust cover |

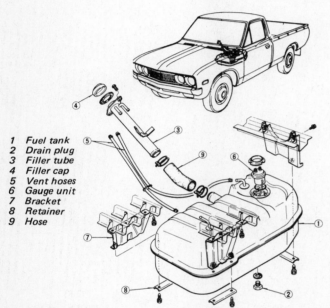

1 Fuel tank
2 Drain plug
3 Filler tube
4 Filler cap
5 Vent hoses
6 Gauge unit
7 Bracket
8 Retainer
9 Hose

**Fig. 3.42. Fuel tank installation - typical for UK models**

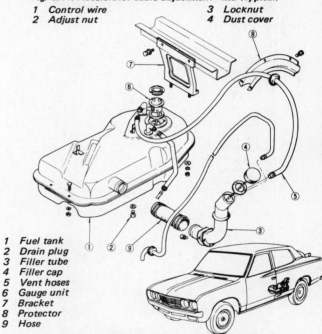

1 Fuel tank
2 Drain plug
3 Filler tube
4 Filler cap
5 Vent hoses
6 Gauge unit
7 Bracket
8 Protector
9 Hose

**Fig. 3.44. Fuel tank installation - double Pick-up**

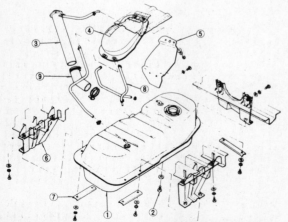

**Fig. 3.43. Fuel tank installation - typical for USA models**

| | |
|---|---|
| 1 Fuel tank | 6 Bracket |
| 2 Drain plug | 7 Retainer |
| 3 Filler tube | 8 Vapor hose |
| 4 Reservoir | 9 Filler hose |
| 5 Protector | |

## 18 Exhaust system - removal and installation

### Standard exhaust

1 Remove the clamp from the front tube and muffler (silencer) joint.

2 Tap around the joint with a hammer to break the sealant used during assembly.

3 Remove the rear mounting tube bolt, and detach the tube complete with the muffler. If necessary, tap the muffler rearwards with a soft-faced hammer to remove it.

4 Where applicable, remove the front tube heat insulator.

5 Remove the nuts securing the front tube to the exhaust manifold then detach the front tube.

6 Installation is the reverse of the removal proeecdure. It is recommended that a proprietary sealant is used at the muffler-to-front tube joint. Ensure that there is no strain on any of the mounting brackets or rubbers and that no part of the system contacts the vehicle floor or propeller shaft.

### Exhaust system with catalytic converter

7 Remove all the heat insulators from the system.

8 Follow the procedure given in paragraphs 1 through 3.

9 Remove the bolts securing the catalytic converter to the centre tube. Remove the center tube mounting bolts and the centre tube itself.

10 Remove the nuts and bolts securing the catalytic converter to the front tube then detach the catalytic converter.

11 Remove the nuts securing the front tube to the exhaust manifold. Remove the front tube mounting bolts the detach the tube itself.

12 Installation is the reverse of the removal procedure. It is recommended that a proprietary sealant is used at the system joints. Ensure that there is no strain or any of the mounting brackets or rubbers, and that no part of the system contacts the vehicle floor or propeller shaft.

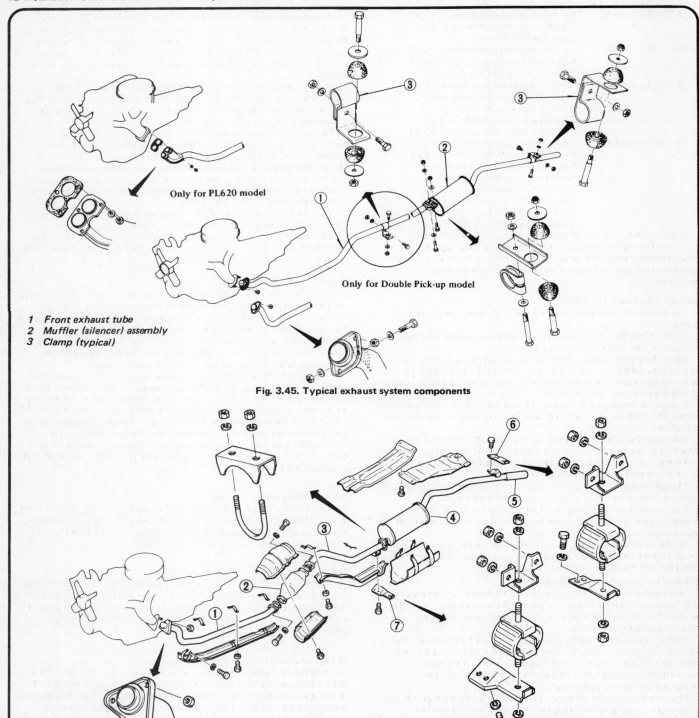

Only for PL620 model

Only for Double Pick-up model

1  Front exhaust tube
2  Muffler (silencer) assembly
3  Clamp (typical)

**Fig. 3.45. Typical exhaust system components**

**Fig. 3.46. California 1976 exhaust system**

| 1  Front exhaust tube | 3  Center exhaust tube | 5  Diffuser | 7  Front tube mounting |
| 2  Catalytic converter | 4  Muffler assembly | 6  Rear tube mounting | |

## 19 Emission control system - description and application

1    The complexity of the system incorporated depends on the vehicle model and intended market, but the following list summarizes the various components or systems:

| | |
|---|---|
| *1973 USA models:* | *Positive crankcase ventilation (PCV)* |
| | *Evaporative emission control (EEC)* |
| | *Spark timing control* |
| *1974 USA models:* | *Positive crankcase ventilation (PCV)* |
| | *Evaporative emission control (EEC)* |
| | *Exhaust gas recirculation (EGR)* |
| *1975 USA models:* | *Positive crankcase ventilation (PCV)* |
| | *Evaporative emission control (EEC)* |
| | *Air injection system (AIS)* |
| | *Exhaust gas recirculation (EGR)* |
| | *Early fuel evaporative system (EFE)* |
| *1976 USA models:* | *Positive crankcase ventilation (PCV)* |
| | *Evaporative emission control (EEC)* |
| | *Spark timing control (automatic transmission, except California)* |
| | *Air injection system (AIS)* |
| | *Exhaust gas recirculation (EGR)* |
| | *Early fuel evaporative system (EFE)* |
| | *Catalytic converter (California only)* |
| *Other models:* | *Positive crankcase ventilation (PCV)* |

2    In addition to the foregoing, the BCDD, anti-dieseling solenoid, altitude compensator and temperature controlled air cleaner can be regarded as emission control items. These are referred to previously in this Chapter.

### Positive crankcase ventilation

3    For details of the system, see Chapter 1. Evaporative emission control.

4    *1973/74 models:* The system comprises a non-vented fuel tank, a separator, a vent line and a flow guide valve.

When the engine is not operating, the system is filled with fuel vapor produced by the fuel in the tank. When the pressure of this vapor reaches a predetermined level, the vapor actuates the flow guide valve and passes into the crankcase.

As soon as the engine is started, the fuel vapor in the crankcase, air cleaner and the inlet manifold is drawn into the combustion chamber and ignited.

Whenever the pressure of vapor in the fuel tank falls (due to reduction in the fuel contents) and a condition of vacuum could prevail within the tank, the flow guide valve opens to admit air to the tank, and this is drawn in through the air cleaner.

5    *1975/76 models:* This system comprises a non-vented fuel tank, a separator, a vent line, carbon canister and a vacuum signal line.

Fuel vapor is emitted from the fuel tank and is stored in the canister (which is filled with activated carbon) during periods when the engine is not running.

As the throttle is opened, vacuum increases in the vacuum signal line and opens the purge control valve to admit vapor through the main valve port and thence to the inlet manifold.

### Spark timing control (1973 models)

6    This system incorporates a dual-point distributor (see Chapter 4) with Advance and Retard sets of prints, a thermo-switch, a throttle switch, a fourth lamp switch which detects top gear (manual transmission only) and a relay.

Under continuous top gear operation (manual transmission) the Advance points are in use;, this condition also applies in other gears when the throttle is more than 45° open or where the passenger compartment temperature is below 1°C (34°F). For all other conditions the Retard points are in use.

Where automatic transmission is installed, the Advance points are in use when cruising with a wide throttle opening or where the passenger compartment temperature is below 1°C (34°F). For all other conditions the Retard points are in use.

### Air injection system

7    This is a method of injecting air (generated in an external compressor) into the exhaust manifold in order to reduce hydrocarbons and carbon monoxide in the exhaust gas by providing conditions favourable for recombustion. The system comprises an air cleaner, engine driven air pump, relief valve, check valve, anti-backfire valve, air gallery and the associated hoses. Models for use in California also have an air control valve and emergency air relief valve to prevent excessive temperature rise in the catalytic converter.

Air is drawn through the air pump air cleaner, compressed, and directed through the check valve to the air gallery and injection nozzles. During high speed operation, excessive pump pressure is vented to ambient through the relief valve in the carburetor air cleaner.

The check valve is fitted in the delivery line at the injection gallery. The function of this valve is to prevent any exhaust gases passing into the air pump should the manifold pressure be greater than the pump injection pressure. It is designed to close against the exhaust manifold pressure should the air pump fail as a result, for example, of a broken drivebelt.

During deceleration, intake manifold vacuum opens the anti-backfire valve to allow fresh air to flow into the intake manifold. This ensures that the combustion cycle is more effective and reduces the amount of unburned gases exhausted.

On California models, the air control valve opens when the combined air pump pressure and intake manifold vacuum reach a predetermined level as happens during lightly loaded conditions. The air from the air pump is bled off to the air cleaner which means that the injection system is less effective, the exhaust gas temperature is lowered and the catalytic converter temperature can be maintained at the optimum operating temperature.

The emergency air relief (EAR) valve bleed air from the air pump when there is a prolonged condition of low manifold suction as happens during high continuous speed operation. This nullifies the air injection system, reduces the exhaust gas temperature and prevents the catalytic converter from overheating.

### Exhaust gas recirculation

8    In this system, a small part of the exhaust gas is introduced into the combustion chamber to lower the spark flame temperature during combustion to reduce the nitrogen oxide content of the exhaust gases. The system used for 1974 models utilizes an EGR control valve, solenoid valve, water temperature switch, relay, EGR tube and vacuum tube. Later systems dispense with the solenoid valve, temperature switch and relay, and substitute a thermal vacuum valve.

When the EGR valve is open, a small amount of exhaust gas is fed from the exhaust manifold to the EGR passage in the intake manifold. On early systems the EGR valve was either open or closed, depending on whether the engine water temperature was above or below 31/41°C (88/106°F). On later systems, the EGR valve position is controlled by the manifold vacuum and temperature, and is a modulating type.

A warning system is incorporated, except on vehicles operating in California and Canada, to warn that the system must be inspected after a pre-determined time.

### Early fuel evaporative system

9    This system utilizes a thermostatically controlled heat control valve in the exhaust manifold to heat the intake manifold during the engine warm-up period. This improves the fuel atomization and results in lower hydrocarbon emissions from the exhaust.

### Spark timing control (1976 models)

10    This system utilizes a sintered steel flow restrictor and an umbrella type non-return valve in the vacuum line between the carburetor and the distributor. Its purpose is to delay the spark advance during rapid acceleration and to cut off the spark advance immediately during deceleration.

### Catalytic converter

11    Installed in the exhaust system of vehicles destined for California, this device speeds up the chemical reaction of the hydrocarbons and carbon monoxide present in the exhaust gases so that they change into harmless carbon dioxide and water. Air for the chemical process is supplied by the air injection pump.

In the event of the system overheating, an increase in the vehicle floor temperature will result. This opens a temperature sensitive floor switch which illuminates a warning lamp through a relay becoming de-energized. During normal operating conditions, the warning lamp is illuminated during the engine start sequence as an indication of its serviceability. It is not unusual for the warning lamp to come on during periods of hard driving, or climbing gradients for long periods in low gears.

**3**

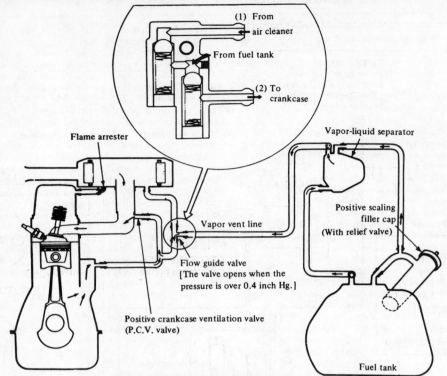

(1) From air cleaner

From fuel tank

(2) To crankcase

Flame arrester

Vapor-liquid separator

Positive scaling filler cap (With relief valve)

Vapor vent line

Flow guide valve [The valve opens when the pressure is over 0.4 inch Hg.]

Positive crankcase ventilation valve (P.C.V. valve)

Fuel tank

**Fig. 3.47. 1973/74 evaporative emission control system**

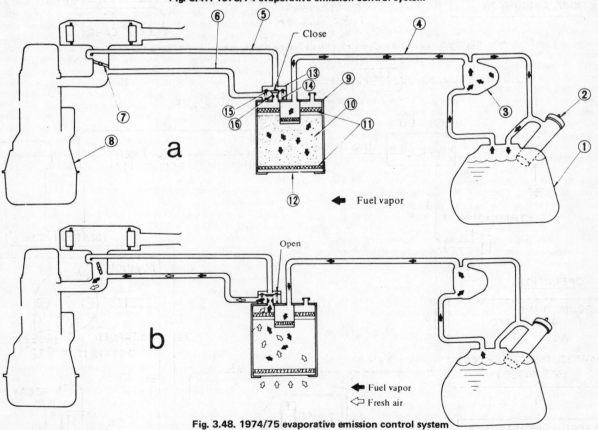

Close

a

Fuel vapor

Open

b

Fuel vapor

Fresh air

**Fig. 3.48. 1974/75 evaporative emission control system**

| | | | | | |
|---|---|---|---|---|---|
| a | Engine idling | b | At rest or running | 12 | Filter |
| 1 | Fuel tank | 4 | Vapor vent line | 13 | Purge control valve |
| 2 | Fuel filler cap with vacuum relief valve | 5 | Vacuum signal line | 14 | Spring |
| | | 6 | Canister purge line | 15 | Diaphragm |
| 3 | Liquid/vapor separator | 7 | Throttle valve | 16 | Fixed orifice |
| | | 8 | Engine | | |
| | | 9 | Carbon canister | | |
| | | 10 | Activated carbon | | |
| | | 11 | Screen | | |

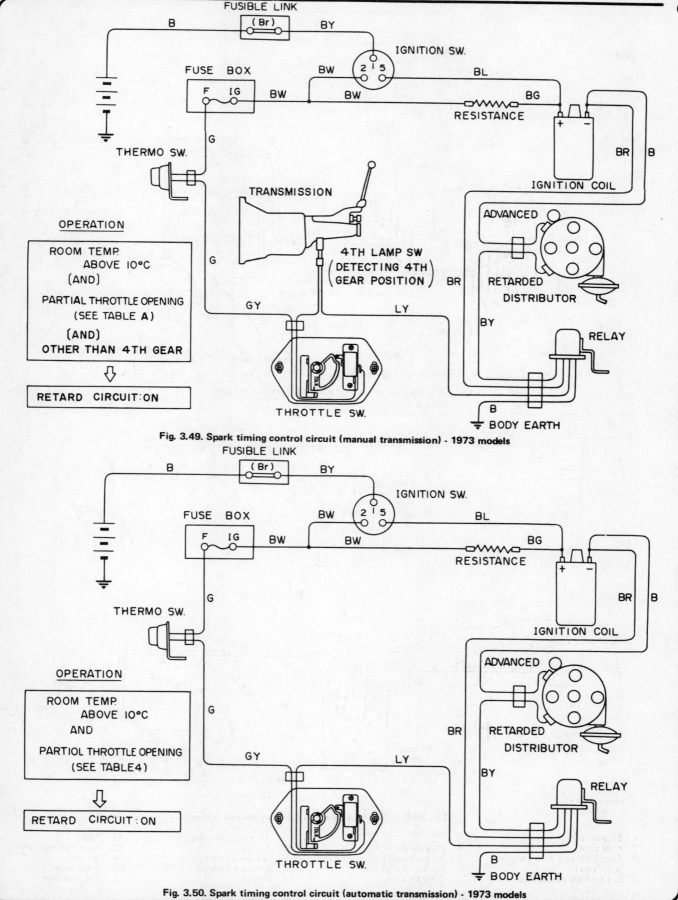

Fig. 3.49. Spark timing control circuit (manual transmission) - 1973 models

Fig. 3.50. Spark timing control circuit (automatic transmission) - 1973 models

3

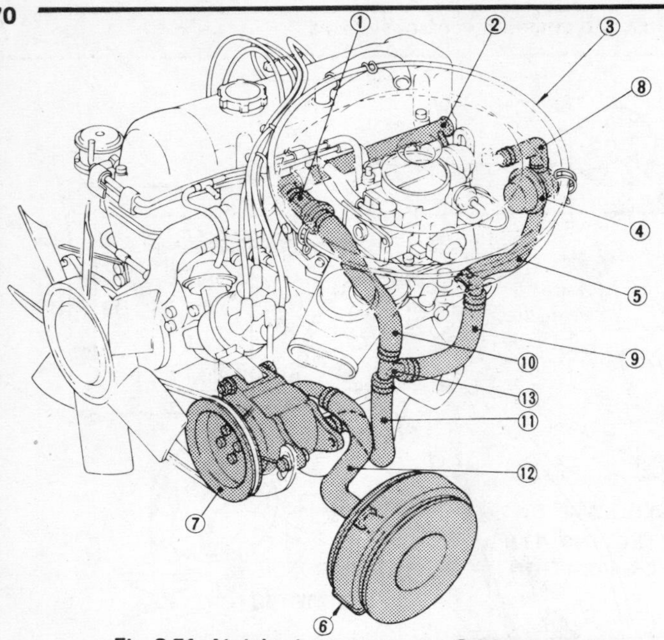

**Fig. 3.51. Air injection system - non-California models**

1  Check valve
2  Air gallery pipe
3  Automatic temperature control air cleaner
4  Anti-backfire valve (A.B. valve)
5  Air hose (A.B. valve to intake manifold)
6  Air pump air cleaner
7  Air pump
9  Hose (carburetor air cleaner to air hose connector)
10  Hose (check valve to air hose connector)
11  Hose (air hose connector to air pump)
12  Hose (air pump to air pump air cleaner)
13  3-way connector

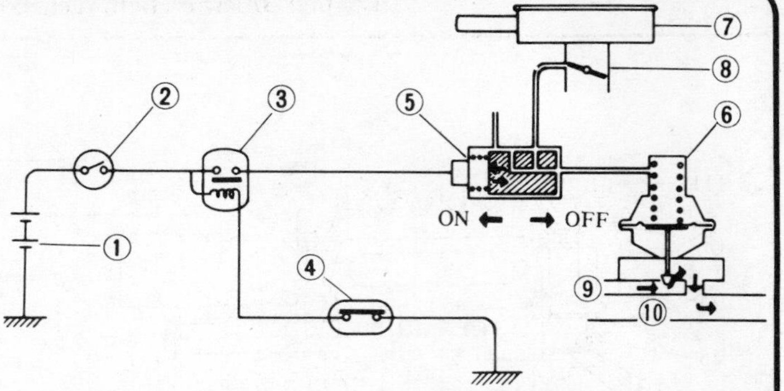

**Fig. 3.53. Schematic diagram of 1974 EGR system**

1  Battery
2  Ignition switch
3  EGR control relay
4  Water temperature switch
5  EGR solenoid valve
6  EGR control valve
7  Air cleaner
8  Throttle valve
9  Exhaust passage
10  Intake manifold

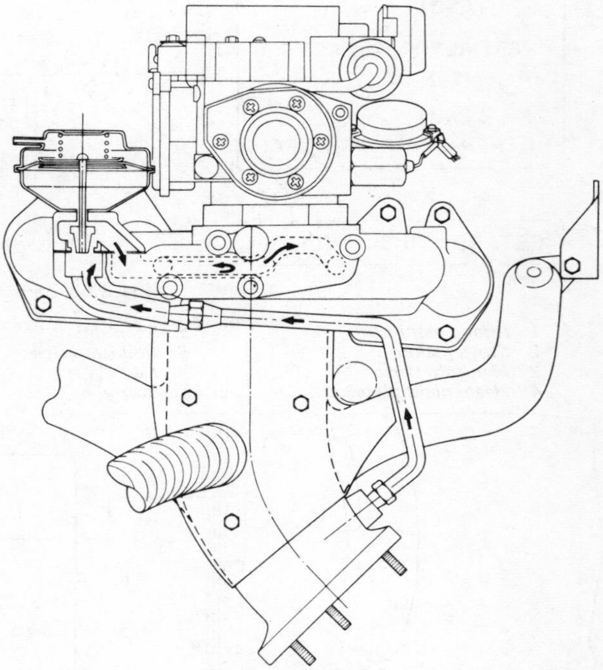

**Fig. 3.52. Air injection system - California models**

1  Air control valve
2  Check valve
3  Air gallery pipe
4  Automatic temperature control air cleaner
5  Anti-backfire valve (A.B. valve)
6  Air relief valve
7  Air hose (A.B. valve to intake manifold)
8  Emergency air relief valve
9  Air pump air cleaner
10  Air pump
11  Hose (carburetor air cleaner to A.B. valve)
12  Hose (carburetor air cleaner to air control valve)
13  Hose (air relief valve to air hose connector)
14  Hose (air hose connector to emergency air relief valve)
15  Hose (air hose connector to air pump)
16  Hose (air pump to air pump air cleaner)
17  Hose (check valve to air hose connector)

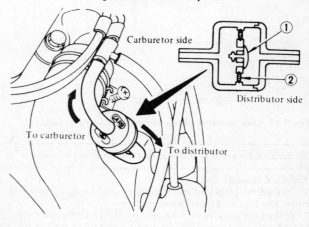

**Fig. 3.54. 1974 EGR system**

**Fig. 3.56. Spark delay valve**

1  One-way valve
2  Sintered metal disc

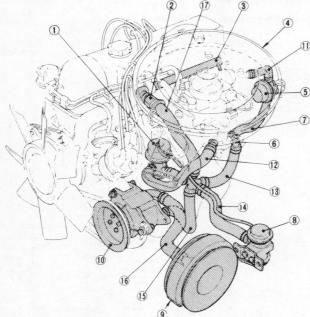

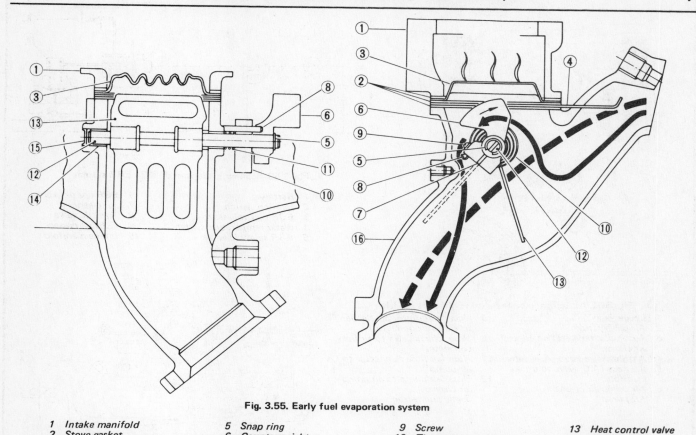

**Fig. 3.55. Early fuel evaporation system**

| | | | |
|---|---|---|---|
| 1 Intake manifold | 5 Snap ring | 9 Screw | 13 Heat control valve |
| 2 Stove gasket | 6 Counterweight | 10 Thermostat spring | 14 Bush |
| 3 Manifold stove | 7 Key | 11 Spring | 15 Cap |
| 4 Heat shield plate | 8 Stop pin | 12 Control valve shaft | 16 Exhaust manifold |

**Fig. 3.57. Location of the floor temperature warning switch**

**Fig. 3.58. Circuit connections to floor temperature warning switch**

**20 Evaporative emission control - maintenance and testing**

*1973/74 models*

1  Inspect the condition and security of all connecting hoses and renew any that have deteriorated.

2  If the flow guide valve is suspected of being faulty disconnect all hoses from it and then apply air pressure of 14.5 in $H_2O$ (1.07 in Hg); If it does not operate correctly, renew it.

3  Check the operation of the filler cap pressure relief valve by sucking it with the mouth. An initial slight resistance followed by the valve making a clicking noise will indicate that it is in good order.

*1975/76 models*

4  Check the security and condition of the connecting hoses.

5  To check the operation of the carbon canister purge control valve, disconnect the hose (which runs between the Tee-connector and the canister diaphragm cover) at the Tee-connector. Suck the end of the hose to verify that there is no leak. If there is, renew the diaphragm.

6  Apply pressure to the purge control valve and check that it opens at an air pressure of 14.5 in $H_2O$ (1.07 in Hg); if it does not operate correctly, renew it.

7  Periodically, renew the filter at the base of the carbon canister.

8  Check the filler cap relief valve, as described in paragraph 3.

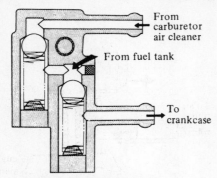

**Fig. 3.59. Floor guide valve**

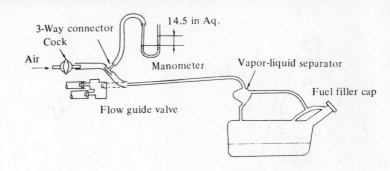

**Fig. 3.60. Evaporative emission control system checks (1973/74)**

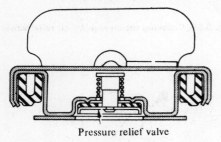

**Fig. 3.61. Filler cap pressure relief valve**

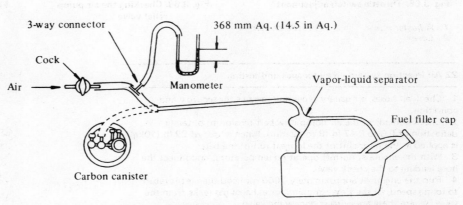

**Fig. 3.62. Evaporative emission control system checks (1975/76)**

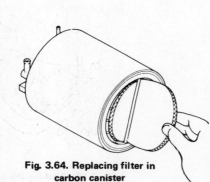

**Fig. 3.63. Carbon canister purge control valve parts**

**Fig. 3.64. Replacing filter in carbon canister**

| | |
|---|---|
| 1  Cover | 3  Retainer ring |
| 2  Diaphragm | 4  Spring |

### 21 Spark timing control system (1973 models) - maintenance and testing

#### Fourth lamp switch

1  The switch can be checked using an ohmmeter or test lamp and battery. The switch should show discontinuity (infinite resistance on an ohmmeter) at its terminals when the gear shift lever is in fourth gear, and continuity at other shift lever positions.

#### Thermo switch

2  The thermoswitch can be checked using an ohmmeter, or test lamp and battery. The switch should show continuity (zero resistance on an ohmmeter) at its terminals when the temperature is above 13°C. At temperatures below 1°C there should be discontinuity at the thermo switch terminals.

#### Throttle switch

3  Press the accelerator pedal slowly to the fully depressed position and check for an audible click as the switch operates.
4  With the throttle pedal fully depressed adjust the switch position if necessary to obtain a clearance of 0.012 in (0.3 mm) between the throttle switch and lever.
5  With the throttle pedal fully depressed, check for discontinuitry between the switch terminals using a ohmmeter, or a lamp and battery. Release the pedal and check that there is continuity after 45° of movement of the switch cam.

#### Wiring

6  Periodically inspect the wiring and terminations for condition and cleanliness.

#### Dual points distributor

7  Refer to Chapter 4 for information as necessary.

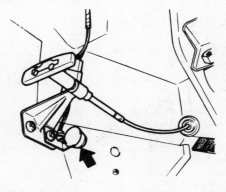

**Fig. 3.65. Thermoswitch location (arrowed)**

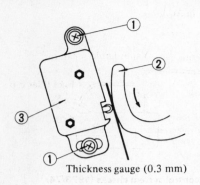

Fig. 3.66. Throttle switch adjustment

1   Adjuster screw     3   Throttle switch
2   Lever

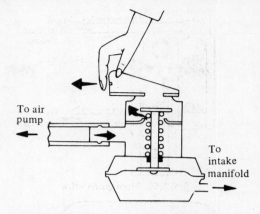

Fig. 3.68. Checking the air pump
relief valve

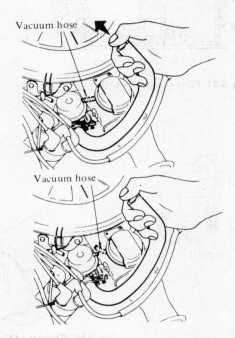

Fig. 3.69. Checking the emergency air relief valve

## 22 Air injection system - maintenance and testing

1   Check all hoses, air gallery pipes and nozzles for security and condition.
2   Check and adjust the air pump drivebelt tension to obtain a deflection of 0.3 to 0.47 in (8 to 12 mm). When a load of 22 lb (10kg) is applied at the midpoint of the longest run of the belt.
3   With the engine at normal operating temperature, disconnect the hose leading to the check valve.
4   Run the engine at approximately 2000 rpm and then let it return to idling speed, all the time watching for exhaust gas leaks from the valve. Where these are evident, renew the valve.
5   Check the operation of the air pump relief valve by first disconnecting the hoses from the non-return valve and then removing the air control valve from the hose connector. Plug the connector.
6   Run the engine at a steady 3000 rpm and place the hand on the air outlet of the emergency relief valve (California models). A good air pressure should be felt but if it is not, renew the valve.
8   Now pull the vacuum hose from the air control valve. If air ejection ceases from the outlet nozzle, the valve is in good condition but if it persists, renew the valve which must be faulty.
9   The anti-backfire valve (flame-trap) can be checked, when the engine is at normal operating temperature, by disconnecting the hose from the air cleaner and placing a finger over the end of the hose. Run the engine at about 3000 rpm and then return it to idling. During this action, a strong suction effect should be felt on the finger which indicates that the valve is in good order. 10 every 12000 miles (19000 km), renew the air pump air cleaner element. The assembly is located on the side of the engine compartment close to the air pump. The element and cleaner lower body are disposable, being an integral unit. A faulty or worn air pump should be renewed on an exchange basis.

Fig. 3.70. Checking the air control valve

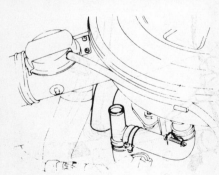

Fig. 3.67. Checking the check valve

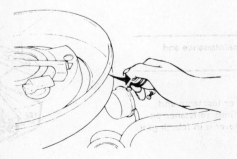

Fig. 3.71. Checking the anti-backfire valve

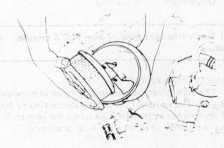

Fig. 3.72. Replacing the air pump
air cleaner element

## 23 Exhaust gas recirculation- maintenance and testing

### 1974 models

1   Check the complete system for insecure or damaged hoses. Tighten or renew as appropriate.

2   Periodically, remove the EGR control valve and clean its seat with a wire brush.

3   The control valve can be checked for correct vacuum operation by connecting a piece of hose to it and sucking with the mouth. The valve should move into its fully extended position and retain this attitude for at least 30 seconds after the vacuum ceases.

4   To check the EGR solenoid valve first connect it to an ohmmeter. If the meter needle deflects, then the solenoid is electrically sound. Now connect the solenoid directly to a battery. Make and break the connecting intermittently. If the solenoid valve clicks then it is in good condition.

5   The only other component which is likely to give trouble is the thermal switch. To test this, partially drain the engine cooling system and unscrew the switch from the cylinder head (adjacent to cooling system water temperature switch).

6   Connect the switch to an ohmmeter and then suspend the switch in a beaker of water being heated. Start with the water temperature below 77°F (25°C) and the switch should be open (reading infinity). As the water is heated, the ohmmeter reading should drop to zero between a water temperature of between 88 and 106°F (31 and 41°C) and remain there as the temperature climbs.

### 1975/76 models

7   The procedure is similar to that described for 1973 but the following additional or modified components should be noted.

8   The system has a warning circuit (except for vehicles operating in California and Canada). Check that the warning lamp lights when the ignition switch is turned to 'Start'. If it does not illuminate, check the wiring, connections and bulb.

9   If the detector drive counter has not reached 50000 counts, the warning lamp should be out but when it exceeds 50000 the lamp should light, indicating that the EGR system needs checking and maintenance. Reset odometer to zero by inserting a screwdriver in the holes provided in the detector drive counter. The hole is normally sealed with a grommet.

10  A thermal type vacuum valve is used in place of the thermal switch, solenoid and relay used in earlier models. To test its operation, unscrew it from the cylinder head and then immerse it in a beaker of water, first having fitted the valve with two lengths of tubing to prevent water entering. Suck the end of the tube to apply vacuum to the valve while heating the water in the beaker and note that the vacuum passage should only open at a temperature between 134 and 145°F (57 to 63°C) and remain open as the temperature climbs.

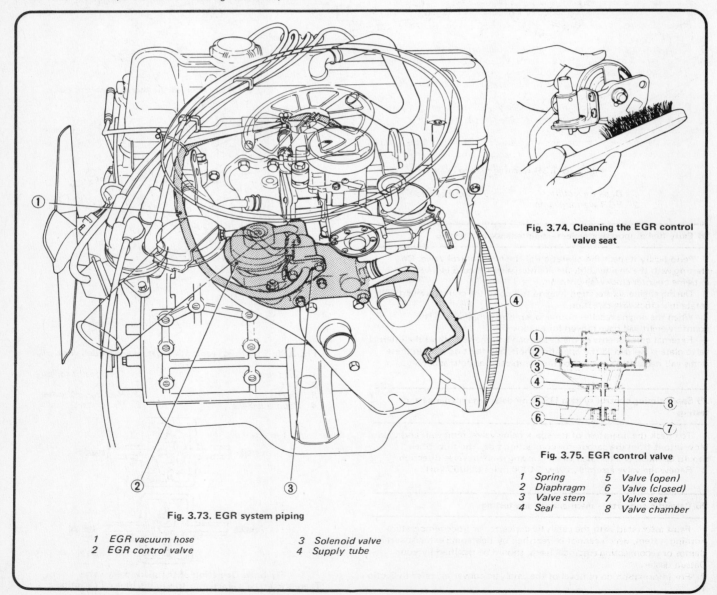

Fig. 3.74. Cleaning the EGR control valve seat

Fig. 3.73. EGR system piping

1   EGR vacuum hose          3   Solenoid valve
2   EGR control valve         4   Supply tube

Fig. 3.75. EGR control valve

1   Spring          5   Valve (open)
2   Diaphragm       6   Valve (closed)
3   Valve stem      7   Valve seat
4   Seal            8   Valve chamber

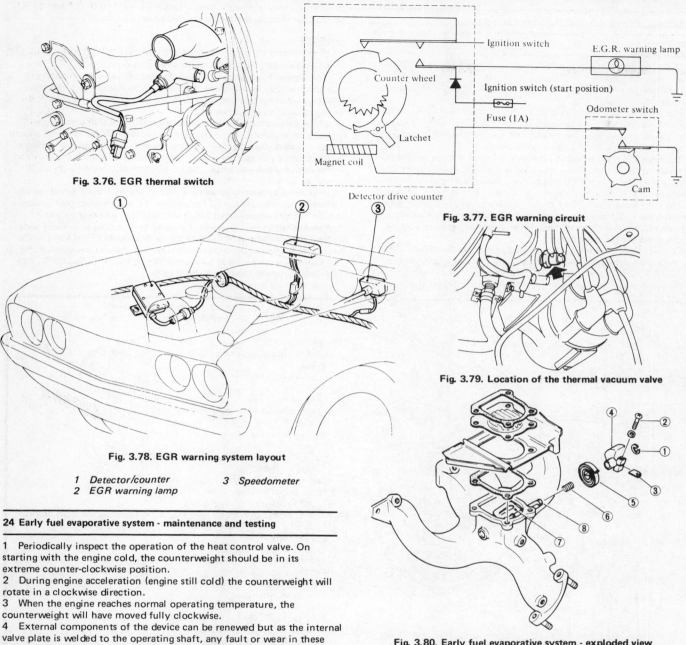

Fig. 3.76. EGR thermal switch

Fig. 3.77. EGR warning circuit

Fig. 3.78. EGR warning system layout

1 Detector/counter     3 Speedometer
2 EGR warning lamp

Fig. 3.79. Location of the thermal vacuum valve

Fig. 3.80. Early fuel evaporative system - exploded view

1 Snap ring     5 Thermostat spring
2 Bolt     6 Spring
3 Key     7 Heat control valve
4 Counterweight     8 Valve shaft

## 24 Early fuel evaporative system - maintenance and testing

1 Periodically inspect the operation of the heat control valve. On starting with the engine cold, the counterweight should be in its extreme counter-clockwise position.
2 During engine acceleration (engine still cold) the counterweight will rotate in a clockwise direction.
3 When the engine reaches normal operating temperature, the counterweight will have moved fully clockwise.
4 External components of the device can be renewed but as the internal valve plate is welded to the operating shaft, any fault or wear in these items will necessitate renewal of the complete manifold assembly.

## 25 Spark timing control system (1976 models) - maintenance and testing

1 To check the operation of the spark delay valve, remove it and then blow into it from the carburetor connecting side. The flow of air should be much greater than when blowing in the reverse direction.
2 Renew the valve assembly every 24000 miles (38000 km).

## 26 Catalytic converter - maintenance and testing

1 Fault associated with the catalytic converter or floor temperature warning system, which cannot be rectified by tightening exhaust system clamps or reconnecting electrical leads, should be rectified by your Datsun dealer.
2 For information on removal of the catalytic converter, refer to Section 18.

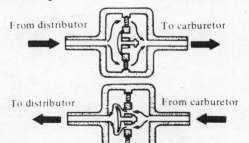

Fig. 3.81. Operation of the spark delay valve
There should be a greater airflow in the lower illustration

## 27 Fault diagnosis - Carburetion; fuel, exhaust and emission control systems

| Symptom | Reason/s |
|---|---|
| Fuel consumption excessive | Air cleaner choked and dirty giving rich mixture |
| | Fuel leaking from carburetor, fuel pump, or fuel lines |
| | Float chamber flooding |
| | Generally worn carburetor |
| | Distributor condenser faulty |
| | Balance weights or vacuum advance mechanism in distributor faulty |
| | Carburetor incorrectly adjusted, mixture too rich |
| | Idling speed too high |
| | Contact breaker gap incorrect |
| | Valve clearances incorrect |
| | Choke valve incorrectly set |
| | Incorrectly set spark plugs |
| | Tires under-inflated |
| | Wrong spark plugs fitted |
| | Brakes dragging |
| | Emission control system faulty (see later in this Section) |
| Insufficient fuel delivery or weak mixture due to air leaks | Partially clogged filter in pump, carburetor or fuel line |
| | Incorrectly seating valves in fuel pump |
| | Fuel pump diaphragm leaking or damaged |
| | Gasket in fuel pump damaged |
| | Fuel pump valves sticking due to fuel gumming |
| | Too little fuel in fuel tank (prevalent when climbing steep hills) |
| | Union joints on pipe connections loose |
| | Split in fuel pipe on suction side of fuel pump |
| | Inlet manifoldto-block or inlet manifold-to-carburetor gaskets leaking |
| | Fuel tank relief valve stuck closed |
| Power reduced | Clogged main jets |
| | Accelerator linkage requires adjustment |
| | Fuel filter blocked |
| | Air cleaner blocked |
| | Power valve faulty |
| Erratic idling | Slow jet clogged |
| | Secondary throttle valve operating incorrectly |
| | Worn throttle valve shafts |
| | Broken carburetor flange gasket |
| | Incorrect adjusted B.C.D.D. |
| Flat spot or hesitation | Clogged jets |
| | Emulsion tube clogged |
| | Secondary throttle valve operating incorrectly |
| | Power valve faulty |
| Engine will not start | Fuel level incorrect |
| | Lack of fuel |
| | Incorrect setting of mixture screw |
| | Faulty anti-dieseling solenoid |
| | Incorrect fast idle adjustment |

### Emission control system faults

| Symptom | Reason/s |
|---|---|
| Erratic idling | Faulty anti-backfire valve |
| | Carbon canister purge line disconnected |
| | Exhaust gas heated valve stuck |
| | Faulty E.G.R. valve |
| Power reduced | Faulty spark timing control valve |
| | Faulty altitude compensator (California) |
| | Faulty E.G.R. valve |
| | Exhaust gas heated valve stuck |

# Chapter 4  Ignition system

*Refer to Chapter 13 for specifications and information applicable to 1977 through 1979 USA models*

## Contents

## Specifications

| | |
|---|---|
| **System type** ... ... ... ... ... ... ... ... | 12 volt, battery and coil |
| **Distributor type** ... ... ... ... ... ... ... | Hitachi D4 series (refer to manufacturer's parts list for model on any paticular vehicle) |
| **Ignition timing (initial advance)** | |
| 1973 N. America models ... ... ... ... ... | 5° BTDC at 800 rpm (manual) |
| | 5° BTDC at 650 rpm (automatic, in 'D') |
| 1974 N. America models ... ... ... ... ... | 12° BTDC at 800 rpm (manual) |
| | 12° BTDC at 650 rpm (autumatic, in 'D') |
| 1975/76 N. America models ... ... ... ... | 12° BTDC at 750 rpm (manual, except California) |
| | 10° BTDC at 750 rpm (manual, California) |
| | 12° BTDC at 650 rpm (automatic, in 'D') |
| J13 & J15 engined models ... ... ... ... ... | 8° BTDC at 600 rpm |
| **Ignition phase difference (1973 USA models)** ... ... ... | 7° lag |
| **Distributor rotation** ... ... ... ... ... ... ... | Counter-clockwise |
| **Dwell angle (except 1976 California)** ... ... ... ... ... | 49 to 55° |
| **Points gap (except 1976 California)** ... ... ... ... ... | 0.018 to 0.022 in (0.45 to 0.55 mm) |
| **Air gap (1976 California)** ... ... ... ... ... ... | 0.008 to 0.016 in (0.2 to 0.4 mm) |
| **Engine firing order** ... ... ... ... ... ... ... | 1, 3, 4, 2 |
| **Condenser capacity (except 1976 California and 1973 retard side)** ... ... ... ... ... ... ... ... | 0.20 to 0.24 mfd |
| **Condenser capacity (1973 retard side)** ... ... ... ... | 0.05 mfd $\pm$ 15% |
| **Coil type** | |
| 1973 N. America models ... ... ... ... ... ... | Hitachi C6R-601 |
| 1974 N. America models ... ... ... ... ... ... | Hanshin H5-15-1 |
| 1975 N. America models ... ... ... ... ... ... | Hanshin H5-15-9 or Hitachi C6R-608 |
| 1976 N. America models (except California) ... ... ... | Hitachi C6R-608 or Hanshin H5-15-9 |
| 1976 models (California) ... ... ... ... ... ... | C1T-16 or STC9 |
| J13 & J15 engined models ... ... ... ... ... ... | Hitachi 6R-200 or C1Z-200 |
| **Coil series resistance** | |
| 1973/1974 N. America models ... ... ... ... ... | 1.3 to 1.7 ohms |
| 1975/76 N. America models (except 1976 California) ... ... | 1.5 ohms |
| 1976 model (California) ... ... ... ... ... ... | 1.3 ohms |
| J13 & J15 engined models ... ... ... ... ... ... | 1.6 ohms (6R-200 coil only) |

## Spark plugs

| | Type | Electrode gap |
|---|---|---|
| 1973/74 N. America    ...    ...    ...    ...    ...    ...    ...    ... | NGK B6ES | 0.028 to 0.031 in (0.7 to 0.8 mm) |
| 1975/76 N. America models (except 1976 California)    ...    ...    ... | NGK BP6ES or Hitachi L45 PW | 0.031 to 0.035 in (0.8 to 0.9 mm) |
| 1976 models (California)    ...    ...    ...    ...    ...    ...    ... | NGK BP6ES-11 or Hitachi L45PW-11 | 0.039 to 0.045 in (1 to 1.1 mm) |
| J13 & J15 engined models    ...    ...    ...    ...    ...    ...    ... | NGK BP-5ES or Hitachi L46PW | 0.31 in (0.8 mm) |

## Torque wrench settings

| | lb f ft | kg f m |
|---|---|---|
| Spark plugs    ...    ...    ...    ...    ...    ...    ...    ...    ... | 11 to 14 | 1.5 to 2 |

## 1  General description

In order that the engine can run correctly, it is necessary for an electrical spark to ignite the fuel/air mixture in the combustion chamber atr exactly the right moment in relation to engine speed and load. The ignition system is based on feeding low tension (LT) voltage from the battery to the coil where it is converted to high tension (HT) voltage. The high tension voltage is powerful enough to jump the spark plug gap in the cylinders many times a second under high compression pressures, providing that the system is in good condition and that all adjustments are correct.

The ignition system is divided into two circuits: the low tension circuit and the high tension circuit.

The low tension (sometimes known as the primary) circuit consists of the battery lead to the ignition switch, lead from the ignition switch to the low tension or primary coil windings (+ terminal) and the lead from the low tension coil windings (− terminal) to the contact breaker points and condenser in the distributor.

The high tension circuit consists of the high tension or secondary coil windings, the heavy ignition lead from the center of the coil to the center of the distributor cap, the rotor arm, and the spark plug leads and spark plugs.

The system functions in the following manner. Low tension voltage is changed in the coil into high tension voltage by the opening and closing of the contact breaker points in the low tension circuit . High tension voltage is then fed via the carbon brush in the centre of the distributor cap to the rotor arm of the distributor cap, and each time it comes in line with one of the four metal segments in the cap, which are connected to the spark plug leads, the opening and closing of the contact breaker points causes the high tension voltage to build up, jump the gap from the rotor arm to the appropriate metal segment and so via the spark plug lead to the spark plug, where it finally jumps the spark plug gap before going to earth.

The ignition is advanced and retarded automatically, to ensure the spark occurs at just the right instant for the particular load at the prevailing engine speed.

The ignition advance is controlled both mechanically and by a vacuum operated system. The mechanical governor mechanism comprises two weights, which move out from the disposition by two light springs, and it is the tension of the springs which is largely responsible for correct spark advancement.

The vacuum control consists of a diaphragm, one side of which is connected via a small bore tube to the carburetor, and the other side to the contact breaker plate. Depression in the inlet manifold and carburetor, which varies with engine speed and throttle opening, causes the diaphragm to move, so moving the contact breaker plate and advancing or retarding the spark. A fine degree of control is achieved by a spring in the vacuum assembly. A resistor is incorporated in the ingition circuit for most models so that during starting, with the engine being cranked by the starter motor, full battery voltage is applied at the coil to maintain a good spark at the plug electrodes which would not be the case should a drop in voltage occur (photo).

On some vehicles for the North American equipped with a full emission control system a spark timing control system is employed. The system is designed to advance or retard the ignition timing in accordance with the prevailing engine operating conditions in order to reduce the emission of noxious exhaust fumes particularly during periods of deceleration for 1973, a dual point distributor was used for this purpose, but for 1976 a spark delay valve was used with a single point distributor. Reference should be made to Chapter 3 for full details of this and the other emission control devices.

Vehicles built for use in California for 1976 use a transistorized ignition system is used. The essential difference between this and the mechanical-type is that the mechanical-type 'make-and-break' contact points are replaced by a reluctor and coil which carry out the function electronically. As each of the projections of the reluctor passes the coil, the coil flux density changes and the resultant electrical signal is passed to transistorized circuit. This circuit cuts off the ignition coil primary feed which generates a high voltage in the coil accordary winding. After a pre-determined time the primary coil circuit is restored until the next reluctor projection passes the coil, when the cycle is repeated. The centrifugal  vacuum advance and retard assemblies are of the same type as used in the mechanical-type distributor.

Distributor models vary with the particular engine type and vehicle, and reference should be made to a main Datsun dealer when spare parts are required.

The description throughout this Chapter apply to all relevant model assemblies, but detail differences will be apparent in the particular components according to vehicle model and year pf production. This is especially the case with distributors.

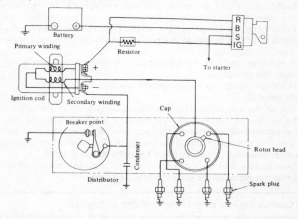

**Fig. 4.1. Ignition circuit - typical for mechanical type contact breaker**

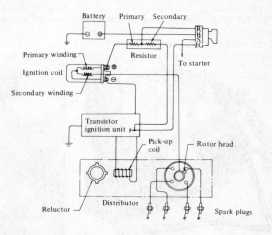

**Fig. 4.2. Ignition circuit - transistorized type**

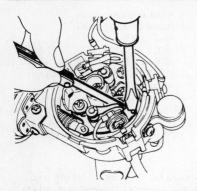

Fig. 4.3. Point gap adjustment
- dual point distributor shown

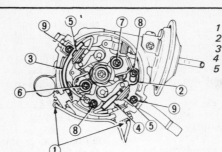

Fig. 4.4a. Breaker assembly - dual point distributor

| | | | |
|---|---|---|---|
| 1 | Lead wire | 6 | Advance point set screw |
| 2 | Adjuster plate | 7 | Retard point set screw |
| 3 | Primary lead (advance point) | 8 | Adjuster plate set screws |
| 4 | Primary lead (retard point) | 9 | Breaker plate set screws |
| 5 | Set screw for primary lead | | |

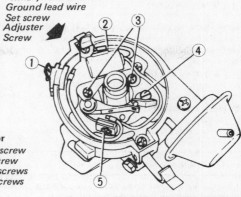

1 Primary lead terminal
2 Ground lead wire
3 Set screw
4 Adjuster
5 Screw

Fig. 4.4b. Breaker assembly - single
point distributor (typical)

## 2 Contact breaker (mechanical type) - adjustment

1 To adjust the contact breaker points to the correct gap, first pull off the two clips securing the distributor cap to the distributor body, and lift away the cap. Clean the cap inside and out with a dry cloth. It is unlikely that the four segments will be badly burned or scored, but if they are the cap will have to be renewed.
2 Inspect the carbon brush contact located in the top of the cap - see that it is unbroken and stands proud of the plastic surface.
3 Check the rotor arm. It must be clean and on the cam shoulder.
4 Gently pry the contact breaker points open to examine the condition of their faces. If they are rough, pitted or dirty, it will be necessary to remove them for resurfacing, or for replacement points to be fitted.
5 Presuming that the points are satisfactory, or have been turning the engine over until the heel of the breaker arm is on the highest point of the cam.
6 A feeler gauge of the specified thickness should now just fit between the points.
7 If the gap varies from this amount, slacken the contact plate securing screw (photo).
8 Adjust the contact gap by inserting a screwdriver in the screw located in the cut-out of the breaker plate (photo). Turn clockwise to increase and anticlockwise to decrease the gap. When the gap is correct tighten the securing screw and check the gap again. For dual point distributors this operation must be carried out for both sets of points.
9 Making sure that the rotor is in position, position the distributor cap and clip the spring blade retainers into position.

## 3 Contact breaker points - removal and installation

1 Slip back the spring clips which secure the distributor cap in position. Remove the distributor cap and lay it to one side, only removing one or two of the HT leads from the plugs if necessary to provide greater movement of the cap.
2 Pull the rotor from the distributor shaft.
3 Unscrew the setscrews just enough to be able to slide out the primary

(LT) lead terminals.
4 Unscrew and remove the contact breaker securing screws and detach the end(s) of the earth lead(s). Pull the contact breaker assembly outwards and upwards to remove it. Remove the pivot circlip to dismantle.
5 Inspect the faces of the contact points. If they are only lightly burned or pitted then they may be ground square on an oilstone or by rubbing a carborundum strip between them. Where the points are found to be severely burned or pitted, then they must be renewed and at the same time the casue of the erosion of the points established. This is most likely to be due to poor earth connections from the battery negative lead to body earth or the engine to earth strap. Remove the connecting bolts at these points, scrape the surfaces free from rust and corrosion and tighten the bolts using a star type lock washer. Other screws to check for security are: the baseplate to distributor body securing screws, the condenser securing screw and the distributor body to lockplate bolt. Looseness in any of these could contribute to a poor earth connection. Check the condenser (Section 4).
6 Refitting the contact breaker assembly is a reversal of removal and when fitted, adjust the points gap(s) as described in the preceeding Section, apply a smear of grease to the high points of the cam.

## 4 Condenser (capacitor) - removal, testing and installation

1 The condenser ensures that with the contact breaker points open, the sparking between them is not excessive to cause severe pitting. The condenser is fitted in parallel, and its failure will automatically cause failure of the ignition system as the points will be prevented from interrupting the low tension circuit.
2 Testing for an unserviceable condenser may be effected by switching on the ignition and separating the contact points by hand. If this action is accompanied by a blue flash then condenser failure is indicated. Difficult starting, missing of the engine after several miles running or badly pitting points are other indications of the faulty condenser.
3 The surest test is by substitution of a new unit.
4 Removal of the condenser is by means of withdrawing the screw(s) which retain(s) it/them from the breaker plate or distributor body.

1 Ignition coil and resistor

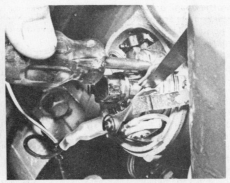

2.8 Contact breaker adjustment

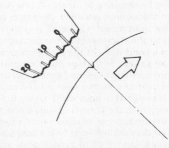

Fig. 4.5. Ignition setting marks

## 5  Distributor - removal and installation

**Note:** If the distributor driveshaft on J series engines is removed after the distributor has been removed, it must be installed as described in the Section of Chapter 1 entitled 'Engine - final stages of assembly after major repair'.

1   To remove the distributor complete with cap from the engine, begin by pulling the plug lead terminals off the spark plugs. Free the HT lead from the centre of the coil to the centre of the distributor by undoing the lead retaining cap from the coil.

2   Pull off the rubber pipe holding the vacuum tube to the distributor vacuum advance and retard take-off pipe.

3   Disconnect the low tension wire from the coil.

4   In order to simplify installation of the distributor, rotate the crankshaft by means of the hexagon on the crankshaft pulley until the notch on the rim of the pulley aligns with the appropriate ignition timing mark (see Specifications) on the engine front cover. Index mark the position of the distributor body with respect to the fixing plate and cylinder block, and the rotor with respect to the distributor body.

5   Undo and remove the bolt which holds the distributor fixing plate to the block and lift the distributor out.

6   Installation is the reverse of the removal procedure, provided that the index marks are aligned correctly. If there is any doubt about the correct positioning of the distributor after it has been installed, the ignition timing **must** be checked, as described in Section 6 or 9.

## 6  Ignition timing (mechanical type contact breaker)

1   Adjust the contact breaker points gap, as described in Section 2.

2   Turn the engine until No. 1 piston is rising on its compression stroke. This may be checked by removing No. 1 spark plug and placing a finger over the plug hole to feel the compression being generated or alternatively removing the distributor cap and observing that the rotor arm is coming up to align with the position of No. 1 contact segment in the distributor cap.

3   There is a notch on the rim of the crankshaft pulley and a scale on the timing cover. Continue turning the crankshaft until the notch on the pulley is opposite the appropriate static ignition setting (initial advance) mark on the scale. Refer to Specifications for this setting as it varies between engine and model types.

4   Slacken the distributor clamp plate bolt.

5   Connect a 12 volt test lamp between the condenser flying lead terminal (on dual points distributors it is the advance condenser flying lead terminal) and the distributor body. Switch on the ignition.

6   Turn the distributor body to the position where even the slightest further movement will illuminate the test bulb.

7   Tighten the distributor clamp plate bolt and remove the test lamp. Switch off the ignition on single point distributors.

8   On dual point distributors connect the test lamp to the retard condenser flying lead terminal and the distributor body. Loosen the adjuster plate screws and, using a screwdriver in the notch of the adjuster plate, move the adjuster plate to give the specified phase difference. One notch of the adjuster plate scale is 4º, rotating the screwdriver clockwise will decrease the phase difference and counterclockwise will increase the phase difference.

9   Tighten the adjuster plate screws.

10 An alternative method of ignition timing is given in Section 9,

of this Chapter. This method uses a stroboscope and is the only satisfactory way of checking ignition timing with the transistorized system.

## 7  Distributor (mechanical type contact breaker) - dismantling and reassembly

**Note:** The procedure given below is for the single point type distributor. The only difference for the dual point distributor is the additional contact point set, and the fact that the condensers are mounted externally.

1   Remove the cap and pull off the rotor.

2   Unscrew and remove the two screws which secure the vacuum capsule to the distributor body. Tilt the capsule slightly to disengage the actuating rod from the pivot of the movable baseplate. Withdraw the vacuum capsule.

3   Remove the contact breaker assembly. Where applicable also remove the condenser from the breaker plate.

4   Unscrew and remove the securing screws from the baseplate assembly and lift out the assembly.

5   If the movable and fixed baseplates are to be separated, remove the securing screws but take care not to lose the balls which are sandwiched between the two components.

6   Knock out the pin from the collar at the base of the distributor shaft using a suitable drift.

7   The shaft and counterweight assembly may now be withdrawn through the upper end of the distributor body.

8   Where it is necessary to remove the cam from the top of the distributor shaft, first mark the relative position of the cam to the shaft, then unscrew and remove the screw from the cam recess.

9   Where the counterweights and their springs are to be dismantled, take care not to stretch the springs.

10 Check all components for wear and renew as appropriate.

11 Grease the counterweight pivots and reassemble by reversing the dismantling procedure but ensure that the rotor positioning flat on the cam is towards the circular hook and also that the circular and rectangular ended springs are correctly located (see Fig. 4.12a and 4.12b for the single and dual point distributors).

## 8  Distributor (transistorized ignition type) - air-gap adjustment

1   On this type of distributor the only adjustment is to ensure that the air gap, measured between the reluctor (rotor) projections and the pole piece of the pick-up coil, is as specified.

2   If adjustment is required, loosen the pick-up coil screws and move the coil until the correct gap is measured using a feeler gauge.

## 9  Ignition timing using a stroboscopic lamp

1   This method of ignition timing is essential for the transistorized ignition system. It is generally accepted as being a preferable method of setting the timing where a mechanical type contact breaker is installed, although for most practical purposes the method given in Section 6 is satisfactory.

2   Initially check the contact breaker points gap (Section 2) or air gap (Section 8)

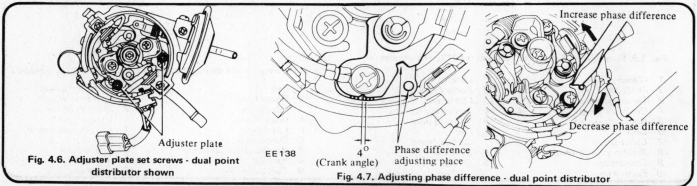

Adjuster plate

**Fig. 4.6. Adjuster plate set screws - dual point distributor shown**

EE 138

4º (Crank angle)

Phase difference adjusting place

Increase phase difference

Decrease phase difference

**Fig. 4.7. Adjusting phase difference - dual point distributor**

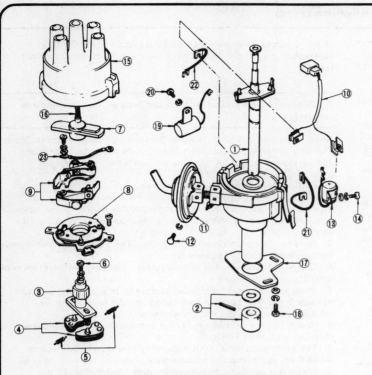

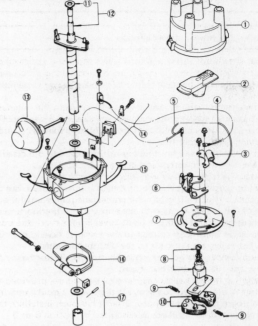

**Fig. 4.10. Single point distributor - typical for 1974 USA models**

| 1 | Cap | 9 | Spring |
|---|---|---|---|
| 2 | Rotor arm | 10 | Counterweight |
| 3 | Condenser | 11 | Thrust washer |
| 4 | Ground lead | 12 | Shaft |
| 5 | LT lead | 13 | Vacuum capsule |
| 6 | Contact breaker | 14 | LT terminal |
| 7 | Baseplate assembly | 15 | Cap clip |
| 8 | Cam | 16 | Clamp plate |
| | | 17 | Collar assembly |

**Fig. 4.8. Dual point distributor - exploded view**

| 1 | Shaft assembly | 13 | Advance point condenser |
|---|---|---|---|
| 2 | Collar set | 14 | Screw |
| 3 | Cam | 15 | Distributor cap |
| 4 | Governor weights | 16 | Carbon brush |
| 5 | Governor springs | 17 | Firing plate |
| 6 | Screw | 18 | Bolt |
| 7 | Rotor | 19 | Retard point condenser |
| 8 | Breaker assembly | 20 | Screw |
| 9 | Contact set | 21 | Advance point lead |
| 10 | Connector assembly | 22 | Retard point lead |
| 11 | Vacuum unit | 23 | Ground wire assembly |
| 12 | Screw | | |

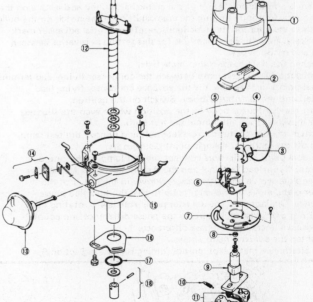

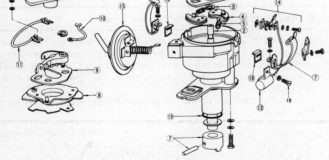

**Fig. 4.9. Single point distributor - typical for J13, J15 engines**

| 1 | Clamp | 11 | Lead wire |
|---|---|---|---|
| 2 | Shaft assembly | 12 | Rotor head |
| 3 | Thrust washer | 13 | Condenser |
| 4 | Governor weight | 14 | Terminal assembly |
| 5 | Governor spring | 15 | Vacuum unit |
| 6 | Cam | 16 | Cap |
| 7 | Collar set | 17 | Carbon brush |
| 8 | Breaker plate assembly | 18 | Dust seal |
| 9 | Contact set | 19 | O-ring |
| 10 | Earth wire | | |

**Fig. 4.11. Single point distributor - typical for 1975/76 USA models**

| 1 | Cap | 10 | Governor spring |
|---|---|---|---|
| 2 | Rotor head | 11 | Governor weight |
| 3 | Condenser | 12 | Shaft assembly |
| 4 | Ground wire | 13 | Vacuum unit |
| 5 | Lead wire | 14 | Terminal assembly |
| 6 | Contact set | 15 | Housing |
| 7 | Breaker plate assembly | 16 | Fixing plate |
| 8 | Packing | 17 | O-ring |
| 9 | Cam assembly | 18 | Collar |

4

3   Mark the notch on the crankshaft pulley with chalk or white paint.
4   Mark in a similar manner, the appropriate line on the timing cover scale (see Specifications for static timing figure according to engine and vehicle type). For dual point distributors also mark the specified phase difference.
5   Disconnect the vacuum pipe (which runs from the vacuum capsule on the distributor to the carburetor. Disconnect the pipe from the distributor end and plug the pipe.
6   Connect a stroboscope in accordance with the makers instructions (usually interposed between No. 1 spark plug and HT lead).
7   Start the engine (which should previously have been run to normal operating temperature) and let it idle (see recommended speeds in Specifications) otherwise the mechanical advance mechanism will operate and give a false ignition timing.
8   Point the stroboscope at the ignition timing marks when they will appear stationary and if the ignition timing is correct, in alignment. If the marks are not in alignment, loosen the distributor clamp plate screw and turn the distributor.
9   For dual point distributors, disconnect the black lead wire from the distributor harness and connect it to the yellow wire, (retard side). With the engine still idling check for the specified phase difference. If necessary, adjust the phase difference by repositioning the adjuster plate as described in paragraph 8, of Section 6.
10  Switch off the ignition, tighten the distributor clamp plate screw and remove the stroboscope.
11  Unplug and reconnect the vacuum pipe.

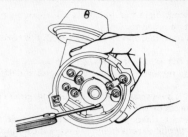

**Fig. 4.13. Checking the air gap - transistor type distributor**

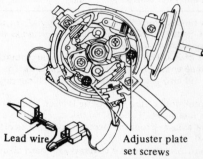

Lead wire                     Adjuster plate
                              set screws

**Fig. 4.14. Lead connects for stroboscopic timing with a dual point distributor**

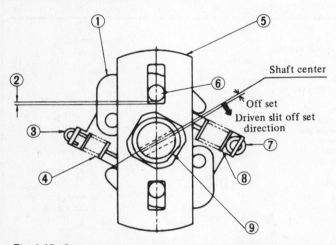

Shaft center

Off set
Driven slit off set direction

**Fig. 4.12a Governor spring and cam setting - dual point distributor**

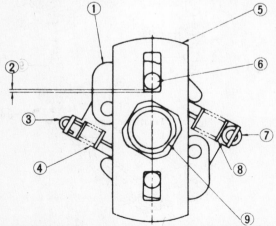

**Fig. 4.12b Governor spring and cam setting - 1974 USA models, and J13, J15 engine models**

1   *Governor weight*                 6   *Pin*
2   *Clearance for start and end*      7   *Circular hook*
    *of advancing angle*              8   *Governor spring (A)*
3   *Rectangular hook*                9   *Rotor positioning*
4   *Governor spring (B)*                 *flat*
5   *Cam plate*

## 10  Distributor (transistor type) - dismantling and reassembly

1   Remove the distributor cap and rotor.
2   Remove the two screws which secure the vacuum capsule, tilt it slightly to disengage the operating rod from the baseplate pivot.
3   Unscrew and remove  the screws which hold the pick-up coils and remove it.
4   Using two bars as levers, pry the reluctor from the distributor shaft and then remove the tension pin.
5   Unscrew and remove the screws which secure the baseplate and lift off the baseplate.
6   Drive out the pin from the lower end of the shaft, remove the collar and then withdraw the upper counterweight assembly and shaft from the top of the distributor.
7   Unscrew and remove the screw from the recess at the end of the shaft then remove the camplate and weight assembly.
8   Where the weights and springs are dismantled, take care not to stretch the springs.
9   Renew any worn components.
10  Reassembly is a reversal of dismantling but ensure that the following conditions are met:
    a)  *The reluctor is correctly orientated on the distributor shaft with regard to the positions of the flat and the tension pin. Note that the slot in the tension pin must face outwards (Fig. 4.15).*
    b)  *If the contactor has been disturbed, adjust the cam to contactor clearance to 0.012 in (0.3 mm) on reassembly (Fig. 4.16).*
    c)  *Grease the counterweight pivots and the top of the rotor shaft sparingly with a general purpose grease.*

## 11  Transistorized ignition unit

1   The unit is located below the left-hand side of the fascia panel within the vehicle.
2   It performs the following functions:
    a)  *It 'makes' and 'breaks' the current in the primary circuit of the ignition coil.*
    b)  *Sets and maintains the make-and-break cycle according to engine speed.*
    c)  *Incorporates a delayed cut-out to disconnect the primary current within a period not exceeding ten seconds if the ignition is left switched on with the engine not running;*
3   A fault in the transistorized ignition system can only be checked and traced using an oscilloscope and this work should therefore be left to an auto-electrician

4   Any fault occuring in the unit itself will require a new unit as the original cannot be repaired.

5   To renew a unit, disconnect the lead from the battery negative terminal.

6   Disconnect the wiring harness from the unit.

7   Unscrew and remove the securing setscrews and lift the unit from its location.

8   Installation is a reversal of removal but take great care to connect the wiring harness correctly.

9   Where a transistorized ignition unit is installed, do not disconnect the spark plug or coil wires when the engine is running.

## 12  Spark plugs and high tension (HT) leads

1   The correct functioning of the spark plugs is vital for the correct running and efficiency of the engine. The plugs fitted as standard are listed on the Specifications page.

2   At intervals of 3000 miles (4800 km) the plugs should be removed, examined, cleaned and, if worn excessively, renewed. The condition of the spark plug will also tell much about the overall condition of the engine.

3   If the insulator nose of the spark plug is clean and white, with no deposits, this is indicative of a weak mixture, or too hot a plug. (A hot plug transfers heat away from the electrode slowly - a cold plug transfers it away quickly).

4   If the top and insulator nose is covered with hard black looking deposits, then this is indicative that the mixture is too rich. Should the plug be black and oily, then it is likely that the engine is fairly worn, as well as the mixture being too rich.

5   If the insulator nose is covered with light tan to greyish brown deposits, then the mixture is correct and it is likely that the engine is in good condition.

6   If there are any traces of long brown tapering stains on the outside of the white portion of the plug, then the plug will have to be renewed, as this shows that there is a faulty joint between the plug body and the insulator, and ccmpression is being allowed to leak away.

7   Plugs should be cleaned by a sand blasting machine, which will free them from carbon more thoroughly than cleaning by hand. The machine will also test the condition of the plugs under compression. Any plug that fails to spark at the recommended pressure should be renewed.

8   The spark plug gap is of considerable importance, as, if it is too large or too small the size of the spark and its efficiency will be seriously impaired. The spark plug gap should be set to the specified gap for the best results.

9   To set it, measure the gap with a feeler gauge, and then bend open, or closed, the outer plug electrode until the correct gap is achieved. The centre electrode should never be bent as this may crack the insulation and cause plug failure, if nothing worse.

10  When replacing the plugs, remember to use new plug washers and install the leads from the distributor in the correct firing order 1—3—4—2, number 1 cylinder being the one nearest the radiator.

11  The plug leads require no attention other than being kept clean and wiped over regularly.

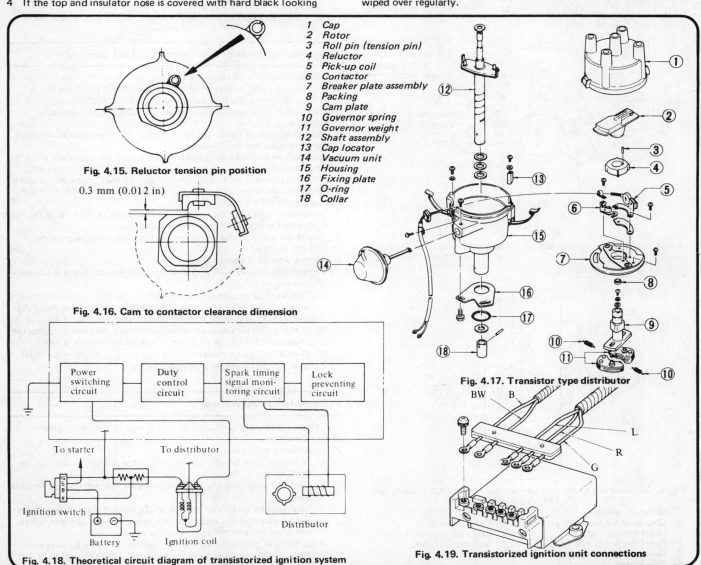

**Fig. 4.15. Reluctor tension pin position**

0.3 mm (0.012 in)

**Fig. 4.16. Cam to contactor clearance dimension**

1   Cap
2   Rotor
3   Roll pin (tension pin)
4   Reluctor
5   Pick-up coil
6   Contactor
7   Breaker plate assembly
8   Packing
9   Cam plate
10  Governor spring
11  Governor weight
12  Shaft assembly
13  Cap locator
14  Vacuum unit
15  Housing
16  Fixing plate
17  O-ring
18  Collar

**Fig. 4.17. Transistor type distributor**

Power switching circuit | Duty control circuit | Spark timing signal monitoring circuit | Lock preventing circuit

To starter | To distributor

Ignition switch

Battery | Ignition coil | Distributor

**Fig. 4.18. Theoretical circuit diagram of transistorized ignition system**

BW   B   L   R   G

**Fig. 4.19. Transistorized ignition unit connections**

# Common spark plug conditions

## NORMAL

**Symptoms:** Brown to grayish-tan color and slight electrode wear. Correct heat range for engine and operating conditions.

**Recommendation:** When new spark plugs are installed, replace with plugs of the same heat range.

### WORN

**Symptoms:** Rounded electrodes with a small amount of deposits on the firing end. Normal color. Causes hard starting in damp or cold weather and poor fuel economy.

**Recommendation:** Plugs have been left in the engine too long. Replace with new plugs of the same heat range. Follow the recommended maintenance schedule.

### CARBON DEPOSITS

**Symptoms:** Dry sooty deposits indicate a rich mixture or weak ignition. Causes misfiring, hard starting and hesitation.

**Recommendation:** Make sure the plug has the correct heat range. Check for a clogged air filter or problem in the fuel system or engine management system. Also check for ignition system problems.

### ASH DEPOSITS

**Symptoms:** Light brown deposits encrusted on the side or center electrodes or both. Derived from oil and/or fuel additives. Excessive amounts may mask the spark, causing misfiring and hesitation during acceleration.

**Recommendation:** If excessive deposits accumulate over a short time or low mileage, install new valve guide seals to prevent seepage of oil into the combustion chambers. Also try changing gasoline brands.

### OIL DEPOSITS

**Symptoms:** Oily coating caused by poor oil control. Oil is leaking past worn valve guides or piston rings into the combustion chamber. Causes hard starting, misfiring and hesitation.

**Recommendation:** Correct the mechanical condition with necessary repairs and install new plugs.

### GAP BRIDGING

**Symptoms:** Combustion deposits lodge between the electrodes. Heavy deposits accumulate and bridge the electrode gap. The plug ceases to fire, resulting in a dead cylinder.

**Recommendation:** Locate the faulty plug and remove the deposits from between the electrodes.

### TOO HOT

**Symptoms:** Blistered, white insulator, eroded electrode and absence of deposits. Results in shortened plug life.

**Recommendation:** Check for the correct plug heat range, over-advanced ignition timing, lean fuel mixture, intake manifold vacuum leaks, sticking valves and insufficient engine cooling.

### PREIGNITION

**Symptoms:** Melted electrodes. Insulators are white, but may be dirty due to misfiring or flying debris in the combustion chamber. Can lead to engine damage.

**Recommendation:** Check for the correct plug heat range, over-advanced ignition timing, lean fuel mixture, insufficient engine cooling and lack of lubrication.

### HIGH SPEED GLAZING

**Symptoms:** Insulator has yellowish, glazed appearance. Indicates that combustion chamber temperatures have risen suddenly during hard acceleration. Normal deposits melt to form a conductive coating. Causes misfiring at high speeds.

**Recommendation:** Install new plugs. Consider using a colder plug if driving habits warrant.

### DETONATION

**Symptoms:** Insulators may be cracked or chipped. Improper gap setting techniques can also result in a fractured insulator tip. Can lead to piston damage.

**Recommendation:** Make sure the fuel anti-knock values meet engine requirements. Use care when setting the gaps on new plugs. Avoid lugging the engine.

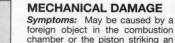

### MECHANICAL DAMAGE

**Symptoms:** May be caused by a foreign object in the combustion chamber or the piston striking an incorrect reach (too long) plug. Causes a dead cylinder and could result in piston damage.

**Recommendation:** Repair the mechanical damage. Remove the foreign object from the engine and/or install the correct reach plug.

## 13 Ignition system (mechanical contact breaker) - fault diagnosis

### Engine fails to start

1 If the engine fails to start and the car was running normally when it was last used, first check there is fuel in the fuel tank. If the engine turns over normally on the starter motor and the battery is evidently well charged, then the fault may be in either the high or low tension circuits. First check the HT circuit. Note: if the battery is known to be fully charged; the ignition light comes on, and the starter motor fails to turn the engine check the tightness of the leads on the battery terminals and also the secureness of the earth lead to its connection to the body. It is quite common for the leads to have worked loose, even if they look and feel secure. If one of the battery terminal posts gets very hot when trying to work the starter motor this is a sure indication of a faulty connection to that terminal.

2 One of the commonest reasons for bad starting is wet or damp spark plug leads and distributor. Remove the distributor cap. If condensation is visible internally, dry the cap with a rag and also wipe over the leads. Replace the cap.

3 If the engine still fails to start, check that current is reaching the plugs by disconnecting each plug lead in turn at the spark plug end, and hold the end of the cable about 3/16th (5 mm) away from the cylinder block. Spin the engine on the starter motor.

4 Sparking between the end of the cable and the block should be fairly strong with a regular blue spark. (Hold the lead with rubber to avoid electric shock). If current is reaching the plugs, then remove them and clean, and regap them. The engine should now start.

5 If there is no spark at the plug leads take off the HT lead from the centre of the distributor cap and hold it to the block as before. Spin the engine on the starter once more. A rapid succession of blue sparks between the end of the lead and the block indicate that the coil is in order and that the distributor cap is cracked, the rotor arm faulty, or the carbon brush in the top of the distributor cap is not making good contact with the spring on the rotor arm. Possibly the points are in bad condition. Clean and reset them as described in this Chapter.

6 If there are no sparks from the end of the lead from the coil check the connections at the coil end of the lead. If it is in order start checking the low tension circuit.

7 Use a 12v voltmeter or a 12v bulb and two lengths of wire. With the ignition switch on and the points open test between the low tension wire to the coil (it is marked SW or +) and earth. No reading indicates a break in the supply from the ignition switch. Check the connections at the switch and resistor to see if any are loose. Reinstall them and the engine should run. A reading shows a faulty coil or condenser, or broken lead between the coil and the distributor.

8 Take the condenser wire off the points assembly and with the point open, test between the moving points and earth. If there now is a reading, then the fault is in the condenser. Install a new one and the fault is cleared.

9 With no reading from the moving point to earth take a reading between earth and the negative terminal of the coil. A reading here shows a broken wire which need to be replaced between the coil and distributor. No reading confirms that the coil has failed and must be replaced, after which the engine will run once more. Remember to reinstall the condenser wire to the points asembly. For these tests it is sufficient to separate the points with a piece of dry paper while testing

with the points open.

### Engine misfires

10 If the engine misfires regularly, run it at a fast idling speed. Pull off each of the plug caps in turn and listen to the note of the engine. Hold the plug cap in a dry cloth or with a rubber glove as additional protection against a shock from the HT supply.

11 No difference in engine running will be noticed when the lead from the defective circuit is removed. Removing the lead from one of the good cylinders will accentuate the misfire.

12 Remove the plug lead from the end of the defective plug and hold it about 3/16th inch (5 mm) away from the block. Restart the engine. If the sparking is fairly strong and regular the fault must lie in the spark plug.

13 The plug may be loose, the insulation may be cracked, or the points may have burnt away giving too wide a gap for the spark to jump. Worse still, one of the points may have broken off. Either renew the plug, or clean it, reset the gap, and then test it.

14 If there is no spark at the end of the plug lead, or if it is weak and intermittent, check the ignition lead from the distributor to the plug. If the insulation is cracked or perished, renew the lead. Check the connections at the distributor cap.

15 If there is still no spark, examine the distributor cap carefully for tracking. This can be recognised by a very thin black line running between two or more electrodes, or between an electrode and some other part of the distributor. These lines are paths which now conduct electricity across the cap thus letting it run to earth. The only answer is a new distributor cap.

16 Apart from the ignition timing being incorrect, other causes of misfiring have already been dealt with under the Section dealing with the failure of the engine to start. To recap - these are that:

   a) *The coil may be faulty giving an intermittent misfire;*
   b) *There may be damaged wire or loose connection in the low tension circuit;*
   c) *The condenser may be short circuiting;*
   d) *There may be a mechanical fault in the distributor (broken driving spindle or contact breaker spring).*

17 If the ignition timing is too far retarded, it should be noted that the engine will tend to overheat, and there will be a quite noticeable drop in power. If the engine is overheating and the power is down, and the ignition timing is correct, then the carburetor should be checked, as it is likely that this is where the fault lies.

## 14 Ignition system (transistorised type) - testing and fault diagnosis

1 Expensive and special equipment is required to test the transistor unit. It is therefore recommended that the unit, which is located on the fascia panel within the car interior, should be removed and tested by a competent automobile electrician.

2 Apart from this, check the security of all HT and LT leads and examine the distributor cap for cracks.

3 The testing procedure described in the preceeding Section will apply except in respect of the contact breaker which of course should be ignored. The air gap between the reluctor and the pick-up coil should however be checked as described earlier in this Chapter (Section 8).

**4**

# Chapter 5 Clutch

## Contents

## Specifications

**Type** ... ... ... ... ... ... ... ... ...     Single dry plate, diaphragm spring, sealed ball type release bearing, hydraulic operation

| Clutch driven plate | 1975/76 USA | 1974 USA | 1973 USA | Other models |
|---|---|---|---|---|
| Friction lining: | | | | |
|   Outside diameter ... ... ... | 8.86 in (225 mm) | 8.86 in (225 mm) | 7.87 in (200 mm) | 7.87 in (200 mm) |
|   Inside diameter ... ... ... | 5.91 in (150 mm) | 5.91 in (150 mm) | 5.12 in (130 mm) | 5.12 in (130 mm) |
|   Thickness ... ... ... ... | 0.138 in (3.5 mm) | 0.138 in (3.5 mm) | 0.138 in (3.5 mm) | 0.138 in (3.5 mm) |
|   Number of torsion springs ... ... | 6 | 6 | 6 | 6 |
| | | | | |
| **Clutch cover type** ... ... ... | C225S | C225R | MF 200K | C200S |
| | | | | |
| **Free-movement at clevis pin** ... | 0.04 to 0.12 in (1 to 3 mm) | 0.04 to 0.12 in (1 to 3 mm) | 0.04 to 0.12 in (1 to 3 mm) | 0.04 to 0.12 in (1 to 3 mm) |
| | | | | |
| **Clutch pedal height from floor** ... | 6.02 in (153 mm) | 6.02 in (153 mm) | 6.42 in (163 mm) | 6.42 (163 mm) |

**Master cylinder diameter** ... ...     5/8 in (15.87 mm)

**Operating cylinder diameter** ...     0.75 in (19.05 mm)

**Fluid type** ... ... ... ...     DOT3 (MVSS 116) or SAE J1703C

| Torque wrench settings | | lb f ft | kg f m |
|---|---|---|---|
| Clutch housing to engine bolts ... ... ... ... ... ... ... | | 35 | 4.8 |
| Clutch to flywheel bolts ... ... ... ... ... ... ... | | 16 | 2.2 |
| Operating cylinder securing bolts ... ... ... ... ... ... ... | | 25 | 3.45 |
| Withdrawal lever ball pivot stud ... ... ... ... ... ... | | 36 | 5.0 |

## 1 General description

The clutch assembly is similar on all models but the design detail of some components varies according to model and date of manufacture. This in no way effects the procedure described in the Sections of this Chapter.

Major components comprise a pressure plate and cover assembly, diaphragm spring and a driven plate (friction disc) which incorporates torsion coil springs to cushion rotational shock when the drive is taken up.

The clutch release bearing is of sealed ball type and clutch actuation is hydraulic.

Depressing the clutch pedal moves the piston in the master cylinder forwards, so forcing hydraulic fluid through the clutch hydraulic pipe to the slave cylinder.

The piston in the slave cylinder moves forward on the entry of the

fluid and actuates the clutch release arm by means of a short pushrod.

The release arm pushes the release bearing forwards to bear against the release plate, so moving the centre of the diaphragm spring inwards. The spring is sandwiched between two annular rings which act as fulcrum points. As the centre of the spring is pushed in, the outside of the spring is pushed out, so moving the pressure plate backwards and disengaging the pressure plate from the clutch disc.

When the clutch pedal is released the diaphragm spring forces the pressure plate into contact with the high friction linings on the clutch disc, and at the same time pushes the clutch disc a fraction of an inch forwards on its splines to engaging the clutch disc with the flywheel. The clutch disc is now firmly sandwiched between the pressure plate and the flywheel so the drive is taken up.

The specified free-movement must be maintained between the face of the clutch release bearing and the pressure plate diaphragm spring fingers. This is carried out by first checking the pedal height and then screwing the master cylinder pushrod in, or out, as necessary and as described in Section 3. This free-movement, once set, is maintained by a special type of operating cylinder which is self-adjusting to compensate for wear on the driven plate friction linings.

## 2  Clutch pedal - removal and installation

1  Remove the cotter pin and clevis pin from the clutch master cylinder pushrod endfitting.
2  Unhook the clutch pedal return spring.
3  Remove the nut from the pedal fulcrum pin.
4  Take off the spring and flat washers, and extract the fulcrum pin.
5  Remove the pedal, taking care that the bushes are not lost.
6  Installation is the reverse of the removal procedure. Apply a little general purpose grease to the pivot points and bushes. Adjust the pedal, if necessary, as described in the following Section.

## 3  Clutch pedal - adjustment

1  Measure the height of the clutch pedal pad upper surface from the floor. This should be as given in the Specifications. If necessary, adjust by releasing the locknut and turning the stop bolt in or out.
2  Now adjust the pushrod to obtain the specified free-movement when the pedal pad is depressed with the fingers.
3  Retighten all locknuts.

## 4  Master cylinder - removal and installation

1  Disconnect the master cylinder pushrod from the pedal arm.
2  Disconnect the fluid line from the master cylinder and drain the fluid into a suitable container.
3  Remove the master cylinder flange mounting bolts and withdraw the unit from the engine compartment rear bulkhead.
4  Installation is the reverse of the removal procedure but check the pedal height and free-movement as previously described, and bleed the hydraulic system (Sec. 8).

## 5  Master cylinder - servicing

1  Unscrew and remove the reservoir cap and drain any fluid.
2  Peel back the dust excluder and extract the snap ring.
3  Withdraw the pushrod and the piston assembly.
4  Remove the valve assembly and return spring.
5  Wash all components in clean hydraulic fluid, isopropyl alcohol or methylated spirit and examine the surface of the piston and the bore of the cylinder for scoring or 'bright' wear areas. Where these are evident, renew the master cylinder complete.
6  Where the components are in good condition, discard the rubber seals and obtain a repair kit. The end of the valve stem can be released from the 'keyhole' in the spring seat by first compressing the return spring and pulling the spring seat to one side.

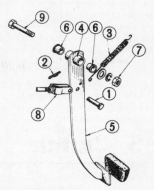

**Fig. 5.2. Clutch pedal - exploded view**

| 1 Clevis pin | 6 Bushes |
| 2 Cotter pin | 7 Nut |
| 3 Spring | 8 Pushrod |
| 4 Pedal boss | 9 Fulcrum pin |
| 5 Pedal assembly | |

**Fig. 5.3. Clutch pedal adjustment**

1  Stop bolt locknut
2  Pushrod locknut

a  —  Pedal height (see Specifications)
b  —  Pedal stroke (approximately 5 in/127 mm)

MG  Apply general purpose grease when reassembling

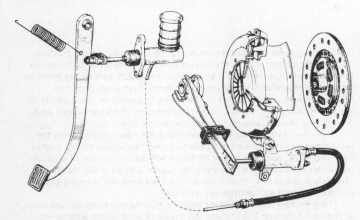

**Fig. 5.1. Layout of clutch components**

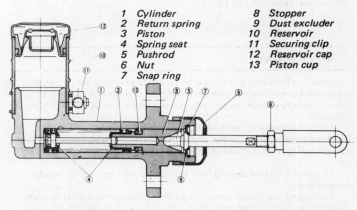

| 1 Cylinder | 8 Stopper |
| 2 Return spring | 9 Dust excluder |
| 3 Piston | 10 Reservoir |
| 4 Spring seat | 11 Securing clip |
| 5 Pushrod | 12 Reservoir cap |
| 6 Nut | 13 Piston cup |
| 7 Snap ring | |

**Fig. 5.4. Master cylinder - sectional view**

5

## 6  Operating cylinder - removal and installation

1   Unscrew and remove the two bolts which secure the operating (slave) cylinder to the clutch bellhousing. Withdraw the cylinder, extracting the end of the pushrod from the clutch withdrawal lever at the same time (photo).

2   Without straining or twisting the hydraulic hose (hold its end fitting securely in a wrench unscrew the cylinder from the end fitting of the hose, and then plug the end fitting to prevent loss of fluid. An alternative method, to prevent loss of fluid, is to remove the reservoir cap and place a piece of polythene sheeting over the open reservoir. Screw on the cap and thus create a vacuum which will stop the fluid running out of the open hose.

3   Installation is the reverse of the removal procedure but check the clutch pedal free-movement and bleed the hydraulic system (Section 8).

## 7  Operating cylinder - servicing

1   Withdraw the pushrod and dust cover from the end of the cylinder body.

2   Extract the piston and the piston rings. If these components are difficult to remove, apply air pressure from a tire pump at the fluid entry port on the cylinder body.

3   Wash all components in clean hydraulic fluid, isoproyl alcohol or methylated spirit, and then examine the surfaces of the piston and cylinder bore. If these are scored, or any 'bright' wear areas are evident, renew the slave cylinder complete.

4   If the components are in good order, discard the seal and obtain a repair kit.

5   Manipulate the new seal into position, ensuring that its lip faces the correct way.

6   Reassembly is the reverse of the dismantling procedure but take care not to nip the piston seal as it enters the cylinder bore. Alway dip the piston assembly in clean hydraulic fluid before commencing to assemble it.

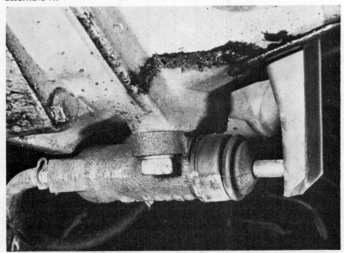

6.1 Clutch operating cylinder installation

## 8  Hydraulic system - bleeding

1   The need for bleeding the cylinders and fluid line arises when air gets into them. Air gets in whenever a joint or seal leaks or a part has to be dismantled. Bleeding is simply the process of getting the air out again.

2   Make sure that the reservoir is filled, and obtain a piece of 3/16 inch (5 mm) bore diameter rubber tube about 2 to 3 feet (0.6 to 0.8 mm) long, and a clean glass jar. A small quantity of fresh, clean hydraulic fluid as also necessary.

3   Detach the cap on the bleed nipple and clean the surrounding area. Unscrew the nipple ¼ turn and fit the tube over it. Put about ½ inch (12 mm) of fluid in the jar and put the other end of the pipe in it. The jar can be placed on the ground under the vehicle.

4   The clutch pedal should then be depressed quickly and released slowly until no more air bubbles come from the pipe. Quick pedal action carries the air along rather than leaving it behind. Keep the reservoir topped up.

5   When the air bubbles stop, tighten the nipple at the end of a down stroke.

6   Check that the operation of the clutch is satisfactory. Even though there may be no exterior leaks, it is possible that the movement of the pushrod from the clutch cylinder is inadequate because fluid is leaking internally past the seals in the master cylinder. If this is the case, it is best to renew all seals in both cylinders.

7   Always use clean hydraulic fluid which has been stored in an airtight container, and has remained unshaken for the preceding 24 hours.

## 9  Clutch - removal

1   Remove the engine/transmission as a unit as described in Chapter 1, or alternatively remove the transmission as described in Chapter 6.

2   Where applicable, separate the transmission from the engine by removing the clutch bellhousing to crankcase securing bolts.

3   The pressure plate need not be marked in relation to the flywheel as it can only be fitted one way due to the positioning dowels.

4   Unscrew the clutch assembly securing bolts a turn at a time in diametrically opposite sequence until the tension of the diaphragm spring is released. Remove the bolts and lift the pressure plate assembly away.

5   At this stage, the driven plate (friction disc) will fall from its location between the pressure plate and the flywheel.

## 10  Clutch - inspection and renovation

1   Due to the slow-wearing characteristics of the clutch, it is not easy to decide when to go to the trouble of removing the transmission in order to check the wear on the friction lining. The only positive indication that something needs doing is when it starts to slip or when squealing noises on engagement indicate that the friction lining has worn down to the rivets. In such instances it can only be hoped that the friction surfaces on the flywheel and pressure plate have not been badly worn or scored.

   A clutch will wear according to the way in which it is used. Much intentional slipping of the clutch while driving - rather then the correct selection of gears - will accelerate wear. It is best to assume however, that the friction disc will need renewal every 35,000 miles (56,000 km)

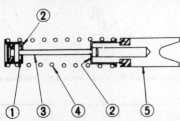

Fig. 5.5. Master cylinder piston assembly

1   Spring            4   Return spring
2   Spring seat       5   Piston
3   Valve assembly

Fig. 5.6. Operating cylinder - exploded view

1   Pushrod           4   Piston
2   Dust cover        5   Operating cylinder
3   Spring            6   Bleed nipple

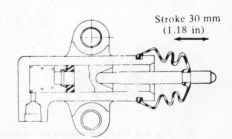

Stroke 30 mm
(1.18 in)

Fig. 5.7. Operating cylinder - sectional view

at least and that it will be worth replacing it after 25,000 miles (40,000 km). The maintenance history of the vehicle is obviously very useful in such cases.

2 Examine the surfaces of the pressure plate and flywheel for signs of scoring. If this is only light it may be left, but if very deep the pressure plate until will have to be renewed. If the flywheel is deeply scored it should be taken off and advice sought from an automobile engineering specialist or Datsun agent. Providing it can be machined completely across the face, the overall balance of engine and flywheel should not be too severely upset. If renewal of the flywheel is necessary, the new one will have to be balanced to match the original.

3 The friction plate lining surfaces should be at least 1/32 in (0.8 mm) above the rivets, otherwise the disc is not worth putting back. If the lining material shows sign of breaking up or black areas where oil contamination has occured, it should also be renewed. If facilities are readily available for obtaining and fitting new friction pads to the existing disc this may be done but the saving is relatively small compared with obtaining a complete new disc assembly which ensures that the shock absorbing springs and the splined hub are renewed also. The same applies to the pressure plate assembly which cannot be readily dismantled and put back together without specialised riveting tools and balancing equipment. An allowance is usually given for exchange units.

## 11 Clutch release bearing - renewal

1 The sealed, ball bearing type release bearing, although designed for long life, is worth renewing at the same time as the other clutch components are being renewed or serviced.
2 Deterioration of the release bearing should be suspected when there are signs of grease leakage or the unit is noisy when spun with the fingers.
3 Remove the rubber dust excluder which surrounds the withdrawal lever at the bellhousing aperture.
4 Disconnect and remove the spring from the release bearing hub (photos).
5 Disconnect the withdrawal lever from the release bearing hub.
6 Withdraw the release bearing/hub assembly from the front cover of the transmission.
7 Remove the release bearing from its hub using a two or three legged puller and a bridge piece across the end-face of the hub.
8 Press on the new bearing but apply pressure only to the center track.
9 Reassembly is the reverse of the removal procedure but apply high melting point grease to the internal recess of the release bearing hub. (Fig. 5.11).
10 Also apply similar grease to the pivot points of the clutch withdrawal lever and front cover.

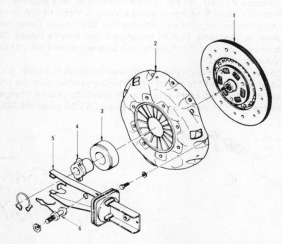

Fig. 5.8. Clutch components - typical for all models

| | |
|---|---|
| 1  Drive plate (friction disc) | 4  Release bearing hub |
| 2  Pressure plate, cover assembly | 5  Withdrawl lever |
| 3  Release bearing | 6  Pivot |

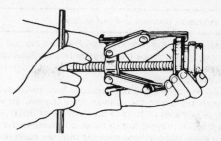

Fig. 5.9. Extracting release bearing from its hub

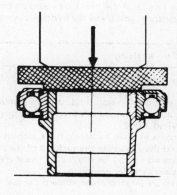

Fig. 5.10. Installing release bearing to its hub

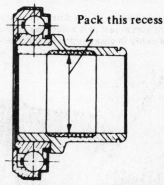

Pack this recess

Fig. 5.11. Lubrication of the release bearing

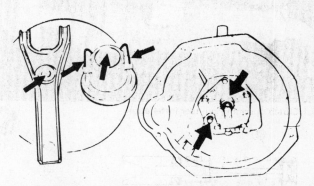

Fig. 5.12. Lubrication points for the withdrawal lever and front cover

## 12 Clutch pilot bearing - renewal

Whenever an engine, clutch or transmission is removed, it is a good policy to check the condition of the clutch pilot bearing at the rear end of the crankshaft. Further information will be found in Chapter 1 under 'Crankshaft and main bearings - examination and renovation!'

### 13 Clutch - installation

1   Clean the face of the flywheel and the pressure plate.
2   Apply a little high melting point grease to clutch pilot bearing in the centre of the flywheel.
3   Locate the driven plate against the flywheel so that its larger projecting boss is furthest from the engine.
4   Position the pressure plate assembly on the flywheel so that the positioning dowels engage.
5   Screw in each of the pressure plate bolts finger tight and then centralise the driven plate. This is accomplished by passing an old input shaft or stepped dowel rod through the splined hub of the driven plate and engaging it in the spigot bush. By moving the shaft or rod in the appropriate directions, the position will be established where the centralising tool can be withdrawn without any side pressure from the driven plate, proving that the driven plate is centralised (Fig. 5.13).
6   Without disturbing the setting of the driven plate, tighten the pressure plate bolts, a turn at a time, in diametrically opposite sequence to the specified torque.
7   Install the transmission to the engine (Chapter 6) when, if the driven plate has been correctly centralised, the input shaft of the gearbox will pass easily through the splined hub of the driven plate to engage with the spigot bush in the centre of the flywheel. Do not allow the weight of the transmission to hang upon the input shaft while it is passing through the clutch mechanism, or damage to the clutch components may result.

11.4a Clutch release bearing and withdrawal lever

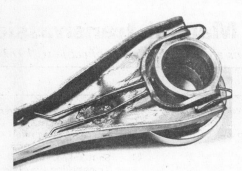

11.4b Release bearing to withdrawal lever retaining springs

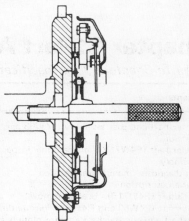

Fig. 5.13. Centralising the clutch driven plate

### 14 Fault diagnosis - clutch

| Symptom | Reason/s |
| --- | --- |
| Judder when taking up drive | Loose engine transmission mountings<br>Badly worn friction surfaces or contaminated with oil<br>Worn splines on transmission input shaft or driven plate hub<br>Worn input shaft spigot bush (pilot bearing) in flywheel |
| Clutch spin (failure to disengage) so that gears cannot be meshed | Incorrect release bearing to diaphragm spring finger clearance<br>Driven plate sticking on input shaft splines due to rust. May occur after vehicle standing idle for long period<br>Damaged or misaligned pressure plate assembly |
| Clutch slip (increase in engine speed does not result in increase in vehicle road speed - particularly on gradients) | Incorrect release bearing to diaphragm spring finger clearance<br>Friction surfaces worn out or oil contaminated |
| Noise evident on depressing clutch pedal | Dry, worn or damaged release bearing<br>Insufficient pedal free travel<br>Weak or broken pedal return spring<br>Weak or broken clutch release lever return spring<br>Excessive play between driven plate hub splines and input shaft splines |
| Noise evident as clutch pedal released | Distorted driven plate<br>Broken or weak driven plate cushion coil springs<br>Insufficient pedal free travel<br>Weak or broken clutch pedal return spring<br>Weak or broken release lever return spring<br>Distorted or worn input shaft<br>Release bearing loose on retainer hub |

# Chapter 6: Part A Manual transmission

*Refer to Chapter 13 for specifications and information applicable to 1977 through 1979 USA models*

## Contents

**6A**

## Specifications

### Type
| | |
|---|---|
| 1974 USA models onwards ... ... ... ... ... ... ... ... | F4W71B, floor shift |
| Other models ... ... ... ... ... ... ... ... ... | F4W63, floor shift or R4W63, column shift |

### Gears
Gears ... ... ... ... ... ... ... ... ... ...     Four forward and 1 reverse. Synchromesh on all forward gears.

### Ratios

*Note: The ratios given are those in most common use. Other ratios are available for certain vehicles and can be traced from the manufacturer's parts list by quoting the vehicle model number.*

1973 models:
| | |
|---|---|
| 1st ... ... ... ... ... ... ... ... ... ... | 3.657 : 1 |
| 2nd ... ... ... ... ... ... ... ... ... ... | 2.177 : 1 |
| 3rd ... ... ... ... ... ... ... ... ... ... | 1.419 : 1 |
| 4th ... ... ... ... ... ... ... ... ... ... | 1.000 : 1 |
| Reverse ... ... ... ... ... ... ... ... ... | 3.638 : 1 |
| Speedometer gear ... ... ... ... ... ... ... ... | 16 : 5 |

1974 models onwards (except UK):
| | |
|---|---|
| 1st ... ... ... ... ... ... ... ... ... ... | 3.592 : 1 |
| 2nd ... ... ... ... ... ... ... ... ... ... | 2.246 : 1 |
| 3rd ... ... ... ... ... ... ... ... ... ... | 1.415 : 1 |
| 4th ... ... ... ... ... ... ... ... ... ... | 1.000 : 1 |
| Reverse ... ... ... ... ... ... ... ... ... | 3.657 : 1 |
| Speedometer gear ... ... ... ... ... ... ... ... | 20 : 6 |

UK models:
| | |
|---|---|
| 1st ... ... ... ... ... ... ... ... ... ... | 4.234 : 1 |
| 2nd ... ... ... ... ... ... ... ... ... ... | 2.558 : 1 |
| 3rd ... ... ... ... ... ... ... ... ... ... | 1.589 : 1 |
| 4th ... ... ... ... ... ... ... ... ... ... | 1.000 : 1 |
| Reverse ... ... ... ... ... ... ... ... ... | 4.367 : 1 |
| Speedometer gear ... ... ... ... ... ... ... ... | 17 : 5 |

## Fits and clearances (F4W63 and R4W63)

| | |
|---|---|
| Gear backlash ... ... ... ... ... ... ... ... ... | 0.002 to 0.004 in (0.05 to 0.10 mm) |
| Gear endplay ... ... ... ... ... ... ... ... ... | 0.002 to 0.006 in (0.05 to 0.15 mm) |
| Baulk ring/gear clearance ... ... ... ... ... | 0.047 to 0.063 in (1.2 to 1.6 mm) |
| 3rd/4th synchro hub snap-ring sizes ... ... ... ... ... | 0.055 to 0.057 in (1.40 to 1.45 mm) |
| | 0.057 to 0.059 in (1.45 to 1.50 mm) |
| | 0.059 to 0.061 in (1.50 to 1.55 mm) |
| | 0.061 to 0.063 in (1.55 to 1.60 mm) |
| | 0.063 to 0.065 in (1.60 to 1.65 mm) |
| Main drive gear (input shaft) snap-ring sizes ... ... ... ... | 0.0587 to 0.0610 in (1.49 to 1.55 mm) |
| | 0.0614 to 0.0638 in (1.56 to 1.62 mm) |
| | 0.0638 to 0.0661 in (1.62 to 1.68 mm) |
| | 0.0661 to 0.0685 in (1.68 to 1.74 mm) |
| | 0.0685 to 0.0709 in (1.74 to 1.80 mm) |
| | 0.0709 to 0.0732 in (1.80 to 1.86 mm) |
| | 0.0732 to 0.0756 in (1.86 to 1.92 mm) |
| Reverse idler gear snap-ring sizes ... ... ... ... ... ... | 0.0453 to 0.0492 in (1.15 to 1.25 mm) |
| | 0.0531 to 0.0571 in (1.35 to 1.45 mm) |
| | 0.0492 to 0.0531 in (1.25 to 1.35 mm) |
| | 0.0571 to 0.0610 in (1.45 to 1.55 mm) |
| | 0.0413 to 0.0453 in (1.05 to 1.15 mm) |
| Counter gear (lay gear) rear thrust washer sizes ... ... ... ... | 0.0925 to 0.0945 in (2.35 to 2.4 mm) |
| | 0.0945 to 0.0965 in (2.40 to 2.45 mm) |
| | 0.0965 to 0.0984 in (2.45 to 2.5 mm) |
| | 0.0984 to 0.1004 in (2.50 to 2.55 mm) |
| | 0.1004 to 0.1024 in (2.55 to 2.60 mm) |

## Fits and clearances (F4W71B)

| | |
|---|---|
| Gear backlash: | |
| Main gear ... ... ... ... ... ... ... ... ... | 0.002 to 0.004 in (0.05 to 0.10 mm) |
| Other gears ... ... ... ... ... ... ... ... ... | 0.002 to 0.008 in (0.05 to 0.20 mm) |
| Gear endplay: | |
| 1st gear ... ... ... ... ... ... ... ... ... | 0.0126 to 0.0154 in (0.32 to 0.39 mm) |
| 2nd and 3rd gears ... ... ... ... ... ... ... | 0.0047 to 0.0075 in (0.12 to 0.19 mm) |
| Baulk ring/gear clearance ... ... ... ... ... ... | 0.049 to 0.063 in (1.25 to 1.6 mm) |
| Mainshaft front snap-ring sizes ... ... ... ... ... ... | 0.055 in (1.4 mm) |
| | 0.059 in (1.5 mm) |
| | 0.063 in (1.6 mm) |
| Main drive gear (input shaft) snap-ring sizes ... ... ... ... ... | 0.0709 in (1.8 mm) |
| | 0.0736 in (1.87 mm) |
| | 0.0764 in (1.94 mm) |
| | 0.0791 in (2.01 mm) |
| | 0.0819 in (2.08 mm) |
| | 0.0681 in (1.73 mm) |
| Counter gear (lay gear) snap-ring sizes... ... ... ... ... ... | 0.055 in (1.4 mm) |
| (drive gear and revers gear) | 0.059 in (1.5 mm) |
| | 0.063 in (1.6 mm) |
| Countershaft front bearing shims ... ... ... ... ... ... | See text. |

## Transmission lubrication

| | |
|---|---|
| Lubricant type ... ... ... ... ... ... ... ... ... | SAE 90EP gear oil |
| Lubricant capacity (approx) ... ... ... ... ... ... ... | 3.4 US pt/2.9 Imp. pt (1.7 liter) |

## Torque wrench settings
*F4W63 and R4W63*

| | lbf ft | kgf m |
|---|---|---|
| Engine/transmission bolt ... ... ... ... ... ... ... | 17 to 20 | 2.4 to 2.8 |
| Front cover/transmission bolt ... ... ... ... ... ... ... | 5.8 to 7.2 | 0.8 to 1.0 |
| Rear extension/transmission bolt ... ... ... ... ... ... | 10 to 13 | 1.4 to 1.8 |
| Main shaft tightening nut ... ... ... ... ... ... ... | 58 to 80 | 8 to 11 |
| Companion flange nut ... ... . ... ... ... ... ... | 72 to 101 | 10 to 14 |
| Rear engine mount installation bolt ... ... ... ... ... | 24 to 28 | 3.3 to 3.8 |
| Filler plug ... ... ... ... ... ... ... ... ... | 18 to 25 | 2.5 to 3.5 |
| Drain plug ... ... ... ... ... ... ... ... ... | 15 to 22 | 2.0 to 3.0 |
| Back-up lamp switch ... ... ... ... ... ... ... | 15 to 22 | 2.0 to 3.0 |
| Bottom cover bolt ... ... ... ... ... ... ... ... | 5.8 to 7.2 | 0.8 to 1.0 |
| Speedometer pinion bolt ... ... ... ... ... ... ... | 2.2 to 2.9 | 0.3 to 0.4 |
| Interlock plug ... ... ... ... ... ... ... ... | 12 to 15 | 1.7 to 2.1 |
| Shift and select operating levers ... ... ... ... ... | 2.2 to 2.9 | 0.3 to 0.4 |
| Reverse check ... ... ... ... ... ... ... ... | 15 to 22 | 2.0 to 3.0 |
| Transmission gear control (R4W63): | | |
| Transmission outer lever ... ... ... ... ... ... ... | 5.8 to 7.2 | 0.8 to 1.0 |
| Shift and select trunnion nuts ... ... ... ... ... ... | 15 to 20 | 2.0 to 2.8 |
| Select lever pivot bolt ... ... ... ... ... ... ... | 3.6 to 5.8 | 0.5 to 0.8 |
| Lower support bracket ... ... ... ... ... ... ... | 4.3 to 7.2 | 0.6 to 1.0 |

| | | | | | | | | |
|---|---|---|---|---|---|---|---|---|
| Steering wheel tightening nut | ... | ... | ... | ... | ... | ... | 51 to 54 | 7.0 to 7.5 |
| Transmission gear control (F4W63): | | | | | | | | |
| Control lever installation bolt | ... | ... | ... | ... | ... | ... | 14 to 16 | 1.9 to 2.2 |

*F4W71B*

| | | | | | | | | |
|---|---|---|---|---|---|---|---|---|
| Engine to transmission bolt | ... | ... | ... | ... | ... | ... | 30 to 36 | 4.0 to 5.0 |
| Transmission to engine rear plate | ... | ... | ... | ... | ... | ... | 4.0 to 5.4 | 0.55 to 0.75 |
| Clutch operating cylinder bolt | ... | ... | ... | ... | ... | ... | 18 to 25 | 2.5 to 3.5 |
| Exhaust front tube to exhaust manifold | ... | ... | ... | ... | ... | ... | 12 to 15 | 1.6 to 2.1 |
| Rear mounting insulator to transmission | ... | ... | ... | ... | ... | ... | 5.8 to 8.0 | 0.8 to 1.1 |
| Propeller shaft to companion flange | ... | ... | ... | ... | ... | ... | 17 to 24 | 2.4 to 3.4 |
| Crossmember mounting bolt | ... | ... | ... | ... | ... | ... | 23 to 31 | 3.2 to 4.3 |
| Stator motor bolt | ... | ... | ... | ... | ... | ... | 20 to 26 | 2.7 to 3.6 |
| Bearing retainer screws | ... | ... | ... | ... | ... | ... | 14 to 18 | 1.9 to 2.5 |
| Mainshaft nut | ... | ... | ... | ... | ... | ... | 101 to 123 | 14.0 to 17.0 |
| Check ball plug | ... | ... | ... | ... | ... | ... | 14 to 18 | 1.9 to 2.5 |
| Rear extension bolt | ... | ... | ... | ... | ... | ... | 12 to 15 | 1.6 to 2.1 |
| Front cover bolt | ... | ... | ... | ... | ... | ... | 12 to 15 | 1.6 to 2.1 |
| Speedometer pinion sleeve locking plate nut | ... | ... | ... | ... | ... | ... | 2.9 to 3.6 | 0.4 to 0.5 |
| Reverse lamp switch | ... | ... | ... | ... | ... | ... | 14 to 22 | 2.0 to 3.0 |
| Filler plug | ... | ... | ... | ... | ... | ... | 18 to 25 | 2.5 to 3.5 |
| Drain plug | ... | ... | ... | ... | ... | ... | 18 to 25 | 2.5 to 3.5 |
| Withdrawal lever ball pin | ... | ... | ... | ... | ... | ... | 14 to 25 | 2.0 to 3.5 |
| Return spring plug | ... | ... | ... | ... | ... | ... | 5.8 to 7.2 | 0.8 to 1.0 |
| Rear extension upper cover bolt | ... | ... | ... | ... | ... | ... | 2.9 to 3.6 | 0.4 to 0.5 |
| Striking lever bolt | ... | ... | ... | ... | ... | ... | 6.5 to 8.7 | 0.9 to 1.2 |

## 1 General description

The transmission fitted to all models is of the four-forward speed and one reverse type, with synchromesh on all forward gears.

The forward gears are of a helical gear formation, and the reverse gear a sliding mesh type using spur gears.

The main driveshaft gear is meshed weith the counter drive gear (laygear). The forward speed gears on the countershaft are in constant mesh with the main gears. Each of the main gears rides on the mainshaft on needle roller bearings, rotating freely.

When the gearchange lever is operated the relevant coupling sleeve is caused to slide on the synchronizer hub and engages its inner teeth with the outer teeth formed on the mainshaft gear. The synchronizer hub is splined to the mainshaft so enabling them to rotate in unison.

Moving the gearchange lever to the reverse gear position moves the mainshaft reverse gear into engagement with the reverse idler gear.

The gear selector mechanism is controlled from a floor or steering column mounted lever. Movement of the lever is transferred through a striking rod to dogs on the ends of the selector rods, and then through the medium of shift forks which are permanently engaged in the grooves of the synchro. Unit sleeves.

The transmission types differ mainly in their method of construction. The F4W63 comprises the complete case, the rear extension, and the gear assembly (main drive gear, mainshaft and countershaft), where the gear assembly is set-up then installed in the case. With the F4W71B transmission, the mian parts are the case, adapter plate (to which all the shafts and gears are installed), and the rear extension. The R4W63 is essentially the same as the F4W63 except that the former uses a column shift linkage which means that there are differences in the selector mechanism.

**6A**

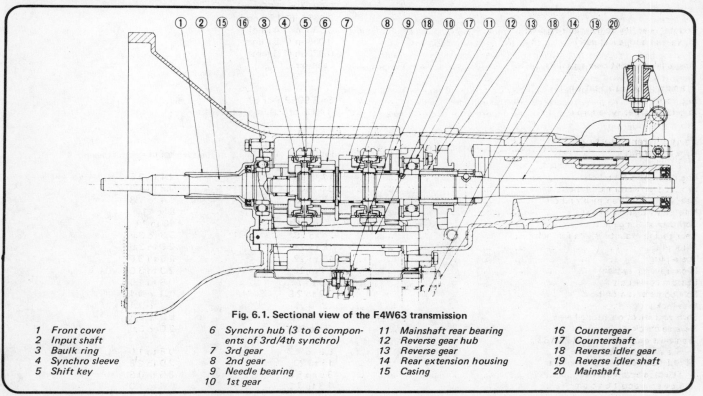

**Fig. 6.1. Sectional view of the F4W63 transmission**

| | | | |
|---|---|---|---|
| 1 Front cover | 6 Synchro hub (3 to 6 compon-ents of 3rd/4th synchro) | 11 Mainshaft rear bearing | 16 Countergear |
| 2 Input shaft | 7 3rd gear | 12 Reverse gear hub | 17 Countershaft |
| 3 Baulk ring | 8 2nd gear | 13 Reverse gear | 18 Reverse idler gear |
| 4 Synchro sleeve | 9 Needle bearing | 14 Rear extension housing | 19 Reverse idler shaft |
| 5 Shift key | 10 1st gear | 15 Casing | 20 Mainshaft |

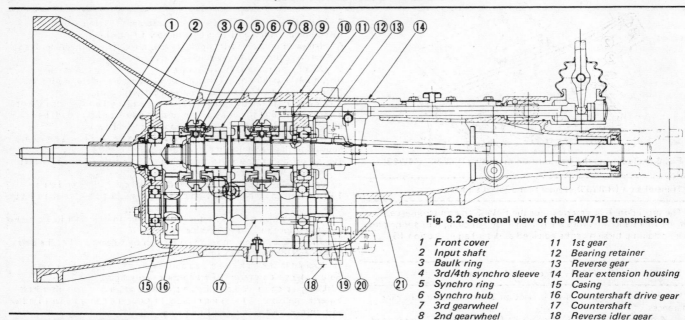

**Fig. 6.2. Sectional view of the F4W71B transmission**

| | | | |
|---|---|---|---|
| 1 | Front cover | 11 | 1st gear |
| 2 | Input shaft | 12 | Bearing retainer |
| 3 | Baulk ring | 13 | Reverse gear |
| 4 | 3rd/4th synchro sleeve | 14 | Rear extension housing |
| 5 | Synchro ring | 15 | Casing |
| 6 | Synchro hub | 16 | Countershaft drive gear |
| 7 | 3rd gearwheel | 17 | Countershaft |
| 8 | 2nd gearwheel | 18 | Reverse idler gear |
| 9 | Needle bearing | 19 | Reverse gear (countershaft) |
| 10 | Adaptor plate | 20 | Reverse idler shaft |
| | | 21 | Mainshaft |

## 2  Transmission (F4W63) - removal and installation

1   Preferably place the vehicle over an inspection pit but if one is not available, raise the vehicle and support it securely on axle stands making sure that there is sufficient clearance below the bodyframe to enable the largest diameter of the clutch bellhousing to pass through during the removal operations.

2   Disconnect the battery ground (earth) lead and drain the transmission oil.

3   Using open-ended wrenches, remove the gearshift control lever (Fig. 6.3) (photo).

4   Disconnect the exhaust downpipe from the exhaust manifold and from the rest of the exhaust system.

5   Disconnect the leads from the reversing lamp switch and then disconnect the speedometer drive cable (photo).

6   Unbolt the clutch operating cylinder from the clutch bellhousing and tie it up out of the way. There is no need to disconnect the hydraulic system.

7   Disconnect the propeller shaft and remove it, as described in Chapter 7. There may be some loss of oil from the rear end of the extension housing and to prevent this, slide a small plastic bag over the end of the extension housing and secure it with a rubber band as soon as the propeller shaft is withdrawn (photo).

8   Support the engine under the oil pan (sump) by using a jack and wooden insulating block to prevent damaging the oil pan.

9   Remove the rear mounting both from the transmission casing and from the bodyframe.

10 Unbolt and remove the starter motor.

11 Unscrew and remove the bolts which secure the clutch bellhousing to the engine.

12 Carefully lower the jack until the transmission can be withdrawn to the rear from below the vehicle. The use of a trolley type jack placed under the transmission will facilitate this operation as it is most important that the weight does not hang on the input shaft while the latter is still engaged with the clutch assembly otherwise the clutch may be seriously damaged. (photo).

13 Installation is the reverse of the removal procedure but first apply a smear of high melting point grease to the input shaft splines. Also check that the clutch pilot bearing at the rear end of the crankshaft is undamaged. For further information refer to Chapter 1.

14 When installation is complete, check the clutch pedal adjustment (Chapter 5) and refill the transmission with the correct grade and quantity of oil.

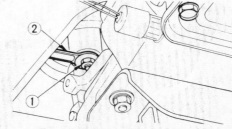

**Fig. 6.3. Removing the gearshift lever**

1   Wrench                          2   Retaining nut

2.3 Gearshift lever retaining nut viewed from below

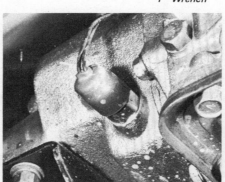

2.5 Reverse light switch leads

2.12 Removing the transmission

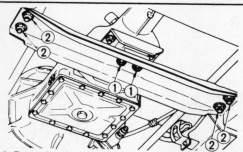

Fig. 6.4. Removing the transmission mounting (F4W63, R4W63)

## 3 Transmission (R4W63) - removal and installation

The procedure is as described for the F4W63 transmission except that the select and shift rods are detached by removing four spring pins. When installing, these must be adjusted as described in Section 16.

## 4 Transmission (F4W71B) - removal and installation

1 Refer to the procedure given in Section 2, but note the following differences:
a) *A different method of attachment for the gearshift lever is used with this transmission. To detach it, remove the C-ring and pin (Fig. 6.6).*
b) *On California models for 1976 it is necessary to remove the exhaust pipe bracket adter the jack has been positioned beneath the engine oil pan (paragraph 8).*

## 5 Transmission (F4W63) - dismantling into major assemblies

1 Before work commences, clean the external surfaces with kerosene (paraffin) or a water soluble solvent.
2 Drain the oil (unless this was done before removal).

3 With the unit secure in the bench, unscrew and remove the speedometer pinion and housing assembly (photos).
4 Remove the dust excluding boot from the clutch bellhousing, then extract the clutch withdrawal lever and release bearing.
5 Unbolt and remove the front cover.
6 Unbolt and remove the transmission lower cover plate, noting the internal magnet which should be wiped clean (photo).
7 Unscrew and remove the reverse lamp (back-up lamp) switch (photo).
8 Make sure that the gears are set in the neutral position and then withdraw the pin from the remote control rod (photo).
9 Unscrew and remove the six bolts which secure the rear extension housing to the transmission casing (photo).
10 Tap off the extension housing using a soft-faced or wooden mallet.
11 Remove the remote control rod.
12 Unscrew the detent ball plugs, and extract the springs and balls.
13 Drive out the tension pins which secure the shift forks to the selector rods.
14 Withdraw each of the selector rods and remove the shift forks, taking care to retrieve the interlock plugs (photo).
15 Using a screwdriver, move the synchronizer sleeves so that the gears engage and lock up the mainshaft.
16 Straighten the lockwasher tab and release the mainshaft end nut. Return the synchronizer sleeves to their neutral positions.
17 Using a piece of rod of suitable diameter, tap out the countershaft towards the front of the transmission. Lift out the countergear together with thrust washers and needle bearings.
18 Pry off the snap ring which retains the reverse idler gear in position. The snap ring is located at the front end of the shaft.
19 Withdraw the idler gear shaft from the rear of the transmission casing.
20 Unscrew and remove the bolts which secure the mainshaft rear bearing retainer.
21 Withdraw the mainshaft assembly from the rear of the casing.
22 Extract the pilot bearing which is located between the mainshaft and the input shaft (main drive gear).
23 Using the wooden handle of a hammer as a drift, tap out the input shaft from the front of the transmission casing.
24 The transmission is now completely dismantled into its major components, further operations should not be undertaken unless the facilities of a press or extractors are available.

5.3a Speedometer gear and retainer

5.3b Withdrawing speedometer gear

5.6 Magnetic plug in transmission cover plate

5.7 Removing the reverse (back-up) lamp switch

5.8 Remote control rod pin and snap ring

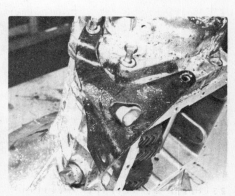

5.9 Removing extension housing bolts

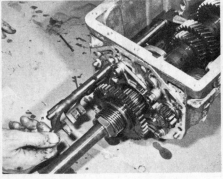

5.14a Remove the reverse selector rod and fork ...    5.14b ... the 3rd/4th selector rod and fork ...    5.14c ... and the 1st/2nd selector rod and fork

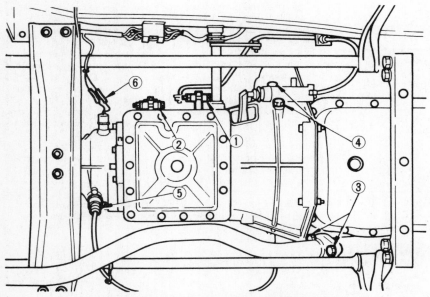

**Fig. 6.5. Transmission detachment points (R4W63 shown)**

| | | |
|---|---|---|
| 1  Select lever | 3  Exhaust | 5  Speedometer drive cable |
| 2  Shift lever | 4  Clutch operating cylinder | 6  Reverse light switch |

## 6  Transmission (R4W63) - dismantling into major assemblies

1    Initially follow the procedure given in paragraph 1 through 10, and paragraph 12 of the previous Section.
2    Remove the lock pins used to secure the internal operating levers to the cross-shafts.
3    Taking care not to damage the oil seals or snap-ring grooves, pry off the shaft snap-rings.
4    Withdraw the cross-shafts complete with their outer levers.
5    Follow the procedure given in paragraph 15 through, 19 of the previous Section.
6    Follow the procedure given in paragraph 13 and 14 of the previous Section.
7    Follow the procedure given in paragraphs 20 through 24 of the previous Section.

## 7  Mainshaft (F4W63 and R4W63) - dismantling, servicing and reassembly

1    Extract the snap-ring from the front end of the mainshaft.
2    Withdraw 3rd/4th synchro unit and 3rd gear.
3    The mainshaft end nut will have already been released (see paragraphs 15 and 16, of Section 5). Now unscrew and remove it, and withdraw reverse gear, reverse gear hub and the speedometer drive

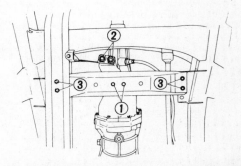

**Fig. 6.6. Control lever attachment (F4W71B)**

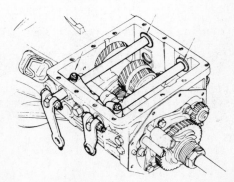

**Fig. 6.7. Removing the transmission mounting (F4W71B)**

1    Insulator bolts
2    Exhaust pipe bracket bolts (California 1976)
3    Mounting bolts

**Fig. 6.8. The cross shafts in the R4W63 transmission**

gear. Make sure that the speedometer gear locking ball is retained.

4   Draw off 1st gear, ball bearing and retainer from the rear end of the mainshaft. This may be carried out by using a puller having its legs engaged behind the front face of 1st gear or otherwise supporting 1st gear and pressing the mainshaft from the gear, bearing and retainer. Do not use 2nd gear front face as a pressure area during these operations or the mainshaft 1st gear spacer may collapse. Extract the thrust washer and locking ball located between the bearing and 1st gear.

5   In a similar manner to that just described in the preceding paragraph, either draw off 1st/2nd gear synchro, and 2nd gear, or press the mainshaft from them.

6   Extract the snap-ring and drive the mainshaft rear bearing from its retainer (photo).

7   The synchro hubs are only too easy to dismantle - just push the centre out and the whole assembly flies apart. The point is to prevent this happening, before you are ready. Do not dismantle the hubs without reason and do not fix up the parts of the two hubs.

8   It is most important to check backlash in the splines between the outer sleeve and inner hub. If any is noticeable, the whole assembly must be renewed.

9   Mark the hubs and sleeve so that you may reassemble them on the same splines. With the hub and sleeve separated, the teeth at the end of the splines which engage with corresponding teeth of the gear wheels, must be checked for damage and wear.

10  Do not confuse the keystone shape at the ends of the teeth. This shape matches the gearteeth shape and it is a design characteristic to minimise jump-out tendencies.

11  If the synchronising cones are being renewed it is sensible also to renew the sliding keys and springs which hold them in position.

12  Place each baulk ring in turn on its gear cone and then, using a feeler gauge, measure the baulk ring to cone clearance. This should be as specified; otherwise renew the baulk ring.

13  Reassemble the synchro, units by placing the hub into its sleeve and insert the shift keys.

14  Install the springs so that they engage in the shift keys. The open Sections of the springs should not be in alignment, but 180º apart.

15  It is assumed that the transmission has been dismantled for reasons of excessive noise, lack of synchromesh action on certain gears or for failure to stay in gear. If anything more drastic than this has occurred (total failure, seizure or main casing cracked) it would be better to leave it alone and look for a replacement, either second-hand or an exchange unit.

16  Examine all gears for excessively worn, chipped or damaged teeth. Any such gears should be renewed. Check that the endfloat and backlash are in accordance with Specifications.

17  All ball-race bearings should be checked for chatter and roughness after they have been flushed out. It is advisable to renew these anyway even though they may not appear too badly worn.

18  Snap-rings which are all important in locating bearings, gears and hubs should be checked to ensure that they are undistorted and undamaged. In any case a selection of new ones of varying thicknesses should be obtained to compensate for variations in new components fitted, and wear in old ones. The Specifications indicate what is available.

19  Needle roller bearings between the input shaft and mainshaft and in the laygear, are usually found in good order, but if in any doubt, replace the needle rollers as necessary.

20  Commence reassembly by installing 2nd gear needle roller bearing, 2nd gear and 2nd gear baulk ring (photo).

21  Install 1st/2nd synchro unit checking that it is fitted the correct way round (photo).

22  Drive on 1st gear spacer using a piece of brass tubing (photo).

23  Install 1st gear baulk ring, the needle bearing, 1st gear, locking ball and the thrust washer (photos).

24  Press on the mainshaft bearing (photo).

25  Install 3rd gear needle roller bearing, 3rd gear and baulk ring (photo).

26  Install 3rd/4th synchro unit checking that it is fitted the correct way round (photo).

27  Fit a snap-ring of the correct size to provide the minimum clearance between the endface of the synchro-hub and the snap-ring groove - see Specifications (photo).

28  To the rear end of the mainshaft, fit the reverse gear, locking ball and speedometer drive gear, lockplate and mainshaft nut. Do not tighten the nut fully at this stage (photos).

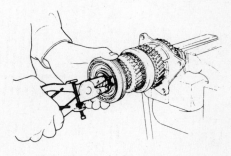

**Fig. 6.9. Removing the mainshaft snap ring**

**6A**

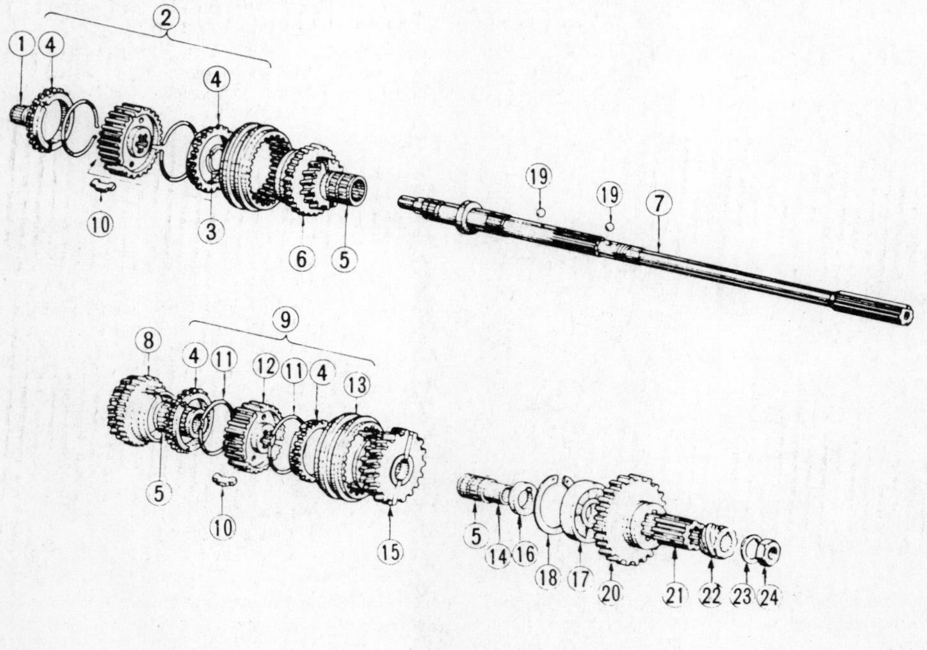

**Fig. 6.10. Mainshaft assembly - exploded view**

1   Pilot bearing
2   3rd & 4th synchro assembly
3   Snap ring
4   Baulk ring
5   Needle bearing
6   3rd gear (mainshaft)
7   Mainshaft
8   2nd gear (mainshaft)
9   1st & 2nd synchro assembly
10  Shifting insert
11  Spreader spring
12  Synchro hub
13  Coupling sleeve
14  Bush, 1st gear
15  1st gear (mainshaft)
16  Thrust washer (mainshaft)
17  Mainshaft bearing
18  Snap ring (mainshaft bearing)
19  Steel ball
20  Reverse gear
21  Reverse hub
22  Speedometer drive gear
23  Lockplate
24  Nut

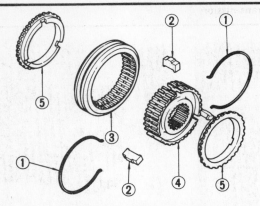
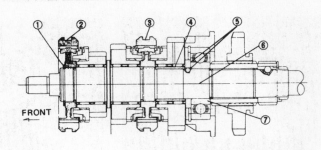

**Fig. 6.11. Synchro assembly - exploded view**

1 Spreader spring
2 Shifting insert
3 Coupling sleeve
4 Synchro hub
5 Baulk ring

**Fig. 6.12. Mainshaft - sectional view**

1 Snap ring
2 3rd/4th synchro assembly
3 1st/2nd synchro assembly
4 1st gear bearing bushing
5 Thrust washer and ball
6 Mainshaft
7 Mainshaft bearing

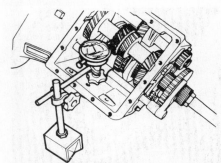
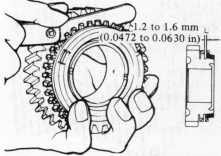

**Fig. 6.13. Gear end-play measurement**

**Fig. 6.14. Gear backlash measurement**

**Fig. 6.15. Baulk ring/cone gap measurement**

7.6 Mainshaft rear bearing and snap ring

7.20 Installing needle roller bearing, 2nd gear and baulk ring to mainshaft

7.21 Installing 1st/2nd synchro unit

7.22 Installing 1st gear spacer

7.23a Installing 1st gear baulk ring and needle roller bearing

7.23b Installing 1st gear and thrust washer locking ball to mainshaft

7.23c 1st gear thrust washer retained by locking ball

7.24 Bearing ready for pressing onto mainshaft

7.25 Installing 3rd gear, baulk ring and needle roller bearing

7.26 Installing 3rd/4th synchro unit

7.27 Installing snap ring to front end of mainshaft

7.28a Installing reverse gear, locking ball and speedometer drive gear

7.28b Lockplate and mainshaft nut installed

8.4 Input shaft bearing, thrust washer and snap ring

10.2 Reverse idler shaft needle roller bearings

6A

## 8 .Input shaft (F4W63 and R4W63) - dismantling and reassembly

1   From the front end of the shaft extract the snap-ring and thrust washer.
2   Using a suitable puller or press, remove the bearing from the shaft.
3   Examine the gearteeth and splines for wear or damage, and check the bearing. Renew components as necessary.
4   Reassembly is a reversal of dismantling, but select a snap-ring from those listed in the Specifications which will provide the minimum endfloat between the face of the spacer and the snap-ring groove (photo).

## 9   Countershaft and gear assembly (F4W63 and R4W63) - inspection

1   Any wear or damage found in the countergear assembly will necessitate renewal of the complete assembly.
2   The needle roller bearings and thrust washers can be renewed separately.
3   When renewing a countershaft, it is normal to renew the corresponding mainshaft gears as matched sets.

## 10  Reverse gear assembly (F4W63 and R4W63) - inspection

1   Examine the gears for wear or chipped teeth.
2   Inspect the idler shaft for wear or distortion and renew as appropriate also the needle roller bearings (photo).

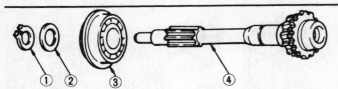

**Fig. 6.16. Input shaft (main drive gear) - exploded view**

1  Snap ring
2  Spacer
3  Bearing end snap ring
4  Main drive gear (input shaft)

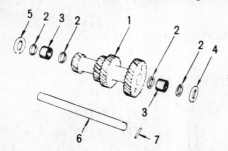

**Fig. 6.17. Counter gear assembly - exploded view**

1  Countergear
2  Washers
3  Needle rollers
4  Thrust washer
5  Thrust washer
6  Countershaft
7  Pin

## 11 Selector mechanism (F4W63 and R4W63) - inspection

1  Inspect the selector rods for wear or distortion. Examine the detent notches particularly carefully for wear.
2  Examine the shift forks. Any excessive wear at the synchro ring engagement surfaces of the forks will necessitate their renewal.

## 12 Oil seals (F4W63 and R4W63) - renewal

1  Whenever the transmission has been dismantled for major overhaul, always renew the front cover oil seal and the rear extension housing oil seal.
2  These are simply driven out and the new ones tapped squarely in, making sure that the lips face the correct way.

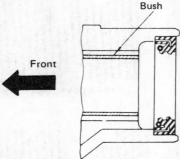

**Fig. 6.18. Correct installation of rear extension oil seal**

## 13 Transmission (F4W63) - reassembly

1  Using a soft faced mallet, tap the input shaft into the front of the transmission casing (photo).
2  Install the pilot bearing and then insert the mainshaft assembly from the rear of the casing (photo).
3  Insert and tighten the mainshaft rear bearing retainer bolts.
4  Install the reverse idler shaft so that the identification mark is towards the rear of the gearbox (photo).
5  Assemble the thrust washer and the helical-type idler gear and secure it with its snap-ring at the front end of the shaft. (photo).
6  Now insert a 0.004 in (0.1 mm) feeler gauge between the helical-type gear and its thrust washer. Push the idler shaft fully rearwards and

install the thrust washer and spur-type gear to the rear end of the idler shaft. Secure the gear with a suitable snap-ring (see Specifications), so that when the feeler gauge is withdrawn from between the helical gear and its thrust washer, the correct endfloat of between 0.004 and 0.012 in (0.10 and 0.30 mm) will be established. Note that the reverse idler shaft thrust washers must be installed so that the sides with the oil grooves are towards the gears (photo).
7  Stick the countershaft thrust washers into position in the interior of the transmission case using a dab of thick grease. Make sure that they are securely held by their lock tabs and that the smaller washer is at the rear (photo).
8  Using a dummy countershaft or rod, inserted through the counter-gear, install the needle rollers and washers at both ends of the countergear, again using thick grease to retain them (21 needle rollers at each end) (photo).
9  Place the countergear assembly into position and then insert the countershaft so that it displaces the dummy shaft or rod without dislodging the needle rollers or thrust washers (photo).
10  Now check the countergear endfloat. This should be between 0.002 and 0.004 in (0.05 and 0.15 mm) and, if otherwise, change the rear thrust washer for one of different thickness (see Specifications for thrust washer sizes).
11  Drive in a new retaining pin (if removed at dismantling) (photo).
12  Move the synchro sleeves to mesh the gears and lock the mainshaft. Tighten the mainshaft nut to the specified torque and bend up the lockplate (photo).
13  Return the synchro sleeves to the neutral position.
14  Engage the 1st/2nd and 3rd/4th shift forks with the sleeve grooves of the respective synchro units (photo).
15  Install the 1st/2nd selector rod so that it passes through the shift fork and secure the fork to the rod with a new tension pin (photo).
16  With the 1st/2nd selector rod in the neutral mode, insert the interlock plunger and then install the 3rd/4th selector rod and secure the 3rd/4th shift fork to it using a new tension pin (photo).
17  Set the 3rd/4th selector rod in the neutral mode and insert the second interlock plunger.
18  Install the reverse selector rod and shift fork. The slot in the reverse selector rod must be positioned as shown (photos).
19  Insert the detent balls, springs and plugs. Apply a non-setting gasket sealant to the threads of the plugs before installing them (photos).
20  Check the operation of the selectors and gear engagement making sure it is smooth and positive.
21  Set the gears in neutral, and then position a new gasket on the rear face of the transmission casing.
22  Install the rear extension housing making sure that before it is pushed fully home, the remote control rod engages correctly with the selector shaft dogs (photo).
23  Insert and tighten the extension housing bolts to the specified torque.
24  Install the front cover, making sure that the gasket and countershaft roll pin are correctly aligned, and that the oil seal is not damaged as it passes over the splines of the input shaft. Tighten the securing bolts to the specified torque (photos).
25  Install the release bearing, withdrawal lever and dust excluder (photo). (Now is the time to renew the release bearing and the clutch components if they are worn - see Chapter 5).
26  Invert the transmission and install the bottom cover plate using a new gasket (photo).

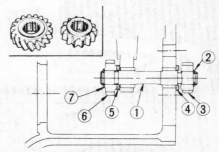

**Fig. 6.19. Reverse idler gear assembly**

1  Idler shaft
2  Snap ring
3  Spur gear
4  Thrust washer
5  Thrust washer
6  Helical gear
7  Snap ring

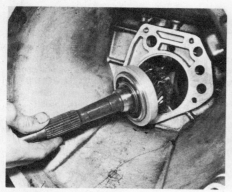
13.1a Installing input shaft

13.1b Mainshaft/input shaft needle roller pilot bearing

13.2 Installing mainshaft assembly from rear of casing

13.4 Reverse idler shaft and thrust washer

13.5 Reverse idler gear and snap ring at front end of shaft

13.6 Reverse idler gear and snap ring at rear end of shaft

13.7 Countershaft thrust washer showing locating tag

13.8 Countershaft needle rollers

13.9 Installing countergear

13.11 Countershaft tension pin installed

13.12 Tightening the mainshaft nut

13.14 Installing shift forks to synchro sleeve grooves - 1 3rd/4th, 2 1st/2nd

6A

**13.15** Securing 1st/2nd shift fork to selector rod

**13.16** Inserting an interlock plunger between 1st/2nd and 3rd/4th selector rods

**13.18a** Installing reverse selector fork

**13.18b** Correct alignment of reverse selector rod

**13.19a** Inserting a detent ball

**13.19b** Inserting detent springs

**13.19c** Installing detent plugs

**13.22** Remote control rod correctly engaged

**13.24a** Front cover gasket and countershaft tension pin correctly aligned

**13.24b** Front cover installation. Note the position of the clutch release lever pivot bolt

**13.25** Clutch release bearing and lever installed

**13.26** Installing transmission lower cover plate

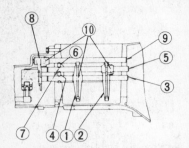

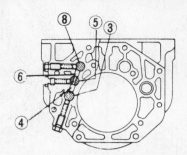

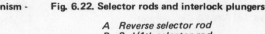

**Fig. 6.20. Selector rods and shift forks (F4W63)**

| | |
|---|---|
| *1* | *1st/2nd shift fork* |
| *2* | *3rd/4th shift fork* |
| *3* | *1st/2nd shift rod* |
| *4* | *Interlock plunger* |
| *5* | *3rd/4th selector rod* |

| | |
|---|---|
| *6* | *Interlock plunger* |
| *7* | *Spring* |
| *8* | *Reverse shift fork* |
| *9* | *Reverse shift rod* |
| *10* | *Tension pin* |

**Fig. 6.21. Selector interlock mechanism - sectional view**

*3 1st/2nd selector rod*
*4 Interlock plunger*
*5 3rd/4th selector rod*
*6 Interlock plunger*
*8 Reverse selector rod*

**Fig. 6.22. Selector rods and interlock plungers**

*A Reverse selector rod*
*B 3rd/4th selector rod*
*C 1st/2nd selector rod*

### 14 Transmission (R4W63) - reassembly

1  Follow the procedure given in paragraphs 1 through 19 of the previous Section.
2  Install the cross-shafts complete with outer levers, passing them through the internal operating levers. Use new thrust washers and snap-rings, and retain the internal operating levers with the lock pins.
3  Follow the procedure given in paragraphs 20 through 26 of the previous Section. Ignore this reference to the remote control rod at paragraph 22.

### 15 Shift linkage (R4W63) - removal and installation

1  Detach the battery ground cable then remove horn pad.
2  Pull off the steering wheel.
3  Remove the steering column shells, and the turn signal and lighting switch assembly.
4  Remove the C-ring and flat washer from the end of the control rod.
5  Remove the snap-ring and control lever pivot pin, then withdraw the control lever.
6  Remove the spring pins, plain washers and spring washers at the transmission of the change speed lever and select lever. Separate the upper shift rod and select rod from the levers.
7  Remove the bolts securing the lower bracket and clamp.
8  Loosen the locking screw and remove the change speed lever from the control rod.
9  Remove the lower bracket and select lever by loosening the lower

bracket until its locating pin can be freed from the jacket tube.
10 Remove the control rod from its upper support by pressing downwards then withdrawing it upward.
11 Remove the spring pins, plain washers and spring washers at the select and shift levers.
12 Separate the select rod from the select lever.
13 After separating the upper and lower shift rods, remove the cross-shaft from the transmission case side, pushing it against the retaining spring. Remove the cross-shaft from the side member by compressing the retaining spring.
14 Installation is the reverse of the removal procedure, apply a little general purpose grease to the parts marked with an asterisk in Fig. 6.25. Adjust the shift linkage, as described in the following Section.

### 16 Shift linkage (R4W63) - adjustment

*Shift linkage*
1  Set the outer lever (Fig. 6.26) to neutral and adjust the shift rod transmission nuts so that the control lever is in the neutral position.

*Select linkage*
2  Arrange the linkage so that the reverse check return spring seat contacts the control rod ring, whilst ensuring that the control lever is in the 'B' position (Fig. 6.26).
3  Set the outer lever to the neutral position then tighten the select rod transmission nuts at a position where only a light force is applied to the select rod.

**6A**

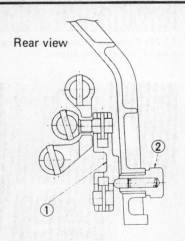

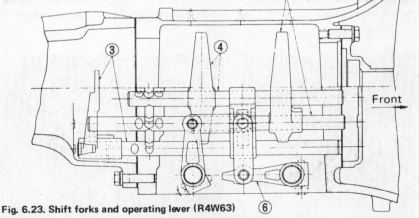

Rear view

Front

**Fig. 6.23. Shift forks and operating lever (R4W63)**

| | |
|---|---|
| *1* | *Arm link (internal operating lever)* |
| *2* | *Reverse check* |

| | |
|---|---|
| *3* | *Reverse shift fork and shift rod* |
| *4* | *1st and 2nd shift fork and shift rod* |

| | |
|---|---|
| *5* | *3rd and 4th shift fork and shift rod* |

| | |
|---|---|
| *6* | *Arm link assembly (internal operating lever assembly)* |

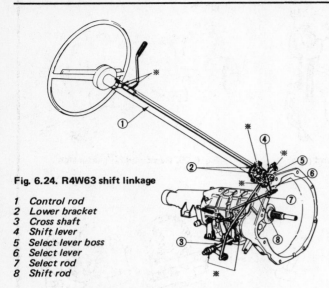

**Fig. 6.24. R4W63 shift linkage**

1  *Control rod*
2  *Lower bracket*
3  *Cross shaft*
4  *Shift lever*
5  *Select lever boss*
6  *Select lever*
7  *Select rod*
8  *Shift rod*

\* Apply grease to these points when reassembling.

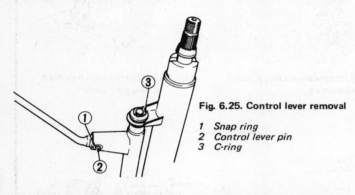

**Fig. 6.25. Control lever removal**

1  *Snap ring*
2  *Control lever pin*
3  *C-ring*

## 17 Transmission (F4W71B) - dismantling into major assemblies

1   With the transmission removed, thoroughly clean the external surfaces with kerosene (paraffin) or a water soluble solvent.

2   Remove the rubber dust excluder from the withdrawal lever aperature in the clutch bellhousing.

3   Remove the release bearing and hub, and the withdrawal lever (Chapter 5).

4   Remove the reverse lamp switch (photo).

5   Unbolt the lockplate from the rear extension housing and remove the speedometer pinion and sleeve (photo).

6   Remove the snap-ring and stop guide pin, also the return spring plug assembly, all from the rear extension housing (Figs. 6.27 and 6.28).

7   Unscrew the securing bolts and drive the rear extension housing from the main transmission casing, using a soft faced mallet.

8   Remove the front cover bolts and the cover, and extract the countershaft bearing shim and the input shaft bearing snap ring.

9   Drive off the one-piece bellhousing (transmission casing from the adaptor plate (Fig. 6.32).

10  Make up a suitable support plate and bolt it to the adaptor plate and then secure the support plate in a vise (Fig. 6.32).

11  Drive out the securing pins from each of the shift forks, using a small diameter drift.

12  Unscrew and remove the three check ball plugs (Fig. 6.34).

13  Withdraw the selector rods from the adaptor plate.

14  Catch the shift forks, and extract the balls and springs as the selector rods are withdrawn. The four smaller balls are the interlock balls (Fig. 6.34).

15  Lock the gears and, using a suitable two legged extractor, draw the front bearing from the countershaft (Fig. 6.35).

16  Now is the time to check the gears for backlash, using a dial gauge. The backlash should be between 0.002 and 0.004 in (0.05 and 0.10 mm). Where this is exceeded, renew the drive and driven gears as a matched set. Now check the gear endfloat using a feeler gauge. For first gear this should be between 0.0126 and 0.0154 in (0.32 and 0.39 mm) and for second and third gears between 0.0047 and 0.0075 in (0.12 and 0.19 mm). Selective snap-rings are available to provide the specified endfloat - see Specifications.

17  Extract the snap-ring (now exposed) from the countershaft.

18  Withdraw the countershaft gear together with the input shaft. (Fig. 6.37). Take care not to drop the needle roller bearing which is located on the front of the mainshaft.

19  Extract the snap-ring from the front end of the mainshaft followed by the thrust washer.

20  Withdraw 3rd/4th synchro unit followed by 3rd gear.

21  Relieve the staking on the mainshaft nut and then slacken it.

22  Remove the mainshaft nut, the thrust washer and reverse gear.

23  Extract the snap-ring from the rear end of the countershaft and remove the reverse idler gear.

24  Drive the mainshaft and countershaft assemblies simultaneously from the adaptor plate, using a soft faced mallet (Fig. 6.38).

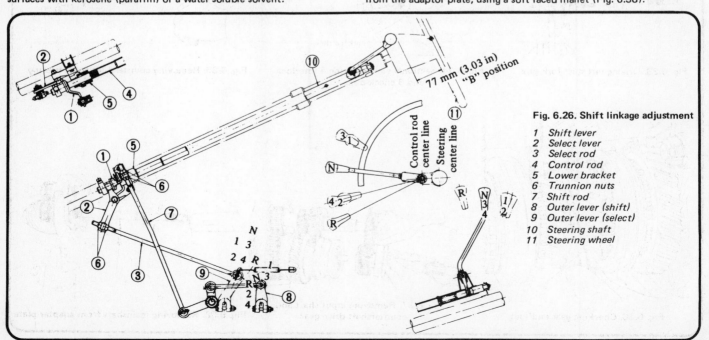

**Fig. 6.26. Shift linkage adjustment**

1   *Shift lever*
2   *Select lever*
3   *Select rod*
4   *Control rod*
5   *Lower bracket*
6   *Trunnion nuts*
7   *Shift rod*
8   *Outer lever (shift)*
9   *Outer lever (select)*
10  *Steering shaft*
11  *Steering wheel*

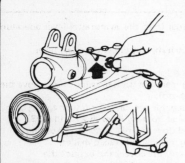

Fig. 6.27. Removing striking rod snap ring and stop pin

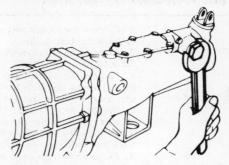

Fig. 6.28. Removing return spring and plug

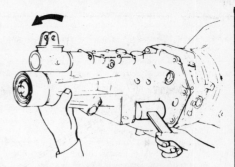

Fig. 6.29. Removing rear extension

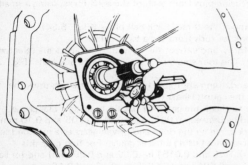

Fig. 6.30. Removing input shaft bearing snap ring

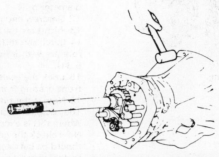

Fig. 6.31. Removing transmission casing/clutch bellhousing

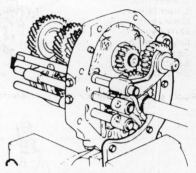

Fig. 6.32. Transmission mounted on support plate

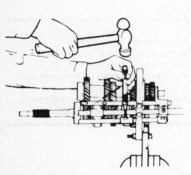

Fig. 6.33. Driving out shift fork pins

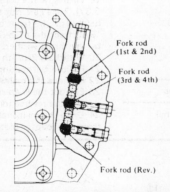

Fork rod (1st & 2nd)

Fork rod (3rd & 4th)

Fork rod (Rev.)

Fig. 6.34. Sectional view showing 4 interlock and 3 check balls

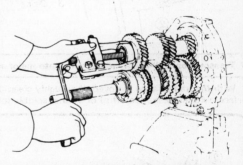

Fig. 6.35. Removing countershaft front bearing

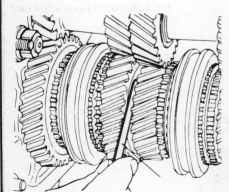

Fig. 6.36. Checking gear endfloat

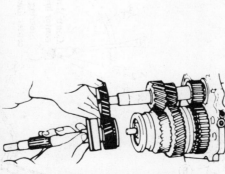

Fig. 6.37. Removing input shaft and countershaft drive gear

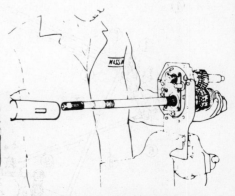

Fig. 6.38. Removing mainshaft from adapter plate

6A

### 18 Mainshaft (F4W71B) - dismantling, servicing and reassembly

1    Carefully examine the gearwheels and shaft splines for chipping of the teeth or wear, and then dismantle the gear train into its components parts, renewing any worn or damaged items. Now that the mainshaft has been removed from the adaptor plate, the gears, bearings and synchro assemblies can be taken off. The parts are shown in Fig. 6.39.

2    Examine the shaft itself for scoring or grooving; also the splines for twist, taper or general wear.

3    Examine the synchro units for cracks wear or general slackness in the assembly renew if evident, particularly if there has been a history of noisy gearchange or where the synchromesh can be easily 'beaten'

4    Press the baulk ring tight against the synchro cone and measure the gap between the two components. If it is less than specified, renew the components (Fig. 6.40).

5    When reassembling the synchro unit ensure that the ends of the springs on opposite sides of the unit do not engage in the same slot.

6    Commence assembly of the mainshaft by installing the 2nd gear needle bearing, 2nd gearwheel, the baulk ring followed by the 1st/2nd synchro unit, noting carefully the direction of fitting the latter (Fig. 6.42).

7    Now install the 1st gear baulk ring, 1st gear bush and the needle bearing followed by the 1st gearwheel and the steel ball (well greased), and the thrust washer (Fig. 6.43).

### 19 Input shaft (F4W71B) - bearing renewal

1    Remove the snap-ring and spacer.

2    Withdraw the bearing using a two legged extractor or a press. Once removed (by means of its outer track) discard the bearing.

3    Press on the new bearing, applying pressure to the center track only. Snap-rings are available in a range of thicknesses as given in the Specifications to eliminate endplay.

### 20 Countershaft (F4W71B) - dismantling, inspection and reassembly

1    Remove the countershaft drive gear and extract the two woodruff keys.The countershaft cannot be further dismantled and if worn must be renewed complete.

2    Check all components for wear especially, the gearteeth and shaft splines for chipping. Renew the Woodruff keys and selective fit snap-ring.

3    Reassembly is the reverse of the dismantling procedure.

### 21 Mainshaft and countershaft adaptor plate bearings (F4W71B) - renewal

1    Before commencing to reassemble the transmission the mainshaft adaptor plate bearing should be removed, examined and renewed if worn. To do this, unscrew the six screws which retain the bearing retainer plate to the adaptor plate. The use of an impact type driver will probably be required for this operation.

2    Check the bearings for wear by first washing them in clean fuel and drying in air from a pump. Spin them with the fingers and if they are noisy or slack in operation, renew them.

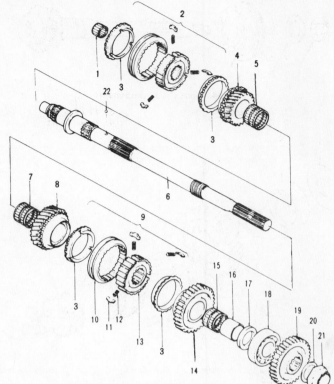

Fig. 6.39. Mainshaft assembly

| | | | |
|---|---|---|---|
| 1 | Needle bearing | 11 | Blocker bar |
| 2 | 3rd/4th synchro unit | 12 | Spring |
| 3 | Baulk ring | 13 | Synchro hub |
| 4 | 3rd gearwheel | 14 | 1st gear |
| 5 | Needle bearing | 15 | Needle bearing |
| 6 | Mainshaft | 16 | Bush |
| 7 | Needle bearing | 17 | Thrust washer |
| 8 | 2nd gearwheel | 18 | Mainshaft rear bearing |
| 9 | 1st/2nd synchro unit | 19 | Reverse gear |
| 10 | Synchro sleeve | 20 | Thrust washer |
| | | 21 | Mainshaft nut |
| | | 22 | Steel ball |

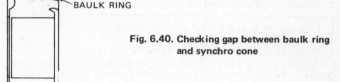

1.2 to 1.4 mm
(0.0472 to 0.0550 in)

BAULK RING

Fig. 6.40. Checking gap between baulk ring and synchro cone

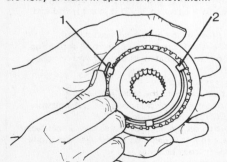

Fig. 6.41. Synchro unit spring (1) and blocker bar (insert) (2)

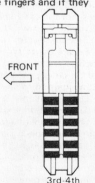

FRONT

3rd-4th          1st-2nd

Fig. 6.42. Correct directional installation of the synchro units

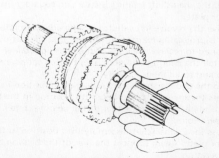

Fig. 6.43. Installing the steel ball and thrust washer

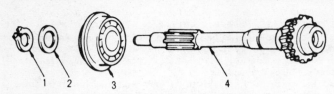

**Fig. 6.44. Input shaft components**

1  Snap ring            3  Bearing
2  Spacer               4  Input shaft

9   Install the thrust washer and a selective snap-ring, and check for endfloat. See Section 17.
10  Insert the needle pilot bearing in its recess at the end of the input shaft.
11  Mesh the countershaft drive gear with the 4th gear on the input shaft. Push the drive gear and input shaft into the countershaft and mainshaft simultaneously, but a piece of tubing will be needed to drive the countershaft gear into position while supporting the rear end of the countershaft.

**Front**

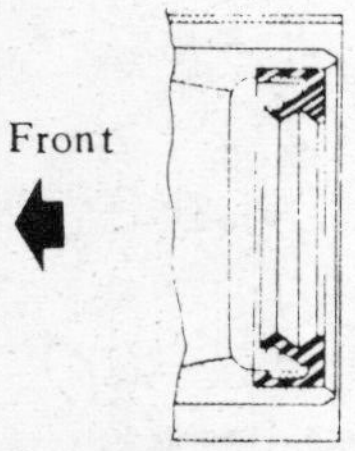

**Fig. 6.46. Installation of rear extension oil seal**

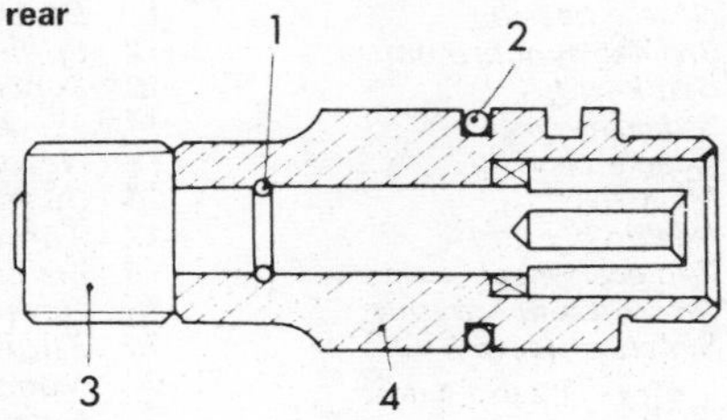

**Fig. 6.47. Speedometer pinion - sectional view**

1  Retaining pin
2  O-ring
3  Pinion
4  Sleeve

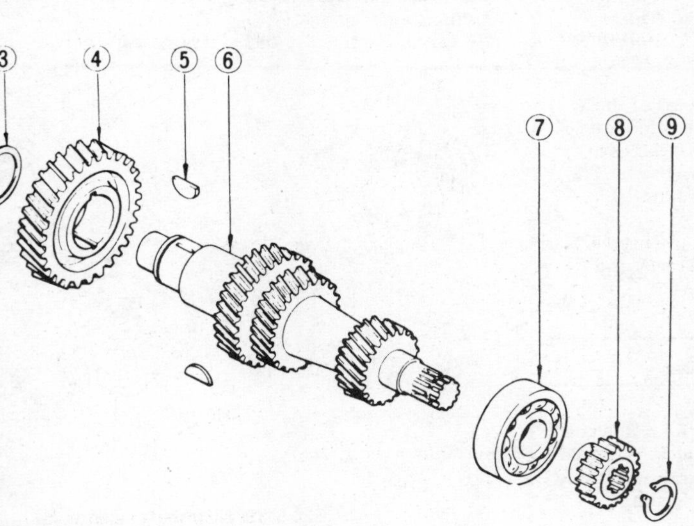

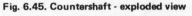

**Fig. 6.45. Countershaft - exploded view**

1  Shim
2  Front bearing
3  Circlip
4  Drive gear
5  Woodruff key
6  Countershaft
7  Rear bearing
8  Reverse gear
9  Circlip

**6A**

12  Install a snap-ring to the front of the countershaft, checking the endfloat and selecting the snap-ring as described in Section 17.
13  Using a tubular drift, drive the front bearing into the countershaft.
14  To the rear of the mainshaft, install the reverse gear, the plain washer and screw on the nut, finger-tight.
15  Install the reverse gear to the rear of the countershaft and use a snap-ring to provide the minimum or no endfloat (see Specifications).
16  Install the reverse idler gear to the reverse idler shaft.
17  Tighten the mainshaft nut (after locking the gears) to the specified torque.
18  Stake the collar of the nut into the groove of the mainshaft.
19  Turn the transmission so far assembled, upside down and again secure the support plate in the vise.
20  Engage the reverse shift fork with reverse idler gear, and install the selector rod, detent ball and spring. Screw in the detent ball plug, first having coated its threads with a non-setting jointing compound. Drive in the fork-to-rod retaining pin.
21  Locate the two interlock balls between the reverse selector rod and the 3rd/4th selector rod.
22  Engage the 3rd/4th shift fork with the groove in the 3rd/4th synchromesh sleeve and fit the selector rod, the detent ball and spring and screw in the detent ball plug, again coating its threads with thread locking compound. The 3rd/4th detent plug is shorter than the plug for reverse or the one for 1st/2nd. Drive in the fork to rod retaining pin.
23  Locate the two interlock balls between 1st/2nd selector rod and the 3rd/4th selector rod.
24  Engage the 1st/2nd shift fork in the groove of the 1st/2nd synchromesh unit and fit the selector rod, the detent ball and spring and the detent ball plug, first having coated its threads with a non-setting jointing compound.
25  Drive in the fork to rod retaining pin.
26  Tighten all three detent ball plugs to the specified torque.
27  Clean the mating faces of the adaptor plate and the transmission casing, and apply gasket sealant to both surfaces.
28  Tap the casing into position on the adaptor plate using a soft faced mallet, taking particular care that it engages correctly with the input shaft bearing and countershaft front bearing.
29  Install the outer snap ring to the input shaft bearing.
30  Clean the mating faces of the adaptor plate and rear extension housing, and apply gasket sealant.

## 22 Oil seals (F4W71B) - renewal

1  Prise out the oil seal from the rear extension and drive in a new one with the lips facing inwards.
2  Renew the speedometer pinion sleeve 'O' ring seal.
3  Renew the oil seal in the front cover by prying out the old one and driving in the new one with a piece of tubing used as a drift.

## 23 Transmission (F4W71B) - reassembly

1  Check that the dowel pin and oil trough are correctly positioned on the adaptor plate (Fig. 6.48).
2  Tap the mainshaft bearing lightly and squarely into position in the adaptor plate.
3  Drive the reverse idler shaft into the adaptor plate so that 2/3 of its length is projecting rearwards. Ensure that the cut-out in the shaft is positioned to receive the edge of the bearing retainer plate.
4  Install the bearing retainer plate, tighten the screws to the specified torque and stake them securely.
5  Tap the countershaft rear bearing into position in the adaptor plate.
6  Press the mainshaft assembly into position in the bearing in the adaptor plate. Support the rear of the bearing center track during this operation.
7  Press the countershaft assembly into position in the bearing in the adaptor plate. Again support the rear of the bearing center track during this operation.
8  Install the needle bearing, 3rd gear, baulk ring and the 3rd/4th synchromesh unit to the front of the mainshaft.

31 Arrange the shift forks in their neutral mode, and then lower the rear extension housing onto the adaptor plate so that the striking lever engages correctly with the selector rods.

32 Install the tie bolts which secure the sections of the transmission together, and tighten them to the specified torque.

33 Measure the amount by which the countershaft front bearing stands proud of the casing front face. Use feeler gauges for this and then select the appropriate shims after reference to the following table:

| Projection (A) - see Fig. 6.54 | Shim to use (thickness) |
|---|---|
| 0.1150 to 0.1185 in (2.92 to 3.01 mm) | 0.0236 in (0.6 mm) |
| 0.1189 to 0.1224 in (3.02 to 3.11 mm) | 0.0197 in (0.5 mm) |
| 0.1228 to 0.1264 in (3.12 to 3.21 mm) | 0.0157 in (0.4 mm) |
| 0.1268 to 0.1303 in (3.22 to 3.31 mm) | 0.0118 in (0.3 mm) |
| 0.1307 to 0.1343 in (3.32 to 3.41 mm) | 0.0079 in (0.2 mm) |
| 0.1346 to 0.1382 in (3.42 to 3.51 mm) | 0.0039 in (0.1 mm) |

34 Stick the shim in position using a dab of thick grease and then install the front cover to the casing (within the clutch bellhousing) complete with a new gasket, taking care not to damage the oil seal as it passes over the input shaft splines.

35 Tighten the securing bolts to the specified torque making sure that the bolt threads are coated with gasket sealant to prevent oil seepage.

36 Install the speedometer pinion assembly to the rear extension housing.

37 Install the reverse lamp switch.

38 Install the release bearing and withdrawal lever within the clutch bellhousing (Chapter 5).

39 Check the security of the drain plug.

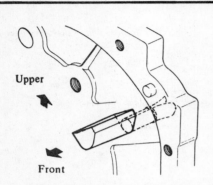
Fig. 6.48. Location of oil trough and dowel

Fig. 6.49. Installing snap ring to mainshaft

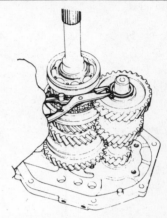
Fig. 6.50. Installing countershaft snap ring

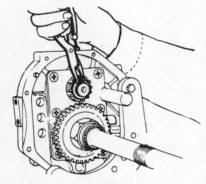
Fig. 6.51. Installing reverse gear snap ring to countershaft

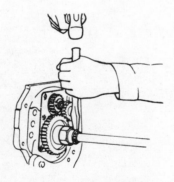
Fig. 6.52. Staking mainshaft nut

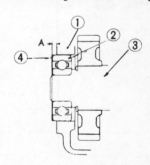
Fig. 6.54. Countershaft front bearing shim selection diagram

1  Gearbox casing        3  Countershaft
2  Front bearing         4  Shim

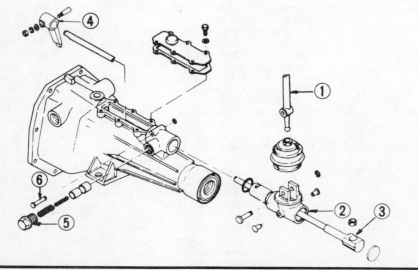

Fig. 6.53. Rear extension housing

1  Gearchange lever
2  Striking rod guide
3  Striking rod
4  Striking lever
5  Plug
6  Stop pin

## 24 Fault diagnosis - Manual transmission

| Symptom | Reason/s |
| --- | --- |
| Weak or ineffective synchromesh | Synchro, cones worn or damaged. Baulk rings worn. Defective synchro unit. |
| Jumps out of gear | Worn interlock plunger. Worn detent ball. Weak or broken detent spring. Worn shift fork or synchro sleeve groove. Worn gear. |
| Excessive noise | Incorrect oil grade. Oil level too low. Worn gear teeth. Worn mainshaft bearings Worn thrust washers. Worn input or mainshaft splines. |
| Difficult gear changing or selection | Incorrect clutch free movement. Incorrect shift linkage adjustment (column gearshift). |

# Chapter 6: Part B Automatic transmission

## Contents

## Specifications

| | |
|---|---|
| **Type** ... ... ... ... ... ... ... ... ... | JATCO 3N71B, three forward speeds and reverse, three element torque converter with planetary geartrain. |
| **Model code (USA models)** ... ... ... ... ... | X2401 - 16B (1973/74)     X2402 - 16B (1975/76) |

**Ratios**

| | |
|---|---|
| 1st ... ... ... ... ... ... ... ... ... ... | 2.458 : 1 |
| 2nd ... ... ... ... ... ... ... ... ... ... | 1.458 : 1 |
| 3rd ... ... ... ... ... ... ... ... ... ... | 1.000 : 1 |
| Reverse ... ... ... ... ... ... ... ... ... | 2.182 : 1 |

| | |
|---|---|
| **Engine idling speed** ... ... ... ... ... ... ... | 650 rpm in 'D' (800 rpm with air-conditioning system) |
| **Stall speed** ... ... ... ... ... ... ... ... | 2000 rpm (approx) |
| **Fluid capacity** ... ... ... ... ... ... ... | 11.6 US pt/9.5 Imp. pt (5.5 liters) |
| **Fluid type** ... ... ... ... ... ... ... ... | Dexron |

**Torque wrench settings**

| | lbf ft | kgf m |
|---|---|---|
| Driveplate to crankshaft bolts ... ... ... | 100 | 13.8 |
| Driveplate to torque converter ... ... ... ... ... | 35 | 4.8 |
| Torque converter housing to engine ... ... ... ... | 35 | 4.8 |
| Transmission casing to converter housing ... ... ... | 40 | 5.5 |
| Transmission casing to rear extension ... ... ... ... | 20 | 2.8 |
| Fluid cooler connection to transmission ... ... ... | 35 | 4.8 |
| Selector range lever nut ... ... ... ... ... ... | 25 | 3.5 |

## 25 General description

1 The automatic transmission unit installed in some USA models is the JATCO 3N71B.

2 The unit provides three forward ratios and one reverse. Changing of the forew ard gear ratios is completely automatic in relation to the vehicle speed and engine torque input and is dependent upon the vacuum pressure in the manifold and the vehicle road speed to actuate the gear change mechanism at the precise time.

3 The transmission has six selector positions:

**P** - parking position which locks the output shaft to the interior wall of the transmission housing. This is a safety device for use when the vehicle is parked on an incline. The engine may be started with 'P' selected and this position should always be selected when adjusting the engine while it is running. Never attempt to select 'P' when the vehicle is in motion.

**R** - reverse gear.

**N** - neutral. Select this position to start the engine or when idling in traffic for long periods.

**D** - drive, for all normal motoring conditions.

**2** - locks the transmission in second gear for wet road conditions or steep hill climbing or descents. The engine can be over revved in this position.

**1** - the selection of this ratio above road speeds of approximately 25 mph (40 kph) will engage second gear and as the speed drops below 25 mph (40 kph) the transmission will lock into first gear. Provides maximum retardation on steep descents.

4 Due to the complexity of the automatic transmission unit, any internal adjustment or servicing should be left to a Datsun agent or automatic transmission specialist.; The information given in this Chapter is therefore confined to those operations which are considered within the scope of the home mechanic. An automatic transmission should give many tens of thousands of miles service provided normal maintenance and adjustment is carried out. When the unit finally requires major overhaul consideration should be given to exchange the old transmission

for a factory reconditioned one, the removal and installation being well within the capabilities of the home mechanic as described later in this Chapter. The hydraulic fluid does not require periodic draining or refilling, but the fluid level must be regularly checked (see next Section).
5   Periodically clean the outside of the transmission housing as the accumulation of dirt and oil is liable to cause overheating of the unit under extreme conditions.
6   Adjust the engine idling speed as specified.

## 26 Fluid level-checking

1   Run the vehicle on the road until normal operating temperature is attained. This will normally take a minimum of 6 miles (10 km) to achieve.
2   With the engine idling, select each gear position in turn and then place the speed selector lever in 'P:;
3   Allow the engine to continue to idle and after a period of two minutes, withdraw the dipstick, wipe it on a piece of clean lint-free cloth; re insert it, quickly withdrawing it and reading off the oil level.
4   Top-up as necessary but do not overfill.
5   Switch off the engine.
6   The need for frequent topping-up indicates a leak either in the tranmission unit itself, or from the fluid cooler or connecting pipes.

## 27 Automatic transmission - removal and installation

1   Removal of the engine and automatic transmission as a combined unit is described in Chapter 1 of this manual. Where it is decided to remove the transmission leaving the engine in position in the vehicle, proceed as follows:
2   Disconnect the battery ground lead.
3   Jack the vehicle to an adequate working height and support on stands or blocks. Alternatively position the vehicle over a pit.
4   Disconnect the exhaust downpipe from the manifold.
5   Disconnect the leads from the starter inhibitor switch.
6   Disconnect the wire from the downshift solenoid.
7   Disconnect the vacuum pipe from the vacuum capsule which is located just forward of the downshift solenoid.
8   Separate the selector lever from the selector linkage.
9   Disconnect the speedometer drive cable from the rear extension housing.
10 Disconnect the fluid filler tube. Plug the opening.

11 Disconnect the fluid cooler tubes from the transmission casing and plug the openings.
12 Remove the propeller shaft; for further information see Chapter 7.
13 Support the engine oil pan with a jack; use a block of wood to prevent damage to the surface of the oil pan.
14 Remove the rubber plug from the lower part of the engine rear plate. Mark the torque converter housing and drive plate in relation to each other for exact alignment.
15 Unscrew and remove the four bolts which secure the torque converter to the drive plate. Access to each of these bolts, in turn is obtained by rotating the engine slowly, using a wrench on the crankshaft pulley bolt.
16 Unbolt and withdraw the starter motor.
17 Support the transmission with a jack (preferably a trolley type).
18 Detach the rear transmission mounting from the transmission housing and the vehicle body frame.
19 Unscrew and remove the transmission to engine securing bolts.
20 Lower the two jacks sufficiently to allow the transmission unit to be withdrawn from below and to the rear of the vehicle. The help of an assistant will probably be required due to the weight of the unit. Do not forget that the transmission is still filled with fluid. If necessary, this can be drained by removing the oil pan (sump) or standing the unit on end to allow the fluid to drain from the extension housing.
21 Installation is basically the reverse of the removal procedure but should the torque converter have been separated from the main assembly, ensure that the notch on the converter is correctly aligned with the corresponding one on the oil pump. To check that the torque converter has been correctly installed, the dimension 'A' should exceed 0.846 in (21.5 mm). See Fig. 6.58.
22 Tighten all bolts to the specified torque settings. Refill the unit with the correct grade and quantity of fluid if any was spilled or drained.
23 Check the operation of the inhibitor switch and the selector linkage and adjust, if necessary, as described later in this Chapter.

## 28 Selector linkage - removal and installation

1   Remove the two small screws which secure the knob to the speed selector lever. Remove the knob.
2   Remove the console from the transmission tunnel.
3   Unbolt the selector lever bracket and the lever on the side of the transmission, and withdraw the complete selector linkage.
4   Installation is the reverse of the removal procedure but adjust the linkage as described in the following Section before installing the control knob.

**6B**

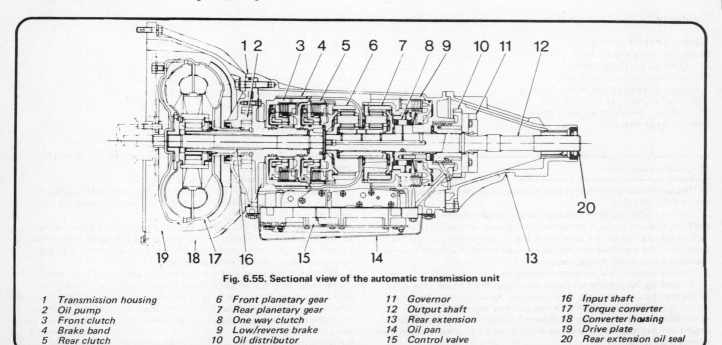

Fig. 6.55. Sectional view of the automatic transmission unit

| 1 | Transmission housing | 6 | Front planetary gear | 11 | Governor | 16 | Input shaft |
|---|---|---|---|---|---|---|---|
| 2 | Oil pump | 7 | Rear planetary gear | 12 | Output shaft | 17 | Torque converter |
| 3 | Front clutch | 8 | One way clutch | 13 | Rear extension | 18 | Converter housing |
| 4 | Brake band | 9 | Low/reverse brake | 14 | Oil pan | 19 | Drive plate |
| 5 | Rear clutch | 10 | Oil distributor | 15 | Control valve | 20 | Rear extension oil seal |

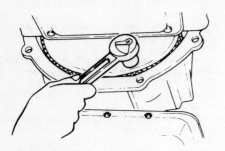

**Fig. 6.56. Removing driveplate/converter bolt**

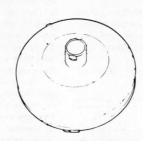

**Fig. 6.57. Torque converter alignment notch**

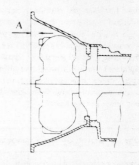

**Fig. 6.58. Torque converter installation dimension**

**Fig. 6.59. Automatic transmission selector linkage**

1  *Control lever knob*      *E  Pivot*
2  *Pusher*                  *F  Range lever nut*
3  *Control lever*           *G  Bracket nuts*
*D  Retainer*                *H  Trunnion nuts*

*A = 0.43 to 0.47 in (11.0 to 12.0 mm)*
*B = 0.004 to 0.043 in (0.1 to 1.1 mm)*
*C = 0.039 in (1.0 mm)*

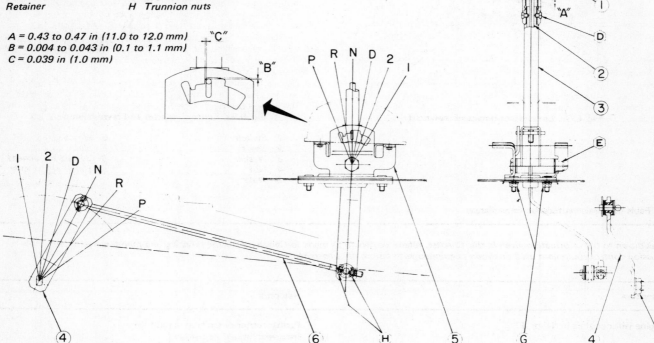

## 29 Selector linkage - adjustment

1  Set dimension 'A' (Fig. 6.59) with the control knob removed, then install the control knob again.
2  Check dimension 'B' (Fig. 6.59) and adjust, if necessary, by rotating the pusher.
3  Loosen trunnion nuts 'H' (Fig. 6.59), set the control lever and selector lever at 'N' and obtain clearance 'C' by adjustment of the nuts as necessary.
4  Ensure that the linkage operates satisfactorily throughout the selection range.

## 30 Kick-down switch and downshift solenoid - checking

1  If the kick-down facility fails to operate or operates at an incorrect change point, first check the security of the switch on the accelerator pedal arm and the wiring between the switch and the solenoid.
2  Turn the ignition key so that the ignition and oil pressure lamps illuminate but without operating the starter motor. Depress the accelerator pedal fully and as the switch actuates, a distinct click should be heard from the solenoid. Where this is absent a replacement switch

or solenoid must be installed. **Note:** when the solenoid is removed, fluid will drain out. This can be re-used if collected in a clean container, do not forget to refill with fluid on completion.

## 31 Starter inhibitor and reverse lamp switch - testing and adjustment

1  Check that the starter motor operates only in 'N' and 'P' and the reversing lamps illuminate only with the selector lever in 'R'.
2  Any deviation from this arrangement should be rectified by adjustment, first having checked the correct setting of the selector linkage (Fig. 6.59).
3  Detach the range selector lever (9) from the selector rod which connects it to the hand control. Now move the range selector lever to the 'N' position, (slot in shaft vertical) (Fig. 6.61).
4  Connect an ohmmeter (or a test lamp) to the black and yellow wires of the inhibitor switch. With the ignition switch on, the meter should indicate continuity of circuit when the range select lever is within 3 degrees (either side) of the 'N' and 'P' positions.
5  Repeat the test with the meter connected to the red and black wires and the range lever in 'R'.
6  Where the switch requires adjusting to provide the correct moment of contact in the three selector positions, move the range level to 'N'

and then remove the retaining nut (6), the two inhibitor switch securing bolts and the screw located below the switch.

7   Align the hole, from which the screw was removed, with the pinhole in the manual shaft (2). A thin rod or piece of wire may be used to do this. Holding this alignment, install the inhibitor switch securing bolts and tighten them. Remove the alignment rod and install the screw.

8   Install the remaining switch components and test for correct operation as previously described. If the test procedure does not prove positive, renew the switch.

## 32 Rear extension oil seal - renewal

1   After a considerable mileage, leakage may occur from the seal which surrounds the shaft at the rear end of the automatic transmission extension housing. This leakage will be evident from the state of the underbody and from the reduction in the level of the hydraulic fluid.

2   Remove the propeller shaft as described in Chapter 7.

3   Taking care not to damage the splined output shaft and the alloy housing, pry the old oil seal from its location. Drive in the new one using a tubular drift.

4   Should the seal be very tight in its recess, then support the transmission on a jack and remove the rear mounting. Unbolt the rear extension housing from the transmission casing.

5   Pull the extension housing straight off over the output shaft and governor assembly.

6   Using a suitable drift applied form the interior of the rear extension housing, remove the old oil seal. At the same time check the bush and renew it if it is scored or worn.

7   Installation is the reverse of the removal procedure, but always use a new gasket between the rear extension and main housing.

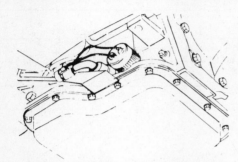

Fig. 6.60. Location of downshift solenoid

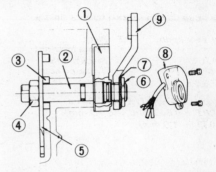

Fig. 6.61. Starter inhibitor and reverse lamp switch

| | | | |
|---|---|---|---|
| 1 | Switch | 6 | Washer |
| 2 | Shaft | 7 | Nut |
| 3 | Washer | 8 | Switch (detached) |
| 4 | Nut | 9 | Range select lever |
| 5 | Plate | | |

## 33 Fault diagnosis - automatic transmission

*In addition to the information given in this Chapter, reference should be made to Chapter 3 for the servicing and maintenance of the emission control equipment used on models equipped with automatic transmission.*

| Symptom | Reason/s |
|---|---|
| Engine will not start in 'N' or 'P' | Faulty starter or ignition circuit.<br>Incorrect linkage adjustment.<br>Incorrectly installed inhibitor switch. |
| Engine starts in selector positions other than 'N' or 'P' | Incorrect linkage adjustment.<br>Incorrectly installed inhibitor switch. |
| Severe bump when selecting 'D' or 'R' and excessive creep when idling | Idling speed too high.<br>Vacuum circuit leaking. |
| Poor acceleration and low maximum speed | Incorrect oil level.<br>Incorrect linkage adjustment. |

**The most likely causes of faulty operation are incorrect oil level and linkage adjustment. Any other faults or mal-operation of the automatic transmission unit must be due to internal faults and should be rectified by your Datsun dealer. An indication of a major internal fault may be gained from the colour of the oil which under normal conditions should be transparent red. If it becomes discoloured or black then burned clutch or brake bands must be suspected.**

**6B**

# Chapter 7 Propeller shaft

**Contents**

**Specifications**

| | |
|---|---|
| **Type** ... ... ... ... ... ... ... ... ... | Two-piece, tubular, with 3 universal joints and centre bearing. |
| **Maximum dynamic unbalance at 5800 rpm** ... ... ... ... | 0.49 oz in (35 gm cm) |
| **Maximum axial play of spider journal** ... ... ... ... | 0.0008 in (0.02 mm) |

| Torque wrench settings | lb f ft | kg f m |
|---|---|---|
| Propeller shaft/axle flange bolt ... ... ... ... ... | 17 to 24 | 2.4 to 3.3 |
| Front shaft self-locking nut ... ... ... ... ... ... | 145 to 174 | 20 to 24 |
| Rear shaft flange yoke/front shaft companion flange bolt ... ... ... | 17 to 24 | 2.4 to 3.3 |
| Centre bearing bracket bolt ... ... ... ... ... ... | 11.6 to 15.9 | 1.6 to 2.2 |

## 1 General description

On all models covered by this Manual, a twopiece propeller shaft is used. This is supported by a centre bearing mounted on one of the chassis frame crossmembers, and incorporates three universal joints, one at the transmission end, one behind the centre bearing and one at the axle companion flange end. Although the propeller shafts used on manual transmission, automatic transmission and long wheelbase models are similar, they are not interchangeable due to their different lengths.

The propeller shaft is finely balanced during manufacture and it is recommended that an exchange unit is obtained rather than dismantle the universal joints when wear is evident. However, this is not always possible and provided care is taken to mark each individual yoke in relation to the one opposite then the balance will usually be maintained. Do not drop the assembly during servicing operations.

## 2 Universal joints - testing for wear

1 Wear in the needle roller bearing is characterized by vibration in the transmission, 'clonks' on taking up the drive, and in extreme cases of lack of lubrication, metallic squeaking and ultimately grating and shrieking sounds as the bearings break up.

2 It is easy to check whether the needle roller bearings are worn with the propeller shaft in position, by trying to turn the shaft with one hand the other hand holding the rear axle flange when the rear universal joint is being checked, and the front half coupling when the front universal joint is being checked. Any movement between the propeller shaft and the front half couplings, and round the rear half couplings, is indicative of considerable wear.

3 If wear is evident, either fit a new propeller shaft assembly complete or renew the universal joints, as described later in this Chapter.

4 A final test for wear is to attempt to lift the shaft and note any movement between the yokes of the joints.

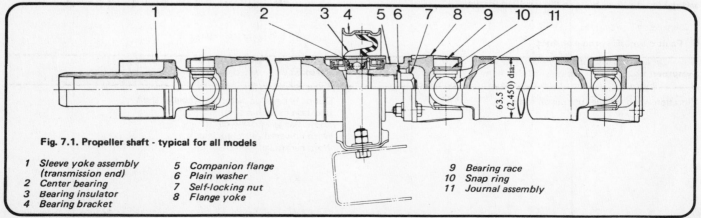

**Fig. 7.1. Propeller shaft - typical for all models**

1 Sleeve yoke assembly (transmission end)
2 Center bearing
3 Bearing insulator
4 Bearing bracket
5 Companion flange
6 Plain washer
7 Self-locking nut
8 Flange yoke
9 Bearing race
10 Snap ring
11 Journal assembly

### 3  Propeller shaft - removal and installation

1   Jack-up the rear of the vehicle, or position the rear of the vehicle over a pit.
2   If the rear of the vehicle is jacked-up, supplement the jack with support blocks so that danger is minimized should the jack collapse.
3   If the rear wheels are off the ground, place the vehicle in gear and apply the handbrake to ensure that the propeller shaft does not turn when an attempt is made to loosen the four bolts securing the propeller shaft to the rear axle.
4   The propeller shaft is carefully balanced to fine limits and it is important that it is in exactly the same position it was in prior to removal. Scratch index marks on the propeller shaft and mating flanges to ensure accurate positioning when the time comes for installation.
5   Unscrew and remove the four bolts and spring washers which hold the flange on the propeller shaft to the flange on the rear axle.
6   Unscrew and remove the bolts which secure the bearing carrier to the bodyframe.
7   Slightly push the shaft forward to separate the two flanges, then lower the end of the shaft and pull it rearwards to disengage it from the transmission mainshaft splines.
8   Place a large can or tray under the rear of the transmission to catch any oil which is likely to leak past the oil seal when the propeller shaft is removed.
9   Installation is a reversal of removal but ensure that the flange index marks are in alignment, and tighten all securing bolts to the specified torque. Check the oil level in the transmission and top-up if necessary.

### 4  Centre bearing - dismantling and reassembly

1   With the propeller shaft removed as already described, disconnect the rear section of the shaft from the front section by unbolting the flanges which are located just to the rear of the center bearing, (index mark the flange alignment first).
2   Relieve the staking on the locknut which is now exposed and unscrew and remove the locknut. This nut will be very tight and the best method of holding the shaft still while it is unscrewed is to pass two old bolts through two of the flange holes and secure them in a vice. Alternatively, a special flange securing wrench can be used.
3   Index mark the relative positions of the center bearing assembly to the clamp/support and the bearing and clamp/support to the propeller shaft itself.
4   Unbolt and remove the bearing clamp/support and draw off the center bearing complete with insulator.
5   Commence reassembly by inserting the center bearing into its insulator. If a new bearing is being fitted, do not lubricate it as it is of a grease-sealed type.
6   Install the bearing/insulator to the propeller shaft making sure to align the marks made before dismantling or in the case of new components. Locate them in similar relative positions.
7   Install the washer and locknut, and tighten to the specified torque. Stake the nut into the shaft groove using a punch.
8   Reconnect the propeller shaft flanges, tightening the securing bolts to the specified torque.
9   Install the clamp/support to the center bearing, aligning it correctly, and tighten the inner bolts to the specified torque.

### 5  Universal joints - servicing

**Note:** Selective fit snap-rings are used to retain the universal joint spiders in the yokes. In order to maintain the propeller shaft balance it is essential to fit replacement snap-rings of the same size as originally used Selective snap-rings are available in the following sizes:

| Thickness | Color |
|---|---|
| 0.0787 in (2.00 mm) | White |
| 0.0795 in (2.02 mm) | Yellow |
| 0.0803 in (2.04 mm) | Red |
| 0.0811 in (2.06 mm) | Green |
| 0.0819 in (2.08 mm) | Blue |
| 0.0827 in (2.10 mm) | Light brown |
| 0.0835 in (2.12 mm) | Unpainted |

1   Clean away all dirt from the ends of the bearings on the yokes so that the snap-rings may be removed during a pair of contracting snap-ring pliers or a small screwdriver. If they are very tight, tap the end of the bearing cup (inside the snap-ring) with a drift and hammer to relieve the pressure.
2   Once the snap-rings are removed, tap the universal joints at the yoke with a wooden or plastic faced hammer; the bearings and cups will come out of the housing and can be removed easily.
3   If they are obstinate they can be gripped in a self-locking wrench for final removal provided that they are to be renewed.
4   Once the bearings are removed from each opposite journal yoke the trunnion can be easily disengaged.
5   Installation of the new yokes and needle rollers and cups is the reverse of the removal procedure.
6   Position the needles in each cup and fill the cup one third full of general purpose grease prior to placing it over the yoke, and tap each one home with a brass drift. Any grease exuding from the further bearing journal after three have been installed should be removed before installing the fourth race.
7   Install the snap-rings ensuring that they are correctly seated (refer to the note at the beginning of this Section).
8   In cases of extreme wear or neglect, it is conceivable that the bearing housings in the propeller shaft, sliding sleeve or rear flange have worn so much that the bearing cups are a slack fit in them. In such cases it will be necessary to replace the item affected as well. Check also that the sliding sleeve splines are in good condition and not a sloppy fit on the transmission mainshaft.

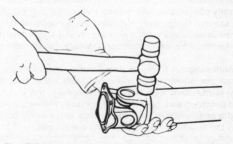

Fig. 7.2. Removal of the universal joint bearings

**7**

### 6  Fault diagnosis - propeller shaft

| Symptom | Reason/s |
|---|---|
| Vibration when vehicle running on road | Out of balance or distorted propeller shaft<br>Backlash in splines shaft<br>Loose flange securing bolts<br>Worn universal joint bearings<br>Worn centre bearing |

# Chapter 8 Rear axle

## Contents

## Specifications

| | |
|---|---|
| **Type** ... ... ... ... ... ... ... ... ... ... | Rigid; semi-floating with hypoid gear. |

**Construction**

| | |
|---|---|
| Axle casing ... ... ... ... ... ... ... ... | Pressed steel |
| Differential carrier ... ... ... ... ... ... ... | Aluminium alloy (with collapsible spacer) or cast iron (with rigid spacer). |

**Ratio**

| | |
|---|---|
| Manual transmission (USA) ... ... ... ... ... ... ... | 4.375 : 1 (35 : 8) |
| Automatic transmission (USA) J15 engined pick-up and J13 engined double pick-up ... ... ... ... ... ... | 4.625 : 1 (37 : 8) |
| J15 engined pick-up (optional) ... ... ... ... ... ... | 4.875 : 1 (39 : 8) |
| J15 engined double pick-up ... ... ... ... ... ... | 4.375 : 1 (35 : 8) |

**Lubricant**

| | |
|---|---|
| Capacity (approx) ... ... ... ... ... ... ... ... | 2 US pt/1¾ Imp. pt (1 liter) |
| Lubricant type ... ... ... ... ... ... ... ... | SAE 90EP hypoid gear oil to spec. MIL-L-2105B |

**Torque wrench settings**

| | lbf ft | kgf m |
|---|---|---|
| Drive pinion nut (rigid spacer axle) ... ... ... ... ... | 101 to 123 | 14 to 17 |
| Differential carrier ... ... ... ... ... ... | 12 to 18 | 1.7 to 2.5 |
| Companion flange bolts ... ... ... ... ... ... | 17 to 24 | 2.4 to 3.3 |
| Drain and filler plugs ... ... ... ... ... ... | 43 to 72 | 6 to 10 |
| Side bearing cap bolts ... ... ... ... ... ... | 28 to 36 | 3.8 to 4.9 |
| Axle-shaft bearing locknut ... ... ... ... ... ... | 108 to 145 | 15 to 20 |
| Axle bearing cage (backplate) nut ... ... ... ... ... | 26.8 to 34.7 | 3.7 to 4.8 |

## 1 General description

The rear axle is of the semi-floating type and is held in place by two semi-elliptic springs. These provide the necessary lateral and longitudinal support for the axle.

The banjo type/casing carries the differential assembly which consists of a hypoid crownwheel and pinion, and a two pinion differential bolted in a carrier to the nose piece.

Either a collapsible spacer or rigid spacer is used to preload the pinion bearing. Rigid spacer axles are identified by the type number H190.

All repairs can be carried out to the component parts of the rear axle without removing the axle casing from the car. It will be found simpler in practice to fit a guaranteed second-hand axle from a car breakers yard rather than dismantle the differential unit which calls for special tools which very few garages will have.

As an alternative a replacement differential carrier assembly can be fitted which means that the axle can be left in position and dismantling is reduced to a minimum.

## 2 Axle-shaft (halfshaft) bearing and oil seal - removal and installation

1 Jack-up the rear of the vehicle and support the rear axle and the bodyframe securely on stands.
2 Remove the rear roadwheel, and brake drum.
3 Disconnect the rear handbrake cable; refer to Chapter 9, if necessary.
4 Disconnect the brake pipe at the wheel cylinder union and plug the pipe to prevent the entry of dirt and loss of hydraulic fluid. In order to prevent loss of fluid from the hydraulic system, the fluid reservoir cap can be removed and a piece of plastic film placed over the opening and the cap installed. This will cause a vacuum to be created and prevent the fluid running from the disconnected pipe.
5 Remove the nuts securing the brake backplate to the wheel bearing cage at the end of the axle tube.
6 A slide hammer must now be attached to the wheel studs and the axleshaft removed complete with brake assembly and backplate. It is quite useless to attempt to pull the axleshaft from the axle casing. Where a slide hammer is not available, an old road wheel can be bolted onto the axle flange and its inner rims struck simultaneously at two

opposite points.

7  Always renew the oil seal in the end of the axle casing whenever the axleshaft is removed. Pry it from its seat with a screwdriver and tap the new one squarely into position.

8  Oil seepage into the rear brake drums is an indication of failure of the axle housing oil seals. Where oil contamination is observed, always check that this is not, in fact, hydraulic brake fluid leaking from a faulty wheel operating cylinder.

9  The removal and installation of axleshaft bearings and spacer/collars is best left to a service station having suitable extracting and pressing equipment. Where the home mechanic has such tools and facilities available, proceed as follows.

10  With the axleshaft removed, as previously described, secure it in a vise fitted with jaw protectors.

11  Using a screwdriver fold back the lockwasher tabs. Remove the lockwasher and discard it.

12  Using a suitable ring wrench (Datsun tool no. ST 38020000 is available for this purpose), remove the nut which retains the wheel bearing.

13  Using a suitable extractor (Datsun tool no. ST 37140000 is available for this purpose) withdraw the wheel bearing cage and bearing assembly, complete with the brake backplate, from the axle shaft.

14  Remove the oil seal at the outer side of the bearing cage.

15  The wheel bearing outer race can be carefully driven out of the cage using a hammer and brass drift.

16  Installation is basically the reverse of the removal procedure. However, the following points must be noted.

   a)  Use new oil seals during assembly, and fill the seal cavity with a general purpose grease.

   b)  Use a new lockwasher for the bearing locknut, and ensure that the faced side of the locknut is towards the washer.

   c)  Apply general purpose grease to the wheel bearing and the cavity in the end of the axle tube (see shaded area in Fig. 8.3).

   d)  Apply rear axle oil to the axleshaft splines, and take care that the oil seal is not damaged as the shaft is installed.

   e)  If both axleshafts have been removed, install the first one (left or right) and obtain an axial end play of 0.012 to 0.059 in (0.3 to 0.9 mm) by shimming between the bearing cage and axle tube end. If only one axleshaft was removed, or when installing the second one, an endplay of 0.0008 to 0.0059 in (0.02 to 0.15 mm) is required. Shims are available in the following sizes:

   0.002 in (0.05 mm)
   0.0028 in (0.07 mm)
   0.0039 in (0.10 mm)
   0.0079 in (0.20 mm)
   0.0197 in (0.50 mm)

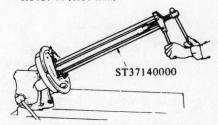

**Fig. 8.2. Removing the bearing using an extractor**

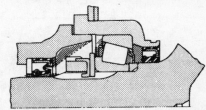

**Fig. 8.3. Part sectioned view of the wheel bearing showing the grease (shaded area)**

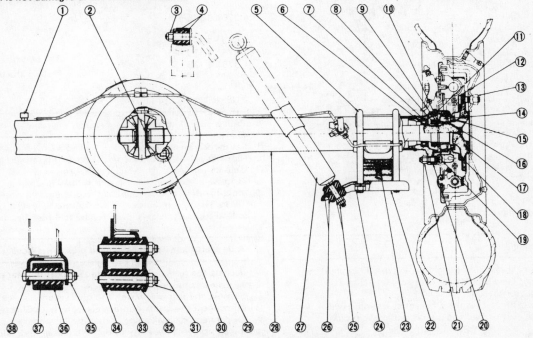

**Fig. 8.1. Rear axle - sectional view**

| 1  Breather | 10  Plain washer | 20  Axle case and shim | 30  Drain plug |
| 2  Thrust block | 11  Axle bearing cage | 21  Nut | 31  Nut |
| 3  Nut | 12  Wheel bolt | 22  Spring pad | 32  Rear spring rear bush |
| 4  Shock absorber mounting rubber bush | 13  Wheel nut | 23  Rear spring | 33  Rear spring |
| 5  Rear spring U-bolt | 14  Wheel bearing | 24  Nut | 34  Rear spring shackle |
| 6  Axle oil seal spacer | 15  Axle bearing grease seal | 25  Nut | 35  Nut |
| 7  Axle shaft oil seal | 16  Axle bearing spacer | 26  Rubber bush | 36  Rear spring |
| 8  Axle bearing locknut | 17  Axle shaft | 27  Shock absorber | 37  Rear spring front bush |
| 9  Axle bearing locknut | 18  Grease catcher | 28  Axle case | 38  Rear spring front pin |
| | 19  Bearing cage bolt | 29  Filler plug | |

**8**

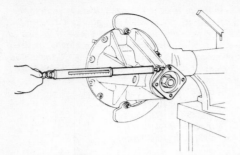

**Fig. 8.6. Measuring pinion preload**

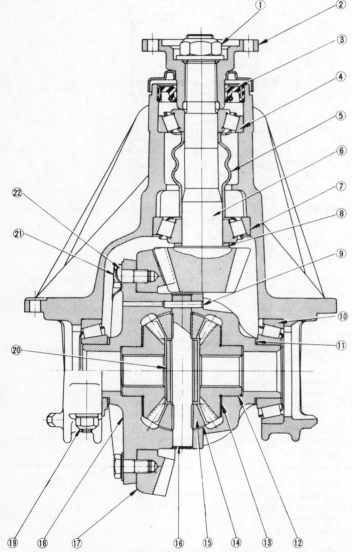

**Fig. 8.5. Collapsible spacer differential - sectional view**

| | |
|---|---|
| 1   Drive pinion nut | 12   Side gear |
| 2   Companion flange | 13   Thrust washer |
| 3   Oil seal | 14   Thrust washer |
| 4   Pinion front bearing | 15   Pinion mate |
| 5   Collapsible spacer | 16   Differential pinion shaft |
| 6   Drive pinion | 17   Ring gear |
| 7   Pinion rear bearing | 18   Differential case |
| 8   Pinion height adjusting washer | 19   Bearing cap nut |
| 9   Lock pin | 20   Thrust block |
| 10  Side bearing | 21   Ring gear bolt |
| 11  Side bearing adjusting shim | 22   Lock strap |

## 3   Pinion oil seal (axle with collapsible spacer) - renewal

1   The pinion oil seal cannot be renewed with the differential carrier still in position in the vehicle. This is due to the use of a collapsible type spacer, between the pinion bearings, which must be renewed if the pinion adjustment is disturbed by removal of the pinion nut.

2   Remove the differential carrier, as described in Section 5.

3   Unbolt and remove the side bearing caps.

4   Withdraw differential case assembly.

5   Unscrew and remove the drive pinion nut and coupling. Extract the pinion oil seal.

6   Withdraw the pinion to the rear and the front pinion bearing race to the front.

7   Extract the collapsible spacer.

8   Insert a new collapsible spacer onto the pinion and fit the front bearing race.

9   Tap a new oil seal into position and apply some grease to the seal lips.

10  Install pinion coupling and screw on the pinion nut finger-tight.

11  Now tighten the pinion nut (coupling flange held quite still until any endfloat in drive pinion is just eliminated.

12  The pinion nut should now be tightened a fraction at a time until, with a spring balance attached to one of the coupling flange bolt holes, the force required to turn it (preload) is between 4.5 and 9.5 lb f (2.0 and 4.3 kg). This is approximately equal to a torque of 115 lb f ft (16 kg f m). Turn the pinion in both directions during the tightening process to settle the bearings.

13  Install the differential case assembly and side bearing caps, and install the carrier to the axle casing, as described in Section 5.

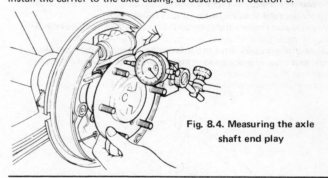

**Fig. 8.4. Measuring the axle shaft end play**

## 4   Pinion oil seal (axle with rigid spacer) - renewal

1   On models manufactured from 1974 onwards the pinion oil seal can be renewed with the differential carrier in position in the vehicle.

2   Jack-up the rear of the vehicle and support the axle on stands.

3   Remove the propeller shaft, as described in Chapter 7.

4   Hold the drive pinion coupling flange quite still while the pinion nut is unscrewed and removed. This nut will be very tight and the flange must be secured by inserting two old bolts through two of the flange holes and then passing a long rod or bar between them as a lever, or alternatively using a special ring wrench.

5   Withdraw the coupling using a suitable extractor.

6   Remove the defective oil seal by drifting in one side of it as far as it will go in order to force the opposite side from the housing.

7   Tap the new seal squarely into position and apply some grease to the seal lips.

8   Fit the pinion coupling and tighten it to the specified torque, whilst keeping the coupling quite still.

9   Install the propeller shaft and top-up the rear axle oil level.

## 5   Differential carrier - removal and installation

1   The overhaul of the rear axle differential unit is not within the scope of the home mechanic due to the specialized gauges and tools which are required. Where the unit requires servicing or repair due to wear or excessive noise, it is most economical to exchange it for a factory reconditioned assembly and this Section is limited to a description of the removal and installation procedure.

2   Drain the oil from the rear axle.

3   Jack-up the axle, remove the roadwheels and partially withdraw the axleshafts, as described in Section 2, of this Chapter.
4   Disconnect and remove the propeller shaft as described in Chapter 7.
5   Unscrew, evenly and in opposite sequence, the nuts from the differential unit securing studs. Pull the differential unit from the axle casing.
6   Scrape all trace of old gasket from the mating surface of the axle casing. Position a new gasket on the axle casing having first smeared it on both sides with jointing compound.
7   Install the differential carrier so that the pinion assembly is at the lowest point. Tighten the securing nuts to the specified torque.
8   Install the axleshafts and the propeller shaft.
9   Install the roadwheels and lower the jack.
10  Fill the differential unit to the correct level with oil of the specified grade.

## 6   Rear axle - removal and installation

1   Remove the hub caps from the rear roadwheels and loosen the wheel nuts.
2   Jack-up the bodyframe at the rear of the vehicle and support it securely on stands.
3   Place a jack under the center of the rear axle casing and raise the axle sufficiently to take its weight.
4   Disconnect the propeller shaft from the rear axle pinion driving flange, as described in Chapter 7.
5   Disconnect the handbrke cables; for further information, see Chapter 9.
6   Disconnect the brake pipes and plug the openings.
7   Disconnect the shock absorber lower mountings.
8   Unscrew and remove the spring 'U' bolt nuts and detach the lower plates.
9   Lower the axle jack until the axle casing is separated from the road springs, and then withdraw the complete rear axle assembly sideways through the space between the spring and the bodyframe.
10  Installation is the reverse of the removal procedure.

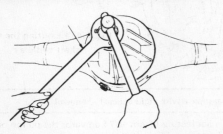

Fig. 8.8. Unscrewing the pinion nut (pinion coupling flange wrench arrowed)

## 7   Fault diagnosis - rear axle

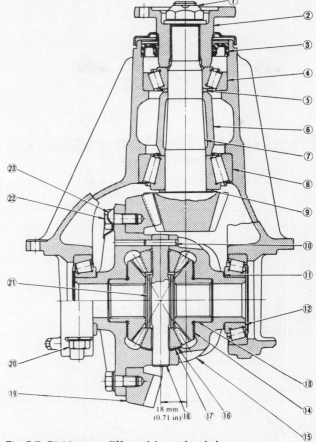

Fig. 8.7. Rigid spacer differential - sectional view

| | | | |
|---|---|---|---|
| 1 | Drive pinion nut | 11 | Side bearing adjusting shim |
| 2 | Companion flange | 12 | Side bearing |
| 3 | Oil seal | 13 | Side gear |
| 4 | Front bearing | 14 | Thrust washer |
| 5 | Drive pinion bearing adjusting washer | 15 | Differential gear case |
| 6 | Drive pinion bearing spacer (rigid) | 16 | Thrust washer |
| 7 | Drive pinion | 17 | Pinion mate |
| 8 | Drive pinion | 18 | Differential pinion shaft |
| 9 | Drive pinion adjusting washer | 19 | Ring gear |
| 10 | Lock pin | 20 | Bearing cap bolt |
| | | 21 | Thrust block |
| | | 22 | Ring gear bolt |
| | | 23 | Lock strap |

| Symptom | Reason/s |
|---|---|
| Noise on drive, coasting or overrun | Shortage of oil. Incorrect crownwheel to pinion mesh. Worn pinion bearings. Worn side bearings. Loose bearing cap bolts. |
| Noise on turn | Differential side gears worn, damaged or tight. |
| Knock on taking up drive or during gearchange | Excessive crownwheel to pinion backlash. Worn gears. Worn axle-shaft splines. Pinion bearing preload too low. Loose drive coupling nut. Loose securing bolts or nuts within unit. Loose roadwheel nuts or elongated wheel nut holes. |
| Oil leakage | Defective gaskets or oil seals possibly caused by clogged breather or oil level too high. |

8

# Chapter 9 Braking system

*Refer to Chapter 13 for specifications and information applicable to 1977 through 1979 USA models*

## Contents

## Specifications

**System type** ... ... ... ... ... ... ... ...
Hydraulic, drums front and rear with vacuum servo unit (except some rhd models). Rear wheel load sensing valve used on 1976 USA models.

### Front brakes
| | |
|---|---|
| Type ... ... ... ... ... ... ... | Leading and trailing shoe, uni-servo. |
| Wheel cylinder diameter ... ... | ¾in (19.05 mm) |
| Lining width x thickness x length ... ... | 1.77 x 0.177 x 9.61 in (45 x 4.5 x 244 mm) |
| Lining wear limit ... ... ... ... | 0.039 in (1.0 mm) |
| Drum diameter: | |
|   Nominal ... ... ... ... ... | 10 in (254 mm) |
|   Maximum permissible ... ... ... ... | 10.059 in (255.5 mm) |

### Rear brakes
| | |
|---|---|
| Type ... ... ... ... ... ... ... | Leading and trailing shoes, due-servo. |
| Wheel cylinder diameter ... ... | ¾ in (19.05 mm) |
| Lining width x thickness x length ... ... ... | 1.77 x 0.177 x 9.61 in (45 x 4.5 x 244 mm) |
| Lining wear limit ... ... ... ... ... | 0.039 in (1.0 mm) |
| Drum diameter: | |
|   Nominal ... ... ... ... | 10 in (254 mm) |
|   Maximum permissible ... ... ... ... | 10.059 in (255.5 mm) |

### Brake pedal free travel (dimension 'A' - Fig. 9.3)
| | |
|---|---|
| Rhd models ... ... ... ... ... ... ... | 6.42 in (163 mm) |
| Lhd 1973/1974/1975 ... ... ... ... ... | 5.51 in (140 mm) |
| Lhd 1976 ... ... ... ... ... ... | 5.83 in (148 mm) |

### Master cylinder
Inner diameter:
| | |
|---|---|
|   1973 models, single and dual master cylinders without vacuum unit ... ... ... ... ... ... | 11/16 in (17.46 mm) |
|   1973 models dual master cylinder with vacuum unit ... | ¾ in (19.05 mm) |
|   1974 models onwards without vacuum unit ... ... | 11/16 in (17.46 mm) |
|   1974 models onwards with vacuum unit ... | ¾ in (19.05 mm) |
| Piston to cylinder clearance ... ... ... ... | 0.0059 in (0.15 mm) |
| Brake fluid specification ... ... ... ... | DOT 3 (MUSS 116) or SAE J1703 C |

### Parking brake (handbrake)
| | |
|---|---|
| Type ... ... ... ... ... ... ... | Stick type, cable operated to rear wheels. |
| Normal stroke ... ... ... ... ... ... | 3.15 to 3.94 in (80 to 100 mm) |

## Vacuum unit

| Type | ... | ... | ... | ... | ... | ... | ... | ... | ... | ... | Master-vac |
|---|---|---|---|---|---|---|---|---|---|---|---|
| Diaphragm diameter | ... | ... | ... | ... | ... | ... | ... | ... | ... | ... | 6 in (152.4 mm) |
| Shell seal depth | ... | ... | ... | ... | ... | ... | ... | ... | ... | ... | 0.264 to 0.276 in (6.7 to 7.0 mm) |
| Pushrod length | ... | ... | ... | ... | ... | ... | ... | ... | ... | ... | 0.394 to 0.413 in (10 to 10.5 mm) |

## Torque wrench settings

| | | | | | | | | | | | lbf ft | kgf m |
|---|---|---|---|---|---|---|---|---|---|---|---|---|
| Master cylinder-to-master-vac | ... | ... | ... | ... | ... | ... | ... | | | | 5.8 to 8.0 | 0.8 to 1.1 |
| Brake tube flare nut | ... | ... | ... | ... | ... | ... | ... | ... | | | 11 to 13 | 1.5 to 1.8 |
| Brake hose connector | ... | ... | ... | ... | ... | ... | ... | ... | | | 13 to 15 | 1.8 to 2.1 |
| Bleed valve | ... | ... | ... | ... | ... | ... | ... | ... | ... | | 5.1 to 6.5 | 0.7 to 0.9 |
| Fulcrum pin of brake pedal | ... | ... | ... | ... | ... | ... | ... | | | | 8.7 to 11 | 1.2 to 1.5 |
| Connector and clip fixing bolts | ... | ... | ... | ... | ... | ... | | | | | 2.5 to 3.3 | 0.35 to 0.45 |
| 3-way connector fixing bolt (on axle case) | ... | ... | ... | ... | | | | | | | 5.8 to 8.0 | 0.8 to 1.1 |
| Brake pedal stop lock nut | ... | ... | ... | ... | ... | ... | ... | | | | 8.7 to 11 | 1.2 to 1.5 |
| NLSV | ... | ... | ... | ... | ... | ... | ... | ... | ... | | 5.8 to 8.0 | 0.8 to 1.1 |
| Wheel cylinder mounting nut: | | | | | | | | | | | | |
| Front | ... | ... | ... | ... | ... | ... | ... | ... | | | 39 to 48 | 5.4 to 6.6 |
| Rear | ... | ... | ... | ... | ... | ... | ... | ... | ... | | 11 to 13 | 1.5 to 1.8 |
| Wheel cylinder connector bolt | ... | ... | ... | ... | ... | ... | ... | | | | 14 to 18 | 1.9 to 2.5 |
| Backplate nut: | | | | | | | | | | | | |
| Front | ... | ... | ... | ... | ... | ... | ... | ... | | | 30 to 36 | 4.2 to 5.0 |
| Rear | ... | ... | ... | ... | ... | ... | ... | ... | ... | | 39 to 46 | 5.4 to 6.4 |
| Master-Vac: | | | | | | | | | | | | |
| Master-Vac to body nut | ... | ... | ... | ... | ... | ... | ... | | | | 5.8 to 8.0 | 0.8 to 1.1 |
| Flange to shell cover nut | ... | ... | ... | ... | ... | ... | ... | | | | 5.8 to 8.0 | 0.8 to 1.1 |
| Operating rod lock nut | ... | ... | ... | ... | ... | ... | ... | | | | 12 to 16 | 1.6 to 2.2 |
| Pushrod adjusting nut | ... | ... | ... | ... | ... | ... | ... | | | | 14 to 17 | 1.9 to 2.4 |

## 1  General description

1   The braking system used on models covered by this manual incorporates hydraulically operated drum brakes operated from a foot pedal through a Master-Vac vacuum servo. (On some right-hand drive models the Master-Vac was not a standard installation, but these vehicles were not marketed in the USA or UK). Models manufactured during 1976 for the USA market also incorporated a load sensing valve which prevents the rear wheels from locking under adverse braking conditions.
2   The front drum brakes are of the leading and trailing shoe, single servo type. In this sytem the single wheel cylinder contains one operating piston only which contacts the leading (front) brake shoe. Adjustment is effected by the use of an adjuster assembly which incorporates a star wheel (accessible through the brake backplate). The adjuster floats in a slot in the backplate.
3   The rear brakes are of a similar type but incorporate wheel cylinders with two pistons; these are a dual servo type.
4   The parking brake (handbrake) is cable operated from a dash mounted handle to the rear wheels.
5   The Master-Vac vacuum servo and rear brake load sensing valve (NLSV) are described separately in this Chapter.

## 2  Brakes - adjustment

### Front brakes

1   Apply the parking brake and raise the front wheel(s).
2   Remove the rubber boot from the rear of the brake backplate (photo).
3   Ensure that the adjuster assembly is free to move in its location and move it forward slightly if necessary for access to the adjuster wheel.
4   Rotate the adjuster wheel downwards to spread the brake shoes until it is no longer possible to rotate the wheel by hand.
5   Turn back the adjuster at least twelve notches, until there is no longer contact between the shoes and the drum as the wheel is rotated.
6   Install the rubber boot to the backplate aperture.

### Rear brakes

7   The procedure for adjusting the rear brakes is identical to that given for the front brakes except that the parking brake (handbrake) must be released. For safety reason also chock the front wheels.

### Brake pedal

8   Adjust the travel of the brake pedal at the stop bracket to give a

pedal height of dimension 'A' in Fig. 9.3 (see Specifications).
9   Adjust the brake lamp switch by repositioning the locknuts on the switch body so that the switch plunger is depressed when the brake pedal is released.
10   Adjust the length of the brake master cylinder or Master-Vac pushrod to obtain dimension 'C' in Fig. 9.3. This corresponds to a free-play of the pushrod of 0.024 to 0.047 in (0.6 to 1.2 mm).
11   Operate the brake pedal several times to ensure that the pedal action is satisfactory.

### Parking brake (handbrake)

12   Adjust the front and rear brakes as already described in this Section.
13   Chock the front wheels and raise the rear of the vehicle so that the wheels are clear of the floor.
14   Adjust the locknut (Fig. 9.4 or 9.5) to obtain a total travel of the parking brake lever of 3.15 to 3.94 in (80 to 100 mm).
15   Operate the parking brake several times to ensure satisfactory operation; ensure that when released, the brake shoes do not rub on the drum when they are rotated.

### Parking brake warning lamp switch

16   Bend the warning lamp switch bracket as necessary so that the lamp illuminates when the lever is pulled out one notch, and extinguishes when the lever is fully released.

2.2 Remove the rubber boot from the rear of the backplate

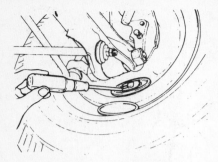

Fig. 9.1. Front brake adjustment

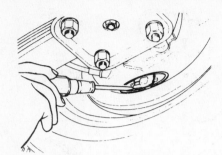

Fig. 9.2. Rear brake adjustment

Fig. 9.4. Early type parking brake
adjustment (arrowed)

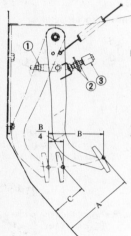

Fig. 9.3. Brake pedal adjustment

A  –  See Specifications
B  –  5.25 in (133 mm) approximately
C  –  1.8 in (46 mm) approximately

1  Master Vac pushrod adjustment nut
2  Brake lamp switch adjusting nuts
3  Brake lamp switch

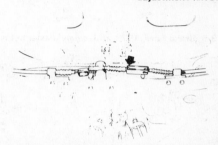

Fig. 9.5. Later type parking brake adjustment (arrowed)

## 3  Bleeding the hydraulic system

1  Removal of all air from the hydraulic system is essential to the correct working of the braking system. Before undertaking this, examine the fluid reservoir cap to ensure that the vent hole is clear. Check the level of fluid in the reservoir(s) and top up if required.
2  Check all brake line unions and connections for seepage, and at the same time check the condition of the rubber hoses which may be perished.
3  If the condition of the wheel cylinder is in doubt, check up for signs of fluid leakage.
4  If there is any possibility that incorrect fluid has been used in the system, drain all the fluid out and flush through with isopropyl alcohol or methylated spirits. Renew all piston seals and cups since they will be affected and could fail under pressure.
5  Gather together a clean glass jar, as 12 inch (300 mm) length of tubing which fits tightly over the bleed valve and a tin of the correct brake fluid.
6  To bleed the system, clean the area around the bleed vlaves and start at the rear left-hand wheel by removing the rubber or plastic cover from the end of the bleed valve.
7  Place the end of the tube in the clean jar which should contain sufficient fluid to keep the end of the tube underneath during the operation.
8  Open the bleed valve ¼ turn with a wrench, depress the brake pedal and close the bleed valve again just before full travel of the brake pedal is reached. This will expel brake fluid and air from the end of the tube.
9  Repeat this operation until no more air is expelled from that particular bleed valve then tighten the valve to the specified torque. During the bleeding operation ensure that the master cylinder reservoir(s) are topped-up as necessary or more air will be introduced into the system.
10  Repeat this operation on the second rear brake, and then the front

brakes, starting with the left-hand brake unit.
11  When completed, check the level of the fluid in the reservoir and then check the feel of the brake pedal, which should be firm and free from any 'spongy' action, which is normally associated with air in the system.
12  It will be noticed that during the bleeding operation, where a servo unit is fitted, the effort required to depress the pedal the full stroke will increase because of loss of the vacuum assistance as it is destroyed by repeated operation of the servo unit. Although the servo unit will be inoperative as far as assistance is concerned it does not affect the brake bleeding operation.

## 4  Brake hoses - inspection, removal and installation

1  Inspect the condition of the flexible hydraulic hoses. If they are swollen, damaged or chafed they must be renewed.
2  Wipe the top of the brake master cylinder reservoir and unscrew the cap. Place a piece of polythene sheet over the top of the reservoir and install the cap. This is to stop hydraulic fluid syphoning out during subsequent operations. Note that tandem master cylinders have two reservoirs but it is not necessary to cover both cylinders unless both front and rear hoses are being removed.

*Front brake hose*
3  First jack-up the vehicle to take the weight off the suspension. To remove the hose, wipe the unions and bracket free of dust, and undo the union nut from the metal pipe end.
4  Withdraw the metal clip securing the hose to the bracket and detach the hose from the bracket. Unscrew the hose from the wheel cylinder.
5  Installation is the reverse of the removal procedure but ensure that the hose is connected at the wheel cylinder end first, with the wheels in the 'straight-ahead' position. On completion, the front brakes must be bled of air, as described in the previous Section.

*Rear brake hose*
6  To remove a rear flexible hose, wipe the unions, bracket and three way adaptor free of dust, and undo the union nut from the metal pipe end.
7  Withdraw the metal clip securing the hose to the bracket and detach the hose from the bracket. Unscrew the hose from the three-way adaptor.
8  Installation is the reverse of the removal procedure. Ensure that the hose is connected at the three-way adaptor end first, and on completion bleed the rear brakes as described in the previous Section.

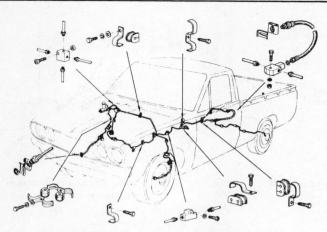

Fig. 9.6. Brake lines, 1973, rhd, single master cylinder

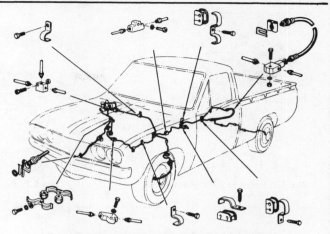

Fig. 9.7. Brake lines, rhd, tandem master cylinder

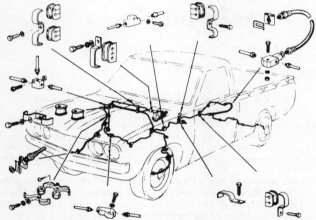

Fig. 9.8. Brake lines, general markets and 1974 lhd, tandem master cylinder

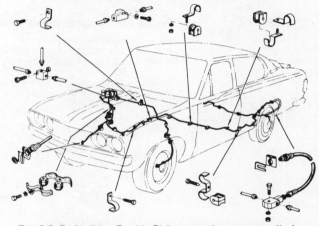

Fig. 9.9. Brake lines, Double Pick-up, tandem master cylinder

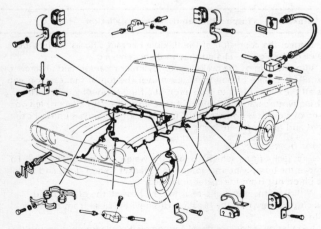

Fig. 9.10. Brake lines, 1973, lhd tandem master cylinder

## 5  Front drum brake shoes - inspection, removal and installation

1  Chock the rear wheels, apply the parking brake, jack-up the front of the vehicle and support on firmly based stands. Remove the road wheel.

2  Back-off the brake adjuster (refer to Section 2, if necessary).

3  Remove the brake drum. If it is tight, use a soft-faced hammer and tap outwards at the circumference whilst rotating the drum. On later models two M8 x 1.25 bolts can be inserted in the tapped holes in the drum and tightened evenly to draw the drum off (photo).

4  Inspect the linings for wear, and if this has exceeded that given in the Specifications, replacements must be fitted.

5  Back-off the adjuster completely and carefully pry the ends of the brake shoes from the wheel cylinder.

6  Repeat this operation for the lower ends of the brake shoes.

7  Detach the trailing (secondary) shoes pull-off spring from the backplate, then seprarate the brake shoes and pull-off springs, noting the spring colors.

8  If the shoes are to be left off for a while, do not depress the brake pedal otherwise the piston will be ejected from the cylinder causing unnecessary work.

9  Thoroughly clean all traces of dust from the shoes, backplate and brake drums using a stiff brush. It is recommended that compressed air is not used as it blows up dust, which should not be inhaled. Brake dust can cause judder or squeal and, therefore, it is important to clean out the drums as described.

10 Check that the piston is free to move in the cylinder, that the rubber dust cover is undamaged and in position, and that there are no hydraulic fluid leaks.

11 Apply a little brake grease to the adjuster threads.

12 Prior to reassembly, smear a little brake grease to the steady platforms and shoe locations on the cylinder and adjuster. Do not allow any grease to come into contact with the linings or rubber parts.

13 When installing the shoes, install the upper and lower springs then position the lower end of the rear shoe in the adjuster slot followed by the lower end of the front shoe. The shoes can then be spread and slotted into the wheel cylinder. Finally install the pull-off spring to the backplate and trailing shoe. **Note:** The upper spring slightly longer and smaller in diameter than the lower spring (photos).

14 Install the brake drum and roadwheel.

15 Adjust the brake and lower the car to the ground. If there is any chance that air has entered the system, it is essential that it is bled, as described in Section 3. Do not forget to remove the polythene from the top of the master cylinder.

9

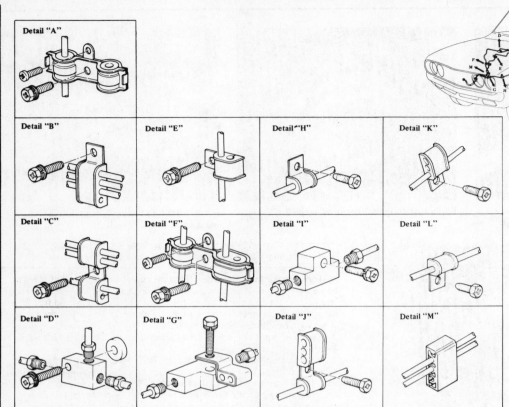

Detail "A"

Detail "B"  Detail "E"  Detail "H"  Detail "K"

Detail "C"  Detail "F"  Detail "I"  Detail "L"

**Fig. 9.11. Brake lines, 1975, USA**

Detail "D"  Detail "G"  Detail "J"  Detail "M"

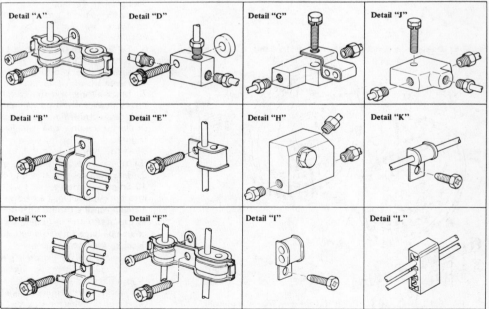

Detail "A"  Detail "D"  Detail "G"  Detail "J"

Detail "B"  Detail "E"  Detail "H"  Detail "K"

Detail "C"  Detail "F"  Detail "I"  Detail "L"

**Fig. 9.12. Brake lines, 1976, USA**

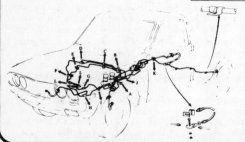

5.3 Brake drum removal on later models

5.13a Installing the rear shoe in the adjuster

5.13b Installing the pull-off spring to the backplate

5.13c The shoes and springs correctly installed

## 6  Front brake wheel cylinder - removal, servicing and installation

If hydraulic fluid is leaking from the brake wheel cylinder, it may be necessary to dismantle it and replace the seal. Should brake fluid be found running down the side of the wheel or a pool of liquid forms alongside one wheel and the level in the master cylinder has dropped, it is indicative that the seals have failed.

1  Remove the brake drum and shoes as described in the previous Section.

2  Clean down the rear of the backplate using a stiff brush. Place a quantity of rag under the backplate to catch any hydraulic fluid that may issue from the open pipe or wheel cylinder.

3  Wipe the top of the brake master cylinder reservoir and unscrew the cap. Place a piece of thick polythene over the top of the reservoir and install the cap. This is to stop hydraulic fluid syphoning out.

4  If considered necessary, disconnect the flexible hose, (refer to Section 4).

5  Unscrew the connector bolt and packing washer; detach the connector and second packing washer. Unscrew the remaining nut and washer.

6  To dismantle the wheel cylinder, first remove the rubber boot; then withdraw the piston and seal assembly, and spring, from the cylinder bore. Take care to note which way round and in what order the parts are removed.

7  Inspect the inside of the cylinder for score marks. If any are found, the cylinder and piston will require renewal. **Note:** If the wheel cylinder requires renewal always ensure that the replacement is exactly similar to the one removed. The cylinders are marked L (left) and R (right).

8  If the cylinder is sound, thoroughly clean it out with fresh hydraulic fluid.

9  The old rubber seal will probably be swollen and visibly worn.

10 Smear all internal parts with clean hydraulic fluid and reassemble into the cylinder in the reverse order to dismantling.

11 Replace the rubber dust cover and then install the wheel cylinder to the backplate, this being the reverse sequence to removal. It will of course be necessary to bleed the hydraulic system as described in Section 3 (photo).

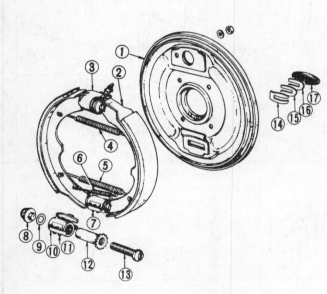
**Fig. 9.13. Front brake component parts**

| | |
|---|---|
| 1   Brake backplate | 8    Adjuster head |
| 2   Brake shoe assembly | 9    Adjuster head shim |
| 3   Wheel cylinder assembly | 10  Lock spring |
| 4   Brake shoe upper pull-off spring | 11  Adjuster housing |
| 5   Brake shoe lower pull-off spring | 12  Adjuster wheel |
| 6   After (trailing) shoe pull-off spring | 13  Adjuster screw |
| 7   Adjuster assembly | 14  Retaining spring |
| | 15  Lockplate |
| | 16  Adjuster shim |
| | 17  Rubber boot |

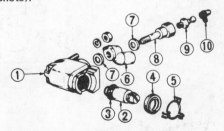
**Fig. 9.14. Front wheel cylinder parts**

| | |
|---|---|
| 1  Wheel cylinder | 6   Connector |
| 2  Piston | 7   Packings |
| 3  Piston cup | 8   Connector bolt |
| 4  Dust cover | 9   Bleed valve |
| 5  Retainer | 10  Bleed valve cap |

9

## 7 Front brake backplate - removal and installation

1 Remove the front wheel hub, as described in Chapter 11.
2 Remove the brake shoes, as described in Section 5, and the brake hose, as described in Section 4.
3 Bend back the lock tabs and remove the four securing bolts to free the backplate from the steering knuckle.
4 Installation is the reverse of the removal procedure. Do not forget to adjust the brakes and bleed the hydraulic system, as described previously in this Chapter.

## 8 Rear drum brakes shoes - inspection, removal and installation

1 Chock the front wheels, jack-up the rear of the vehicle and support it on firmly based axle stands. Remove the roadwheel and release the parking brake.
2 Back-off the brake adjuster (refer to Section 2, if necessary).
3 Remove the brake drum, as described in Section 5.
4 Inspect the linings for wear, and if this has exceeded that given in the Specifications, replacements must be fitted.
5 Depress the retainers and rotate the anti-rattle pins through 90°. Remove the retainer, spring and spring seat.
6 Back-off the adjuster completely, then carefully pry the shoes apart and remove extension link.
7 Carefully pry the shoes apart again, and remove them from the slots in the adjuster and wheel cylinder pistons. Note that the trailing (secondary) shoe must be detached from the toggle lever by removing the clevis pin. If the wheel cylinder pistons can be prevented from coming out, by using a rubber band or adhesive tape to hold them in position, it will not be necessary to bleed the brakes on completion.
8 Disconnect the parking brake cable from the toggle lever.
9 Refer to Section 5, paragraphs 8 thru 15, for information on cleaning and also reassembly which is the reverse of the removal procedure (photo). Note that a clearance of 0 to 0.012 in (0 to 0.3 mm) should exist between the toggle lever and the trailing brake shoe. This is obtained by selecting a toggle pin washer as given in the following table:

| Washer number | Washer thickness |
|---|---|
| 1 | 0.079 in (2.0 mm) |
| 2 | 0.091 in (2.3 mm) |
| 3 | 0.102 in (2.6 mm) |
| 4 | 0.114 in (2.9 mm) |
| 5 | 0.126 in (3.2 mm) |

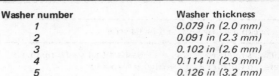

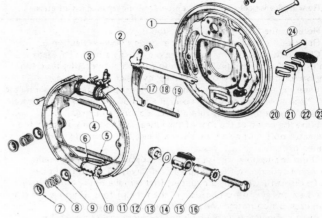

**Fig. 9.15. Rear brake component parts**

| | | | |
|---|---|---|---|
| 1 | Brake backplate | 13 | Lock spring |
| 2 | Brake shoe assembly | 14 | Adjuster housing |
| 3 | Wheel cylinder assembly | 15 | Adjuster wheel |
| 4 | Upper pull-off spring | 16 | Adjuster screw |
| 5 | Lower pull-off spring | 17 | Toggle lever |
| 6 | After shoe pull-off spring | 18 | Extension link |
| 7 | Retainer | 19 | Return spring |
| 8 | Anti-rattle spring | 20 | Adjuster spring |
| 9 | Spring seat | 21 | Lock plate |
| 10 | Adjuster assembly | 22 | Adjuster shim |
| 11 | Adjuster head | 23 | Rubber boot |
| 12 | Adjuster head shim | 24 | Anti-rattle pin |

6.11 Front brake wheel cylinder correctly installed

8.5 Depress the retainer to remove the anti-rattle pins

8.9a When installing the rear brake shoes, install the link first, followed by the upper spring

8.9b Install the shoes into the wheel cylinder slots then install the lower spring before slotting the screws into the adjuster

8.9c Finally install the pull-off spring to the rear shoe and backplate

11.5 Front brake adjuster correctly installed

## 9 Rear brake backplate - removal and installation

The backplate is removed during the axleshaft (halfshaft) removal procedure. Refer to Chapter 8, for further information

## 10 Rear brake wheel cylinder - removal, servicing and installation

1 Refer to the introduction to Section 6.
2 Remove the brake drum and shoes as described in Section 8.
3 Clean down the rear of the backplate using a stiff brush. Place a quantity of rag under the backplate to catch any hydraulic fluid that may issue from the open pipe or wheel cylinder.
4 Wipe the top of the brake master cylinder reservoir and unscrew the cap. Place a piece of polythene over the top of the reservoir and install the cap. This is to stop hydraulic fluid syphoning out.
5 Wipe the union at the rear of the wheel cylinder and unscrew the connector bolt. Lift away the two washers, one each side of the connector.
6 Undo and remove the four nuts and spring washers that secure the wheel cylinder to the backplate. Lift away the wheel cylinder.
7 To dismantle the wheel cylinder, first remove the two dust covers. Withdraw the two piston heads and then the pistons. Remove the seal from each piston noting which way round it is installed.
8 Inspect the inside of the cylinder for score marks caused by impurities in the hydraulic fluid. **Note:** If the wheel cylinder requires renewal always ensure that the replacement is exactly identical to the one removed.
9 If the cylinder is sound, thoroughly clean it out with clean hydraulic fluid.
10 The old rubber seals will probably be swollen and visibly worn. Smear the new rubber seals with hydraulic fluid and install to the pistons making sure that the lips face inwards when assembled.
11 Insert the pistons into the bore taking care not to roll the lip of the seal. Install the two piston heads and then dust cover covers.
12 Installation of the wheel cylinder is the reverse of the removal procedure. It will of course be necessary to bleed the hydraulic system, as described in Section 3.

## 11 Drum brake adjusters - removal, inspection and installation

1 Remove the brake drums and shoes, as described in Section 5 or 8.
2 Press the adjuster firmly against the brake backplate, and remove the spring, lockplate and shim from the rear of the backplate.
3 Examine the parts for damage, corrosion and distortion, renewing as necessary.
4 Reassemble the adjuster using a little brake grease on all the moving parts.
5 Installation is the reverse of the removal procedure, but smear a little brake grease on the rubbing surface of the adjuster and in the backplate slot (photo).

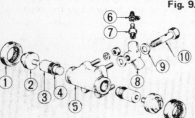

**Fig. 9.16. Rear wheel cylinder parts**

| | |
|---|---|
| 1 | Dust cover |
| 2 | Piston head |
| 3 | Piston |
| 4 | Piston cup (seal) |
| 5 | Wheel cylinder |
| 6 | Bleed valve cap |
| 7 | Bleed valve |
| 8 | Connector |
| 9 | Washer |
| 10 | Connector bolt |

## 12 Master cylinder - removal and installation

1 Where no vacuum servo (Master-Vac) is installed, straighten the ends of the split pin on the brake pedal pushrod and remove the clevis pin.
2 Wipe the master cylinder with a rag to remove any dirt and grease which may contaminate the hydraulic fluid.
3 On all models, unscrew the hydraulic union(s) from the master cylinder and drain the fluid into a suitable container. (If the master cylinder is not going to be dismantled, place a piece of polythene sheet over the reservoir top - see Section 6, paragraph 3).
4 Undo and remove the two nuts and spring washers securing the master cylinder to the bulkhead or servo unit. Carefully lift away ensuring no hydraulic fluid drips on the paintwork.
5 Installation is the reverse of the removal procedure. After topping up the reservoirs, bleed the master cylinder at the bleed nipples then bleed the hydraulic system, as described in Section 3. (photo)

## 13 Brake master cylinder (tandem) - dismantling and reassembly

**Note: Where a Nabeo master cylinder is installed, do not dismantle the primary piston.**
1 Remove both reservoir caps and rain out the hydraulic fluid (if not already drained).
2 Withdraw the pushrod assembly from the end of the cylinder body (applicable to non servo unit model).
3 Remove the rubber dust cover and then, using a pair of circlip pliers, release the circlip retaining the piston stopper in the end of the bore. Lift away the circlip and stopper.
4 Undo and remove the stopper screw located on the underside of the cylinder body.
5 The primary and secondary piston assemblies may now be withdrawn from the cylinder bore. Make a special note of the assembly order as the parts are removed.
6 Carefully remove the seals making a note of which way round they are installed.
7 Unscrew the plugs located on the underside of the cylinder body and withdraw the check valve parts. These must be kept in their respective sets.
8 Thoroughly clean the parts in brake fluid, isopropyl alcohol or methylated spirits. After drying the items, inspect the seals for signs of distortion, swelling, splitting or hardening although it is recommended new rubber parts are always fitted after dismantling as a matter of course.
9 Inspect the bore and piston for signs of deep scoring marks which, if evident, means a new cylinder should be fitted. Make sure that the ports in the bore are clean by poking gently with a piece of wire.
10 As the parts are refitted to the cylinder bore make sure that they are thoroughly wetted with clean hydraulic fluid.
11 Install new seals to the pistons making sure they are the correct way round as noted during removal.
12 With the cylinder bore well lubricated, insert the secondary return spring, secondary piston, primary return spring and primary piston into the bore. Take care not to roll the seal lips whilst inserting into the bore.

## 14 Brake master cylinder (single) - dismantling and reassembly

The basic procedures given in the previous Section are applicable to single master cylinders. Make sure that the lips of both piston seals face towards the front of the piston when reassembling.

## 15 Nissan load sensing valve (N.L.S.V.) - general

This device is used on some later models to prevent the rear wheels from locking under adverse braking conditions. The valve operates by changing the front and rear brake fluid pressure distribution in response to vehicle loading.
To check the operation of the N.L.S.V., first ensure that the braking system is operating satisfactorily and is correctly adjusted. Drive the vehicle, first with a full payload and then with the driver only, on a dry, flat road at 30 mph (40 km/hr).
Apply the brakes suddenly. If the vehicle stops in a distance of 43 ft (13.1 mm) or less, and the front wheels lock before or at the same time as the rear wheels, the N.L.S.V. is satifactory; this applies for a loaded or unloaded vehicle. If the vehicle stops in a distance of 43 ft (13.1 mm) or less, and the rear wheels lock before the front wheels, a replacement N.L.S.V. should be installed.

**9**

12.5 Correct installation of typical master cylinder

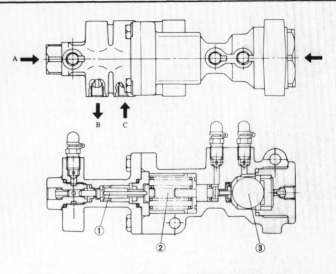

Fig. 9.19. Sectional view of Nissan load sensing valve (NLSV)

| | |
|---|---|
| A  From brake master cylinder front pressure side | 1  Plunger |
| B  To rear brake wheel cylinder | 2  Spring |
| C  From brake master cylinder rear pressure side | 3  Retainer ball |

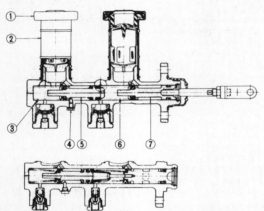

Fig. 9.17. Sectional view of Tokico (top) and Nabco (bottom) master cylinders

1  Reservoir cap
2  Reservoir
3  Secondary piston return spring
4  Stopper screw
5  Secondary piston
6  Primary piston return spring
7  Primary piston

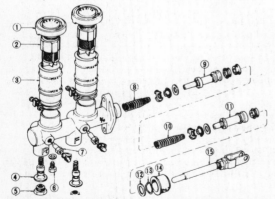

Fig. 9.18. Brake master cylinder (typical) - exploded view

1  Reservoir cap
2  Oil filter
3  Oil reservoir
4  Packing
5  Valve cap
6  Secondary piston stopper
7  Bleeder screw
8  Secondary return spring
9  Secondary piston
10  Primary return spring
11  Primary piston
12  Piston stopper
13  Piston stopper ring
14  Dust cover
15  Pushrod assembly

### 16 Master-Vac vacuum servo unit - description

A Master-Vac vacuum servo unit is fitted on most models in the Datsun pick-up range. It is in series with the master cylinder to provide assistance to the driver when the brake pedal is depressed. This reduces the effort required by the driver to operate the brakes under all braking conditions.

The unit operates by vacuum obtained from the intake manifold, and comprises basically a booster diaphragm and control valve assembly.

The servo unit and hydraulic master cylinder are connected together so that the servo unit piston rod (valve rod) acts as the master cylinder pushrod. The driver's braking effort is transmitted through another pushrod to the servo unit piston and its built-in control system. The servo unit piston is attached to a rolling diaphragm which ensures an airtight seal between the two major parts of the servo unit casing. The forward chamber is held under vacuum conditions created in the intake manifold of the engine and, during periods when the brake pedal is not in use, the controls open a passage to the rear chamber so placing it under vacuum conditions as well. When the brake pedal is depressed, the vacuum passage to the rear chamber is cut off and the chamber opened to atmospheric pressure. The consequent pressure difference across the servo piston pushes the piston forward in the vacuum chamber and operates the main pushrod to the master cylinder.

The controls are designed so that assistance is given under all conditions and, when the brakes are not required, vacuum in the rear chamber is established when the brake pedal is released.

Under normal operating conditions the vacuum servo unit is very reliable and does not require overhaul except at very high mileage. In this case it is far better to obtain a service exchange unit, rather than repair the original unit. If overhaul is to be carried out make sure that the necessary kit is available.

Although the vacuum unit is similar in appearance for all models, vehicles manufactured for the USA for 1976 have a stronger unit which must not be interchanged with other types. A caution label is fitted to these units, whereas other units have a yellow colored label.

### 17 Master-Vac vacuum servo unit - removal and installation

1  Remove the suction hose from the connection on the servo unit.
2  Remove the master cylinder; refer to Section 2, if necessary.

3 Using a pair of pliers, extract the split pin in the end of the brake pedal to pushrod clevis pin. Withdraw the clevis pin. To assist this it may be necessary to release the pedal return spring.

4 Undo and remove the four nuts and spring washers that secure the unit to the bulkhead. Lift the unit away from the engine bulkhead.

5 Installation of the servo unit is the reverse sequence to removal. Check the brake pedal movement and adjust as necessary as described in Section 2.

### 18 Master-Vac vacuum servo unit - dismantling, inspection and reassembly

Thoroughly clean the outside of the unit using a stiff brush and wipe with a lint-free rag. It cannot be too strongly emphasised that cleanliness is important when working on the servo unit. Before any attempt is made to dismantle, refer to Fig. 9.21 where it will be seen that two items of equipment are required. Firstly, a base plate must be made to enable the unit to be safely held in the vise. Secondly, a lever must be made similar to the form shown. Without these items it is impossible to dismantle satisfactorily.

To dismantle the unit proceed as follows:

1 Using a file or scriber, mark a line across the two halves of the unit to act as a datum for alignment.

2 Fit the previously made base-plate into a firm vice and attach the unit to the plate using the master cylinder studs.

3 Fit the lever over the four studs on the rear shell.

4 Use a piece of long rubber hose and connect one end to the adaptor on the engine inlet manifold and the other end to the servo unit. Start the engine and this will create a vacuum in the unit so drawing the two halves together.

5 Rotate the lever in a counter-clockwise direction until the front shell indentations are in line with the recesses in the rim of the rear shell. Then press the lever assembly down firmly whilst an assistant stops the engine and quickly removes the vacuum pipe from the inlet manifold connector. Depress the operating rod so as to release the vacuum, whereupon the front and rear halves should part. If necessary, use a soft faced hammer and slightly tap the front half to break the bond.

6 Unscrew the locknut and yoke from the pushrod and then remove the valve body rubber gaiter. Separate the diaphragm assembly from the rear shell.

7 Using a screwdriver, carefully pry out the retainer and then remove the bearing and seal from the shell. This operation should only be done if it is absolutely necessary to renew the seal or bearing.

8 Carefully detach the diaphragm from the diaphragm plate.

9 Using a screwdriver, carefully and evenly remove the air silencer retainer from the diaphragm plate.

10 Withdraw the valve plunger stop key by lightly pushing on the valve operating rod and sliding it from its location.

11 Withdraw the silencer and plunger assembly.

12 Next remove the reaction disc.

13 Remove the two nuts and spring washers, and withdraw the front seal assembly from the front cover. It is recommended that unless the seal is to be renwed it should be left in its housing.

14 Thoroughly clean all parts and wipe with a clean lint-free rag. Inspect for signs of damage, stripped threads etc, and obtain new parts as necessary. All seals must be renewed and for this a 'Major Repair Kit' should be purchased. This will also contain the special grease required during reassembly.

15 To reassemble, first apply a little of the special grease to the sealing surface and lip of the seal. Install the seal to the rear shell using a drift of suitable diameter. Ensure that dimension A (Fig. 9.22) is maintained.

16 Apply a little special grease to the sliding contact portions on the circumference of the plunger assembly.

17 Fit the plunger assembly and silencer into the diaphragm plate and retain in position with the stop key. As the plate is made of bakelite take care not to damage it during this operation.

18 Install the diaphragm into the cover and then smear a little special grease on the diaphragm plate. Install the reaction disc.

19 Smear a little special grease onto the inner wall of the seal and front shell with which the seal comes into contact. Install the front seal assembly.

20 Install the front shell to the base plate, and the lever to the rear shell Reconnect the vacuum hose. Position the diaphragm return spring in

the front shell. Lightly smear the outer head of the diaphragm with special grease and locate the diaphragm assembly in the rear shell. Position the rear shell assembly on the return spring and align the previously-made scribed marks.

21 Adjust the end of the pushrod to obtain dimension 'B' as in Fig. 9.23.

22 An assistant should start the engine. Watching one's fingers very carefully, press the two halves of the unit together and, using the lever tool, turn clockwise to lock the two halves together. Stop the engine and disconnect the hose.

23 Install the servo unit for correct operation after overhaul, first start the engine and run for a minimum period of two minutes and then switch off. Wait for ten minutes and apply the footbrake very carefully, listening to hear the rush of air into the servo unit. This will indicate that vacuum was retained and the unit is operating correctly.

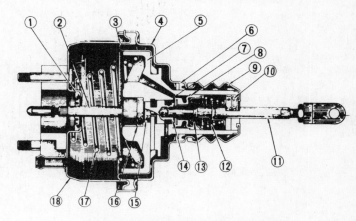

**Fig. 9.20. Master-Vac - sectional view**

| | | | |
|---|---|---|---|
| 1 | Plate and seal | 10 | Air silencer filter |
| 2 | Pushrod | 11 | Valve operating rod |
| 3 | Rolling diaphragm | 12 | Return spring |
| 4 | Rear shell | 13 | Poppet return spring |
| 5 | Diaphragm plate | 14 | Exhaust valve |
| 6 | Seal | 15 | Valve plunger |
| 7 | Vacuum valve | 16 | Reaction disc |
| 8 | Poppet assembly | 17 | Diaphragm return spring |
| 9 | Valve body rubber gaiter | 18 | Front shell |

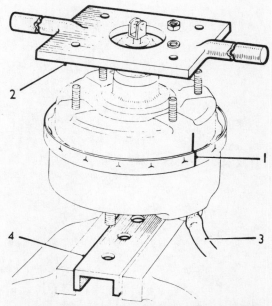

**Fig. 9.21. Special tools required to dismantle servo unit**

| | | | |
|---|---|---|---|
| 1 | Scribe marks | 3 | Vacuum applied |
| 2 | Lever | 4 | Base plate |

**9**

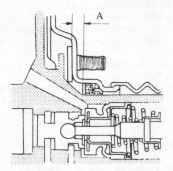

**Fig. 9.22. Installation dimension for the seal**
*A = 0.264 to 0.276 in (6.7 to 7.0 mm)*

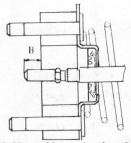

**Fig. 9.23. Master-Vac pushrod setting dimension**
*B = 0.394 to 0.413 in (10 to 10.5 mm)*

## 19 Check valve - removal and installation

1   On models fitted with a vacuum servo unit a small check valve is fitted in the vacuum line and attached to the bulkhead. If its operation be suspect the car should be taken to the local dealer for a pressure test.
2   To remove the valve, undo and remove the securing bracket retaining screws and lift away the bracket. Slacken the two clips and detach the two hoses.
3   Installation is the reverse of the removal procedure.

## 20 Brake pedal - removal and installation

1   Note which way round the pedal return spring is fitted and remove the spring.
2   Withdraw the spring pin that secures the brake pedal to pushrod cotter pin. Remove the cotter pin and washer, and then separate the pushrod from the pedal.
3   Undo and remove the nut securing the pedal fulcrum pin. Note that on RHD models the fulcrum pin nut must be unscrewed counter clockwise whereas on LHD models it must be unscrewed clockwise.
4   Lift away the washer and withdraw the fulcrum pin. The pedal may now be lifted from its support bracket.
5   If the pedal split bushes have worn they may be removed by tapping out with a small drift.
6   Installation is the reverse sequence to removal. Lubricate the bushes with a little general purpose grease.
7   Check the pedal height and fully depressed positons, and adjust as necessary at the pushrod yoke or switch until correct movement is obtained (see Section 2).

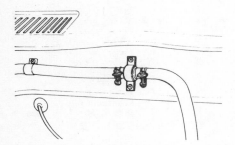

**Fig. 9.24. Check valve location**

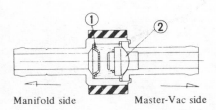

**Fig. 9.25. Sectional view of check valve**

*1  Spring*        *2  Valve head*

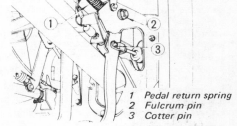

*1  Pedal return spring*
*2  Fulcrum pin*
*3  Cotter pin*

**Fig. 9.26. Brake pedal location**

## 21 Parking brake (handbrake) - removal and installation

### Control handle
1   Disconnect the wire from the parking brake switch terminal.
2   Remove the nuts securing the control bracket beneath the dash panel.
3   Pull out the lock pin and cotter pin, then remove the control handle assembly.
4   Installation is the reverse of the removal profedure; apply a little general purpose grease to all sliding surfaces and pivot points.

### Cable (UK and 1973/74 models)
5   Release the parking brake then loosen the adjusting nut at the cable lever (photo).
6   Disconnect the cable from the control lever.
7   Remove both rear brake drums and disconnect the rear cable from the toggle levers. Refer to Section 8, for further information, if necessary.
8   Detach the lockplate, spring and clip, and carefully pull out the cable from the cable lever.
9   Withdraw the spring pin and remove the cotter pin located at the cable lever. Finally disconnect the cable.
10  Installation of the cable is the reverse of the removal procedure; apply a little general purpose grease to all sliding surfaces and pivot points.

**21.5 Parking brake cable lever - UK model shown**

*Front cable (1975/1976 USA models)*
11 Release the parking brake then loosen the adjusting nut at the balance lever.
12 Disconnect the cable from the balance lever.
13 Remove the retainer spring at the cable guide bushing.
14 Disconnect the rear cables at the balance lever bracket.
15 Remove the balance lever brackets from the vehicle crossmember.
16 Detach the front cable clip, then pull the cable rearward to remove it.
17 Installation of the front cable is the reverse of the removal procedure; apply a little general purpose grease to all sliding surfaces and pivot points.

*Rear cable (1975/76 USA models)*
18 Release the parking brake.
19 Remove both rear brake drums and disconnect the rear cables from the toggle levers. Refer to Section 8 for further information, if necessary.
20 Detach the spring and spring retainer, and remove the rear cable from the brake backplate.
21 Disconnect the rear cables from the balance lever bracket.
22 Detach the cable clips and remove the rear cables.
23 Installation is the reverse of the removal procedure; apply a little general purpose grease to all sliding surfaces and pivot points.

*Parking brake and parking brake warning lamp switch - adjustment*
24 The adjustment procedure is given in Section 2.

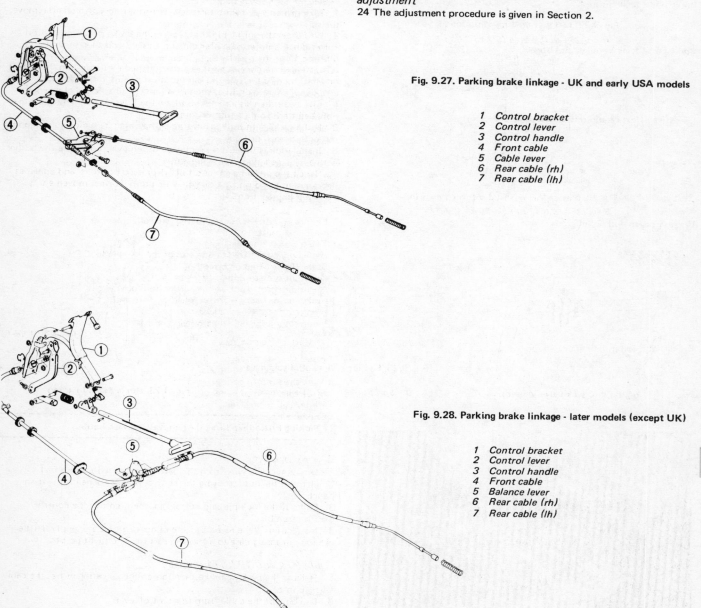

Fig. 9.27. Parking brake linkage - UK and early USA models

1  Control bracket
2  Control lever
3  Control handle
4  Front cable
5  Cable lever
6  Rear cable (rh)
7  Rear cable (lh)

Fig. 9.28. Parking brake linkage - later models (except UK)

1  Control bracket
2  Control lever
3  Control handle
4  Front cable
5  Balance lever
6  Rear cable (rh)
7  Rear cable (lh)

**9**

## 22 Fault diagnosis - braking system

| Symptom | Reason/s |
| --- | --- |
| Pedal travels almost to floor before brakes operate | Brake fluid level too low.<br>Wheel cylinder leaking.<br>Master cylinder leaking (bubbles in master cylinder fluid).<br>Brake flexible hose leaking.<br>Brake line fractured.<br>Brake system unions loose.<br>Shoes linings excessively worn. |
| Brake pedal feels 'springy' | New linings not yet bedded-in.<br>Brake drums badly worn or cracked.<br>Master cylinder securing nuts loose. |
| Brake pedal feels 'spongy' and 'soggy' | Wheel cylinder leaking.<br>Master cylinder leaking (bubbles in master cylinder reservoir).<br>Brake pipe line or flexible hose leaking.<br>Unions in brake system loose.<br>Blocked reservoir cap vent hole. |
| Excessive effort required to brake vehicle | Shoe linings badly worn.<br>New shoes recently fitted - not yet bedded-in.<br>Harder linings fitted than standard resulting in increase in pedal pressure.<br>Linings and brake drums contaminated with oil, grease or hydraulic fluid.<br>Servo unit inoperative or faulty.<br>Scored drums. |
| Brakes uneven and pulling to one side | Linings and drums contaminated with oil, grease or hydraulic fluid.<br>Tire pressure unequal.<br>Radial ply tires fitted at one end of the vehicle only.<br>Brake shoes fitted incorrectly.<br>Different type of linings fitted at each wheel.<br>Anchorages for front or rear suspension loose.<br>Brake drums badly worn, cracked or distorted.<br>Incorrect front wheel alignment.<br>Incorrectly adjusted front wheel bearings. |
| Brakes tend to bind, drag or lock-on | Air in hydraulic system.<br>Wheel cylinders seized.<br>Handbrake cables too tight.<br>Weak shoe return springs.<br>Incorrecly set foot pedal or pushrod.<br>Master cylinder seized.<br>Brakes over-adjusted. |

# Chapter 10 Electrical system

*Refer to Chapter 13 for specifications and information applicable to 1977 through 1979 USA models*

## Contents

## Specifications

| | |
|---|---|
| **System type** ... ... ... ... ... ... ... ... ... | 12V, negative ground (earth) |
| Battery: | |
| Type ... ... ... ... ... ... ... ... ... ... | Lead acid. |
| Rating ... ... ... ... ... ... ... ... ... | Varies according to market, consult your Datsun dealer or battery specialist for a replacement. |

### Alternator

| | |
|---|---|
| Type ... ... ... ... ... ... ... ... ... ... | Hitachi LT 135-13B (LT 135-19B or LT 150-05 option) |
| Rating: | |
| LT135 series ... ... ... ... ... ... ... | 35 amps at 12 volts. |
| LT150 series ... ... ... ... ... ... ... | 50 amps at 12 volts. |
| Output current (hot) at rpm: | |
| LT135 series ... ... ... ... ... ... ... | 28 amps at 2500 rpm |
| LT150 series ... ... ... ... ... ... ... | 37.5 amps at 2500 rpm |
| Pulley ratio ... ... ... ... ... ... ... | 2.25 : 1 |
| Brush length (minimum) ... ... ... ... ... | 0.295 in (7.5 mm) |
| Brush spring pressure ... ... ... ... ... ... | 9.0 to 12.2 oz (255 to 345 gm) |
| Slip ring outer diameter (minimum) ... ... ... ... | 1.181 in (30 mm) |

### Charge regulator

| | |
|---|---|
| Type: | |
| 1973/74 USA ... ... ... ... ... ... ... | TL 1Z-57 |
| 1975/76 USA ... ... ... ... ... ... ... | TL 1Z-85 |
| Other markets ... ... ... ... ... ... ... | TL 1Z-61 |

| | TL 1Z-57 and 85 | TL 1Z-61 |
|---|---|---|
| Regulating voltage (with fully charged battery) ... ... ... ... ... | 14.3 to 15.3V at 68°F (20°C) | 13.8 to 14.8V at 68°F (20°C) |
| Voltage coil resistance ... ... ... ... | 10.5 ohms at 68°F (20°C) | 10.3 ohms at 68°F (20°C) |
| Core gap ... ... ... ... ... ... ... | 0.024 to 0.039 in (0.6 to 1.0 mm) | 0.024 to 0.039 in (0.6 to 1.0 mm) |
| Points gap ... ... ... ... ... ... ... | 0.012 to 0.016 in (0.3 to 0.4 mm) | 0.012 to 0.016 in (0.3 to 0.4 mm) |

## Cut-out

|  | TL 1Z-57 and 85 | TL 1Z-61 |
|---|---|---|
| Release voltage ... ... ... ... | 8 to 10V at 'A' terminal | 8 to 10V at 'A' terminal |
| Voltage coil resistance ... ... ... | 37.8 ohms at 68°F (20°C) | 31.9 ohms at 68°F (20°C) |
| Core gap ... ... ... ... ... | 0.032 to 0.039 in (0.8 to 1.0 mm) | 0.032 to 0.039 in (0.8 to 1.0 mm) |
| Points gap ... ... ... ... | 0.016 to 0.024 in (0.4 to0.6 mm) | 0.016 to 0.024 in (0.4 to 0.6 mm) |

## Starter motor

Manufacturer and type ...   ...   ...   ...   ...   ...   ...   Hitachi pre-engaged

|  | General usage, including UK. | 1973, 1974 USA Manual Transmission | 1973, 1974 USA Automatic Transmission | 1975, 1976 USA Manual Transmission | 1975, 1976 USA Automatic Transmission |
|---|---|---|---|---|---|
| Model ... ... ... ... ... | S114-92K | S114-103P | S114-126M | S114-170 | S114-180 |
| Output ... ... ... ... ... | 1.0 kw | 1.0 kw | 1.2 kw | 1.2 kw | 1.2 kw |
| Starting current ... ... ... ... | less than 420 | less than 480A (6V) | less than 540A (5V) | less than 540A (5V) | less than 500A (5V) |
| No load current ... ... ... |  |  | less than 60A (12V) |  |  |
| No load speed ... ... ... | in excess of 7000 rpm | in excess of 7000 rpm | in excess of 6000 rpm | in excess of 7000 rpm | in excess of 6000 rpm |

## Fuses

| Fusebox location ... ... ... ... ... ... ... ... | Beneath instrument panel, between steering column and driver's side door |
|---|---|
| Fuse rating and protected circuits ... ... ... ... | Stated on fusebox cover. |

## Fusible link

| Color ... ... ... ... ... ... ... ... ... | Green |
|---|---|
| Location ... ... ... ... ... ... ... ... | In battery positive lead |
| Rating ... ... ... ... ... ... ... ... | 20 amp continuous |
|  | 200 amp for 5 seconds |

## Bulbs

|  | WATTAGE | |
|---|---|---|
|  | USA and Canada | General areas. including UK. |
| Headlamp: | | |
|     Inner - high beam ... ... ... ... ... ... ... | 37.5 | 37.5 |
|     Outer - low beam/high beam ... ... ... ... ... ... | 37.5/50 | 37.5/50 |
| Front combination lamp: | | |
|     Turn signal ... ... ... ... ... ... ... ... | 8/23 | 21 |
|     Parking lamp ... ... ... ... ... ... ... | — | 5 |
| Side flasher ... ... ... ... ... ... ... ... | — | 5 |
| Side marker ... ... ... ... ... ... ... ... | 8 | — |
| License plate ... ... ... ... ... ... ... | 7.5 | 10 |
| Rear combination lamp: | | |
|     Turn signal ... ... ... ... ... ... ... | — | 21 |
|     Turn signal/stop lamp ... ... ... ... ... ... ... | 23 | — |
|     Tail/stoplamp ... ... ... ... ... ... ... | — | 5/21 |
|     Tail/turn signal and stoplamp ... ... ... ... ... | 8/23 | — |
|     Tail lamp ... ... ... ... ... ... ... ... | 8 | 5 |
| Back-up lamp (reverse lamp) ... ... ... ... ... ... | 23 | 21 |
| Cab light ... ... ... ... ... ... ... ... | 5 | 5 |
| Engine compartment light ... ... ... ... ... ... | 6 | 6 |
| Wiper/washer illumination lamp ... ... ... ... ... | 3.4 | — |
| Heater control illumination lamp ... ... ... ... ... | 3.4 |  |
| Instrument panel and warning lamps (except tachometer) ... ... ... ... | 1.7 | 1.7 |
| Tachometer illumination lamp ... ... ... ... ... ... | 3.4 | 3.4 |

## 1  General description

The electrical system is of 12 volt negative ground (earth) type. The major components comprise the battery, a belt-driven alternator and a pre-engaged starter motor.

The battery supplies a steady current to the ignition system (see Chapter 4), and for the operation of the electrical accessories.

The alternator maintains the charge in the battery, and the voltage regulator adjusts the charging rate according to the system demands. Silicon diodes within the alternator rectify the alternating current produced into direct current. A cut-out prevents the battery discharging when the engine is switched off or when it is running at idle speed.

## 2  Battery - removal and installation

1   The battery is located within the engine compartment at the right

front side.

2   When removing the battery, always disconnect the negative (ground) cable first, followed by the positive cable. Then remove the nuts from the battery clamps and lift out the battery.

3   Installation is the reverse of the removal procedure but before fitting the terminals smear them with a little petroleum jelly.

## 3  Battery - maintenance and inspection

1   Keep the top of the battery clean by wiping away dirt and moisture.

2   Remove the plugs or lid from the cells and check that the electrolyte level is just above the separator plates. If the level has fallen, add only distilled water until the electrolyte level is just above the separator plates.

3   As well as keeping the terminals clean and covered with petroleum jelly, the top of the battery, and especially the top of the cells, should be kept clean and dry. This helps prevent corrosion and ensures that the

battery does not become partially discharged by leakage through dampness and dirt.

4   Once every three months, remove the battery and inspect the battery securing bolts, the battery clamp plate, tray and battery leads for corrosion (white fluffy deposits on the metal which is brittle to touch). If any corrosion is found, clean off the deposits with an ammonia or soda solution and paint over the clean metal with a fine base primer and/or underbody paint.

5   At the same time inspect the battery case for cracks. If a crack is found, clean and plug it with one of the proprietary compounds marketed for this purpose. If leakage through the crack has been excessive then it will be necessary to refill the appropriate cell with fresh electrolyte as detailed later. Cracks are frequently caused to the top of the battery cases by pouring in distilled water in the middle of winter after instead of before a run. This gives the water no chance to mix with the electrolyte and so the former freezes and splits the battery case.

6   If topping-up the battery becomes excessive and the case has been inspected for cracks that could cause leakage, but none are found, the battery is being over-charged and the voltage regulator will have to be checked and reset.

7   With the battery on the bench at the three monthly interval check, measure its specific gravity with a hydrometer to determine the state of charge and condition of the electrolyte. There should be very little variation between the different cells and if a variation in excess of 0.025 is present it will be due to either:

   *a) Loss of electrolyte from the battery at some time caused by spillage or a leak, resulting in a drop in the specific gravity of electrolyte when the deficiency was replaced with distilled water instead of fresh electrolyte.*

   *b) An internal short circuit caused by buckling of the plates or a similar malady pointing to the likelihood of total battery failure in the near future.*

8   The specific gravity of the electrolyte for fully charged conditions at the electrolyte temperature indicated, is listed in Table A. The specific gravity of a fully discharged battery at different temperatures of the electrolyte is given in Table B.

### Table A
*Specific Gravity - Battery Fully Charged*
1.268 at 100°F or 38°C electrolyte temperature
1.272 at  90°F or 32°C electrolyte temperature
1.276 at  80°F or 27°C electrolyte temperature
1.280 at  70°F or 21°C electrolyte temperaute
1.284 at  60°F or 16°C electrolyte temperature
1.288 at  50°F or 10°C electrolyte temperature
1.292 at  40°F or  4°C electrolyte temperature
1.296 at  30°F or-1.5°C electrolyte temperaute

### Table B
*Specific Gravity - Battery Fully Discharged*
1.098 at 100°F or 38°C electrolyte temperature
1.102 at  90°F or 32°C electrolyte temperature
1.106 at  80°F or 27°C electrolyte temperature
1.110 at  70°F or 21°C electrolyte temperature
1.114 at  60°F or 16°C electrolyte temperature
1.118 at  50°F or 10°C electrolyte temperature
1.112 at  40°F or  4°C electrolyte temperature
1.126 at  30°F or-1.5°C electrolyte temperature

## 4   Electrolyte replenishment

1   If the battery is in a fully charged state and one of the cells maintains a specific gravity reading which is 0.025 or more lower than the others, and a check of each cell has been made with a battery testing meter to check for short circuits (a four to seven second test should give a steady reading of between 1.2 to 1.8 volts), then it is likely that electrolyte has been lost from the cell with the low reading at some time.

2   Top up the cell with a solution of 1 part sulphuric acid to 2.5 parts water. If the cell is already fully topped up draw some electrolyte out of it with a pipette.

3   When mixing the sulphuric acid and water **never add water to sulphuric acid** - always pour the acid slowly onto the water in a glass container. **If water is added to sulphuric acid it will explode.**

4   Continue to top-up the cell with the freshly made electrolyte and

then recharge the battery and check the hydrometer readings.
**Note: If the battery is not removed from the vehicle when being charged it is essential that the cables are disconnected as described in Section 2.**

## 5   Battery charging

1   Under normal operating conditions there should be no need to charge a battery from an external source, and if it is found to be necessary either the battery or alternator is at fault.

2   When a vehicle has not been used for a period of time (particularly in very cold conditions) and it s found that the battery condition will not allow the engine to start, it is a good idea to charge the battery for about five hours at an initial charging current of around five amps (The amount of charge and charging time will obviously depend on the battery condition, but the charging current will fall as the battery charge builds up). Alternatively a trickle charge at an initial current of about 1.5 amps can safely be used overnight.

3   The use of rapid boost chargers, which are claimed to restore the full charge of a battery in a very short time, should be avoided if at all possible as the battery plates are likely to suffer damage.

## 6   Alternator - general description, maintenance and precautions

1   Briefly, the alternator comprises a rotor and stator. Current is generated in the coils of the stator as soon as the rotor revolves. This current is three-phase alternating, which is then rectified by positive and negative silicon diodes; the charging current required to maintain the battery charge is controlled by a regulator unit.

2   Maintenance consists of occasionally wiping away any oil or dirt which may have accumulated on the outside of the unit.

3   No lubrication is required as the bearings are grease-sealed for life.

4   Check the drivebelt tension periodically to ensure that its specified deflection is correctly maintained (See Chapter 2).

5   Take extreme care when making circuit connections to a vehicle fitted with an alternator and observe the following. When making connections to the alternator from a battery, always match correct polarity. Before using electric-arc welding equipment to repair any part of the vehicle, disconnect the connector from the alternator and disconnect the battery cables. Never start the car with the battery charger connected. Always disconnect both battery cables before using a mains charger. If boosting from another battery, always connect in parallel using heavy cable.

## 7   Alternator - testing in the vehicle

1   Where a faulty alternator is suspected, first ensure that the battery is fully charged; If necessary charge from an outside source.

2   Obtain a 0 to 30 voltmeter.

3   Disconnect the leads from the alternator terminals.

4   Connect a test probe from the voltmeter positive terminal to the 'N' or 'BAT' terminal of the alternator. Connect the voltmeter negative terminal to earth and check that the voltmeter indicates battery voltage (12 volts).

5   Switch the headlamps to main beam.

6   Start the engine and gradually increase its speed to approximately 1100 rev/min and check the reading on the voltmeter. If it registers over 12.5 volts then the alternator is in good condition; if it registers below 12.5 volts then the alternator is faulty, and must be removed and repaired.

## 8   Alternator - removal and installation

1   Disconnect the battery ground cable.

2   Disconnect the two lead wires and the electrical connector from the rear of the alternator.

3   Loosen the alternator pivot (mounting) bolts, and the bolt on the adjusting link.

4   Push the alternator towards the engine and remove the fanbelt.

5   Remove the bolts completely and lift away the alternator.

6   Installation is the reverse of the removal procedure. Adjust the fanbelt tension, as described in Chapter 2.

**10**

## 9 Alternator - brush renewal

1 These are the most likely components to require renewal, and their wear should be checked at 50000 mile (80000 km) intervals or whenever the alternator is suspected of being faulty (indicated by a discharged battery).

2 Remove the brush holder cover securing screws and withdraw the cover.

3 Remove the brush holder complete with brushes. Do not disconnect the 'N' terminal from the stator coil lead.

4 If the brushes have worn down to the limit line marked on them, renew them.

5 Check that the brushes move smoothly in their holders; otherwise clean the holders free from any dust or dirt.

6 Installation of the new brushes is the reverse of the removal procedure.

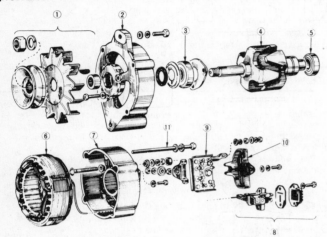

**Fig. 10.1. Alternator - exploded view (typical)**

| | | |
|---|---|---|
| 1 *Pulley group* | 5 *Rear bearing* | 9 *Diode set* |
| 2 *Front cover* | 6 *Stator* | 10 *Diode cover* |
| 3 *Front bearing* | 7 *Rear cover* | 11 *Through bolts* |
| 4 *Rotor* | 8 *Brush assembly* | |

**Fig. 10.2. Alternator 'A' terminal assembly**

| | |
|---|---|
| 1 *Insulator bush* | 4 *Rear cover* |
| 2 *'A' terminal bolt* | 5 *Diode set* |
| 3 *Diode cover* | |

## 10 Alternator - dismantling, servicing and reassembly

1 Components of any alternator have a very long life and apart from the brushes, any malfunction is most economically overcome by fitting an exchange unit. For those who prefer to overhaul the original unit however, the following procedure will apply. **Note:** When using the soldering iron it is important that the minimum ammount of heat is applied when soldering or unsoldering diode connections, to avoid permanent damage to the diodes. Wherever possible use a pair of pliers on the diode lead between the diode body and the soldered joint to act as a heat shunt.

2 Clean dirt, dust and oil from the external surfaces.

3 From the front of the alternator, remove the nut, pulley and fan.

4 Remove the brush holder assembly, as described in the preceeding Section.

5 Unscrew and remove the tie-bolts.

6 Separate the front cover (complete with rotor) from the rear cover and stator, by gently tapping the front mounting bracket with a soft-faced hammer.

7 Remove the bearing retainer setscrews from the front face of the front cover and separate the rotor from the front cover.

8 If necessary, remove the rear bearing from the rotor shaft with a suitable puller.

9 Remove the diode cover fixing screw and withdraw the cover.

10 Disconnect the three stator coil leads from the diode terminals using a soldering iron.

11 Unscrew the alternator 'A' terminal nut and the diode assembly securing nut and withdraw the assembly.

12 To avoid unnecessary expense in the purchase of sound components, carry out the following tests.

13 Using an ohmmeter, test the rotor coils for continuity. Apply the probes of the meter to the slip rings, the meter should indicate 4.4 ohms. If there is no reading then there is probably a break in the field coils and the rotor mustbe renewed.

14 Next test the rotor for insulation breakdown by placing the probes, one on the slip ring and one on the rotor core. If the meter shows any reading then the slip ring or rotor coil is earthing, probably due to faulty insulation.

15 Check the stator for continuity by connecting the meter probes to the stator coil terminals. If no reading is indicated on the meter then the coil wiring is broken.

16 Now connect one probe to each of the stator coil terminals in turn. No reading should be indicated, otherwise the insulation of the coil has broken down.

17 Check that the diodes conduct in one direction only by connecting the ohmmeter probes to terminal lead and the case of each diode in turn. It will be necessary to reverse the polarity of the probes, according to which set of three diodes is being checked. If a diode conducts in both directions or neither direction, a replacement must be obtained.

18 Reassembly is basically the reverse of the dismantling procedure. Ensure that the diode 'A' terminal is correctly assembled with the insulating bush and tube (Fig. 10.2).

## 11 Regulator - description, testing and adjustment

1 The regulator is located on the right side of the engine compartment, and incorporates a separate voltage regulator and cut-out (photo).

2 The voltage regulator controls the output from the alternator depending upon the state of the battery and the demands of the vehicle electrical equipment, and it ensures that the battery is not overcharged. The cut-out is virtually an automatic switch which completes the charging circuit as soon as the alternator starts to rotate and isolates it when the engine stops so that the battery cannot be discharged through the alternator. One visual indication of the correct functioning of the cut-out is the ignition warning lamp. When the lamp is out, the system is charging.

3 Before testing, check that the alternator drivebelt is not broken or slack, and that all electrical leads are secure.

4 Test the regulator voltage with the unit still installed in the vehicle. If it has been removed make sure that it is positioned with the connector plug hanging downward. Carry out the testing with the engine compartment cold, and complete the test within one minute to prevent the regulator heating up and affecting the specified voltage readings.

5 Establish the ambient temperature within the engine compartment, turn off all vehicle electrical equipment and ensure that the battery is in a fully charged state. Connect a d.c. (0 to 20v) voltmeter a.d.c. (0 to 10A) ammeter and a 0.25 ohm 25 watt resistor, as shown (Fig. 10.3).

6 Start the engine and immediately detach the short circuit wire. Increase the engine speed to 2500 rpm and check the voltmeter reading according to the pre-determined ambient temperature table below.

7 If the voltage does not conform to that specified, continue to run the engine at 2500 rpm for several minutes and then with the engine idling check that the ammeter reads below 5 amps. If the reading is above this, the battery is not fully charged and must be removed for charging as otherwise accurate testing cannot be carried out.

| Ambient temperature | | Rated regulating voltage |
|---|---|---|
| °C | (°F) | (V) |
| −10 | (14) | 14.75 to 15.75 |
| 0 | (32) | 14.60 to 15.60 |
| 10 | (50) | 14.45 to 15.45 |
| 20 | (68) | 14.30 to 15.30 |
| 30 | (86) | 14.15 to 15.15 |
| 40 | (104) | 14.00 to 15.00 |

8 Switch off the engine, remove the cover from the voltage regulator and inspect the surfaces of the contacts. If, these are rough or pitted, clean them by drawing a strip of very fine emery cloth between them.

9 Using feeler gauges, check and adjust the core gap, if necessary, to between 0.024 and 0.040 in (0.6 and 1.0 mm).

10 Check and adjust the contact point gap if necessary, to between 0.012 and 0.16 in (0.3 and 0.4 mm).

11 By now the voltage regulator will have cooled down so that the previous test may be repeated. If the voltage/temperature are still not compatible, switch off the engine and adjust the regulator screw. Do this by loosening the locknut and turning the screw clockwise to increase the voltage reading and counter clockwise to reduce it.

12 Turn the adjuster screw only fractionally before retesting the voltage charging rate again with the unit cold. Finally tighten the locknut.

13 If the cut-out is operating incorrectly, first check the fan belt and the ignition warning lamp bulb. Connect the positive terminal of a d.c. voltmeter to the 'N' socket of the regulator connector plug, and the voltmeter negative terminal to ground as shown (Fig. 10.4).

14 Start the engine and let it idle. Check the voltmeter reading. If the reading is zero volts, check for continuity between the 'N' terminals of the regulator unit and the alternator. If the reading is below 5.2 volts and the ignition warning lamp remains on, check and adjust the

core gap to between 0.032 and 0.040 in (0.8 and 1.0 mm) and the points gap to between 0.016 and 0.024 in (0.4 and 0.6 mm). Remember that this time the adjustments are carried out to the cut-out not the voltage regulator although the procedure is similar.

15 If the reading is over 5.2 volts with the ignition warning lamp on, and the core and points gap are correctly set, the complete regulator unit must be renewed.

16 The cut-out is operating correctly if the voltmeter shows a reading of more than 5.2 volts (ignition lamp out).

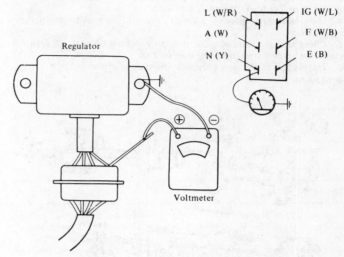

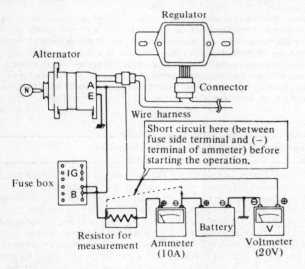

Fig. 10.3. Regulating voltage measurement

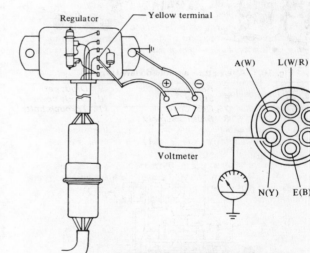

Fig. 10.4. Charging relay checks
Alternative arrangements shown

**10**

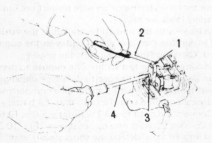

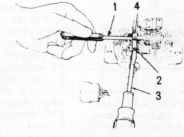

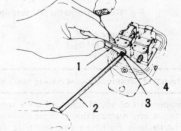

Fig. 10.5. Checking and adjusting voltage regulator core gap

Fig. 10.6. Checking and adjusting voltage regulator points gap

Fig. 10.7. Adjusting voltage regulating screw on voltage regulator

| 1  Contacts | 3  Adjusting screw |
|---|---|
| 2  Feeler blade | 4  Screwdriver |

| 1  Feeler blade | 3  Screwdriver |
|---|---|
| 2  Adjusting screw | 4  Upper contact |

| 1  Spanner | 3  Adjusting screw |
|---|---|
| 2  Screwdriver | 4  Locknut |

11.1 Regulator location on right side of engine compartment

## 12 Starter motor - general description

1   This type of starter motor incorporates a solenoid mounted on top of the starter motor body. When the ignition switch is operated, the solenoid moves the starter drive pinion, through the medium of the shift lever, into engagement with the flywheel or driveplate starter ring gear. As the solenoid reaches the end of its stroke and with the pinion by now partially engaged with the flywheel ring gear, the main fixed and moving contacts close and energize the starter motor to rotate the engine. This fractional pre-engagement of the starter drive does much to reduce the wear on the flywheel ring gear associated with inertia type starter motors.

## 13 Starter motor - removal and installation

1   Disconnect the battery ground lead.
2   Disconnect the black and yellow wire from the 'S' terminal on the solenoid, and the black cable from the 'B' terminal (also on the end cover of the solenoid).
3   Unscrew and remove the two starter motor securing bolts, pull the starter forward, tilt it slightly to clear the motor shaft support from the flywheel ring gear and withdraw it.
4   Installation is the reverse of the removal procedure.

## 14 Starter motor - dismantling, servicing and reassembly

1   Disconnect the lead from the 'M' terminal of the solenoid.
2   Remove the solenoid securing screws and withdraw the solenoid from the starter motor.
3   Remove the dust cover, the 'E' ring and the two thrust washers from the rear cover S114-170/180 starter motors only).
4   Unscrew and remove the two screws which secure the brush holder.
5   Unscrew and remove the two tie-bolts and the rear cover.
6   Using a length of wire with a hook at its end, remove the brushes by pulling the brush springs aside.
7   Remove the brush holder.
8   Withdraw the yoke assembly and extract the armature assembly and shift lever. Push the pinion stop towards the pinion to expose the circlip. Extract the circlip and then withdraw the stop and clutch assembly.
9   Check the brushes for wear. If their length is less than 0.472 in (12.0 mm), renew them.
10 If the ohmmeter is available, test the field coil for continuity. To do this, connect one probe of the meter to the field coil positive terminal and the other to the positive brush holder. If no reading is indicated then the field coil circuit has a break in it.
11 Connect one probe of the meter to the field coil positive lead and the other one to the yoke. If there is a low resistance, then the field coil is earthed due to a breakdown in insulation. When this fault is discovered, the field coils should be renewed by an automotive electrician as it is very difficult to remove the field coil securing screws without special equipment. In any event, it will probably be more economical to exchange the complete starter motor for a reconditioned unit.
12 Undercut the separators of the commutator using an old hacksaw blade ground to suit to a depth of 0.02 to 0.03 in (0.5 to 0.8 mm). The commutator may be polished with a piece of very fine glass paper - never use emery cloth as the carborundum particles will become embedded in the copper surfaces.
13 The armature may be tested for insulation breakdown again using the ohmmeter. To do this, place one probe on the armature shaft and the other on each of the commutator segments in turn. If there is a reading inidcated at any time during the test then the armature must be renewed.
14 Wash the components of the drive gear in kerosene (paraffin) inspect for wear or damage, particularly to the pinion teeth and renew as appropriate. Refitting is a reversal of dismantling but stake a new stop washer in position and lubricate the sliding surfaces of the pinion assembly with a light oil, applied sparingly.
15 Reassembly of the remaining components of the starter motor is the reverse of the dismantling procedure.
16 When the starter motor has been fully reassembled, actuate the solenoid which will throw the drive gear forward into its normal flywheel engagement position. Do this by connecting jumper leads between the battery negative terminal and the solenoid 'M' terminal and between the battery positive terminal and the solenoid 'S' terminal. Now check the gap between the end face of the drive pinion and the mating face of the thrust washer. This should be between 0.012 and 0.059 in (0.3 to 1.5 mm) measured either with a vernier or feeler gauge. Adjusting washers are available in different thicknesses.

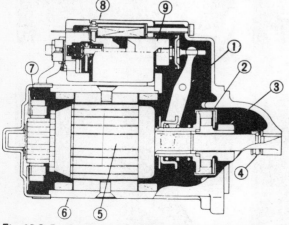

Fig. 10.8. Sectional view of typical Hitachi starter motor

1   *Shift lever*        5   *Armature*
2   *Over-running clutch*  6   *Yoke*
3   *Pinion*             7   *Brush*
4   *Pinion stop*        8   *Solenoid*
                         9   *Plunger*

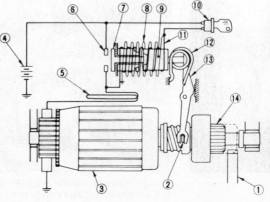

Fig. 10.9. Starting circuit

1   *Flywheel ring gear*
2   *Shift lever guide*
3   *Armature*
4   *Battery*
5   *Field coil*
6   *Stationary contact*
7   *Moving contact*
8   *Shunt coil*
9   *Plunger*
10  *Ignition switch*
11  *Series coil*
12  *Torsion spring*
13  *Shift lever*
14  *Pinion*

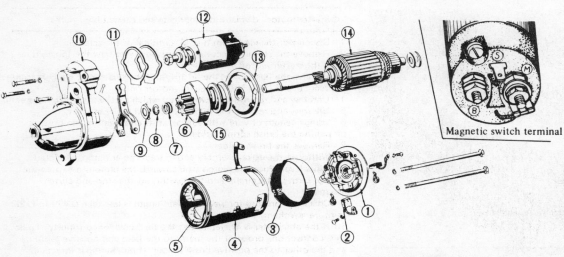

**Fig. 10.10. Exploded view of typical starter motor**

1  Rear cover
2  Brush
3  Brush cover
4  Yoke
5  Field coil
6  Pinion gear
7  Pinion stopper
8  Stopper clip
9  Stopper washer
10  Gear case
11  Shift lever
12  Solenoid assembly
13  Center bracket
14  Armature
15  Over-running clutch

Magnetic switch terminal

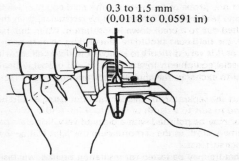

0.3 to 1.5 mm
(0.0118 to 0.0591 in)

**Fig. 10.11. Gap measurement, drive pinion end face-to-thrust washer face**

### 15  Fuses and fusible link

1  The fusebox is located beneath the instrument panel between the steering column and the driver's door. Fuse ratings and the circuits protected are marked on the fusebox (photos).

2  A fusible link is incorporated in the battery-to-alternator wiring harness within the engine compartment. It provides an additional protection for the starting, charging, lighting and accessory circuits (photo).

3  In the event of a fuse or fusible link blowing, always establish the cause before installing a new one. This is most likely to be due to faulty insulation somewhere in the wiring circuit. Always carry a spare fuse for each rating, and never be tempted to substitute a piece of wire or a nail for the correct fuse as a fire may be caused or, at least, the electrical component ruined.

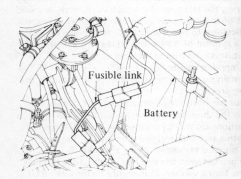

Fusible link

Battery

**Fig. 10.12. Fusible link location - typical**

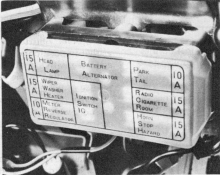

15.1a Fusebox cover ...

15.1b ... and fuses

10

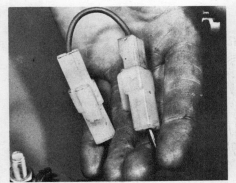

15.2 Fusible link

16.2 Headlamp removal. The screw at the top is for beam aiming and should not be removed

16.4 Removing the headlamp connector

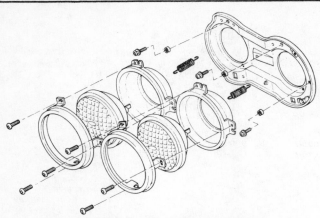

**Fig. 10.13. Headlamp assembly - exploded view**

### 16 Headlamp unit - removal and installation

1 Remove the radiator grille, refer to Chapter 12, if necessary.
2 Remove the three headlamp retaining screws. Do not disturb the beam aiming adjustment screws (photo).
3 Rotate the retaining ring clockwise and remove it.
4 Remove the headlamp unit from the retaining ring, remove the rubber cover from the connector (where applicable) then pull off the connector (photo).
5 Installation is the reverse of the removal procedure, but ensure that the headlamp unit is the correct way up. It is recommended that the beam alignment is checked on completion (see next Section).

### 17 Headlamp aiming (beam alignment)

1 The only entirely satisfactory way of checking headlamp beam alignment is by the use of special optical testers.
2 However, where this equipment is not available, the following beam aiming procedure may be used.
3 Ensure that the tires are correctly inflated and that the vehicle is on a flat level surface facing a flat wall. Ensure that the fuel tank, radiator and oil pan (sump) are full or topped-up to the recommended levels.
4 Mark up the wall using chalk or similar, to the dimension shown in Fig. 10.15. Note that these dimensions are for right-hand drive vehicles, but the only difference for left-hand drive vehicles is that dimension 'd' will be to the right of the 'straight-ahead' position instead of the left.
5 Position the car 32.8 ft (10 m) from the wall and adjust the beam aiming screws to obtain the correct alignment pattern.

### 18 Front combination lamp

#### Bulb renewal

1 Remove the retaining screws and take off the lens (photo).
2 Press in the bulb and rotate it counterclockwise to remove it from

its socket.
3 Install the new bulb, ensuring that it is locked in the socket.
4 Position the gasket to the lamp body and install the lens (and lamp body) using the two screws.

#### Lamp removal and installation

5 Disconnect the lamp wires at the connector, and remove the grommet from the body panel.
6 Remove the lens as described in paragraph 1 then withdraw the lamp body.
7 Installation is the reverse of the removal procedure.

### 19 Side marker lamp

#### Bulb renewal

1 Remove the retaining screws and take off the lens and rim (photo).
2 According to the particular type, either press in the bulb and rotate it counter-clockwise to remove it, or pull the bulb and socket forward and take the bulb out.
3 Install the new bulb (and socket, where applicable).
4 Position the gasket to the lamp body and install the lens and rim.

#### Lamp removal and installation

5 Disconnect the two lamp wires at the connectors, and remove the grommet (where applicable) from the body panel.
6 Remove the two retaining screws, the lens and the rim, and withdraw the lamp from the vehicle.
7 Installation is the reverse of the removal procedure.

### 20 Cab light

#### Bulb renewal

1 Remove the lens from the lamp housing and pull the bulb forward to remove it from its socket.
2 Push in the new bulb and install the lens.

#### Light removal and installation

3 Disconnect the battery ground cable.
4 Remove the lens from the lamp housing then remove the two lamp retaining screws.
5 Detach the lamp housing from the roof rail and disconnect the two wires at the connectors.
6 Installation is the reverse of the removal procedure.

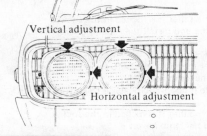

Fig. 10.14. Headlamp aim adjustment screws

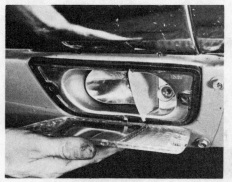

18.1 Front combination lamp lens removal

19.1 Side marker lamp lens removal

21.1 Rear combination lamp lens removal

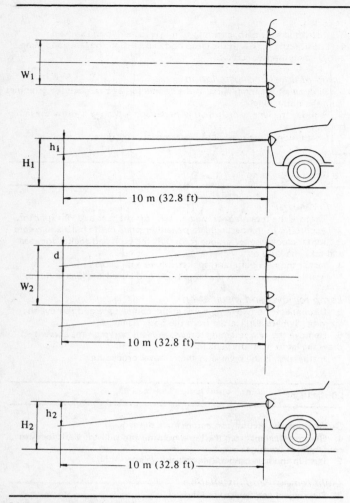

| Vehicle/Dimension | | (High beam) | |
|---|---|---|---|
| | $H_1$ mm (in) | $W_1$ mm (in) | $h_1$ mm (in) |
| Pick-up | 715 (28.15) | 780 (30.71) | 140 (5.51) |
| Double Pick-up | 680 (26.77) | 780 (30.71) | 122 (4.80) |

| Vehicle/Dimension | | (Low beam) | | |
|---|---|---|---|---|
| | $H_2$ mm (in) | $W_2$ mm (in) | $h_2$ mm (in) | d mm (in) |
| Pick-up | 715 (28.15) | 1,160 (45.67) | 392 (15.43) | 349 (13.74) |
| Double Pick-up | 680 (26.77) | 1,160 (45.67) | 268 (10.55) | 349 (13.74) |

**Fig. 10.15. Headlamp aim diagram**

## 21 Rear combination lamp

### Bulb renewal - pick-up
1  Remove the six retaining screws and take off the lens (photo).
2  Press in the bulb and rotate it counter-clockwise to remove it from its socket.
3  Install the rear bulb, ensuring that it is locked in the socket.
4  Position the lens to the lamp and install the retaining screws.

### Bulb renewal - double pick-up
5  Remove the tail lamp cover then turn the bulb socket counter-clockwise to remove it from the lamp body.
6  Press in the bulb and rotate it counter-clockwise to remove it from its socket.
7  Install the new bulb, ensuring that it is locked in the socket.
8  Install the bulb socket and tail lamp cover.

### Lamp removal and installation
9  On double pick-up models remove the tail lamp cover.
10  Disconnect the wiring assembly at the connector.
11  Remove the two nuts from the studs at the rear of the conbination lamp, and remove the lamp.
12  Installation is the reverse of the removal sequence.

## 22 License plate (number plate) lamp

### Bulb renewal - pick-up
1  Remove the lens retaining screw (where applicable) and remove the lens.
2  Pull out the bulb and install a replacement, then install the lens (photo).

### Bulb renewal - double pick-up
3  Remove the two retaining screws trhen take off the rim, lens and gasket.
4  Press in the bulb and rotate it counter-clockwise to remove it from its socket.
5  Install the new bulb, ensuring that it is locked in the socket.
6  Position the gasket, lens and rim, and install the retaining screws.

### Lamp removal and installation - pick-up
7  Disconnect the lead wire at the connector
8  Remove the lamp bracket retaining screws and the lamp assembly.
9  Installation is the reverse of the removal procedure.

### Lamp removal and installation - double pick-up
10  Disconnect the lead wire at the connector.
11  Remove the flange nuts from the rear of the rear bumper.
12  Pull out the lamp assembly.
13  Installation is the reverse of the removal procedure.

22.2 License plate lamp bulb

**10**

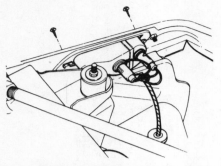

**Fig. 10.16. Front combination lamp leads**
Some models have one bulb socket only.

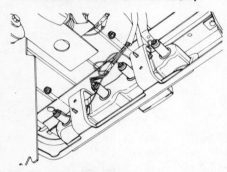

**Fig. 10.17. Rear combination lamp leads - Pick-up**
Some models have 3 bulb sockets

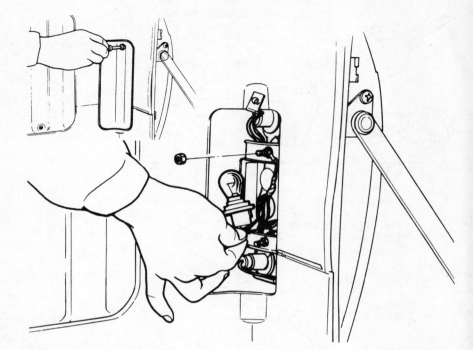

**Fig. 10.18. Rear combination lamp - Double Pick-up**

**23 Engine compartment lamp**

*Bulb renewal*
1   Press in the bulb and rotate it counter-clockwise to remove it from its socket.
2   Install the new bulb, ensuring that it is locked in the socket.

*Lamp removal and installation*
3   Remove the single screw retaining the lamp bracket to the upper dash panel and disconnect the wires at the connectors.
4   Installation is the reverse of the removal procedure.

*Lamp switch removal and installation*
5   Disconnect the lead wire at the connector and the switch assembly from the bracket.
6   Installation is the reverse of the removal procedure, but ensure that the bracket is free from dirt, rust etc.,

**24 Light switch - removal and installation**

1   Disconnect the battery ground cable.
2   Press in the switch knob, rotate it counter-clockwise and pull it off the switch.
3   Unscrew the escutcheon and remove the spacer.
4   Reach up behind the instrument panel and disconnect the lighting switch connector.
5   Remove the spacer and lighting switch.
6   Installation is the reverse of the removal procedure.

**25 Illumination control switch**

1   The switch incorporates a 35 ohm variable resistance to control the brightness of the heater control illumination lamp, wiper switch illumination lamp and lighting switch illumination lamp.

*Removal and installation*
2   Pull off the switch knob.

3   Unscrew the escutcheon and remove the spacer.
4   Disconnect the switch lead wires at the connector and remove the switch from the panel.
5   Installation is the reverse of the removal procedure.

**26 Turn signal and headlamp dimmer (dip) switch - removal and installation**

1   Remove the steering wheel; refer to Chapter 11 if necessary.
2   Unhook the wiring assembly from its clip behind the lower instrument panel.
3   Disconnect the multiple connector and lead wires from the instrument harness wiring.
4   Remove the upper and lower steering column shell covers.
5   Loosen the two screws attaching the switch assembly to the steering column jacket and remove the switch assembly.
6   Installation is the reverse of the removal procedure, but ensure that the switch locating tab (or screw) fits into the hole of the steering column jacket.

**27 Stoplamp switch - removal and installation**

1   Disconnect the battery ground cable.
2   Disconnect the lead wires at the connectors (the switch is mounted at the bottom of the pedal and steering shaft bracket).
3   Loosen the locknut and unscrew the switch.
4   Installation is the reverse of the removal procedure but ensure that the switch is positioned so that it operates satisfactorily. Also see the Section in Chapter 9 dealing with brake pedal adjustment.

**28 Door switch - removal and installation**

1   Disconnect the battery ground cable.
2   Carefully pry the switch from the door hinge pillar.
3   Withdraw the switch and wiring, disconnecting the lead wire from the connector.
4   Installation is the reverse of the removal procedure.

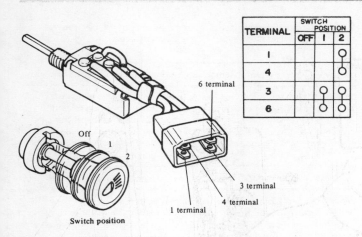

| TERMINAL | SWITCH POSITION | | |
|---|---|---|---|
| | OFF | 1 | 2 |
| 1 | | | ○ |
| 4 | | | ○ |
| 3 | | ○ | ○ |
| 6 | | ○ | ○ |

**Fig. 10.19. Light switch**
Some switches are marked with the word 'Lights'

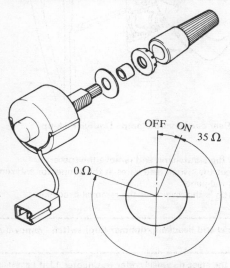

**Fig. 10.20. Illumination control switch**

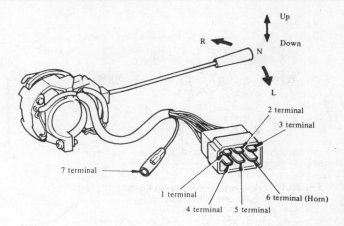

| TERMINAL | LEVER POSITION | | |
|---|---|---|---|
| | L | N | R |
| 1 LH | ○ | | |
| 2 RH | | | ○ |
| 7 FLASH | ○ | | ○ |

TURN SIGNAL SWITCH

| TERMINAL | LEVER POSITION | |
|---|---|---|
| | DOWN | UP |
| 3 LIGHT | ○ | ○ |
| 4 HIGH | | ○ |
| 5 LOW | ○ | |

DIMMER SWITCH

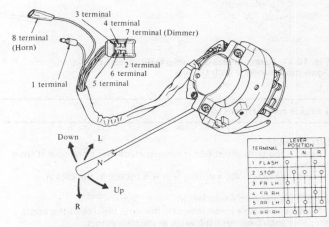

| TERMINAL | LEVER POSITION | | |
|---|---|---|---|
| | L | N | R |
| 1 FLASH | ○ | | |
| 2 STOP | ○ | ○ | ○ |
| 3 FR LH | ○ | | |
| 4 FR RH | | | ○ |
| 5 RR LH | ○ | | |
| 6 RR RH | | | ○ |

**Fig. 10.21. Turn signal and headlamp dimmer switch**
Alternative arrangements shown

## 29 Hazard switch - removal and installation

1 Disconnect the multiple connector and the lead wire from the instrument wiring harness.
2 Remove the upper shell cover.
3 Remove the two screws attaching the switch to the lower shell cover and remove the switch.
4 Installation is the reverse of the removal procedure.

## 30 Instrument panel meters and gauges

**Note:** Refer to Chapter 12 for the instrument panel removal and installation procedure, if necessary.

### Combination meter (left-hand drive vehicle) removal and installation

1 Disconnect the battery ground cable.
2 Working through the meter apertures of the cluster remove the three screws retaining the cluster lid the instrument panel.
3 From beneath the instrument panel remove the single screw retaining the meter assembly to the lower panel.
4 Draw the cluster slightly forward then unscrew the speedometer cable ferrule from the rear of the speedometer and the instrument wire assembly multiple connector from the printed circuit (Refer to the appropriate Sections if it is found necessary to remove any of the switch knobs).

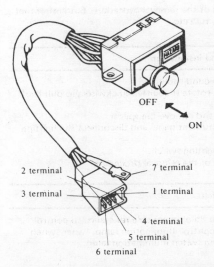
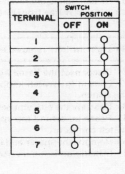

| TERMINAL | SWITCH POSITION | |
|---|---|---|
| | OFF | ON |
| 1 | | ○ |
| 2 | | ○ |
| 3 | | ○ |
| 4 | | ○ |
| 5 | | ○ |
| 6 | ○ | |
| 7 | ○ | |

**10**

**Fig. 10.22. Illumination control switch**

5   Where applicable, disconnect the clock wires from the meter printed circuit.
6   Remove the four screws which secure the meter assembly to the cluster lid; remove the meter.
7   Installation is the reverse   of the removal procedure.

### Combination meter (right-hand drive vehicle) - removal and installation
8   Initially follow the procedure given in paragraphs 1, 4 and 5.
9   Working through the centre and right meter openings of the instrument panel, remove the two screws retaining the combination meter assembly to the instrument panel.
10  From beneath the instrument panel remove the single screw retaining the meter assembly to the lower panel.
11  Remove the combination meter.
12  Installation is the reverse of the removal procedure.

### Speedometer - removal and installation
13  Remove the combination meter as described previously.
14  Remove the meter front cover and shadow plate by removing the clips and screws.
15  Remove the screws retaining the speedometer to the printed circuit housing; remove the speedometer.
16  Installation is the reverse of the removal procedure.

### Odometer (mileage recorder) - removal and installation
17  Remove the speedometer as described previously.
18  Remove the odometer retaining screws,
19  Installation is the reverse of the removal procedure.

### Fuel and water temperature gauges - removal and installation
20  Initially proceed as described in paragraphs 13 and 14.
21  Remove the retaining nuts at the rear of the combination meter; remove the meter(s).
22  Installation is the reverse of the removal procedure.

### Clock (left-hand drive vehicle) - removal and installation
23  Initially follow the procedure given in paragraphs 1 thru **4.**
24  Disconnect the three clock wire connectors from the combination meter printed circuit and instrument harness wiring.
25  Remove the three screws to remove the clock from the cluster lid.

### Clock (right-hand drive vehicle) - removal and installation
26  Disconnect the battery ground cable.
27  Disconnect the two wire connectors from the combination meter printed circuit and one from the instrument harness wiring.
28  Remove the single screw from the clock opening of the instrument panel.
29  Remove the single screw retaining the clock to the lower panel.
30  Installation is the reverse of the removal procedure.

### Tachometer - bulb renewal
31  Remove the tachometer as described in the following Sub-Section.
32  Twist the bulb socket from the rear of the tachometer and remove the bulb.
33  Installation is the reverse of the removal procedure.

### Tachometer - removal and installation
34  Initially follow the procedure given in paragraph 1 through 4.
35  Disconnect the four tachometer lead wire connectors (these are connected to the combination meter and tachometer cable).
36  Remove the three screws to remove the tachometer from the cluster lid.
37  Installation is the reverse of the removal procedure, but note the following tachometer lead connections:

| | |
|---|---|
| Black/white | *To black/white cable from engine compartment* |
| Red/green | *To flat plate terminal at rear of combination meter.* |
| Black | *To T-shaped terminal at rear of combination meter.* |
| Yellow/red | *To pole terminal at rear of combination meter.* |

### 31  Oil pressure switch - removal and installation

1   Disconnect the lead wire from the oil pressure switch then unscrew the switch from the rear right side of the cylinder block.
2   Installation is the reverse of the removal procedure, but apply a little non-setting gasket sealant to the screw thread.

### 32  Parking brake warning lamp switch - removal and installation

1   Disconnect the switch lead wire, pull the switch out of the parking brake control bracket and withdraw the switch and wiring assembly.
2   Installation is the reverse of the removal procedure; bend the switch plate down so that the switch operates (warning light on) when the parking brake is moved one notch from the fully released position.

### 33  Meter illumination, indicator and warning light bulbs - renewal

**Note:** Refer to Section 30 for tachometer bulb renewal.
1   To remove a bulb, turn the bulb socket counter-clockwise to detach it from the combination meter. If necessary, disconnect the lead wire connector from the printed circuit.
2   Remove the bulb from the socket.
3   Installation is the reverse of the removal procedure.

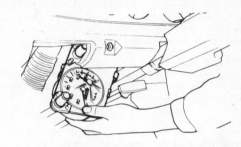

Fig. 10.23. Removing the combination meter

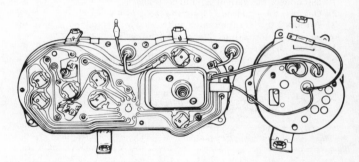

Fig. 10.24. Clock connections

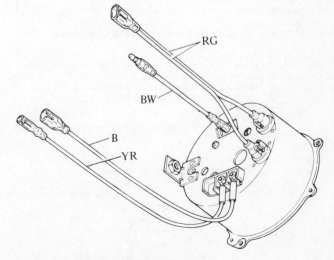

Fig. 10.25. Tachometer connections

## 34 Horn(s), horn relay and horn operating button - removal and installation

### Horn

1 Disconnect the horn wire at the terminal on the horn body (photo).
2 Remove the retaining bolts that retain the horn and bracket assembly to the hood (bonnet) ledge.
3 Installation is the reverse of the removal procedure.

### Horn relay

4 Disconnect the battery ground cable.
5 Disconnect the three lead wires from the horn relay terminals and remove the retaining screw.
**Note:** According to the particular model, the horn relay is mounted on the radiator core support, the bulkhead on the rear side of the instrument panel or beneath the dash panel.
6 Installation is the reverse of the removal procedure.

### Horn operating button

7 In most cases the horn operating button is integral with the turn signal and headlamp dimmer switch (see Section 26). Alternatively it is incorporated in the steering wheel pad and is accessible after removing the two screws from behind the steering wheel crosspiece. The wires from the two screws link at a single spede-type centre terminal (photo).

### Horn adjustment

8 In most cases the horn is adjustable. To obtain the most satisfactory note, together with an operating current of 3 to 5 amps, slacken the locknut and turn the adjusting screw.

## 35 Ignition switch (standard) - removal and installation

1 Disconnect the battery ground cable.
2 Unscrew the escutcheon from the front of the switch.
3 Withdraw the ignition switch and wiring assembly, complete with spacer, from the steering column wheel cover.
4 Detach the wiring connector from the rear of the switch.
5 Installation is the reverse of the removal procedure.

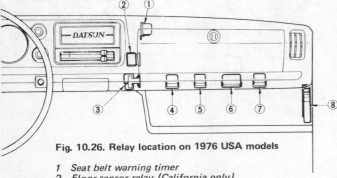

Fig. 10.26. Relay location on 1976 USA models

1  Seat belt warning timer
2  Floor sensor relay (California only)
3  Buzzer
4  Inhibitor relay automatic transmission
5  Ignition relay (California only)
6  Horn relay
7  Light relay
8  Full transistor amplifier (California only)

Fig. 10.27. Horn adjustment

## 36 Ignition switch (steering lock type) - removal and installation

1 Disconnect the battery ground cable.
2 Detach the wiring assembly from the rear of the switch.
3 Remove the two retaining screws from the rear of the switch on the steering lock cylinder.
4 Installation is the reverse of the removal procedure.

## 37 Steering lock - removal and installation

1 Disconnect the battery ground cable.
2 Detach the wiring assembly from the rear of the ignition switch.
3 Carefully drill into the heads of the shear type screws and use a suitable extractor to remove them. Alternatively it may be possible to make a small sawcut or chisel cut in the screw end to permit it to be rotated and unscrewed.
4 Remove the lock assembly from the steering column.
5 Installation is the reverse of the removal procedure, but ensure that new shear type screws are used for securing the lock to the steering column.

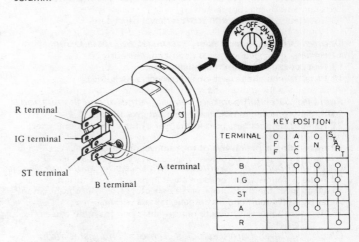

| TERMINAL | KEY POSITION | | | |
|---|---|---|---|---|
| | OFF | ACC | ON | START |
| B | | o | o | o |
| IG | | | o | o |
| ST | | | | o |
| A | | o | o | |
| R | | | | o |

Fig. 10.28. Standard ignition switch connections

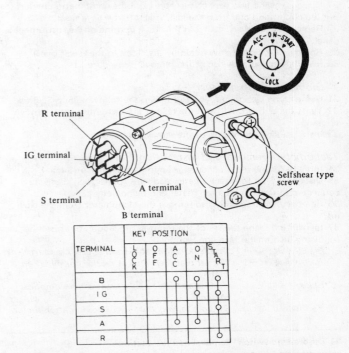

| TERMINAL | KEY POSITION | | | | |
|---|---|---|---|---|---|
| | LOCK | OFF | ACC | ON | START |
| B | | | o | o | o |
| IG | | | | o | o |
| S | | | | | o |
| A | | | o | o | |
| R | | | | | o |

Fig. 10.29. Steering lock type ignition switch connections

**10**

### 38 Windshield wipers and washers

*Wiper blade and arm - removal and installation*
1   To remove a wiper arm, loosen the single screw retaining the arm to the spindle then pull the arm off (photo).
2   The wiper blade can be removed by depressing the retaining clips and sliding the two items apart (photo).
3   Installation of the blade and arm is straighforward. Ensure that the arms are set so that they come to rest in the position shown in Fig. 10.30.

*Wiper linkage - removal and installation*
4   Remove the wiper blade and arm, as described in the previous sub-Section.
5   Remove the cowl top grille; refer to Chapter 12, if necessary.
6   Remove the two flange nuts retaining the wiper linkage pivot to the top of the cowl.
7   Remove the stop ring retaining the connecting link to the wiper motor arm, and remove the wiper motor linkage assembly.
8   Installation is the reverse of the removal procedure but set the wiper arm so that they come to rest in the position shown in Fig. 10.30.

*Wiper motor - removal and installation*
9   Remove the cowl top grille. refer to Chapter 12, if necessary.
10  Remove the stop ring retaining the connecting link to the wiper motor arm.
11  From beneath the instrument panel, disconnect the wiper motor harness at the connector or the wiper motor body (photo).
12  Remove the three retaining screws and pull the wiper motor forward and out.
13  Installation is the reverse of the removal procedure.

*Wiper motor - testing*
14  Disconnect the wiring connector from the wiper motor.
15  Connect a jumper lead between the battery positive lead and the motor 'B' terminal.
16  Connect a jumper cable between the battery negative lead or vehicle ground and the motor 'H' terminal; the motor should run at high speed.
17  Transfer the humper lead from the 'H' terminal to the 'L' terminal and check that the motor runs at low speed.
18  Transfer the jumper lead from the 'L' terminal to the 'E' terminal. Additionally connect a jumper lead between the 'P' and 'L' terminals and check that the motor stops automatically.
19  If the above tests are unsatisfactory, the motor is unsatisfactory, the motor is unserviceable and a replacement item should be installed.

*Wiper and washer switch - removal and installation*
20  Press in the switch knob, rotate it counter-clockwise and pull it off the switch.
21  Unscrew the excutcheon and remove the spacer.
22  Reach up behind the instrument panel and disconnect the switch connector.
23  Remove the spacer and switch.
24  Installation is the reverse of the removal procedure.

*Washer pump - removal and installation*
**Note:** Under normal operating conditions the washer pump should not be operated for more than ten seconds at a time. Under no circumstances should it be operated for more than thirty seconds if ther is no fluid in the washer reservoir.
25  Disconnect the two washer pump lead wires at the connectors.
26  Remove the washer pump hose and drain the fluid.
27  Pull out the washer tank and motor assembly from the tank bracket. These are integral parts and must be serviced as an assembly (photo).
28  Installation is the reverse of the removal procedure.

*Washer nozzle - removal and installation*
29  Disconnect the washer tube and remove the single retaining screw from the cowl top.
30  Installation is the reverse of the removal procedure; if necessary bend the nozzle tube to obtain a satisfactory spray pattern.

34.1 Horn location

34.7 Horn pad removal

38.1 Wiper arm removal

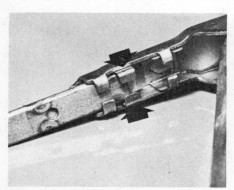
38.2 Wiper blade retaining clips (arrowed)

38.11 Wiper motor installation

38.28 Washer pump/reservoir removal

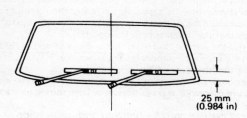

Fig. 10.30. The 'at rest' position of the wiper arms for right-hand drive models. Left-hand drive models are the opposite to this

25 mm
(0.984 in)

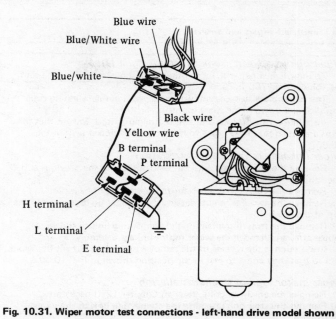

Fig. 10.31. Wiper motor test connections - left-hand drive model shown

| TERMINAL | SWITCH POSITION | | | |
|---|---|---|---|---|
| | OFF | 1 | 2 | TWIST |
| 1 | ○ | | | |
| 2 | ○ | ○ | | |
| 3 | | ○ | ○ | ○ |
| 4 | | | ○ | ○ |
| 5 | | | | ○ |

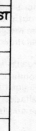

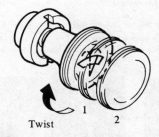

Twist

Switch position

1 terminal
2 terminal
3 terminal
4 terminal
5 terminal

Fig. 10.32. Wiper switch connections

10

## 39 Fault diagnosis - electrical system

| Symptom | Reason/s |
| --- | --- |
| Starter motor fails to turn engine | Battery discharged.<br>Battery defective internally.<br>Battery terminal leads loose or ground lead not securely attached to body.<br>Loose or broken connections in starter motor circuit.<br>Starter motor solenoid switch faulty.<br>Starter motor pinion jammed in mesh with flywheel gear ring.<br>Starter brushes badly worn, sticking or brush wires loose.<br>Commutator dirty, worn or burnt.<br>Starter motor armature faulty.<br>Field coils grounded. |
| Starter motor turns engine very slowly | Battery in discharged condition.<br>Starter brushes badly worn, sticking or brush wires loose.<br>Loose wires in starter motor circuit. |
| Starter motor operates without turning engine | Pinion or flywheel gear teeth broken or worn. |
| Starter motor noisy or engagement excessively rough | Pinion or flywheel teeth broken or worn.<br>Starter motor retaining bolts loose. |
| Starter motor remains in operation after ignition key released | Faulty ignition switch.<br>Faulty solenoid. |
| Charging system indicator on with ignition switch off | Faulty alternator diode. |
| Charging system indicator light on - engine speed above idling | Loose or broken drivebelt.<br>Shorted negative doide.<br>No output from alternator. |
| Charge indicator light not on when ignition switched on but engine not running | Burnt out bulb.<br>Field circuit open.<br>Lamp circuit open. |
| Battery will not hold charge for more than a few days | Battery defective internally.<br>Electrolyte level too weak or to low.<br>Battery plates heavily sulphated. |
| Horn will not operate or operates intermittently | Loose connections.<br>Defective switch.<br>Defective relay.<br>Defective horn. |
| Horns blow continually | Faulty relay.<br>Relay wiring grounded.<br>Horn button stuck (grounded). |
| Lights do not come on | If engine not running, battery discharged.<br>Light bulb filament burnt out or bulbs broken.<br>Wire connections loose, disconnected or broken.<br>Light switch shorting or otherwise faulty. |
| Lights come on but fade out | If engine not running battery discharged.<br>Light bulb filament burnt out, or bulbs or sealed beam units broken.<br>Wire connections loose, disconnected or broken.<br>Light switch shorting or otherwise faulty. |
| Lights give very poor illumination | Lamp glasses dirty.<br>Lamps badly out of adjustment. |
| Lights work erratically - flashing on and off, especially over bumps | Battery terminals or ground connectrion loose.<br>Lights not grounding properly.<br>Contacts in light switch faulty. |
| Wiper motor fails to work | Blown fuse.<br>Wire connections loose, disconnected, or broken.<br>Brushes badly worn.<br>Armature worn or faulty.<br>Field coils faulty. |

| | |
|---|---|
| Wiper motor works very slowly and takes excessive current | Commutator dirty, greasy or burnt.<br>Armature bearings dirty or unaligned.<br>Armature badly worn or faulty. |
| Wiper motor works slowly and takes little current | Brushes badly worn.<br>Commutator dirty, greasy or burnt.<br>Armature badly worn or faulty. |
| Wiper motor works but wiper blades remain static | Wiper motor gearbox parts badly worn or teeth stripped. |

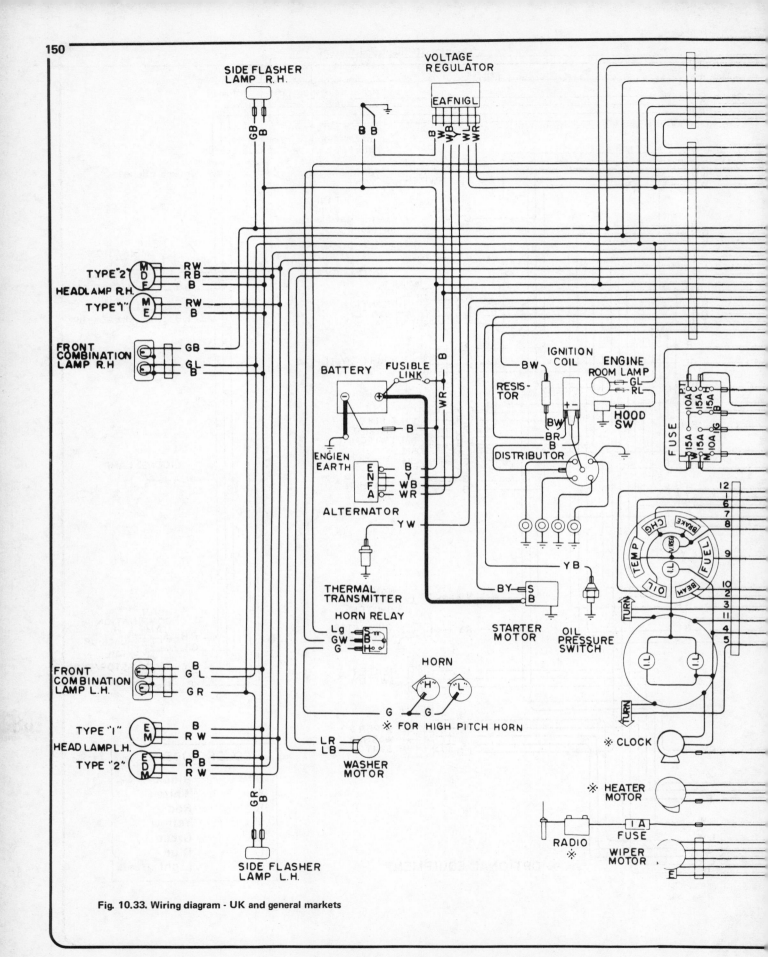

Fig. 10.33. Wiring diagram - UK and general markets

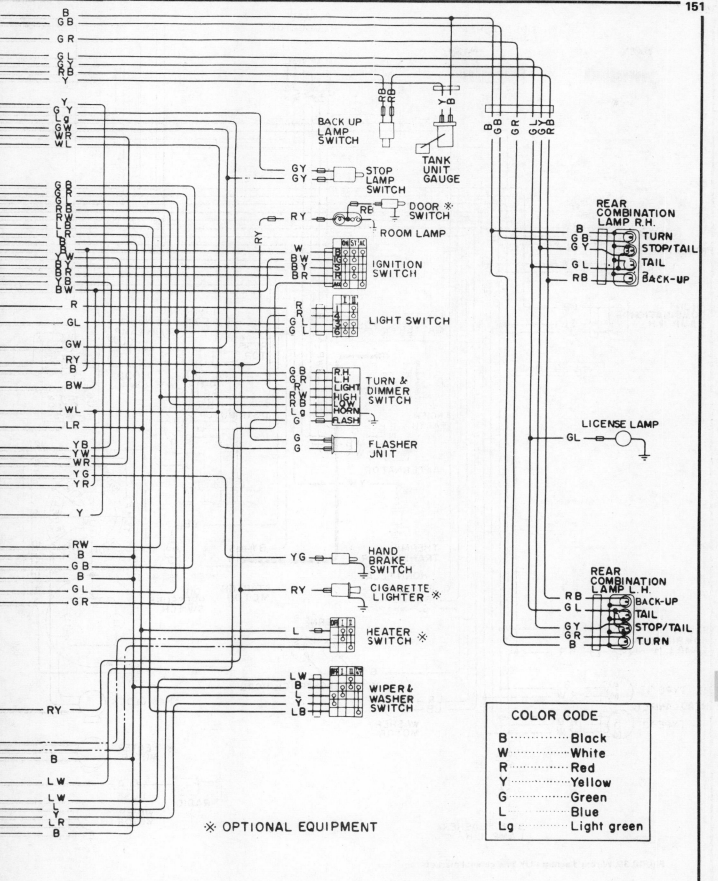

BACK UP LAMP SWITCH

TANK UNIT GAUGE

STOP LAMP SWITCH

DOOR SWITCH ※

ROOM LAMP

IGNITION SWITCH

LIGHT SWITCH

TURN & DIMMER SWITCH

FLASHER UNIT

HAND BRAKE SWITCH

CIGARETTE LIGHTER ※

HEATER SWITCH ※

WIPER & WASHER SWITCH

REAR COMBINATION LAMP R.H.

B — TURN
GB — STOP/TAIL
GY — TAIL
GL — TAIL
RB — BACK-UP

LICENSE LAMP

REAR COMBINATION LAMP L.H.

RB — BACK-UP
GL — TAIL
GY — STOP/TAIL
GR — TURN
B — TURN

※ OPTIONAL EQUIPMENT

COLOR CODE

B ·········· Black
W ·········· White
R ·········· Red
Y ·········· Yellow
G ·········· Green
L ·········· Blue
Lg ·········· Light green

10

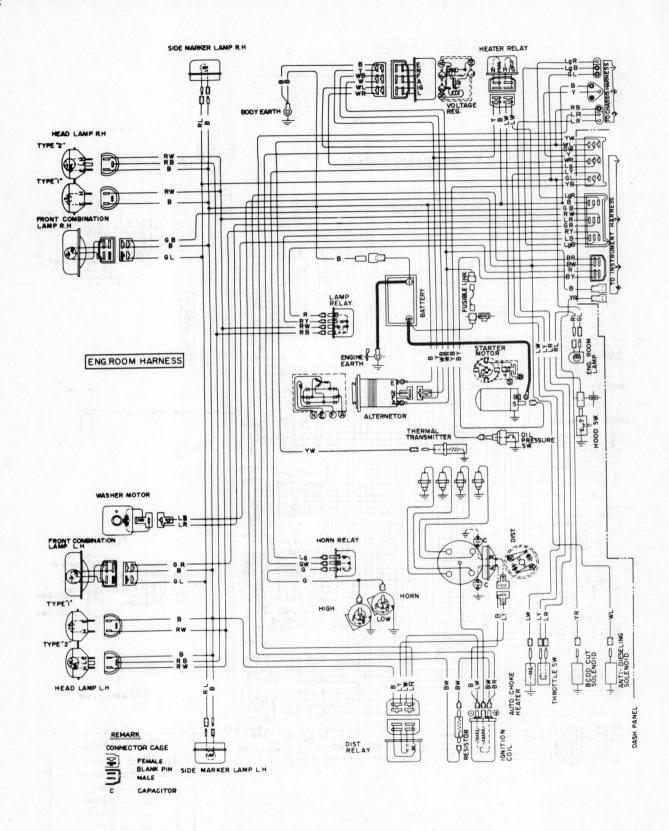

Fig. 10.34. Wiring diagram - 1973 USA - manual transmission

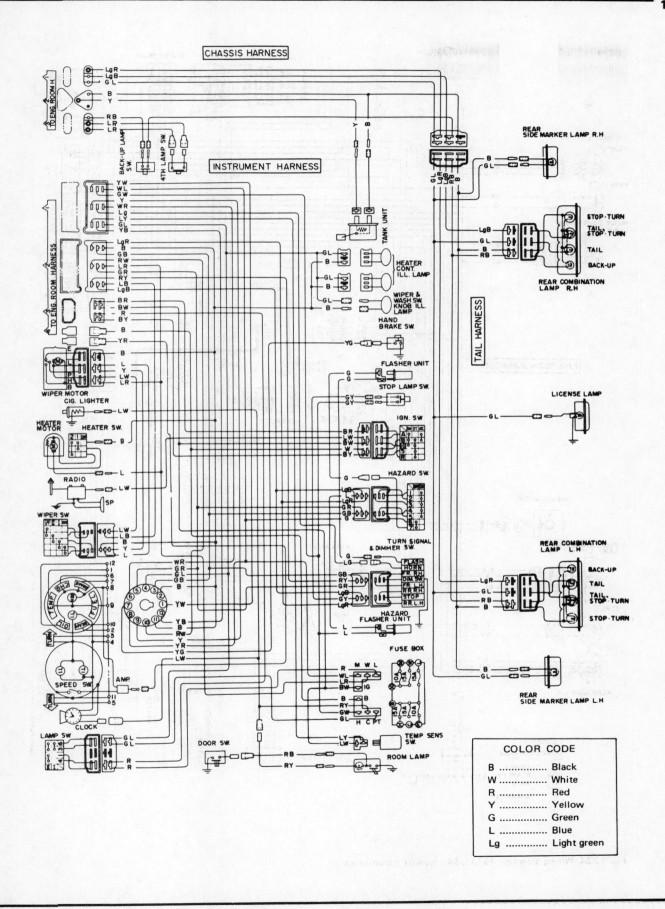

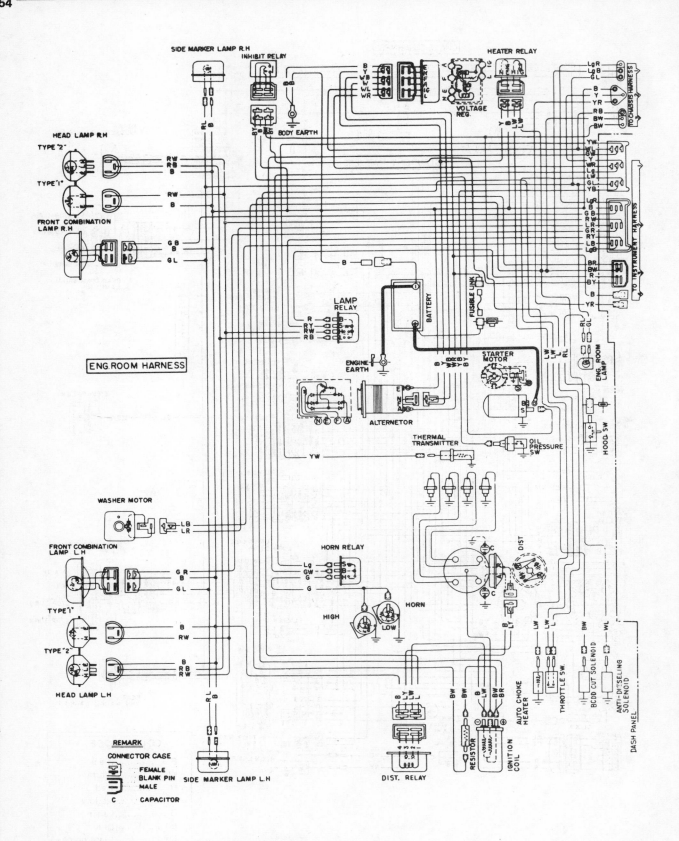

Fig. 10.35. Wiring diagram - 1973 USA - automatic transmission

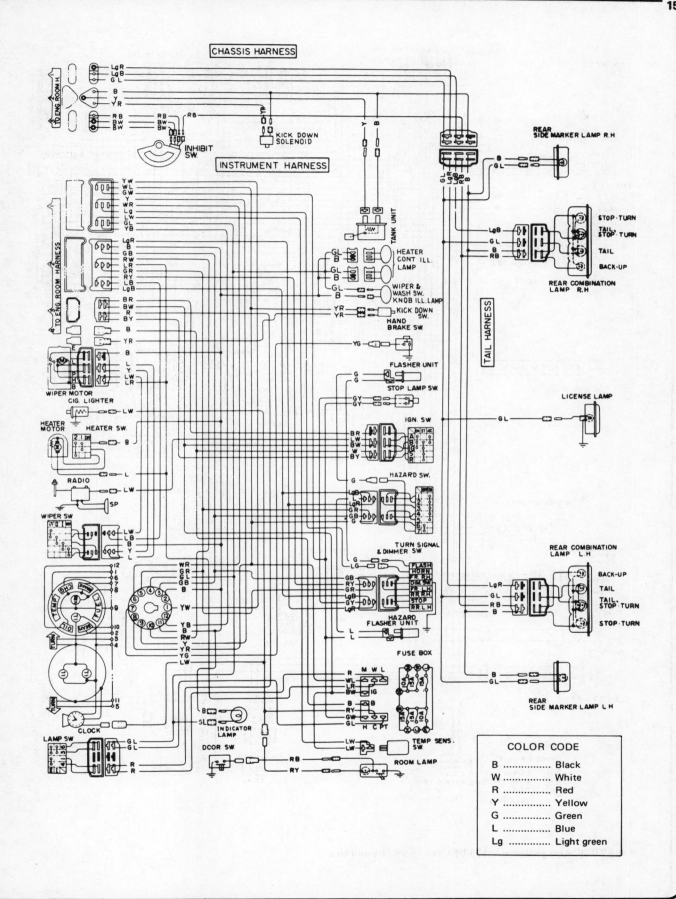

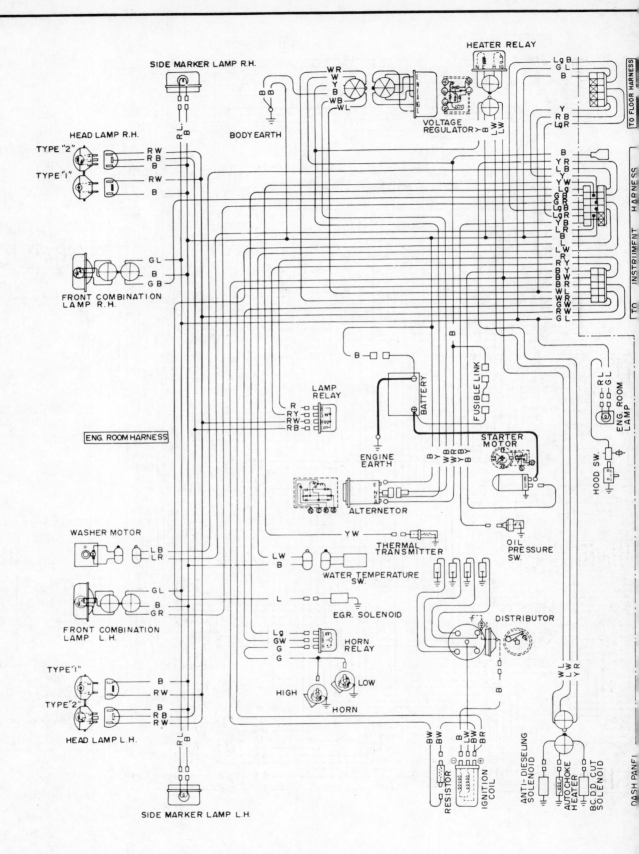

Fig. 10.36. Wiring diagram - 1974 USA - manual transmission

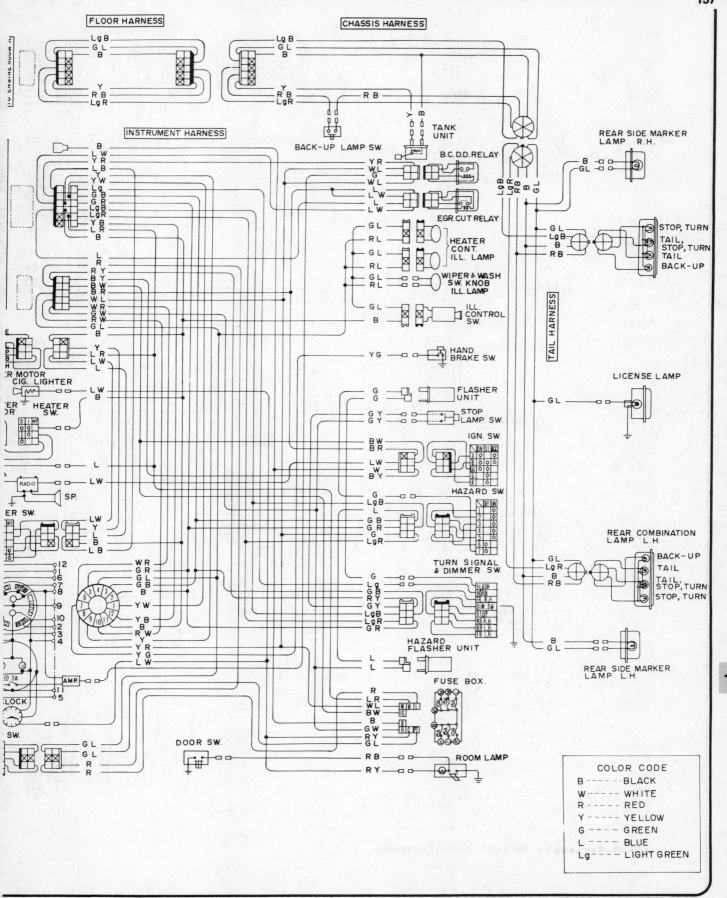

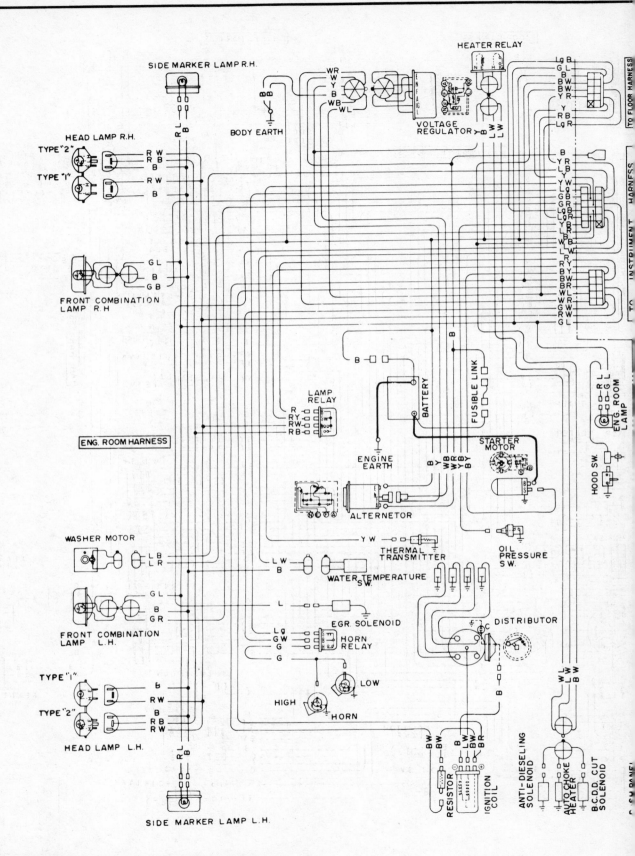

**Fig. 10.37. Wiring diagram - 1974 USA - automatic transmission**

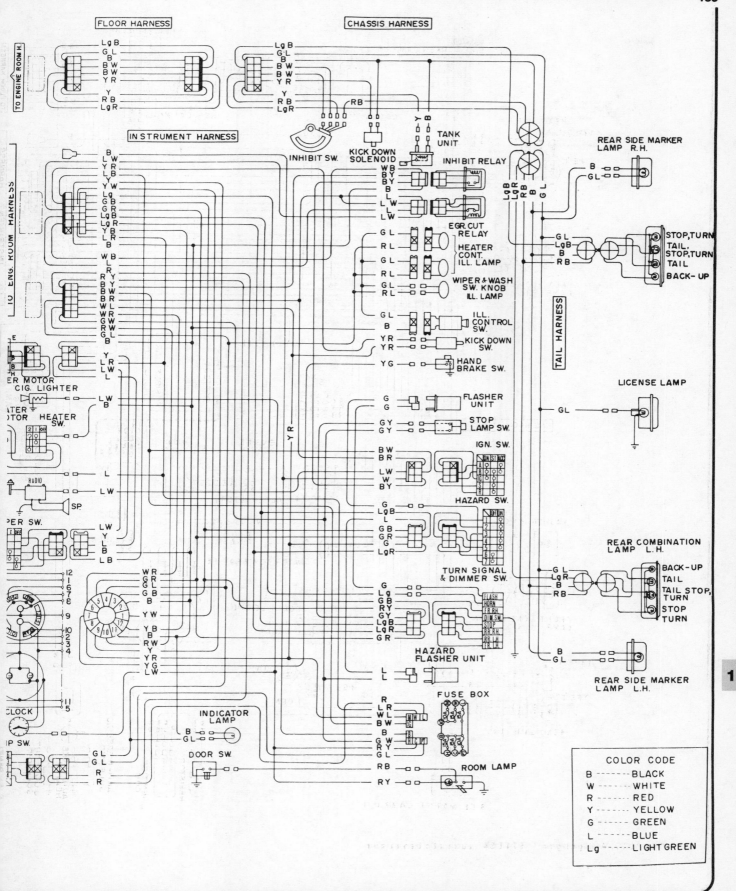

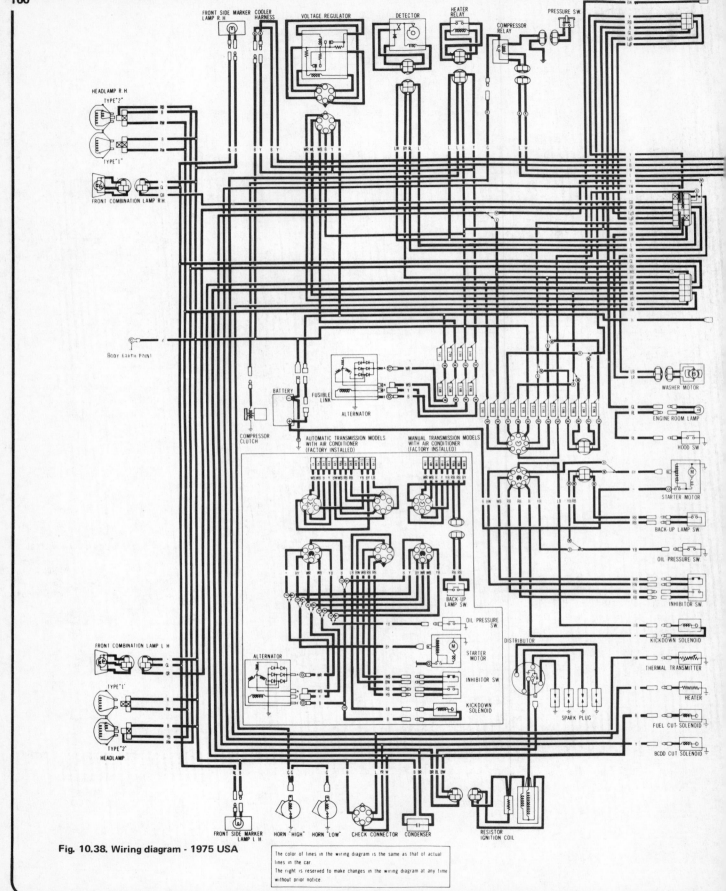

**Fig. 10.38. Wiring diagram - 1975 USA**

The color of lines in the wiring diagram is the same as that of actual lines in the car

The right is reserved to make changes in the wiring diagram at any time without prior notice

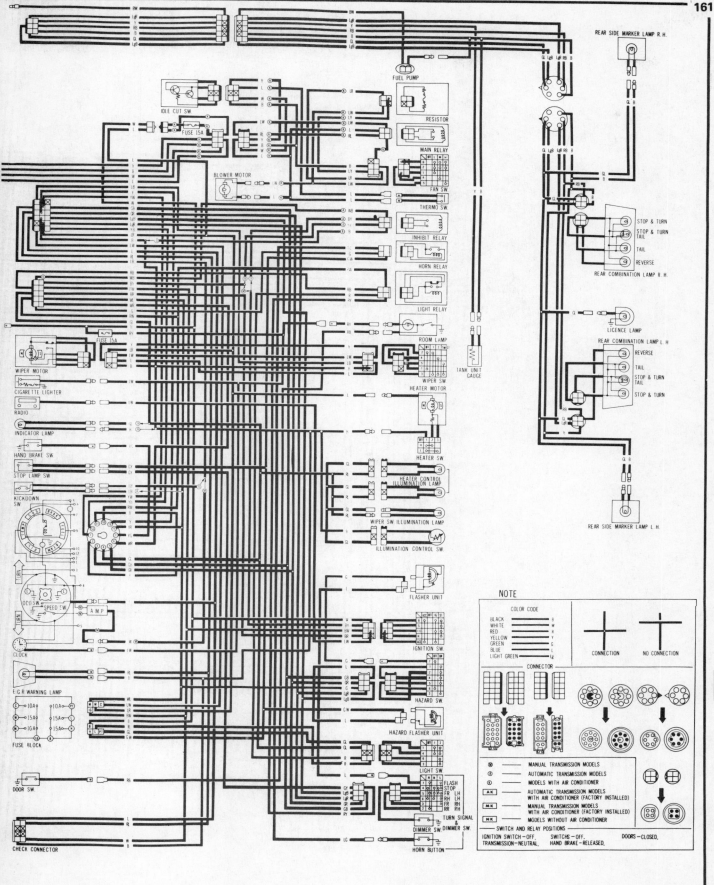

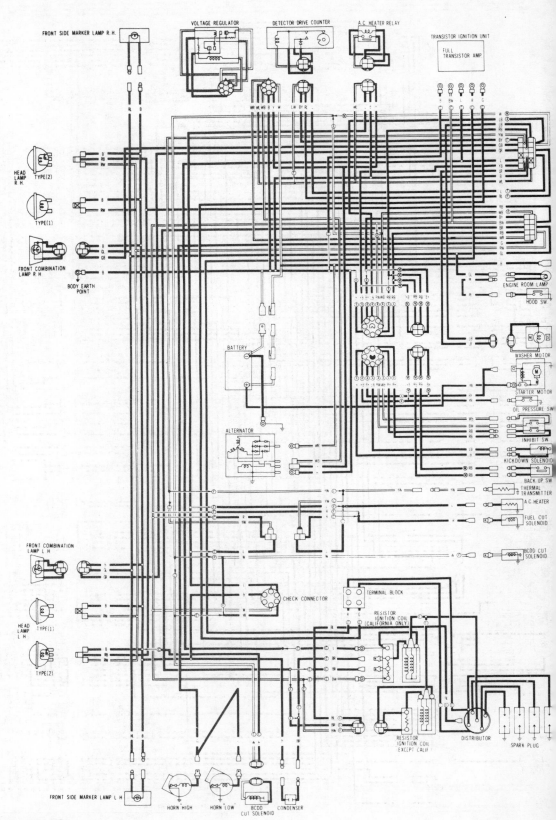

**Fig. 10.39. Wiring diagram - 1976 USA**

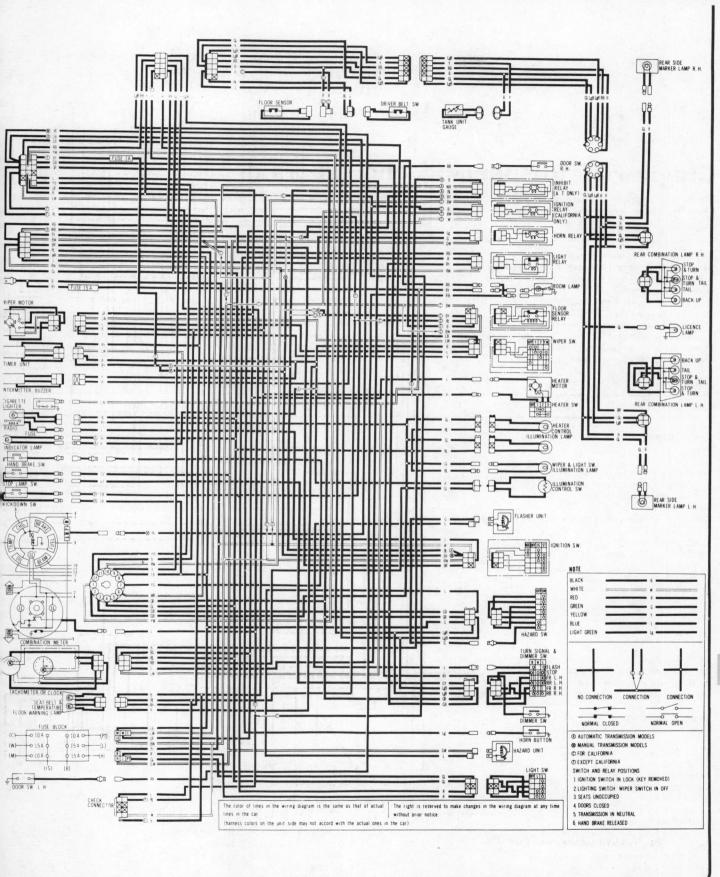

# Chapter 11 Suspension and steering

*Refer to Chapter 13 for specifications and information applicable to 1977 through 1979 USA models*

## Contents

## Specifications

### Front suspension

| | |
|---|---|
| Type ... ... ... ... ... ... ... ... ... | Independant, torsion bar with double wishbones, stabilizer bar (optional), tension rods and hydraulic shock absorbers |

Torsion bar torsional rigidity:

| | kg fm/degree | lb f ft/degree |
|---|---|---|
| Standard wheelbase and Double pick-up ... ... ... ... | 2.99 | 21.6 |
| Long wheelbase ... ... ... ... ... | 3.74 | 27.1 |

Wheel alignment:
Toe-in, measured at extreme front and rear of tire centre:

| | |
|---|---|
| Pick-up ... ... ... ... ... ... ... ... | 0.039 to 0.197 in (1 to 5 mm) |
| Double pick-up ... ... ... ... ... ... | 0.079 to 0.118 (2 to 3 mm) |

Camber angle:

| | |
|---|---|
| Pick-up ... ... ... ... ... ... ... ... | $1^{\circ}\ 15' \pm 1^{\circ}$ |
| Double pick-up ... ... ... ... ... ... | $1^{\circ}\ 30' \pm 1^{\circ}$ |
| Caster angle ... ... ... ... ... ... ... | $1^{\circ}\ 50' \pm 45'$ |

King pin inclination:

| | |
|---|---|
| Pick-up ... ... ... ... ... ... ... ... | $6^{\circ}\ 15'$ |
| Double pick-up ... ... ... ... ... ... | $6^{\circ}$ |

Steering angle:

| | |
|---|---|
| Inner wheel ... ... ... ... ... ... ... | $36 \pm 1^{\circ}$ |
| Outer wheel ... ... ... ... ... ... ... | $31 \pm 1^{\circ}$ |
| King pin clearance limit in bush ... ... ... ... | 0.0059 in (0.15 mm) |
| Bushing inner diameter (when fitted) ... ... ... ... ... | 0.7878 to 0.7888 in (20.01 to 20.035 mm) |
| Clearance between knuckle spindle support and spindle ... ... ... | Less than 0.004 in (0.1 mm) |

### Rear suspension

| | |
|---|---|
| Type ... ... ... ... ... ... ... ... ... | Live axle with semi-elliptic springs and hydraulic shock absorbers |

### Steering

| | |
|---|---|
| Type ... ... ... ... ... ... ... ... ... | Recirculating ball nut and worm |
| Gear ratio ... ... ... ... ... ... ... ... | 19.8 : 1 |
| Worm bearing adjusting shims ... ... ... ... ... | 0.059 in (1.5 mm) |

Initial turning torque of steering column:

| | lb f in | kg fm |
|---|---|---|
| New worm bearing ... ... ... ... ... ... | 3.5 to 5.2 | 4.0 to 6.0 |
| Used worm bearing ... ... ... ... ... ... | 2.1 to 3.8 | 2.4 to 4.4 |

| | |
|---|---|
| Sector shaft adjusting screw and clearance ... ... ... | 0.0004 to 0.0012 in (0.01 to 0.03 mm) |
| Backlash at top end of gear arm ... ... ... ... | 0 to 0.004 in (0 to 0.1 mm) |
| Balljoint axial endplay ... ... ... ... ... ... | 0.004 to 0.020 in (0.1 to 0.5 mm) |
| Standard cross rod length ... ... ... ... ... | 20 to 31 in (516 mm) |
| Steering gear oil type ... ... ... ... ... ... | SAE 90EP Gear oil |
| Steering gear oil capacity ... ... ... ... ... | 3/8 US pt (¼ Imp. pt/0.33 liter) |

## Wheels and tires

| | | | | | | | | | |
|---|---|---|---|---|---|---|---|---|---|
| Wheel type | ... | ... | ... | ... | ... | ... | ... | ... | 4½J - 14 |
| Tire size: * | | | | | | | | | |
| USA | ... | ... | ... | ... | ... | ... | ... | ... | 6.00 - 14 - 6PR |
| UK | ... | ... | ... | ... | ... | ... | ... | ... | 6.70 - 14C - 8PR |
| Double pick-up | ... | ... | ... | ... | ... | ... | ... | ... | 5.50 - 14 - 8PR |

*Tire size depends on the vehicle usage. It is recommended that a Datsun agent or tire specialist is consulted when replacements are required.*

| Tire pressures (measured cold): ** | Under 60mph (100 km/h) | Over 60 mph (100 km/h) |
|---|---|---|
| Long wheelbase: | | |
| Unloaded: | | |
| Front | 21 (1.5) | 26 (1.8) |
| Rear | 39 (2.75) | 46 (3.25) |
| Loaded: | | |
| Front | 21 (1.5) | 26 (1.8) |
| Rear | 60 (4.25) | 67 (4.75) |
| Standard wheelbase: | | |
| Unloaded: | | |
| Front | 21 (1.5) | 26 (1.8) |
| Rear | 25 (1.75) | 32 (2.25) |
| Loaded: | | |
| Front | 21 (1.5) | 26 (1.8) |
| Rear | 42 (3.0) | 49 (3.5) |
| Double pick-up: | | |
| Unloaded: | | |
| Front | 21 (1.5) | 26 (1.8) |
| Rear | 25 (1.75) | 32 (2.25) |
| Loaded: | | |
| Front | 21 (1.5) | 26 (1.8) |
| Rear | 53 (3.75) | 60 (4.25) |

**Tire pressures are in lb f/sq. in (kg f/sq.cm) and are for general usage. For special applications consult your Datsun agent or a tire specialist.*

## Torque wrench settings

| | lb f ft | kg f m |
|---|---|---|
| *Front suspension* | | |
| Brake hose connecting nut | 1.9 to 2.5 | 14 to 18 |
| Wheel bearing locknut | 3.0 to 3.5 | 22 to 25 |
| Brake disc fixing bolt | 4 2 to 5.0 | 30 to 36 |
| Knuckle arm fixing bolt | 10.3 to 12.1 | 74 to 88 |
| King pin lock bolt | 2.1 to 2.5 | 15 to 18 |
| Torsion bar: | | |
| Arm end | 2.7 to 3.7 | 20 to 27 |
| Serration boss | 1.8 to 2.6 | 13 to 19 |
| Lower arm spindle nut | 7.4 to 8.0 | 54 to 58 |
| Upper arm screw bushing | 35 to 55 | 253 to 398 |
| Upper arm spindle bolt fixing to bracket | 7 to 9 | 51 to 65 |
| Cotter pin lock nut | 0.8 to 1.1 | 5.8 to 8.0 |
| Lower arm screw bushing | 20 to 30 | 145 to 217 |
| Fulcrum bolt | 3.9 to 5.3 | 28 to 38 |
| Torsion rod: | | |
| Locknut | 12 to 16 | 1.6 to 2.2 |
| Bracket bolt | 12 to 16 | 1.6 to 2.2 |
| Shock absorber: | | |
| Locknut of the upper end | 12 to 16 | 1.6 to 2.2 |
| Lower end | 22 to 30 | 3.1 to 4.1 |
| Stabilizer bar bracket bolt | 12 to 16 | 1.6 to 2.2 |
| Locknut of the anchor bolt | 22 to 30 | 3.1 to 4.1 |
| Bumper rubber bolt | 5.8 to 8.0 | 0.8 to 1.1 |
| | | |
| *Rear suspension* | | |
| Shock absorber upper end nut | 22 to 30 | 3.1 to 4.1 |
| Shock absorber lower end nut | 12 to 16 | 1.6 to 2.2 |
| Rear spring U-bolt (clip) | 53 to 72 | 7.3 to 9.9 |
| Spring front pin | 83 to 94 | 11.5 to 13.0 |
| Spring shackle | 83 to 94 | 11.5 to 13.0 |
| Bearing cage fixing bolt | 39 to 46 | 5.4 to 6.4 |
| Wheel bearing locknut | 108 to 145 | 15 to 20 |
| Bumper rubber bolt | 12 to 16 | 1.6 to 2.2 |
| | | |
| *Steering* | | |
| Steering column jacket to gear housing | 11 to 18 | 1.5 to 2.5 |
| Sector shaft cover | 11 to 18 | 1.5 to 2.5 |
| Sector shaft locknut | 22 to 29 | 3.0 to 4.0 |
| Gear housing | 33 to 38 | 4.6 to 5.3 |
| Gear arm | 94 to 108 | 13 to 15 |

**11**

| | | | | | | | | | | |
|---|---|---|---|---|---|---|---|---|---|---|
| Steering wheel | ... | ... | ... | ... | ... | ... | ... | ... | 51 to 54 | 7 to 7.5 |
| Ball studs of cross rod | ... | ... | ... | ... | ... | ... | ... | ... | 40 to 72 | 5.5 to 10.0 |
| Ball studs of side rod (tie-rod): | | | | | | | | | | |
|    Knuckle arm side | ... | ... | ... | ... | ... | ... | ... | ... | 40 to 72 | 5.5 to 10.0 |
|    Gear or idler arm side | ... | ... | ... | ... | ... | ... | ... | 40 to 72 | 5.5 to 10.0 |
| Steering idler screw bushing | ... | ... | ... | ... | ... | ... | ... | 80 to 94 | 11 to 13 |
| Wheel nuts | ... | ... | ... | ... | ... | ... | ... | ... | 58 to 65 | 8 to 9 |

## 1  General description

The front suspension is of the independant double wishbone type with torsion bar springing. The steering knuckle is connected to the upper link through a rubber bushing, and to the lower link through a screw bushing. Fore-and-aft loads on the wishbones are absorbed through tension rods mounted on rubber bushes on the lower suspension arm and chassis frame (photo).

The front end of the torsion bar is attached to a torque arm which connects with the lower link. The rear arm is attached to a spring anchor firmly mounted on the chassis frame.

The shock abosrber is a double acting, telescopic, hydraulic type connected at the upper end to a bracket on the chassis frame and at the lower end to a bracket on the lower wishbone.

Vertical movement of the suspension arms is limited by a rubber bumper attached to a bracket on the chassis frame.

An optional stabilizer bar is available.

The rear suspension comprises semi-elliptic leaf springs mounted in rubber bushings on the chassis frame sidemembers, and a line rear axle connected to the springs by U-bolts. Hydraulic shock absorbers are rubber mounted through brackets at the spring mountings, and bushes on one of the chassis frame crossmembers.

The steering system comprises a steering wheel and column, recirculating ball-nut steering gear, idler arm assembly, cross rod, side rods (tie-rods), steering knuckle arms and kingpins. The steering gear is adjustable for worn bearing preload by the use of shims, and for sector shaft endplay by means of an adjusting screw.

The front wheel hubs are supported on opposed taper roller bearings on the steering knuckle spindle (stub axle). The rear hubs are supported at their outer ends in single roller bearings; details of removal procedures etc, will be found in Chapter 8.

1 General view of left side front suspension looking forward

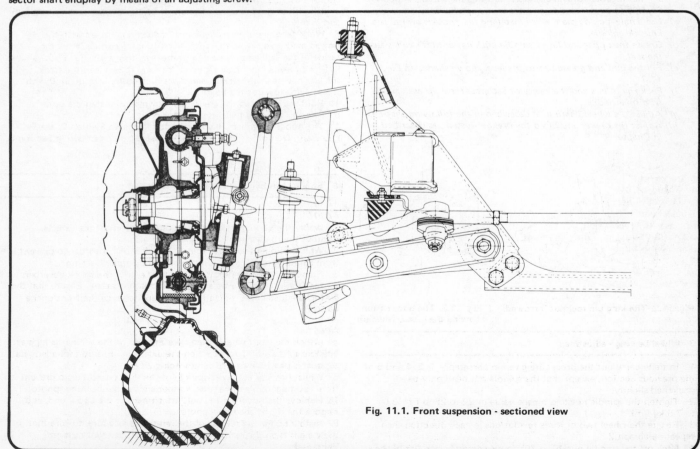

Fig. 11.1. Front suspension - sectioned view

## 2 Steering knuckle - removal and installation

1 Apply the parking brake then jack-up the front of the vehicle and support it on a firmly based axle stand on the chassis frame sidemember.
2 Remove the front wheel.
3 Remove the brake hose, together with the connector, the wheel cylinder; refer to Chapter 9, if necessary.
4 Remove the brake drum; refer to Chapter 9, if necessary.
5 Remove the hub grease cap, then remove the cotter pin, adjusting cap and spindle nut from the spindle.
6 Pull off the wheel hub. Unless the hub is to be dismantled (Section 5), leave the thrust washer and grease seal in position to retain the roller races.
7 Remove the brake backplate; refer to Chapter 9, if necessary.
8 Remove the steering knuckle arm from the knuckle spindle. Discard the locking plate.
9 Slacken the nut of the king pin (swivel) lock bolt, then drive the bolt free using a soft-faced hammer. Remove the nut completely and withdraw the bolt.
10 Remove the air breather from the top of the kingpin, then drill a hole 0.413 in/10.5 mm diameter (Letter drill Z) in the plug. Drill and tap the hole, and install a suitable bolt (M12 thread suits the drill size quoted, but the actual size of the hole and bolt can be altered slightly, if necessary, to suit available tools and bolts). Screw in the bolt to extract the plug.
11 Liberally apply penetrating oil to the kingpin and drive it out downwards using a hammer and brass drift.
12 Tap the spindle with a soft-faced hammer to detach it from the knuckle spindle support. Do not lose the thrust bearing.
13 Installation of the steering knuckle is basically the reverse of the removal procedure. However, the following points should be noted:

    *a) Grease all moving parts using lithium based general purpose grease.*
    *b) Do not forget to insert the 'O'-ring on the lower end of the steering knuckle support. Install the thrust bearing and spindle shim(s) together with the spindle, towards the spindle support. Shim(s) to be selected to give the specified clearance.*
    *c) Use a new locking plate when installing the knuckle arm to the knuckle spindle.*
    *d) Grease the upper and lower spindle bushings until it exudes from the seal.*
    *e) Fill the hub and grease cap to the level shown shaded in Fig. 11.3.*
    *f) Pack the rollers and the cavity of the grease seal lip with grease (if dismantled).*
    *g) Adjust the wheel bearing, as described in the following Section.*
    *h) Adjust the brakes and bleed the braking system, as described in Chapter 9.*

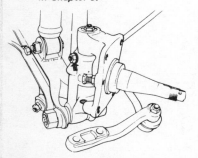
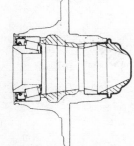

**Fig. 11.2. The king pin locknut (arrowed)**     **Fig. 11.3. The hub section showing the grease (shaded)**

## 3 Wheel bearing - adjustment

1 Initially carry out the procedure given in paragraphs 1, 2, 4 and 5 of the previous Section, except that the spindle nut need only be slackened slightly.
2 Tighten the spindle nut to a torque value of 22 to 25 lb f ft (3.0 to 3.5 kg f m).
3 Rotate the wheel two or three revolutions in each direction then repeat paragraph 2.
4 Back off the spindle nut 40 to 70° (approximately one flat of the

nut) then locate the adjusting cap to align the castellations and the cotter pin hole.
5 Ensure that the hub rotates freely. If it does not, either the bearing is incorrectly adjusted, or is unserviceable and should be dismantled as described in Section 5.
6 Install a new cotter pin, bending over the ends (photo).
7 Install the grease cap, brake drum and wheel then lower the vehicle to the ground.

## 4 Steering knuckle - renewal of bushes

This operation is considered beyond the scope of the home mechanic since it requires the use of special tools to remove and install the bushes, ream them to the correct size and install the grease seal. Therefore, it is recommended that the steering knuckle is removed as described in Section 2, and passed to a Datsun main dealer or automobile engineering workshop for renewal of the bushes.

## 5 Front wheel hub - dismantling and reassembly

1 Having removed the hub as described in paragraphs 1, 2, 4, 5 and 6, of Section 2, pry out the rear grease seal with a screwdriver.
2 Take out the inner bearing inner race and roller assembly.
3 Working through the hub, push out the outer bearing inner race and roller assembly. Remove the thrust washer which is adhering to the race.
4 Using a hammer and brass drift, carefully and evenly tap out the bearing outer tracks.
5 Wash the parts carefully in gasoline (petrol) or kerosene (paraffin), taking care that the left and right assemblies are not mixed up.
6 Examine the bearings and tracks for scoring, pitting, corrosion and signs of overheating (a bluish color). Brown staining can be ignored as this is a residue from the bearing grease. Ensure that the bearings run freely after cleaning; if replacements are required renew the inner and/or outer bearings as a complete assembly.
7 Install the bearing outer tracks in the hub, tapping them in carefully and evenly.
8 Work general purpose grease into the bearing rollers with the fingers, and smear it on the outer track running surface. Pack the inside of the hub and grease cap to the level shown in Fig. 11.3.
9 Position the inner bearing inner race and rollers into the track, smear a new seal with grease and press it carefully into the hub with the seal lips towards the bearing.
10 Hold the hub with the grease seal downward, install the outer bearing and position the thrust washer on it.
11 The hub is now ready for installation. Refer to Section 2, as necessary. Do not forget to adjust the bearing, as described in Section 3.

## 6 Shock absorbers - removal and installation

### Front
1 Apply the parking brake and jack-up the front of the vehicle. Remove the roadwheel.
2 Whilst holding the upper spindle of the shock absorber to prevent it from rotating, remove the nuts, washer and rubber bushing.
3 Remove the through-bolt at the lower end of the shock absorber.
4 Installation is the reverse of the removal procedure. Ensure that the bolt at the lower end is fitted with its head towards the front of the vehicle.

### Rear
5 Chock the front wheels then raise the rear of the vehicle as high as possible so that it is supported on the axle tube. Ensure that adequate support is provided before commencing work.
6 Whilst holding the lower spindle of the shock absorber to prevent it from rotating, remove the nuts, washer and rubber bushing (photo).
7 Remove the nut from the bolt attachment at the upper end, and remove the shock absorber (photo).
8 Installation is the reverse of the removal procedure. Ensure that the weight is on the rear wheels before the attachment nuts are tightened.

**11**

3.6 Bend over the ends of the cotter pin

6.6 Lower attachment of rear shock absorber

6.7 Upper attachment of rear shock absorber

## 7  Stabilizer bar - removal and installation

1   Apply the parking brake then jack-up the front of the vehicle and support it on firmly based axlestands on the chassis frame sidemembers.
2   Remove the roadwheels.
3   Loosen the securing nut at each end of the lower suspension arm mounting.
4   Remove the bolts securing the stabilizer mounting brackets to the frame.
5   Installation is the reverse of the removal procedure but ensure that new bushes are used where there is any deterioration of the original ones. Attach and tighten the frame mounting first, then tighten the nuts on the lower suspension arm attachment points for the stabilizer bar to obtain the dimension given in Fig. 11.7. Tighten the locknut to the specified torque whilst maintaining this dimension.

## 8  Tension (radius) rods - removal and installation

1   Apply the parking brake then jack-up the front of the vehicle and support it on firmly based axlestands.
2   Remove the roadwheel.
3   Remove the nuts from the ends of the tension rods.
4   Remove the bracket bolt from the front end of the tension rod then remove the tension rod from the bracket.
5   Installation is basically the reverse of the removal procedure but ensure that new bushes are used where there is any deterioration of the original ones. The following points should be noted:
   a) *Install the rear end of the tension rod and tighten the nut to obtain a dimension of 1.315 in (33.4 mm) between the shoulder on the rod and the nut face (Fig. 11.9a).*
   b) *Install the bracket to the forward end of the tension rod to obtain a dimension of 1.441 in (36.6 mm) as shown in Fig. 11.9b.*

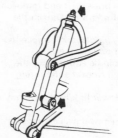

Fig. 11.4. Wheel bearing - sectional view

1   *Outer race*
2   *Roller*
3   *Small collar*
4   *Inner race installed surface*
5   *Collar surface*
6   *Inner race surface*
7   *Outer race installed surface*
8   *Outer race surface*
9   *Roller rolling surface*
10  *Inner race*
11  *Large collar*
12  *Supporter (cage)*

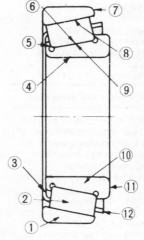

Fig. 11.5. Front shock absorber retaining nuts (arrowed)

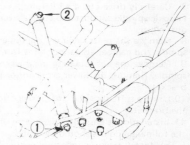

Fig. 11.6. Rear shock absorber

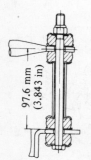

Fig. 11.7. Stabilizer installation dimensions

97.6 mm (3.843 in)

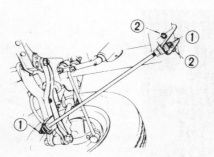

Fig. 11.8. Tension rod attachment points (1 and 2)

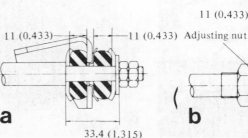

a

11 (0.433)          11 (0.433)

33.4 (1.315)

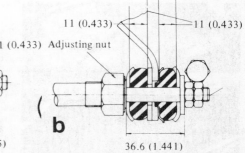

b

11 (0.433)          11 (0.433)   Adjusting nut

36.6 (1.441)

Fig. 11.9. Tension rod installation dimensions - mm (in)

a   *Rear end*                    b   *Front end*

### 9 Torsion bar - removal and installation

1   Apply the parking brake then jack-up the front of the vehicle and support it on firmly based axle stands.
2   Remove the roadwheel.
3   Loosen the nuts at the torsion bar anchor bolt.
4   Remove the dust cover at the rear end of the torsion bar spring, then remove and discard the snap-ring (circlip).
5   Withdraw the torsion bar from the rear after pulling out the anchor arm.
6   Installation is basically the reverse of the removal procedure, but the following points must be noted:
   a) *The torsion bars are marked L H (left) or R H (right) on the end surface, and must not be interchanged (photo).*
   b) *Smear grease on the torsion bar splines, prior to installation.*
   c) *Install the anchor arm to obtain 'A' dimension' of 0.197 to 0.591 in (5 to 15 mm) for a standard wheelbase vehicle, 0.591 to 0.984 in (15 to 25 mm) for a long wheelbase vehicle or 0.925 in (23.5 mm) for a double pick-up when the lower suspension arm is contacting the rubber bumper (Fig. 11.10). (photo).*
   d) *Install the new snap-ring and dust cover, and obtain 'B' dimension of 2.362 to 2.756 in (60 to 70 mm) for a standard long wheelbase vehicle, or 2.421 in (61.5 mm) for a Double pick-up, by tightening the adjusting nut.*

### 10 Upper and lower suspension arms - removal and installation

1   Initially carry out the procedure of Section 2, paragraphs 1 thru 8.
2   Remove the torsion bar, stabilizer bar, shock absorber and tension rod in this order, by reference to the appropriate preceding Sections.
3   Remove the upper fulcrum bolt securing the steering knuckle support to the upper suspension arm, and separate the parts.
4   Carefully drive out the upper arm bushes from the knuckle spindle support.
5   Remove the screw bushings from each end of the lower link fulcrum pin.
6   Loosen the nut from the inside at the lower part of the knuckle spindle support, and remove the cotter pin retaining the fulcrum pin.
7   Carefully drive out the fulcrum pin using a brass drift and remove the knuckle spindle support and spndle from the lower arm. Detach the dust cover.
8   Remove the bolts retaining the upper arm spindle, and remove the spindle and camber adjusting shims from the body bracket.
9   Remove the nut retaining the lower arm spindle and remove the spindle. Remove the lower arm and torque arm from the mounting bracket.
10  Using a suitably sized drift, drive out the lower link bushing from the bracket.
11  Installation is basically the reverse of the removal procedure, but the following points should be noted:
   a) *Install the original camber shims to prevent the camber angle from being upset.*
   b) *Grease the screw bushing threads before installation. Position the knuckle spindle support at the centre of the lower link and loosely install the screw bushings. Tighten the screw bushings to*

obtain the dimensions shown in Fig. 11.12.
   c) *Remove the grease plug, temporarily install a green nipple and fill with grease until it exudes from the dust cover. Reinstall the grease plug.*
   d) *Ensure that the upper arm fulcrum pin is installed from the rear of the vehicle.*

### 11 Suspension arms - dismantling, inspection and reassembly

*Upper arm*
1   Detach the upper arm spindle from the upper arms. Remove the clamp, dust cover and dust seal. Secure the arm in a vise and loosen the screw bushing. Discard the dust cover and seal.
2   Check that there is no more than 0.0138 in (0.35mm) endplay between the upper arm spindle or fulcrum pin and screw bushing. Replace parts as necessary where the endplay is excessive.
3   Check the screw thread of the upper arm spindle, fulcrum pin and screw bushing; obtain replacement parts as necessary.
4   Reassembly is basically the reverse of the removal procedure, but note the following points:
   a) *Use a new dust seal and dust cover.*
   b) *Grease the screw bushing before installation. Screw the front and rear arm to the arm spindle to obtain the dimensions given in Fig. 11.13.*
   c) *Remove the grease plug, temporarily install a grease nipple and fill with grease until it exudes from the dust cover. Reinstall the grease plug.*

*Lower arm*
5   The dismantling procedure is given in the previous Section.
6   When installing the torque arm to the lower arm, tighten the serration boss to a torque value of 13 to 19 lb f ft (1.8 to 2.6 kg f m), and the arm head to a torque value of 20 to 27 lb f ft (2.7 to 3.7 kg f m).

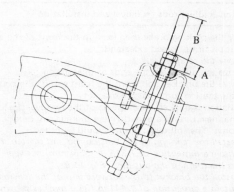

**Fig. 11.10. Installing the anchor arm**
Refer to the text for dimensions A and B

9.6a Right torsion bar marking

9.6c Torsion bar anchor arms

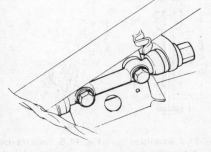

**Fig. 11.11. Upper arm spindle retaining bolts**

**11**

## 12 Vehicle trim height - adjustment

1   If found necessary, the vehicle trim height can be adjusted, although this should only be necessary after a very high mileage has been covered.

2   Apply the parking brake, then jack-up the front of the vehicle and support it on firmly based axle stands.

3   Referring to Fig. 11.14, adjust the H dimension by turning the nut adjusting anchor bolt, according to the values given in the table. The dimension changes approximately 0.138 in (3.5 mm) for every complete turn of the adjuster nut. **Note:** Although the vehicle is raised for access to the adjusting anchor bolt, measurements are taken with the vehicle on the ground.

*Vehicle loaded*      *3.071 to 3.228 in (78 to 82 mm)*
*No payload*          *2.146 in (54.5 mm)*

Vehicle loaded is:
  *Two passengers and 1100 lb (500 kg) payload for a pick-up or five passengers and 880 lb (400 kg) payload for a Double pick-up.*
No payload is:
  *a) Fuel tank, radiator and engine oil level full.*
  *b) Spare tire, wheel, jack and handle correctly installed in their respective positions.*

stubborn wheel can usually be removed by heavy blows with the ball of the hand on the steering wheel spokes near the hub. If this fails, a puller will be required - do not use too much force (photo).

6   Remove the upper and lower steering column shell covers.

7   Remove the turn signal switch assembly; refer to Chapter 10, if necessary.

8   On column change models, draw out the hand lever by removing the snap-ring (circlip).

9   Remove the column clamp by unscrewing the two fixing bolts (Fig. 11.17).

10  Remove the four bolts securing the steering shaft grommet to the dash panel.

11  Remove the nut securing the steering gear arm to the sector shaft. Index mark the arm and shaft as an aid to alignment.

12  Withdraw the arm from the splined taper using a hammer and split wedges or a universal balljoint separator (provided that care is taken it is possible to insert the taper of a cold chisel between the end of the arm and the lower end of the gear housing to remove the arm).

13  Remove the three bolts securing the gear housing to the vehicle frame.

14  Withdraw the complete steering gear downward through the engine compartment.

15  Where applicable, detach the transmission control linkage.

16  Installation is the reverse of the removal procedure.

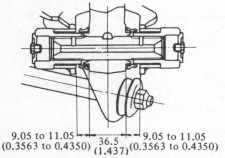

9.05 to 11.05
(0.3563 to 0.4350)      36.5        9.05 to 11.05
                      (1.437)      (0.3563 to 0.4350)

**Fig. 11.12. Screw bushing installation dimensions - mm (in)**

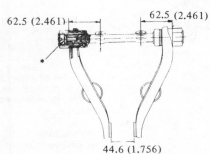

62.5 (2.461)              62.5 (2.461)

44.6 (1.756)

**Fig. 11.13. Upper arm and spindle installation dimensions - mm (in)**

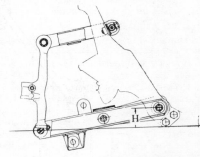

H

**Fig. 11.14. Vehicle trim height adjustment dimension H**

## 13 Rear spring - removal and installation

1   Chock the front wheels, then raise the rear of the vehicle with the jack head on the body sidemember.

2   Place an axle stand beneath the sidemember, remove the jack then position the jack to just take the weight of the axle.

3   Detach the shock absorber lower mounting from the spring plate.

4   Remove the U-bolt nuts then raise the jack beneath the axle to separate the axle from the spring.

5   Remove the nuts from the rear spring shackle. Carefully drive out the bolts to free the rear end of the spring.

6   Remove the pin at the front end of the spring to permit the spring to be removed.

7   Examine the spring for broken or distorted leaves; if any are found a replacement spring must be obtained. If the rubber bushes are damaged they can be pressed out using a suitable diameter drift and spacer between the jaws of a vise. Coat new ones with a soap and water solution to ease their installation.

8   Installation of the spring is the reverse of the removal procedure, but ensure that the weight of the vehicle is on the roadwheel before the front pin nut, shackle nuts, U-bolts nuts and shock absorber mounting are torque tightered.

## 14 Steering gear - removal and installation

1   Disconnect the battery ground cable.

2   Unscrew the two bolts at the rear of the horn pad so that the pad can be removed. Where applicable detach the electrical lead at the center terminal.

3   Remove the single nut from the center of the steering wheel.

4   Index mark the steering wheel hub and the top of the steering shaft as an aid to alignment.

5   If you are lucky you will be able to pull off the steering wheel now. A

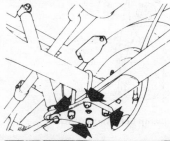

**Fig. 11.15. Rear spring plate attachment points**

14.5 Warning notice on the steering wheel spokes

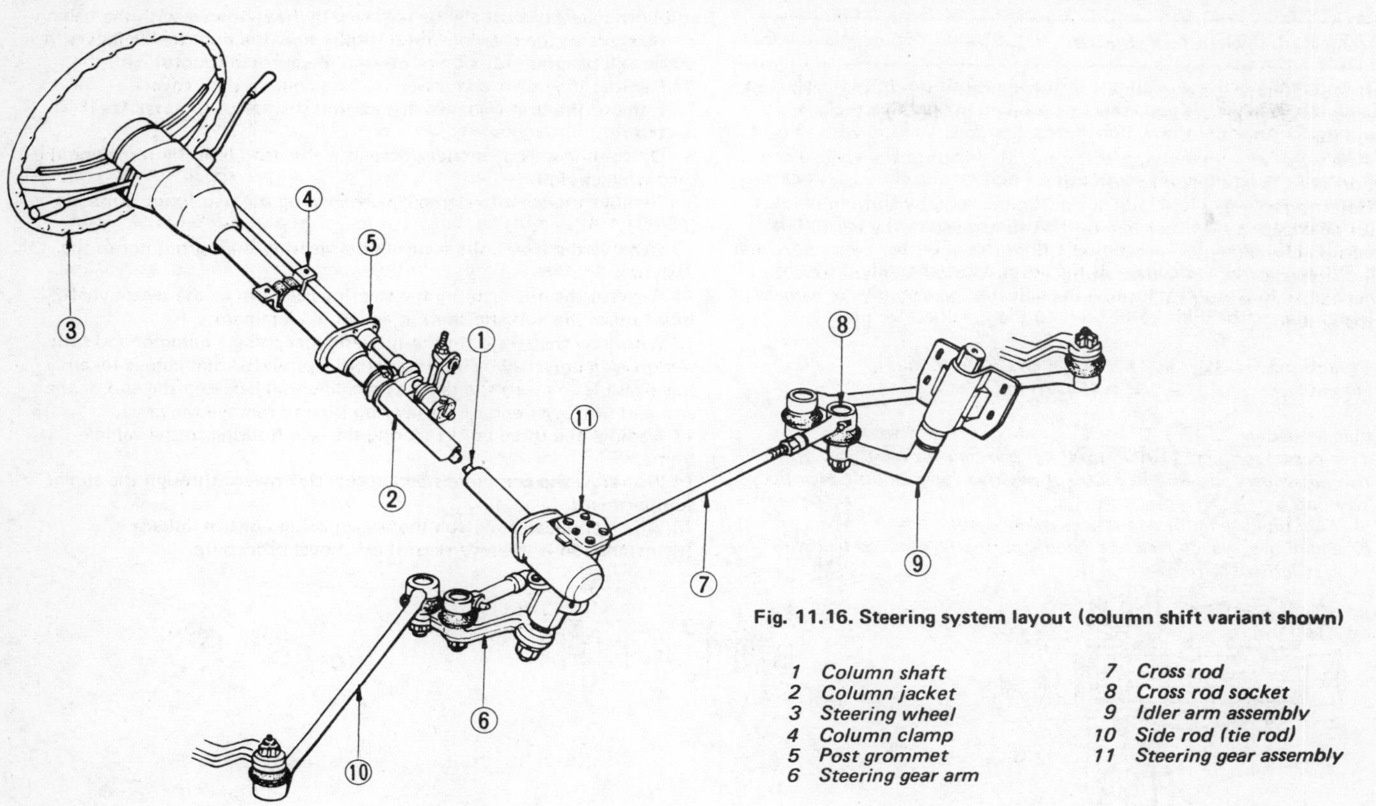

Fig. 11.16. Steering system layout (column shift variant shown)

| 1 | Column shaft | 7 | Cross rod |
| 2 | Column jacket | 8 | Cross rod socket |
| 3 | Steering wheel | 9 | Idler arm assembly |
| 4 | Column clamp | 10 | Side rod (tie rod) |
| 5 | Post grommet | 11 | Steering gear assembly |
| 6 | Steering gear arm | | |

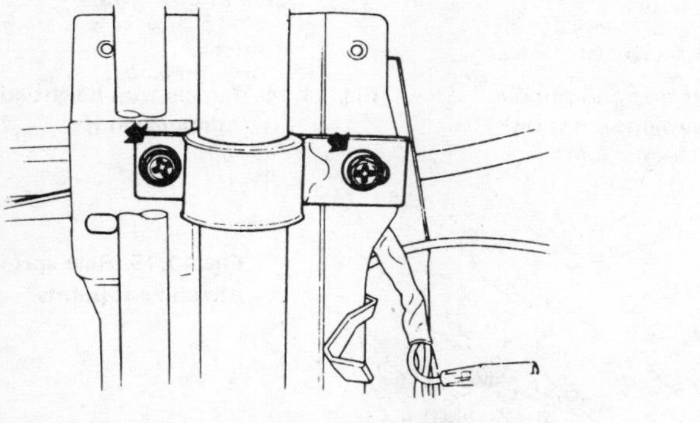

Fig. 11.17. Steering column clamp bolts (arrowed)

## 15 Steering gear - dismantling, inspection and reassembly

1  Unscrew the steering gear filler plug and drain the oil into a suitable receptacle.

2  Secure the steering gear in a vise, then loosen the sector shaft adjuster locknut. Back-off the screw approximately 3 turns.

3  Remove the four cover retaining bolts; take off the cover and gasket.

4  Turn the sector shaft adjusting screw clockwise, and pull the shaft cover and gear from the housing.

5  Separate the shaft, adjusting screw and shim(s) from the cover.

6  Remove the jacket tube by unscrewing the three bolts.

7  Remove the worm assembly from the housing.

8  Taking extreme care that the ball nut does not run suddenly to the end of the worm (for fear of damaging the ball guides), detach the worm bearings and adjusting shims from the gear assembly and column jacket.

9  Pry out the sector shaft oil seal from the gear housing and discard it.

10  Remove the 'O'-ring from the rear cover of the column jacket and discard it.

11  Remove the column jacket bushing. Do not remove the sector

shaft bushing from the housing, if this is worn the gear housing must be renewed. Do not dismantle the ball nut and worm gear; if necessary, replace them with new ones as a worm gear assembly.

12  Wash all the parts in kerosene (paraffin) and dry them carefully with a lint-free cloth.

13  Sector shaft: Check the gear tooth surface for wear and damage, renewing as necessary. Check the shaft splines for wear and damage; if necessary obtain a replacement shaft. If the splines are damaged, also check the gear housing for deformation.

14  Steering column shaft assembly: Examine the gear tooth surface for wear and damage, renewing as necessary. Examine the ball nut for smooth operation; the ball nut should move under its own weight over the full length of the worm gear when the shaft assembly is held vertically, but take care that the ball guide is not damaged during this check.

15  Bearings and bushings: Examine bearings and bushings for wear and damage, renewing as necessary.

16  To commence reassembly, lubricate all parts of the steering gear with the approved type of gear oil.

17  Bond the column jacket bushing to the column jacket using a proprietary contact adhesive; lubricate the inside of the bushing with general purpose grease.

18  Fill a new sector shaft oil seal with grease, and install it in the gear housing.

19  Position the worm assembly into the gear housing together with the worm bearings.

20  Install the column jacket on the gear housing using a new 'O'-ring and the existing shim(s), ensuring that the thickest shims are towards the gear housing side. Tighten the bolts to the specified torque.

21  Check the initial turning torque of the steering gear and comapre the valve obtained with that given in the Specifications. Select suitable shims to obtain the specified torque figure; shims are available in sizes of 0.03 in (0.762 mm), 0.01 in (0.254 mm), 0.005 in (0.127 mm) and 0.002 in (0.05 mm). Note: An Alternative method is to temporarily install the steering wheel and check the turning force at the wheel rim. This should be 0.4 to 0.7 lb (0.2 to 0.3 kg) for a new bearing and 0.3 to 0.5 lb (0.12 to 0.22 kg) for a used bearing.

22  Insert the adjusting screw into the T-shaped groove in the sector shaft head, and adjust the shaft-to-screw endplay by selecting suitable shims, until it is as given in the Specifications. Shims are available in

sizes of 0.0620 in (1.575 mm), 0.0610 in (1.550 mm), 0.0600 in (1.525 mm), 0.0591 in (1.500 mm), 0.0581 in (1.475 mm) and 0.0571 in (1.450 mm).

23 Rotate the ball nut until it is in the mid-position of its travel, then install the sector shaft and adjusting screw together into the gear housing. Ensure that the sector shaft center gear engages with that of the ball nut.

24 Install the sector shaft cover using a non-setting gasket sealant on the gasket surfaces.

25 Rotate the adjusting screw counter-clockwise and install the shaft cover and fixing bolts. Lightly tighten the cover bolts.

26 Pull the sector shaft towards the cover approximately 0.079 to 0.118 in (2 to 3 mm) by turning the adjusting screw counter-clockwise. Tighten the sector shaft cover bolts to the specified torque.

27 Push the sector shaft against the ball nut gear by gradually turning the adjusting screw clockwise until the shaft gear lightly meshes with the ball nut gear. Temporarily secure the adjusting screw with the locknut.

28 Install the gear arm, and ensure that the sector shaft moves smoothly throughout its range of travel.

29 Adjust the steering gear backlash at the mid-position of its travel (by means of the adjusting screw) to obtain the specified backlash when measured at the outer end of the gear arm.

30 Turn the adjusting screw 1/8 to 1/6 of a turn (45 to 60°) then tighten the locknut to the specified torque.

31 Fill the steering gear with the specified type and quantity of gear oil.

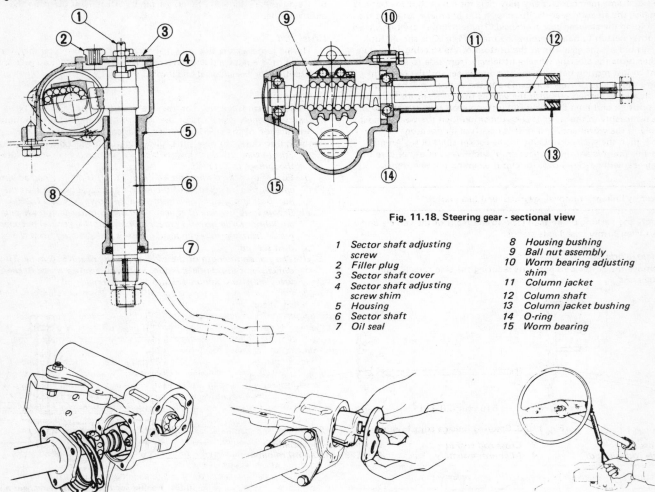

Fig. 11.18. Steering gear - sectional view

| | |
|---|---|
| 1  Sector shaft adjusting screw | 8  Housing bushing |
| 2  Filler plug | 9  Ball nut assembly |
| 3  Sector shaft cover | 10  Worm bearing adjusting shim |
| 4  Sector shaft adjusting screw shim | 11  Column jacket |
| 5  Housing | 12  Column shaft |
| 6  Sector shaft | 13  Column jacket bushing |
| 7  Oil seal | 14  O-ring |
| | 15  Worm bearing |

Fig. 11.19. Withdrawing the sector shaft          Fig. 11.20. Removing the steering worm assembly          Fig. 11.21. Checking the initial turning torque

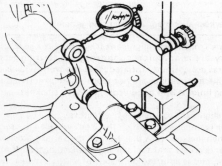

Fig. 11.22. Checking the gear arm backlash

## 16 Steering linkage - inspection for wear

1  Wear in the steering gear and linkage is indicated when there is considerable movement in the steering wheel without corresponding movement at the roadwheels. Wear is also indicated when the vehicle tends to 'wander' off the line one is trying to steer. There are three main steering 'groups' to examine in such circumstances. These are the wheel bearings, the linkage joints and bushes, and the steering gear itself.

2  First jack up the front of the vehicle and support it on stands under the side frame members so that both front wheels are clear of the ground.

3  Grip the top and bottom of the wheel and try to rock it. It will not take any great effort to be able to feel any play in the wheel bearing. If this play is very noticeable it would be as well to adjust it straight away as it could confuse further examinations. It is also possible that during this check play may be found in the steering king pin which

must be rectified accordingly.

4    Next grip each side of the wheel and try rocking it laterally. Steady pressure will, of course, turn the steering but an alternated back and forth pressure will reveal any loose joint. If some play is felt it would be easier to get assistance from someone so that while one person rocks the wheel from side to side, the other can look at the joints and bushes on the track rods and connections. Excluding the steering gear itself there are eight places where the play may occur. The two outer balljoints on the side rods are the most likely, followed by the two inner joints on the same rods there they join the cross rod. Any play in these means renewal of the side rod(s). Next are the two balljoints, one at each end of the cross rod. Finally check the steering gear arm balljoint, and the one on the idler arm which supports the cross rod on the side opposite the steering gear. This unit is bolted to the side frame member and any play calls for renewal of the bushes.

5    Finally, the steering gear itself is checked. First make sure that the bolts holding the steering gear to the side frame member are tight, then get another person to help examine the mechanism. One should look, at or get hold of, the gear arm at the bottom of the steering gear while the other turns the steering wheel a little way from side to side. The amount of lost motion between the steering wheel and the gear arm indicates the degree of wear somewhere in the steering mechanism. This check should be carried out with the wheels first of all in the straight ahead position and then at nearly full lock on each side. If the play only occurs noticeably in the straight ahead position then the wear is most probably in the worm and/or nut. If it occurs at all positions of the steering, then the wear is probably in the rocker shaft bush. An oil leak at this point is another indication of such wear. In either case the steering gear will need removal for closer examination and repair.

---

**17 Steering linkage - removal, overhaul and installation**

---

1    Apply the parking brake then jack-up the front of the vehicle and support it on firmly based axle stands.

### Side (tie) rods
2    Remove the cotter pins and nuts securing the side rods to the knuckle arms.

3    Using a proprietary balljoint separator or a hammer and split wedges, detach the ball studs from the knuckle arms (provided that care is taken it is possible to insert the taper of a cold chisel between the end of the arm and the eye-end of the side rod to remove the side rod).

4    If the crossrod is not going to be removed, detach the inner ends of the side rods in a similar manner.

### Gear arm
5    Index mark the position of the gear arm on the sector shaft splined end to assist with alignment during reassembly. Remove the gear arm in a similar manner to that described for the side rods.

### Idler arm assembly
6    Remove the idler arm assembly from its attachment point on the chassis frame.

### Cross rod
7    Having removed the side rods, gear arm and idler arm assembly, the cross-rod can be removed and detached from the idler arm and gear arm as described for the side rod ball joints.

### Ball joints
8    If the ball studs are worn or the axial play is escessive, it will be necessary to renew a side rod or the cross rod ball-and-socket assemblies.
9    Installation of the steering linkage is basically the reverse of the removal procedure. However, the following points must be noted:

   a) *Ensure that any dust cover which is damaged is renewed before the linkage is installed.*
   b) *Ensure that the dimension 'A' (Fig. 11.23) is maintained at both ends during installation of the idler arm assembly, and that the nut, bolt and washer arrangement is as shown in Fig. 11.24.*
   c) *Before installing the idler arm assembly, remove the grease plug and temporarily install a grease nipple. Apply a general purpose grease from a grease gun until grease is just exuding from the dust seal lip.*
   d) *The standard length of the cross rod is 20.31 in (516 mm). This dimension should be set before any adjustment is made to the vehicle toe-in (Section 18).*

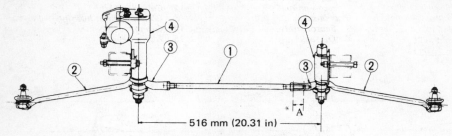

**Fig. 11.23. Steering linkage adjustment**

1    Cross rod
2    Side rod (tie rod)
3    Cross rod socket
4    Idler arm assembly
5    Gear housing assembly
A = 0.79 in (20 mm) minimum

516 mm (20.31 in)

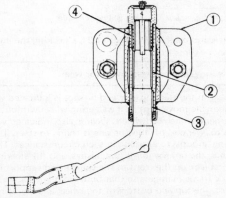

**Fig. 11.25. Idler arm assembly - sectional view**

1    Body
2    Welded collar
3    Plain bushing
4    Screw bushing

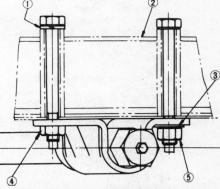

**Fig. 11.24. Washer location for steering gear and idler arm assembly**

1    Spring washer
2    Vehicle frame
3    Flat washer
4    Weld nut
5    Self-locking nut

---

**18 Front wheel alignment and steering geometry**

---

1    Accurate front wheel alignment is essential for good steering and satisfactory tire wear. Before considering the steering geometry, check that the tires are correctly inflated, that the front wheels are not buckled, the hub bearings are not worn or incorrectly adjusted, and that the steering linkage is in good order, without slackness or wear at the joints.
2    Wheel alignment consists of five factors:
   *Camber* is the angle at which the front wheels are set from the vertical when viewed from the front of the vehicle. Positive camber is the amount (in degrees) that the wheels are tilted outwards at the top from the vertical, and is adjusted by means of shims between the suspension upper arm spindle and the arm mounting bracket at the front and rear.

**11**

*Castor* is the angle between the steering axis and a vertical line when viewed from each side of the vehicle. Positive castor is when the steering axis is inclined rearward; the angle is adjusted by means of shims between the suspension upper arm spindle and the arm mounting bracket at the front or rear.

*Steering axis inclination* is the angle, when viewed from the front of the vehicle, between the vertical and an imaginary line drawn through the king pin. The angle is not adjustable. *Steering angle* is the angle through which the front wheels swivel from lock-to-lock, and is adjustable by means of stopper bolts on the steering knuckles.

*Toe-in* is the amount by which the distance between the front inside edges of the roadwheels (measured at hub height) is less than the diametrically opposite distance measured between the rear inside edges of the front roadwheels.

3   Due to the need for special gap gauges and correct weighting of the car suspension it is not within the scope of the home mechanic to check steering geometry other than checking the toe-in and the steering angle. This should be checked however by a properly equipped service stator after any part of the steering or the front end of the vehicle has been damaged in an accident. Front wheel tracking (toe-in) checks are the best carried out with modern setting equippment but a reaonably accurate alternative and adjustment procedure may be carried out as follows:

## Toe-in

4   Place the vehicle on level ground with the wheels in the straight-ahead position.

6   Obtain or make a toe-in gauge. One may be easily made from tubing, cranked to clear the oil pan (sump) having an adjustable nut and set-screw at one end.

6   Using the guage, measure the distance between the two inner wheel rims at hub height at the rear of the wheels.

7   Rotate the wheels (by pushing the car backwards or forwards) through 180° (half a turn) and again using the gauge, measure the distance of hub height between the two inner wheel rims at the front of the wheels. This measurement should be less than that previously taken at the rear of the wheel by the amount given in the Specifications, and represents the correct toe-in.

8   Where the toe-in is found to be incorrect, slacken the locknuts on each end of the cross rod, and rotate the rod until the correct toe-in is obtained. Tighten the locknuts, ensuring that the balljoints are held in the center of their arc of travel during tightening. Ensure that dimension 'A' (Fig. 11.23) at each end of the cross-rod is not less than 0.79 in

(20 mm). **Note:** Toe-in is reduced by rotating the cross rod forwards (ie: clockwise when viewed from the right side of the vehicle), and vise versa.

## Steering angles

9   The steering angles differ between the inner and outer roadwheels during a turn on full steering lock (see Specifications). These angles can only be satisfactorily measured on turn-tables at a service station but in an emergency in order to prevent a tire rubbing against the inside of a wheel arch, the stopper bolts can be adjusted.

10  Remove the caps from the bolt heads (where applicable), and loosen the locknuts.

11  Turn one or both bolts in or out as necessary to reduce or increase one or both steering angles. Tighten the locknuts after any adjustment.

## 19 Roadwheels and tires

1   Whenever the roadwheels are removed it is a good idea to clean the insides of the wheels to remove accumulations of mud.

2   Check the condition of the wheel for rust, and repaint if necessary.

3   Examine the wheel stud holes. If these are tending to become elongated, or the dished recesses in which the nuts seat have worn or become overcompressed, then the wheel will have to be renewed.

4   With a roadwheel removed, pick out any embedded flints from the tire tread, and check for splits in the sidewalls or damage to the tire carcass generally.

5   Where the depth of tread pattern is 1 mm or less, the tire must be renewed. The tires fitted as original equipment have tread markers at six points around the circumference. These markers give warning of 1.6 mm of tread remaining.

6   Rotation of the roadwheels to even out wear is a worthwhile idea if the wheels have been balanced off the car.

7   If the wheels have been balanced on the car then they cannot be moved round the car as the balance of wheel tire and hub will be upset.

8   It is recommended that wheels are balanced whenever new tires are fitted, and re-balanced halfway through the life of the tire to compensate for the loss of tread rubber due to wear.

9   Finally, always keep the tires (including the spare) inflated to the recommended pressures, and always install the dust caps on the valves. Tire pressures are best checked first thing in the morning when the tires are cold.

## 20 Fault diagnosis - suspension and steering

| Symptom | Reason/s |
| --- | --- |
| Steering feels vague, car wanders and floats at speed | Tire pressures uneven |
| | Shock absorbers worn |
| | Spring broken |
| | Steering gear balljoints badly worn |
| | Suspension geometry incorrect |
| | Steering mechanism free play excessive |
| | Front suspension and rear axle pick-up points out of alignment |
| Stiff and heavy steering | Tire pressures too low |
| | No grease in king pin joints |
| | Front wheel toe-in incorrect |
| | Suspension geometry incorrect |
| | Steering gear incorrectly adjusted too tightly |
| | Steering column badly misaligned |
| Wheel wobble and vibration | Wheel nuts loose |
| | Front wheels and tires out of balance |
| | Steering king pins badly worn |
| | Hub bearings badly worn |
| | Steering gear free play excessive |
| | Front springs weak or broken |

# Chapter 12 Bodywork and fittings

**Contents**

**Specifications**

### Torque wrench settings

| | | | | | | | | lb f ft | kg f m |
|---|---|---|---|---|---|---|---|---|---|
| Cab body to frame | ... | ... | ... | ... | ... | ... | ... | 12 to 16 | 1.6 to 2.2 |
| Rear body to frame | ... | ... | ... | ... | ... | ... | ... | 24 to 30 | 3.3 to 4.2 |
| Engine compartment hood bolts | ... | ... | ... | ... | ... | ... | | 3.3 to 4.3 | 0.45 to 0.60 |
| Hood lock dovetail bolt locking nut | ... | ... | ... | ... | ... | | | 14 to 19 | 1.9 to 2.6 |
| Seatbelt attaching bolts | ... | ... | ... | ... | ... | ... | | 20 to 23 | 2.8 to 3.2 |

## 1 General description

The pick-up bodywork and underframe comprise separate cab body and rear body sections bolted onto a pressed steel, box-section chassis frame; transverse crossmember join the two main longitudinal side-members. Apart from the length of the sidemembers, the standard and long wheelbase versions are similar.

A double pick-up is available for some markets, and comprise a 2-door 4 seat body with a small cargo compartment at the rear. This uses an entirely different chassis frame to which the one-piece body is welded.

Procedures which apply to the double pick-up only, are headed separately in the text.

## 2 Maintenance - bodywork and underframe

1 The general condition of a vehicle's bodywork is the one thing that significantly affects its value. Maintenance is easy but needs to be regular. Neglect, particularly after minor damage, can lead quickly to further deterioration and costly repair bills. It is important also to keep watch on those parts of the vehicle not immediately visible, for instance the underside, inside all the wheel arches and the lower part of the engine compartment.

2 The basic maintenance routine for the bodywork is washing - preferably with a lot of water from a hose. This will remove all the loose solids which may have stuck to the vehicle. It is important to flush these off in such a way as to prevent grit from scratching the finish.

The wheel arches and underbody need washing in the same way to remove any accumulated mud which will retain moisture and tend to encourage rust. Paradoxically enough, the best time to clean the underbody and wheel arches is in wet weather when the mud is thoroughly wet and soft. In very wet weather the underbody is usually cleaned of large accumulations automatically and this is a good time for inspection.

3 Periodically it is a good idea to have the whole of the underside of the vehicle steam cleaned, engine compartment included, so that a thorough inspection can be carried out to see what minor repairs and renovations are necessary. Steam cleaning is available at many garages and is necessary for removal of accumulations of oily grime which sometimes is allowed to cake thick in certain areas near the engine, transmission and rear axle. If steam facilities are not available, there are one ot two excellent grease solvents available which can be brush applied. The dirt can then be simply hosed off.

4 After washing paintwork, wipe off with a chamois leather to give an unspotted clear finish. A coat of clear protective wax polish will give added protection against chemical pollutants in the air. If the paintwork sheen has dulled or oxidised, use a cleaner/polisher combination to restore the brilliance of the shine. This requires little effort, but is usually caused because regular washing has been neglected. Always check that the door and ventilator opening drain holes and pipes are completely clear so that water can drain out. Bright work should be treated the same ways as paintwork. Windshields and windows can be kept clear of the smeary film which often appears if a little ammonia is added to the water. If they are scratched, a good rub with a proprietary metal polish will often clear them. Never use any from of wax or other body or chromium polish on glass.

## 3   Maintenance - upholstery and carpets

Mats and carpets should be brushed or vacuum-cleaned regularly to keep them free of grit. If they are badly stained remove them from the vehicle for scrubbing or sponging and make quite sure they are dry before replacement. Seats and interior trim panels can be kept clean by a wipe over with a damp cloth. If they do become stained (which can be more apparent on light coloured upholstery) use a little liquid detergent and a soft nail brush to scour the grime out of the grain of the material. Do not forget to keep the head lining clean in the same way as the upholstery. When using liquid cleaners inside the car do not over-wet the surfaces being cleaned. Excessive moisture could get into the seams and padded interior causing stains offensive odours or even rot. If the inside of the vehicle gets wet accidentally it is worthwhile taking some trouble to dry it out properly particularly where carpets are involved. Do not leave oil or electric heaters inside the car for this purpose.

## 4   Minor body damage - repair

*The photograph sequence on pages 178, 179 and 180 illustrates the operations detailed in the following sub-Sections.*

### Repair of minor scratches in the vehicles bodywork

If the scratch is very superficial, and does not penetrate to the metal of the bodywork, repair is very simple. Lightly rub the area of the scratch with a paintwork renovator, or a very fine cutting paste, to remove loose paint from the scratch and to clear the surrounding bodywork of wax polish. Rinse the area with clean water.

Apply touch-up paint to the scratch using a thin paint brush, continue to apply thin layers of paint until the surface of the paint in the scratch is level with the surrounding paintwork. Allow the new paint at least two weeks to harden, then, blend it into the surrounding paintwork by rubbing the paintwork, in the scratch area with a paintwork renovator, or a very fine cutting paste, Finally apply wax polish.

An alternative to painting over the scratch is to use a paint transfer. Use the same preparation for the affected area; then simply pick a patch of a suitable size to cover the scratch completely. Hold the patch against the scratch and burnish its backing paper; the patch will adhere to the paintwork, freeing itself from the backing paper at the same time. Polish the affected area to blend the patch into the surrounding paintwork. Where the scratch has penetrated right through to the metal of the bodywork, causing the metal to rust, a different repair technique is required. Remove any loose rust from the bottom of the scratch with a penknife, then apply rust inhibiting paint to prevent the formation of rust in the future. Using a rubber or nylon applicator fill the scratch with bodystopper paste. If required, this paste can be mixed with cellulose thinners to provide a very thin paste which is ideal for filling narrow scratches. Before the stopper paste in the scratch hardens, wrap a piece of smooth cotton rag around the top of a finger. Dip the finger in cellulose thinners and then quickly sweep it across the surface of the stopper paste in the scratch; this will ensure that the surface of the stopper paste is slightly hollowed. The scratch can now be painted over as described earlier in this Section.

### Repair of dents in the vehicles bodywork

When deep denting of the vehicle's bodywork has taken place, the first task is to pull the dent out, until the affected bodywork almost attains its original shape. There is little point in trying to restore the original shape completely, as the metal in the damaged area will have stretched on impact and cannot be reshaped fully to its original contour. It is better to bring the level of the dent up to a point which is about 1/8 inch (3 mm) below the level of the surrounding bodywork. In cases where the dent is very shallow anyway, it is not worth trying to pull it out at all.

If the underside of the dent is accessible, it can be hammered out gently from behind, using a mallet with a wooden or plastic head. Whilst doing this, hold a suitable block of wood firmly against the impact from the hammer blows and thus prevent a large area of bodywork from being 'belled-out'.

Should the dent be in a section of the bodywork which has a double skin or some other factor making it inaccessible from behind, a different technique is called for. Drill several small holes through the metal inside the dent area - particularly in the deeper sections. Then screw long self-tapping screws into the holes just sufficient for them

to gain a good purchase in the metal. Now the dent can be pulled out by pulling on the protruding heads of the screws with a pair of pliers.

The next stage of the repair is the removal of the paint from the damaged area, and from an inch or so of the surrounding 'sound' bodywork. This is accomplished most easily by using a wire brush or abrasive pad on a power drill, although it can be done just as effectively by hand using sheets of abrasive paper. To complete the preparations for filling, score the surface of the bare metal with a screwdriver or the tang of a file, or alternatively, drill small holes in the affected area. This will provide a really good 'key' for the filler paste.

To complete the repair see the Section on filling and respraying.

### Repair of rust holes or gashes in the vehicle's bodywork

Remove all paint from the affected area and from an inch or so of the surrounding 'sound' bodywork, using an abrasive pad or a wire brush on a power drill. If these are not available a few sheets of abrasive paper will do the job just as effectively. With the paint removed you will be able to gauge the severity of the corrosion and therefore decide whether to replace the whole panel (if this is possible) or to repair the affected area. Replacement body panels are not as expensive as most people think and it is often quicker and more satisfactory to fit a new panel than to attempt to repair large areas of corrosion.

Remove all fittings from the affected area except those which will act as a guide to the original shape of the damaged bodywork (eg; headlamp shells etc). Then, using tin snips or a hacksaw blade, remove all loose metal and any other metal badly affected by corrosion. Hammer the edges of the hole inwards in order to create a slight depression for the filler paste.

Wire brush the affected area to remove the powdery rust from the surface of the remaining metal. Paint the affected area with rust inhibiting paint; if the back of the rusted area is accessible treat this also.

Before filling can take place it will be necessary to block the hole in some way. This can be achieved by the use of one of the following materials: Zinc gauze, Aluminium tape or Polyurethane foam.

Zinc gauze is probably the best material to use for a large hole. Cut a piece to the approximate size and shape of the hole to be filled, then position it in the hole so that its edges are below the level of the surrounding bodywork. It can be retained in position by several blobs of filler paste around its periphery.

Aluminium tape should be used for small or very narrow holes. Pull a piece off the roll and trim it to the approximate size and shape required, then pull off the backing paper (if used) and stick the tape over the hole; it can be overlapped if the thickness of one piece is insufficient. Burnish down the edges of the tape with the handle of a screwdriver or similar, to ensure that the tape is securely attached to the metal underneath.

Polyurethane foam is best used where the hole is situated in a section of bodywork of complex shape, backed by a small box section (eg; where the sill panel meets the rear wheel arch - mostcars). The unusual mixing procedure for this foam is as follows: Put equal amounts of fluid from each of the two cans provided in the kit, into one container. Stir until the mixture begins to thicken, then quickly pour this mixture into the hole, and hold a piece of cardboard over the larger apertures. Almost immediately the polyurethane will begin to expand, gushing out of any small holes left unblocked. When the foam hardens it can be cut back to just below the level of the surrounding bodywork with a hacksaw blade.

### Bodywork repairs - filling and re-spraying

Before using this Section, see the Sections on dent, deep scratch, rust hole, and gash repairs.

Many types of bodyfiller are available, but generally speaking those proprietary kits which contain a tin of filler paste and a tube of resin hardener are best for this type of repair. A wide, flexible plastic or nylon applicator will be found invaluable for imparting a smooth and well contoured finish to the surface of the filler.

Mix up a little filler on a clean piece of card or board - use the hardener sparingly (follow the maker's instructions on the packet) otherwise the filler will set very rapidly.

Using the applicator, apply the filler paste to the prepared area; draw the applicator across the surface of the filler to achieve the correct contour and to level the filler surface. As soon as a contour that approximates the correct one is achieved, stop working the paste - if you carry on too long the paste will become sticky and begin to 'pick-up' on the applicator. Continue to add thin layers of filler paste at twenty-minute intervals until the level of the filler is just 'proud' of the surrounding bodywork.

Once the filler has hardened, excess can be removed using a Surform plane or Dreadnought file. From then on, progressively finer grades of abrasive paper should be used, starting with a 40 grade production paper and finishing with 400 grade 'wet or dry' paper. Always wrap the abrasive paper around a flat rubber, cork, or wooden block - otherwise the surface of the filler will not be completely flat. During the smoothing of the filler surface the 'wet or dry' paper should be periodically finsed in water. This will ensure that a very smooth finish is imparted to the filler at the final stage.

At this stage the dent should be surrounded by a ring of bare metal, which in turn should be encircled by the finely ,feathered' edge of the good paintwork. Rinse the repair area with clean water, until all of the dust produced by the rubbingdown operation is gone.

Spray the whole repair area with a light coat of grey primer - this will show up any imperfections in the surface of the filler. Repair these imperfections with fresh filler paste or bodystopper, and once more smooth the surface with abrasive paper. If bodystopper is used, it can be mixed with cellulose thinners to form a really thin paste which is ideal for filling small holes. Repeat this spray and repair procedure until you are satisfied that the surface of the filler, and the filler, and the feathered edge of the paintwork are perfect. Clean the repair area with clean water and allow to dry fully.

The repair area is now ready for spraying. Paint spraying must be carried out in a warm, dry, windless and dust free atmosphere. This condition can be created artificially if you have access to a large indoor working area, but if you are forced to work in the open, you will have to pick your day very carefully. If you are working indoors, dousing the floor in the work area with water will 'lay' the dust which would otherwise be in the atmosphere. If the repair area is confined to one body panel, mask off the surrounding panels; this will help to minimise the effects of a slight mis-match in paint colours. Bodywork fittings (eg chrome strips, door handles etc) will also need to be masked off. Use geniune masking tape and several thicknesses of newspaper for the masking operation.

Before commencing to spray, agitate the aerosol can thoroughly then spray a test area (an old tin, or similar) until the technique is mastered. Cover the repair area with a thick coat of primer; the thickness should be built up using several thin layers of paint rather than one thick one. Using 400 grade 'wet or dry' paper, rub down the surface of the primer until it is really smooth. While doing this, the work area should be thoroughly doused with water, and the 'wet or dry' paper periodically rinsed in water. Allow to dry before spraying on more paint.

Spray on the tpp coat, again building up the thickness by using several thin layers of paint. Start spraying in the centre of the repair area and then, using a circular motion, work outwards until the whole repair area and about 2 inches of the surrounding original paintwork is covered. Remove all masking material 10 to 15 minutes after spraying on the final coat of paint.

Allow the new paint at least 2 weeks to harden fully; then, using a paintwork renovator or a very fine cutting paste, blend the edges of the new paint into the existing paintwork. Finally, apply wax polish.

## 5  Major body damage - repair

1  Where damage has occurred to the chassis frame, it is essential that any repair is left to a suitably equipped Datsun main dealer or vehicle repair specialist. This is because it is essential to check the frame alignment using special jigs (which may indicate that straightening is necessary), and where welding operations are required it is essential that the original frame strength is maintained.
2  Where serious damage has occurred to the pick-up cab body or rear body, and it has been ascertained that the chassis frame is fully serviceable, either of the two major body sections can be renewed by reference to the following paragraphs. The weight of the cab body is approximately 485 lb (220 kg) and that of the rear body approximately 286 lb (130 kg).

### Cab body - removal and installation

3  Disconnect and remove the vehicle battery; refer to Chapter 10, if necessary.
4  On automatic transmission models, disconnect the oil cooler hoses from the radiator.
5  Where applicable, disconnect the cooler tubes from the condenser.

6  Drain the cooling system and remove the radiator. refer to Chapter 2, if necessary. Where applicable, also remove the condenser.
7  Remove the hood from the engine compartment, as described in Section 8.
8  Remove the bumper stay and bumper, as described in Section 7.
9  Remove the radiator grille, as described in Section 7.
10 Remove the steering wheel; refer to Chapter 11, if necessary.
11 Detach the steering gear arm from the steering sector shaft, refer to Chapter 11, if necessary.
12 On column shift models, disconnect the select and shift rods at the sector lever and gearchange lever. Free the shift lever from the control rod.
13 Remove the screws securing the steering shaft dust seat and insulator in position.
14 Remove the steering gear housing from the frame and pull it out into the engine compartment.
15 Disconnect the speedometer cable from the transmission.
16 Where applicable, disconnect the carbon canister hoses.
17 Where applicable, disconnect the air pump-to-air cleaner hose at the air cleaner.
18 Where applicable, disconnect the cooler hose from the compressor.
19 Where applicable, disconnect the air cleaner duct from the body.
20 Where applicable, disconnect the brake vacuum unit hose at the intake manifold.
21 On floor change models, remove the snap-ring and control lever pin from the transmission striking guide; remove the control lever.
22 Disconnect the fuel hoses at the fuel strainer or pump (as applicable).
23 Where applicable, disconnect the fuel return hose and evaporation hose at the connectors.
24 Disconnect the brake and clutch master cylinder lines. On models with a single brake master cylinder, disconnect the rear brake tube at the front 4-way connector.
25 Remove all clips securing the fuel lines brake lines and clutch lines to the vehicle body.
26 Block the roadwheels to prevent the vehicle from moving. Loosen the handbrake control cable at the brake control lever, then disconnect the cable at the dash panel; refer to Chapter 9, if necessary.
27 Free the choke and accelerator cables at the carburetor. refer to Chapter 3, if necessary.
28 Disconnect the heater hoses on the engine side.
29 Disconnect the electrical connections from the engine and ancillary fittings. Make a carefull note or sketch of the various connections if there is any possibility of mix-up.
30 Disconnect the engine and chassis harnesses at the connection on the right sidemember rear, the rear engine mounting member.
31 Remove the six bolts securing the body to the frame. Note the position of the washers and rubber backings as shown in Fig. 12.1.
32 Using a suitable hoist, ropes and timber beam (Fig. 12.2), carefully lift off the cab body. Take care that it does not foul the engine or rear body.
33 Installation is the reverse of the removal procedure, noting the following points.

> a) Refer to Fig. 12.1 for the position of the washers and rubber bushings.
> b) Adjust the handbrake, as described in Chapter 9.
> c) Bleed the clutch hydraulic system, as described in Chapter 5.
> d) Bleed the brake hydraulic system, as described in Chapter 9.

### Rear body - removal and installation

34 Initially disconnect the battery ground lead.
35 Apply the handbrake.
36 Disconnect the rear combination lamp wiring harness at the connectors.
37 Drain the contents of the fuel tank then remove the tank itself; refer to Chapter 3, if necessary.
38 Remove the eight bolts attaching the rear body to the chassis frame. Note the positions of the rubber washers and shims (Fig. 12.3).
39 Attach lifting ropes to the rear body. Ensure that the body is balanced, then carefully lift it off.
40 Installation is the reverse of the removal procedure, but ensure that the rubber washers and shims are correctly positioned.

**12**

Typical example of rust damage to a body panel. Before starting ensure that you have all of the materials required to hand. The first task is to ...

... remove body fittings from effected area, except those which can act as a guide to the original shape of the damaged bodywork - the headlamp shell in this case.

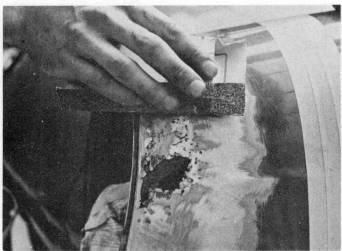

Remove all paint from the rusted area and from an inch or so of the adjoining 'sound' bodywork - use coarse abrasive paper or a power drill fitted with a wire brush or abrasive pad. Gently hammer in the edges of the hole to provide a hollow for the filler.

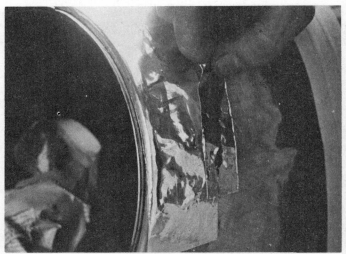

Before filling, the larger holes must be blocked off. Adhesive aluminium tape is one method; cut the tape to the required shape and size, peel off the backing strip (where used), position the tape over the hole and burnish to ensure adhesion.

Alternatively, zinc gauze can be used. Cut a piece of the gauze to the required shape and size; position it in the hole below the level of the surrounding bodywork; then ...

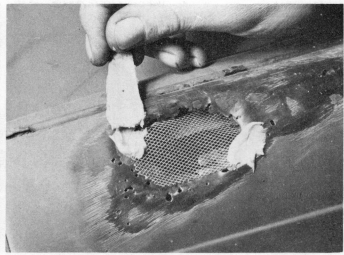

... secure in position by placing a few blobs of filler paste around its periphery. Alternatively, pop rivets or self-tapping screws can be used. Preparation for filling is now complete.

Mix filler and hardener according to manufacturer's instructions - avoid using too much hardener otherwise the filler will harden before you have a chance to work it.

Apply the filler to the affected area with a flexible applicator - this will ensure a smooth finish. Apply thin layers of filler at 20 minute intervals, until the surface of the filler is just 'proud' of the surrounding bodywork. Then ...

... remove excess filler and start shaping with a Surform plane or a dreadnought file. Once an approximate contour has been obtained and the surface is relatively smooth, start using ...

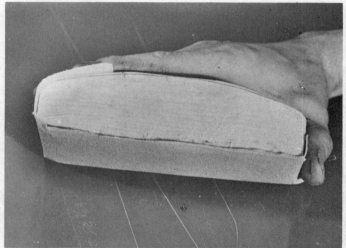

... abrasive paper. The paper should be wrapped around a flat wood, cork or rubber block - this will ensure that it imparts a smooth surface to the filler.

40 grit production paper is best to start with, then use progressively finer abrasive paper, finishing with 400 grade 'wet-and-dry'. When using 'wet-and-dry' paper, periodically rinse it in water ensuring also, that the work area is kept wet continuously.

Rubbing-down is complete when the surface of the filler is really smooth and flat, and the edges of the surrounding paintwork are finely 'feathered'. Wash the area thoroughly with clean water and allow to dry before commencing re-spray.

12

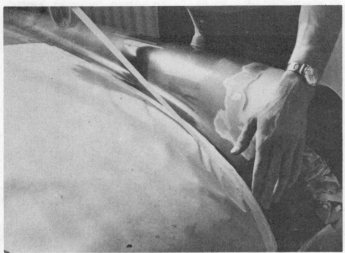

Firstly, mask off all adjoining panels and the fittings in the spray area. Ensure that the area to be sprayed is completely free of dust. Practice using an aerosol on a piece of waste metal sheet until the technique is mastered.

Spray the affected area with primer - apply several thin coats rather than one thick one. Start spraying in the centre of the repair area and then work outwards using a circular motion - in this way the paint will be evenly distributed.

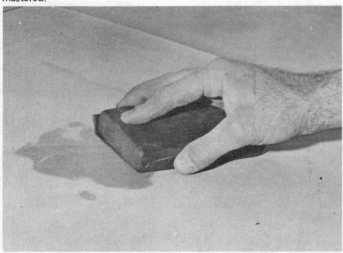

When the primer has dried inspect its surface for imperfections. Holes can be filled with filler paste or body-stopper, and lumps can be sanded smooth. Apply a further coat of primer, then 'flat' its surface with 400 grade 'wet-and-dry' paper.

Spray on the top coat, again building up the thickness with several thin coats of paint. Overspray onto the surrounding original paintwork to a depth of about five inches, applying a very thin coat at the outer edges.

Allow the paint two weeks, at least, to harden fully, then blend it into the surrounding original paintwork with a paint restorative compound or very fine cutting paste. Use wax polish to finish off.

The finished job should look like this. Remember, the quality of the completed work is directly proportional to the amount of time and effort expended at each stage of the preparation.

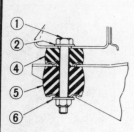
1st mounting

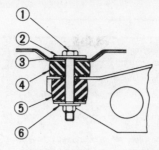
2nd mounting

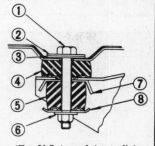
3rd mounting

(For U.S.A. and Australia)

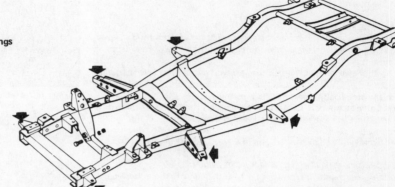

Fig. 12.1. Cab body mounting points and mountings

1  Bolt
2  Plain washer
3  Rubber washer
4  Upper rubber
5  Lower rubber
6  Plain washer
7  Upper washer
8  Lower washer

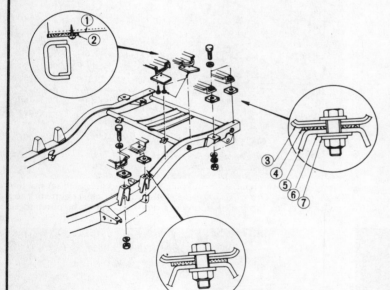

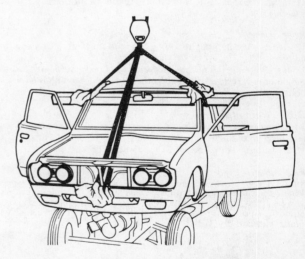

Fig. 12.2. Removing the cab body

Fig. 12.3. Rear body mounting points and mountings

1  Bolster
2  Shim (B)
3  Bolster
4  Shim (A)
5  Frame
6  Rubber washer
7  Plain washer

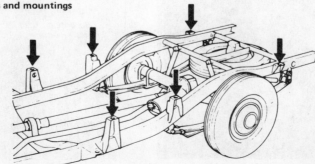

12

### 6  Rear body fittings - removal and installation

#### *Tailgate*
1  Open the tailgate. Remove the chain from the gate (pick-up) or gate stay (Double pick-up).
2  Remove the hinge attaching bolts and lift away the tailgate. Note the shims fitted at the hinges.
3  Installation is a direct reversal of the removal procedure, but ensure that the tailgate is centrally and squarely located before tightening the hinge bolts. If necessary, shims can be added or removed to obtain satisfactory alignment; these are available in 0.063 in (1.6 mm) and 0.032 (0.8 mm) sizes. On Double pick-up versions loosen the bolts and adjust the stays until they are of equal length.

#### *Rear gate lock (Double pick-up)*
4  Open the rear gate and remove the four inside cover attaching screws.
5  Take off the cover and disengage the two remote control rods from the lever assembly.
6  Remove the lever assembly attaching screws; detach the lever assembly and shim(s).
7  Detach the side lock assembly (three screws).
8  Detach the lock handle (two attaching nuts on the inside of the gate).
9  Installation is the reverse of the removal procedure. Adjust the control rod nuts to ensure correct engagement and operation of the strikers. If necessary adjust the strikers in a fore and aft direction also.

#### *Tailgate aperture weather strip (Double pick-up)*
10  Detach the weatherstrip from the body and clean off the adhesive using a lead-free gasoline (petrol). Wipe clean with a damp cloth.
11  Install the replacement weatherstrip using a proprietary contact adhesive.

#### *Rear bumper (Double pick-up)*
12  Remove the bumper attaching nuts and bolts, and lift away the bumper.
13  Installation is the reverse of the removal procedure but ensure that the bumper is properly aligned before finally tightening the nuts and bolts.

#### *Guard frame (pick-up)*
14  To remove the guard frame (where installed) remove the nine retaining bolts and lift the frame away.
15  Installation is the reverse of the removal procedure.

#### *Fuel filler flap lock*
16  To remove the lock (where one is installed), slide up the retaining clip using a screwdriver or similar tool. If necessary, the lock can be dismantled by removing the spring clip and separating the parts (photo).
17  Assembly and installation is the reverse of the removal procedure.

6.16 Fuel filler flap lock removal

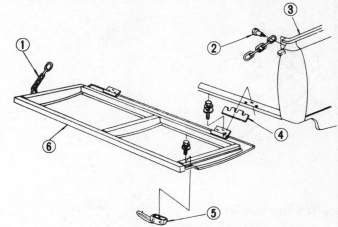

**Fig. 12.4. Tailgate, hinges and chains**

| | | | |
|---|---|---|---|
| 1 | Gate chain | 4 | Shim |
| 2 | Gate chain bolt | 5 | Hook handle |
| 3 | Rear body | 6 | Rear gate |

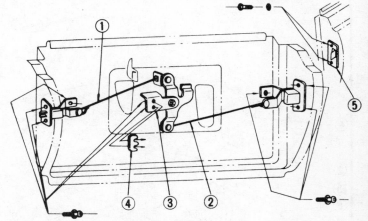

**Fig. 12.5. Double Pick-up gate lock**

| | | | |
|---|---|---|---|
| 1, 2 | Remote control rods | 4 | Shim |
| 3 | Remote control lever assembly | 5 | Striker |

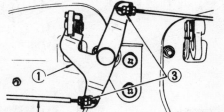

**Fig. 12.6. Double Pick-up rear gate lock adjustment**

| | | | |
|---|---|---|---|
| 1 | Remote control lever | 3 | Adjustment nut |
| 2 | Remote control rod | | |

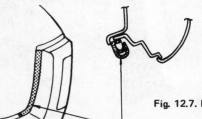

**Fig. 12.7. Double Pick-up weatherstrip**

Weatherstrip

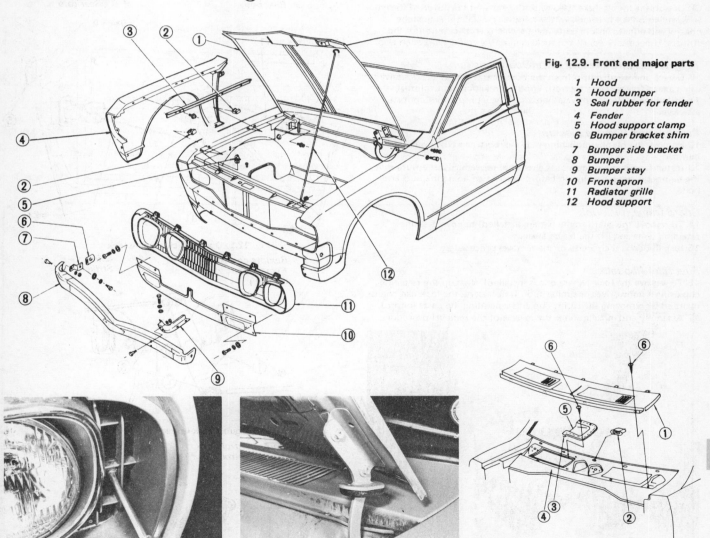

**Fig. 12.8. Rear bumper parts**

1 Stay
2 Side bracket
3 Bumper

### 7 Front end body fittings - removal and installation

#### Front bumper

1 Remove the bumper to fender attaching bolts.
2 Remove the four bumper stay-to-side frame front attaching bolts, and pull the bumper away.
3 Installation is the reverse of the removal procedure, but align the bumper with the front fender and apron before tightening the retaining bolts.

#### Radiator grille

4 Remove the six attaching screws along the top of the grille and the two at each end, then lift away the grille.
5 If necessary, the decorative motif can be removed by removing the nut from behind the grille.
6 Installation is the reverse of the removal procedure but ensure that the locating studs align with the holes in the radiator support lower frame. Before tightening the screws, check that the grille is aligned with the headlamps and fenders.

**Fig. 12.9. Front end major parts**

1 Hood
2 Hood bumper
3 Seal rubber for fender
4 Fender
5 Hood support clamp
6 Bumper bracket shim
7 Bumper side bracket
8 Bumper
9 Bumper stay
10 Front apron
11 Radiator grille
12 Hood support

7.4 Radiator grille removal

8.1 Hood hinge. Before removing hood, mark around hinge positions to assist with installation

**Fig. 12.10. Cowl top grille**

1 Cowl top grille
2 Cap
3 Air box drain seal
4 Cowl top
5 Air box drain
6 Screws

**12**

## Front apron

7 Remove the bumper and radiator grille as already described in this Section.

8 Disconnect the front turn signal wire harness at its connector.

9 Remove the attaching bolts and lift away the apron.

10 Installation is the reverse of the removal procedure.

## Cowl top grille

11 Open the engine compartment hood and detach the windshield wiper blades.

12 Remove the cowl top grille attaching screws, and lift the grille forward to remove it.

13 If necessary, remove the air-box drain.

14 Installation is the reverse of the removal procedure. If the airbox drain was removed, apply adhesive at its lower end. Before tightening the cowl top grille screws, ensure that it is aligned with the fender.

## Front fender (wing)

15 Remove the front bumper, radiator grille, front apron and cowl top grille, as described previously in this Section.

16 Carefully remove the sill moulding (where applicable).

17 Remove the two hood bumpers from the fender.

18 Remove the front side marker lamp; refer to Chapter 10, if necessary.

19 Remove the nine fender attaching screws and lift the fender away.

20 Remove the front fender rubber seals.

21 Installation is the reverse of the removal procedure.

## 8  Hood (bonnet) - removal and installation

1  Open the hood and mark around the hinge positions to assist with installation.

2  Loosen the four bolts securing the hood to the hinges, then with help from an assistant remove the bolts and lift the hood away.

3  To remove the hinges, remove the cowl top panel as described in Section 7. Pry off the pin from the hood hinge and remove the hinge.

4  Installation is the reverse of the removal procedure. Any adjustment and closing action may be made at the hinges, lock control, rubber bumpers or dovetail bolt.

## 9  Hood lock control and cable - removal and intallation

1  To remove the male part of the lock (on the hood), remove the two attaching bolts.

2  To remove the female part of the lock, first remove the radiator grille, as described in Section 7.

3  Back off the bolts securing the female part so that it can be removed.

4  Remove the two bolts attaching the release handle to the dash side panel. Disconnect the cable at the hood lock and remove the cable clamps so that the cable can be pulled into the cab.

5  Installation of the lock assembly parts is the reverse of the removal procedure. Ensure that the cable clamps are tight and secure; note that the hood lock handle bracket is secured by two screws only. Adjustment may be made to ensure satisfactory locking by repositioning the dove-tail bolt after slackening the locknut. Ensure that the safety catch engages properly by reference to the dimensions given in Fig. 12.13.

## 10  Locks and hinges - maintenance

1  Lubricate the hinges of the bonnet, boot and doors with a drop of two of light oil prieriodically. A good time is after the vehicle has been washed.

2  Lubricate the bonnet, the release catch pivot pin and the safety catch pivot pin periodically.

3  Do not over lubricate door latches and strikers. Normaly a little oil on the rotary cam spindle alone is sufficient.

## 11  Doors - tracing and rectifying rattles

1  Check first that the door is not loose at the hinges and that the latch is holding the door firmly in position. Check also that the door lines up with the aperture in the body.

2  If the hinges are loose or the door is out of alignment it will be necessary to reset the hinge positions, as described in Section 12.

3  If the latch is holding the door properly it should hold the door

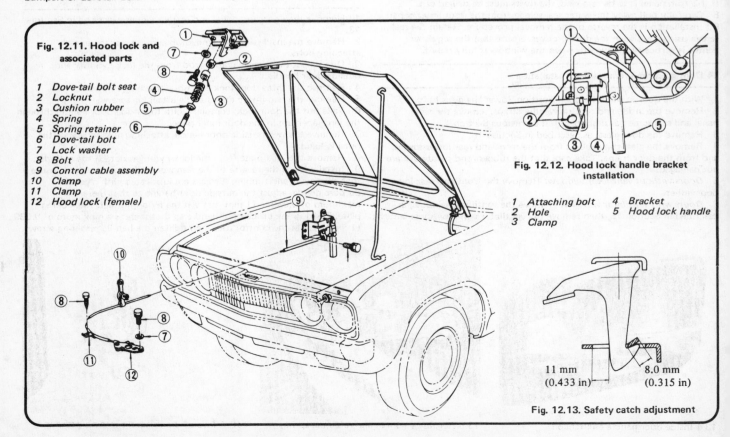

Fig. 12.11. Hood lock and associated parts

1  Dove-tail bolt seat
2  Locknut
3  Cushion rubber
4  Spring
5  Spring retainer
6  Dove-tail bolt
7  Lock washer
8  Bolt
9  Control cable assembly
10 Clamp
11 Clamp
12 Hood lock (female)

Fig. 12.12. Hood lock handle bracket installation

1  Attaching bolt       4  Bracket
2  Hole                 5  Hood lock handle
3  Clamp

11 mm
(0.433 in)        8.0 mm
                  (0.315 in)

Fig. 12.13. Safety catch adjustment

tightly when fully latched and the door should line up with the body. If it is out of alignment it needs adjustment as described. If loose, some part of the lock mechanism must be worn out and requires renewal.
4   Other rattles from the door would be caused by wear or looseness in the window winder, the glass channels and sill strips or the door buttons and interior latch release mechanism.

## 12  Doors - removal and installation

1   Fully open the door then place a jack or suitable blocks beneath the door lower edge to support it when the hinges are loosened. Protect the door paintwork with a wad of rag or similar.
2   Separate the lower door hinge hole cover from the dash trim.
3   Ensure that the door is firmly supported then back-off the three screws at each hinge mounting on the body. Carefully lift the door away.
4   Installation is the reverse of the removal procedure, Ensure that the door closes firmly and squarely by adjusting the hinge and lock striker, as necessary.

## 13  Door weatherstrip, trim panel and seal screen - removal and installation

1   With the door fully open, free the  weatherstrip from the door sash clamp.
2   Pry off the nineteen retaining clips and remove the weatherstrip.
3   Installation is the reverse of the removal procedure.

*Trim panel and seal screen*
4   Remove the screw retaining the inside door handle escutcheon, then remove the escutcheon (photo).
5   Remove the screws retaining the door pull handle, then take off the handle.
6   Pull the retaining spring off the regulator handle, then take off the handle and seat washer (photo).
7   Using a wide bladed screwdriver  or similar tool, pry off the trim panel taking care that the retaining clips, panel and paintwork are not damaged. **Note:** On some models a plate is attached to one door panel If this trim panel is to be removed, the rivets must be drilled out.
8   Carefully pull away the water seal screen from the door inner panel.
9   Installation is the reverse of the removal procedure. Retain the seal screen using adjesive in the door grooves. ensure that the regulator handle is vertically downwards when the window is fully raised.

## 14  Door glass rim - removal and installation

1   With the door in the fully open position, lower the glass fully.
2   Remove the inside and outside weatherstraps; remove the trim panel and seal screen as described in the previous Section.
3   Remove the door glass, as described in Section 16.
4   Remove the glass run rubbers from the front and rear lower sashes, and from the door frame. Take care that the rubbers and paintwork are not damaged.
5   *Doors without ventilator window:* Remove the front and rear lower door sashes.
6   *Doors with ventilator window:* Remove the ventilator window, as described in Section 15, then remove the ventilator window frame and the

rear lower door sash.
7   Installation is the reverse of the removal procedure. Ensure that the run rubbers are bonded to the inside of the sashes using a suitable adhesive.

## 15  Door ventilator window - removal and installation

1   Remove the ventilator window frame, as described in the following Section.
2   Remove the nuts and spring securing the lower end of the ventilator window to the frame.
3   Work off the rivets securing the upper end of the ventilator window to the frame, then take out the window.
4   Installation to the reverse of the removal procedure.

## 16  Door glass and regulator - removal and installation

1   Lower the window fully then remove the door trim panel and seal screen, as described in Section 13.
2   Using a flat bladed screwdriver, carefully remove the door outside and inside weatherstrips.
3   *Doors without ventilator window:* Remove the three door glass bottom channel attaching bolts, then lift the glass straight up and out of the door.
4   *Doors with ventilator window:* Remove the three bolts securing the door glass bottom channel in place then let the glass go down fully. Remove the five ventilator frame attaching bolts and the three retaining screws at the top (accessible after removing the door weatherstrip). Lift the glass straight up and out of the door.
5   Remove the five guide channel-to-regulator base attaching screws, and remove the regulator from the access aperture in the door inner panel (photo).
6   Installation is the reverse of the removal procedure. Ensure that the rear lower sash is parallel to the front lower sash. to reduce play in the window assembly, move the front lower sash to the rear a little if necessary.

## 17  Door lock - removal and installation

1   Remove the door trim panel and seal screen, as described in Section 13.
2   Remove the inside door locking knob and the rear lower sash attaching bolts.
3   Disconnect the remote control rod from the lock cylinder and outside door handle.
4   Remove the three door lock assembly attaching screws.
5   Remove the two inside door handle attaching screws.
6   Take out the door lock, complete with the inside door handle through the large aperture in the door inner panel.
7   Remove the two outside door handle attaching nuts to release the outside handle.
8   Remove the lock plate from the lock cylinder; detach the cylinder.
9   Installation is the reverse of the removal procedure, but first ensure that all moving and rubbing surfaces are lubricated with a general purpose grease. adjust the outside door handle so that there is a maximum of 0.039 in (1 mm) betwen the nylon nut and the locking plate. Position the inside door handle so that there is a maximum of 0.039 (1 mm) play at the control rod, then tighten the handle retaining screws.

**12**

13.4 Inside door handle escutcheon

13.6 Regulator handle and retaining spring

16.5 Two of the regulator retaining screws

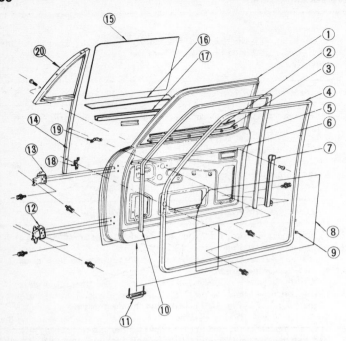

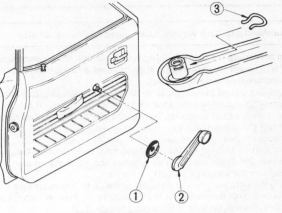

**Fig. 12.16. Regulator handle removal**

1 Seat washer
2 Handle
3 Retaining spring

**Fig. 12.14. Door with ventilator window - parts**

| | | | |
|---|---|---|---|
| 1 | Sash | 11 | Drain hole cover |
| 2 | Outside weatherstrip | 12 | Door hinge |
| 3 | Inside weatherstrip | 13 | Door hinge |
| 4 | Door weatherstrip | 14 | Front lower sash |
| 5 | Rear glass run rubber | 15 | Door glass |
| 6 | Door finish holder | 16 | Glazing rubber |
| 7 | Rear lower sash | 17 | Door glass bottom channel |
| 8 | Seal screen | 18 | Lower support |
| 9 | Weatherstrip clip | 19 | Upper support |
| 10 | Front glass run rubber | 20 | Door ventilator assembly |

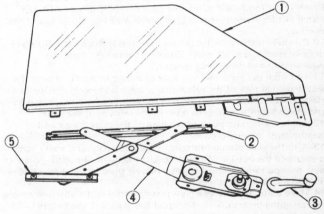

**Fig. 12.17. Door glass and regulator parts**

| | | | |
|---|---|---|---|
| 1 | Glass | 4 | Regulator arm |
| 2 | Bottom channel | 5 | Guide channel |
| 3 | Regulator handle | | |

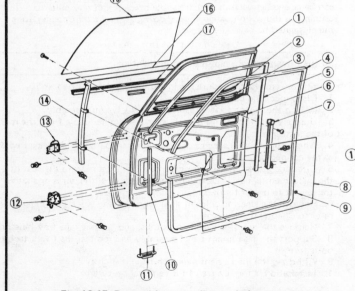

**Fig. 12.15. Door without ventilator window - parts**

| | | | |
|---|---|---|---|
| 1 | Sash | 10 | Front glass run rubber |
| 2 | Outside weatherstrip | 11 | Drain hole cover |
| 3 | Inside weatherstrip | 12 | Door hinge |
| 4 | Door weatherstrip | 13 | Door hinge |
| 5 | Rear glass run rubber | 14 | Front lower sash |
| 6 | Door finish holder | 15 | Door glass |
| 7 | Rear lower sash | 16 | Glazing rubber |
| 8 | Seal screen | 17 | Door glass bottom channel |
| 9 | Weatherstrip clip | | |

**Fig. 12.18. Door lock mechanism**

| | | | |
|---|---|---|---|
| 1 | Escutcheon | 8 | Nylon nut |
| 2 | Inside handle | 9 | Locking plate spring |
| 3 | Spring | 10 | Locking plate |
| 4 | Door lock knob | 11 | Lock cylinder |
| 5 | Grommet | 12 | Lock assembly |
| 6 | Outside handle | 13 | Stopper |
| 7 | Outside handle rod | | |

## 18 Windshield and back window glass - removal and installation

1  The procedure for removing the windshield and back window glass is similar. The windshield weatherstrip has twelve drain holes and the back window weatherstrip has four.

2  If you are unfortunate enough to have a windshield shatter fitting a replacement is one of the few jobs that the average owner is advised to leave to a body repair specialist, but for the owner who wishes to do the job himself the following instructions are given.

3  Remove the rear view mirror and run visors.

4  Place a thick blanket on the hood and fenders to protect the paint.

5  Working inside the cab, carefully loosen the lip of the rubber channel from the windshield aperture flange.

6  Using the palms of the hands apply pressure to the outer edges of the glass and push outwards. At the same time an assistant should ease the rubber channel lip over the aperture flange.

7  When the lip is free, the windshield may be lifted away. (This is of course not applicable if the windscreen has shattered).

8  Remove the rubber from the glass and the remains of the glass from the channel.

9  Now is the time to remove all pieces of glass if the screen has shattered. Use a vacuum cleaner to extract as much as possible. Switch on the heater boost motor and adjust the controls to 'screen defrost' but watch out for flying pieces of glass which might be blown out of the ducting.

10 Carefully inspect the rubber weatherstrip for signs of splitting or deterioration. Clean all traces of sealing compound from the weatherstrip and windshield aperture.

11 To install the glass, insert a piece of strong thin cord around the securing lip groove of the weatherstrip leaving a loop at the top of the glass. The cord should be crossed in the groove where the loop is formed and also where the cord ends meet at the bottom of the glass.

12 Apply sealing compund to the base of the body flange and weatherstrip to body groove.

13 With the glass placed centrally in the body aperture, apply light pressure to the outside of the glass. Lift the lip of the glazing channel over the aperture bottom flange by pulling the cord to within 6.00 in (150 mm) of each corner.

14 Make quite sure that the glass is still central in the aperture before repeating the procedure to the top of the glass and also before refitting the side sections.

15 After installing the glass carefully inject sealing compound between the outside of the glass and glazing channel.

16 Install the windshield mouldings in the weatherstrip, using a soap or detergent solution to ease their installation.

17 Clean off any sealing compound which has excluded using a gasoline soaked cloth.

18 Install the sun visors and rear view mirror.

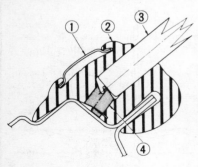

**Fig. 12.19. Windshield glass and weatherstrip**

1  Moulding
2  Weatherstrip
3  Windshield glass
4  Water drain hole

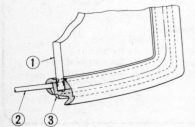

**Fig. 12.20. Inserting drawcord around weatherstrip outer channel**

1  Windshield glass
2  Drawcord
3  Windshield weatherstrip

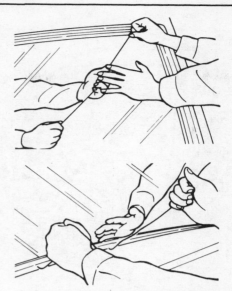

**Fig. 12.21. Installing the weatherstrip**

## 19 Side window and weatherstrip (Double pick-up) - removal, installation and adjustment

1  Remove the two screws retaining the catch handle bracket to the rear pillar.

2  Carefully pry off the two hinge covers using a screwdriver. Take care not to damage the paint surfaces by placing a piece of rag between the screwdriver and the cover.

3  Remove the hinge securing screws and take out the side window.

4  Remove the welt from the glass opening and take off the weatherstrip.

5  Installation is the reverse of the removal procedure.

6  Adjust the glass in the closed position so that there is a clearance of 0.551 in (14 mm) between the welt and the glass. If necessary, a shim can be added between the catch handle bracket and rear pillar to obtain this dimension. Align the window glass and glass opening using the elongated holes of the hinges.

## 20 Instrument panel - removal and installation

**Note:** For removal procedure for instruments refer to Chapter 10.

1  Disconnect the battery ground cable.

2  Detach the heater control cables from the heater assembly.

3  Unscrew the ferrule and detach the speedometer cable from the rear of the instrument.

4  Where applicable, detach the radio antenna (aerial) and speaker wires at the connectors.

5  Disconnect the relative wiring harness connectors from the rear of the instrument panel. If considered necessary label the wires or sketch the layout to prevent mix-up.

6  Remove the steering column shell (and steering wheel, for convenience) refer to Chapter 11, if necessary.

7  Remove the two side ventilator knobs, and the package tray (one bolt).

8  Support the instrument panel assembly and remove the five attaching bolts from it.

9  Withdraw the instrument panel, shifting it slightly.

10 Installation is the reverse of the removal procedure.

## 21 Body side cover panel (Double pick-up) - removal and installation

1  Using a screwdriver, carefully pry off the two clips on the body side cover.

2  Allow the cover panel to bend, and detach it from the upper and lower retainers.

3  Detach the body side screen, if necessary.

4  Installation is the reverse of the removal procedure. Where applicable, retain the seal screen using an adhesive.

**12**

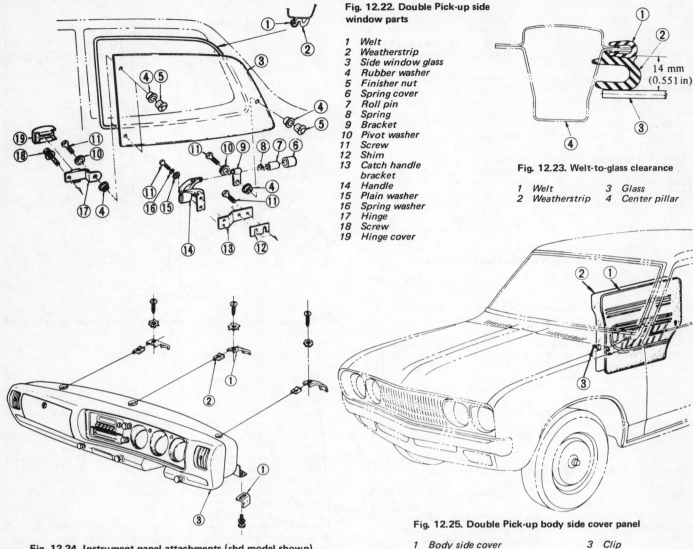

**Fig. 12.22. Double Pick-up side window parts**

1 Welt
2 Weatherstrip
3 Side window glass
4 Rubber washer
5 Finisher nut
6 Spring cover
7 Roll pin
8 Spring
9 Bracket
10 Pivot washer
11 Screw
12 Shim
13 Catch handle bracket
14 Handle
15 Plain washer
16 Spring washer
17 Hinge
18 Screw
19 Hinge cover

**Fig. 12.23. Welt-to-glass clearance**

1 Welt           3 Glass
2 Weatherstrip   4 Center pillar

14 mm (0.551 in)

**Fig. 12.24. Instrument panel attachments (rhd model shown)**

1 Bracket (welded to dash panel)   3 Instrument panel
2 Nut

**Fig. 12.25. Double Pick-up body side cover panel**

1 Body side cover         3 Clip
2 Screen

## 22 Center console - removal and installation

1 Remove the two bolts from the rear of the center console, then pull the console back.
2 When installing, insert the front portion into the bracket on the floor, then install and tighten the two rear attaching bolts.

## 23 Seats and seat belts - general

### Seats

1 Bench seats are used on all models but the Double pick-up has a front seat with separate seat backs.
2 The front or cab seat is adjustable for 5½ in (140 mm) of fore and aft travel. This is achieved by moving the slide lock handle to the side, and moving the seat on its runners.
3 To remove the seat, remove the four slide-to-floor retaining bolts then lift out the complete seat assembly.
4 Installation is the reverse of the removal procedure.
5 The Double pick-up rear seat cushion can be lifted out. To remove the seat back, remove the two screws at the base and lift the seat back up.
6 Installation is the reverse of the removal procedure.

### Seatbelts

7 The seatbelt attachments are shown in Fig. 12.28. If any component part of the seat belts is faulty, the complete belt must be replaced; never renew individual items. The same applies if the belts are strained in an accident.
8 To clean the belt webbing only use a soft bristle brush and a soap or detergent solution, then wipe off the surplus and allow to dry naturally. Never use bleach or chemical cleaners as these may cause the webbing to deteriorate.

## 24 Heater unit - removal and installation

1 Disconnect the battery ground lead.
2 Drain the engine coolant; refer to Chapter 2, if necessary.
3 Remove the defroster hoses.
4 Remove the three cable retaining clips and disconnect the contro cables from the water cork and valves.
5 Disconnect the fan motor leads at their connections.
6 Disconnect the two resistor leads at their connectors.
7 Disconnect the water hoses from the core and water cock.
8 Remove the three heater housing mounting bolts and remove the heater unit from the vehicle.
9 Installation is the reverse of the removal procedure. Adjust the control cables as described in Section 27, fill the cooling system as described in Chapter 2.

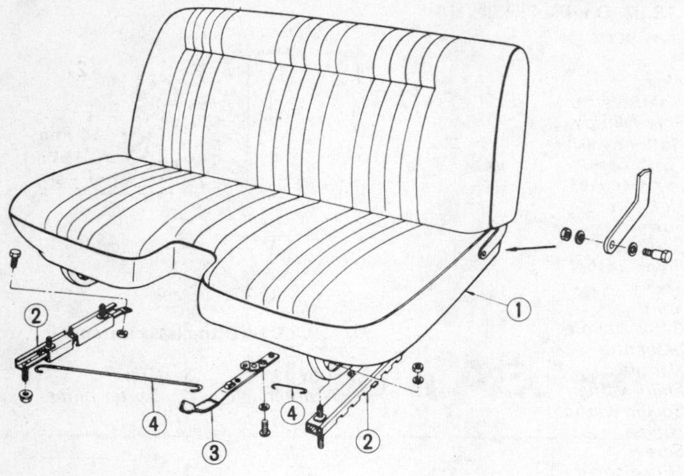

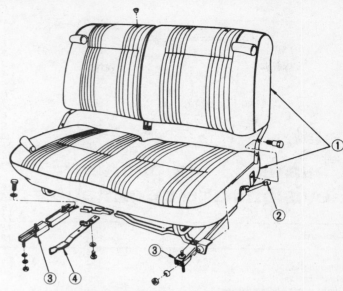

**Fig. 12.26. Front seat attachments (typical for Pick-up)**

1  Seat assembly          3  Slide lock handle
2  Slide                  4  Slide lock wire

**Fig. 12.27. Front seat attachments - Double Pick-up**

1  Seat assembly          3  Slide
2  Seat back latch handle 4  Slide lock handle

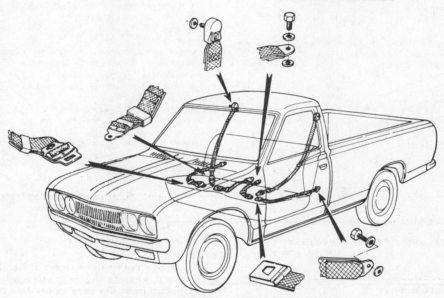

**Fig. 12.28. Seat belt anchorage points - typical**

## 25  Heater core - removal and installation

1  Drain the engine coolant; refer to Chapter 2 if necessary.
2  Remove the defroster hoses.
3  Remove the water hoses from the heater core inlet and outlet pipes.
4  Carefully pry away the four spring clips to release the front cover
5  Withdraw the heater core from the heater housing.
6  Installation is the reverse of the removal procedure; fill the cooling system, as described in Chapter 2.

## 26  Fan motor - removal and installation

1  Remove the heater unit, as described in Section 24.
2  Remove the wire spring clips and disassemble the heater housing.
3  Detach the fan from the fan motor.
4  Remove the fan motor retaining screw; remove the fan from the heater unit.
5  Installation is the reverse of the removal procedure.

## 27  Heater controls - adjustment

### Air lever (OFF/DEFROST/HOT)

1  Move the air lever to the 'Defrost' position.
2  Open the air intake valve and connect the control cable to the intake valve.
3  Secure the control cable with the cable returning clip.
4  Pull the room valve upward and connect the control cable.
5  Secure the control cable with the cable retaining clip.

### Temperature lever

6  Move the temperature lever to 'OFF'.
7  Close the water cock/lever pulled pully forward); connect the control cable to the lever.
8  Install the control cable on the water cock bracket, and secure it with the retaining clip.

**12**

# Chapter 13 Supplement:
# Revisions and information on later USA models

## Contents

## 1  Introduction

The contents of this Chapter update the original information contained in this manual. It covers vehicles produced from 1977 through 1979, otherwise the original details pertaining to 1975/76 model year cars given in Chapters 1 through 12 apply.

## 2  Specifications

**Note:** *The information given in this Section is supplementary to the Specifications in the twelve main Chapters of the manual. Owners of 1977 through 1979 trucks should refer to figures quoted for 1976 trucks when using the original Specifications.*

### Fuel
**Electric fuel pump**  (Air conditioner equipped models)

| | |
|---|---|
| Fuel pressure ... ... ... ... ... ... ... ... ... ... | 4.6 psi (0.32 kg 1cm$^2$) |
| Fuel pump capacity ... ... ... ... ... ... ... ... | 48 fl oz (1400 cc) per minute |

**Carburetor specifications**  (47A & 48A)

| | Primary | Secondary |
|---|---|---|
| Main jet ... ... ... ... ... ... ... ... ... ... ... | 99 | 160 |
| Main air bleed ... ... ... ... ... ... ... ... ... | 70 | 60 |
| Slow jet ... ... ... ... ... ... ... ... ... ... ... | 48 | 100 |
| Power valve ... ... ... ... ... ... ... ... ... ... | 43 | |
| Fast idle gap | | |
|    Manual transmission... ... ... ... ... ... ... ... | 0.0524 to 0.0579 in (1.33 to 1.47 mm) | |
|    Automatic transmission ... ... ... ... ... ... ... | 0.0622 to 0.0677 in (1.58 to 1.72 mm) | |
| BCDD set pressure (at standard sea level conditions) | | |
|    Manual transmission... ... ... ... ... ... ... ... | −20.1 to −21.7 inHg (−510 to −550 mmHg) | |
|    Automatic transmission ... ... ... ... ... ... ... | −19.3 to −20.9 inHg (−490 to −530 mmHg) | |
| Vacuum break gap ... ... ... ... ... ... ... ... | 0.056 in (1.42 mm) | |

## Carburetor specifications (45B & 46A)

| | Primary | Secondary |
|---|---|---|
| Main jet ... ... ... ... ... ... ... ... ... ... | 101 | 160 |
| Main air bleed ... ... ... ... ... ... ... ... ... | 70 | 60 |
| Slow jet (45B) ... ... ... ... ... ... ... ... ... | 48 | 100 |
| Slow jet (46A) ... ... ... ... ... ... ... ... ... | 48 | 80 |
| Power valve ... ... ... ... ... ... ... ... ... | 40 | |
| Fast idle gap | | |
|    Manual transmission ... ... ... ... ... ... ... | 0.0524 to 0.0579 in (1.33 to 1.47 mm) | |
|    Automatic transmission ... ... ... ... ... ... | 0.0622 to 0.0677 in (1.58 to 1.72 mm) | |
| BCDD set pressure (at standard sea level conditions) | | |
|    Manual transmission ... ... ... ... ... ... ... | −20.1 to −21.7 inHg (−510 to −550 mmHg) | |
|    Automatic transmission ... ... ... ... ... ... | −19.3 to −20.9 inHg (−490 to −530 mmHg) | |
| Vacuum break gap | | |
|    (45B) ... ... ... ... ... ... ... ... ... | 0.056 in (1.42 mm) | |
|    (46A) ... ... ... ... ... ... ... ... ... | 0.059 in (1.50 mm) | |

## Carburetor specifications (DCH340—95 & 96)

| | Primary | Secondary |
|---|---|---|
| Main jet ... ... ... ... ... ... ... ... ... ... | 101 | 158 |
| Main air bleed ... ... ... ... ... ... ... ... ... | 70 | 60 |
| Slow jet ... ... ... ... ... ... ... ... ... ... | 48 | 70 |
| Power valve ... ... ... ... ... ... ... ... ... | 40 | |
| Fast idle gap | | |
|    Manual transmission ... ... ... ... ... ... ... | 0.052 to 0.058 in (1.33 to 1.47 mm) | |
|    Automatic transmission ... ... ... ... ... ... | 0.062 to 0.068 in (1.58 to 1.72 mm) | |
| Vacuum break gap ... ... ... ... ... | 0.059 in (1.50 mm) | |

## Carburetor specifications (97 & 98)

| | Primary | Secondary |
|---|---|---|
| Main jet ... ... ... ... ... ... ... ... ... ... | 103 | 160 |
| Main air bleed ... ... ... ... ... ... ... ... ... | 60 | 60 |
| Slow jet ... ... ... ... ... ... ... ... ... ... | 48 | 70 |
| Power valve ... ... ... ... ... ... ... ... ... | 43 | |
| Fast idle gap | | |
|    Manual transmission ... ... ... ... ... ... ... | 0.052 to 0.058 in (1.33 to 1.47 mm) | |
|    Automatic transmission ... ... ... ... ... ... | 0.062 to 0.068 in (1.58 to 1.72 mm) | |
| BCDD set pressure (at standard sea level conditions) | | |
|    Manual transmission ... ... ... ... ... ... ... | −22.05 ±0.79 in Hg (−560 ±20 mmHg) | |
|    Automatic transmission ... ... ... ... ... ... | −22.05 ±0.79 in Hg (−560 ±20 mmHg) | |
| Vacuum break gap ... ... ... ... ... ... | 0.0689 in (1.75 mm) | |

## Carburetor specifications (DCH340—95C & 65A & 96C)

| | Primary | Secondary |
|---|---|---|
| Main jet (95C & 96C) ... ... ... ... ... ... ... ... | 103 | 158 |
| Main jet (65A) ... ... ... ... ... ... ... ... ... | 101 | 150 |
| Main air bleed ... ... ... ... ... ... ... ... ... | 70 | 60 |
| Slow jet (95C & 96C) ... ... ... ... ... ... ... ... | 48 | 70 |
| Slow jet (65A) ... ... ... ... ... ... ... ... ... | 48 | 60 |
| Power valve ... ... ... ... ... ... ... ... ... | 35 | |
| Fast idle gap | | |
|    Manual transmission ... ... ... ... ... ... | 0.0524 to 0.0579 in (1.33 to 1.47 mm) | |
|    Automatic transmission ... ... ... ... ... ... | 0.0622 to 0.0677 in (1.58 to 1.72 mm) | |
| Vacuum break gap | | |
|    95C & 96C ... ... ... ... ... ... ... | 0.1043 in (2.65 mm) | |
|    65A ... ... ... ... ... ... ... ... | 0.0965 in (2.45 mm) | |

## Carburetor specifications (DCH340—97C & 57A & 67A & 98B & 58A)

| | Primary | Secondary |
|---|---|---|
| Main jet (97C & 98B) ... ... ... ... ... ... ... | 103 | 160 |
| Main jet (57A & 58A) ... ... ... ... ... ... ... | 106 | 160 |
| Main jet (67A) ... ... ... ... ... ... ... ... | 105 | 150 |
| Main air bleed ... ... ... ... ... ... ... ... | 60 | 60 |
| Slow jet (97C & 57A & 98B & 58A) ... ... ... | 48 | 70 |
| Slow jet (67A) ... ... ... ... ... ... ... ... | 48 | 50 |
| Power valve (97C & 98B & 57A & 58A) ... ... | 43 | |
| Power valve (67A) ... ... ... ... ... ... ... | 35 | |
| BCDD Set pressure (at standard sea level conditions) | | |
|    Manual transmission ... ... ... ... ... ... | −21.65 ±0.75 inHg (−550 ±20 mmHg) | |
|    Automatic transmission ... ... ... ... ... ... | −21.65 ±0.75 inHg (−550 ±20 mmHg) | |
| Fast idle gap | | |
|    Manual transmission ... ... ... ... ... ... | 0.0524 to 0.0579 in (1.33 to 1.47 mm) | |
|    Automatic transmission ... ... ... ... ... ... | 0.0622 to 0.0677 in (1.58 to 1.72 mm) | |
| Vacuum break adjustment ... ... ... ... ... | 0.1087 in (2.76 mm) | |

## Clutch

| | |
|---|---|
| Pressure plate warpage ... ... ... ... ... ... ... | 0.004 in (0.1 mm) |
| Pedal height from floor ... ... ... ... ... ... ... | 6.42 in (153 mm) |
| Freeplay at clevis pin ... ... ... ... ... ... ... | 0.039 to 0.118 in (1 to 3 mm) |
| Full stroke of pedal ... ... ... ... ... ... ... | 4.61 to 4.84 in (117 to 133 mm) |

## Torque wrench settings

| | |
|---|---|
| Pedal stopper lock nut ... ... ... ... ... ... ... | 8.7 ft—lb (1.2 kg—m) |

13

## Manual gearbox
## 5 speed transmission (FS5W71B)
Gear ratios
|  |  |
|---|---|
| 1st | 3.592 |
| 2nd | 2.246 |
| 3rd | 1.415 |
| 4th | 1.000 |
| 5th | 0.882 |
| Reverse | 3.657 |
| Oil capacity | 4¼ US pints/3½ Imp pints (2.0 liters) |
| Mainshaft rear bearing snap rings | 0.043 in (1.1 mm) |
|  | 0.047 in (1.2 mm) |
|  | 0.051 in (1.3 mm) |
|  | 0.055 in (1.4 mm) |

Final gear ratio
|  |  |
|---|---|
| Standard | 4.111 |
| Optional | 4.375 |

Speedometer gear ratio
|  |  |
|---|---|
| Standard | 19/6 |
| Optional | 20/6 |

## Brakes
## Front disc brake
| Type | Disc — N22A |
|---|---|
| Cylinder inner diameter | 2 1/8 in (53.98 mm) |
| Pad dimensions (width x thickness x length) | 2.08 x 0.36 x 3.00 in (52.9 x 9.2 x 76.2 mm) |
| Rotor outer diameter | 10.67 in (271 mm) |
| Pad wear limit (minimum thickness) | 0.079 in (2.0 mm) |
| Rotor maximum runout | 0.0059 in (0.15 mm) |
| Rotor maximum parrallelism | 0.0028 in (0.07 mm) |
| Rotor minimum thickness | 0.413 in (10.5 mm) |

## Master cylinder
| Inner diameter | 13/16 in (20.64 mm) |
|---|---|
| Cylinder-to-piston clearance (maximum) | 0.0059 in (0.15 mm) |

## Booster (vacuum servo unit)
| Output rod length | 0.384 to 0.394 in (9.75 to 10.00 mm) |
|---|---|

## Brake pedal
| Free play | 0.04 to 0.20 in (1 to 5 mm) |
|---|---|
| Pedal height | 6.06 in (154 mm) |
| Depressed pedal height (minimum) | 2.56 in (65 mm) |

## Suspension and steering
## 1977
Wheel alignment
| Toe-in | 0.079 to 0.118 in (2 to 3 mm) |
|---|---|
| Total angle (degrees) | 10' to 16' |
| Camber | 1°15' ± 1° |
| Caster | 1°50' ± 45' |

## 1978 — 1979
Wheel alignment
| Toe-in | 0.20 to 0.28 in (5 to 7 mm) |
|---|---|
| Camber | −15' to 1°15' |
| Caster | 35' to 2°05' |

## Torque wrench settings
| Front axle | ft—lb | kg—m |
|---|---|---|
| Wheel nut | 58 to 72 | 8.0 to 10.0 |
| Knuckle arm fixing bolt | 53 to 72 | 7.3 to 9.9 |
| Caliper fixing bolt | 53 to 72 | 7.3 to 9.9 |
| Steering stopper lock nut | 20 to 27 | 2.7 to 3.7 |
| Cross rod lock nut | 58 to 72 | 8.0 to 10.0 |
| Shock absorber |  |  |
| Upper end nut | 12 to 16 | 1.6 to 2.2 |
| Lower end nut | 22 to 30 | 3.1 to 4.1 |
| Torsion bar spring |  |  |
| Anchor bolt lock nut | 22 to 30 | 3.1 to 4.1 |
| Upper link and balljoint |  |  |
| Upper balljoint to upper link nut | 12 to 16 | 1.7 to 2.2 |
| Upper link spindle end nut | 56 to 76 | 7.7 to 10.5 |
| Upper link spindle to frame bolt | 80 to 108 | 11.1 to 15.0 |
| Upper balljoint stud nut | 58 to 72 | 8.0 to 10.0 |

| | | | | | | | | | |
|---|---|---|---|---|---|---|---|---|---|
| Tension rod | | | | | | | | | |
| Tension rod end nut | ... | ... | ... | ... | ... | ... | 22 to 30 | | 3.0 to 4.2 |
| Tension rod to lower link bolt | ... | ... | ... | ... | ... | ... | 28 to 38 | | 3.9 to 5.3 |
| Lower link and balljoint | | | | | | | | | |
| Torque arm fixing nut, inner | ... | ... | ... | ... | ... | ... | 26 to 33 | | 3.6 to 4.6 |
| Torque arm fixing nut, outer | ... | ... | ... | ... | ... | ... | 20 to 27 | | 2.7 to 3.7 |
| Bound bumper fixing nut | ... | ... | ... | ... | ... | ... | 5.8 to 8.0 | | 0.8 to 1.1 |
| Lower balljoint stud nut | ... | ... | ... | ... | ... | ... | 124 to 141 | | 17.2 to 19.5 |
| Lower link spindle end nut | ... | ... | ... | ... | ... | ... | 80 to 108 | | 11.1 to 15.0 |
| Lower balljoint to lower link nut | ... | ... | ... | ... | ... | ... | 28 to 72 | | 3.9 to 9.9 |

## 3   Fuel system and emissions

### Fuel pump

1   Disassembly of the fuel pump is the same with the exception of diaphram removal. On 1978/79 model vehicles the diaphram is removed by pressing down its center against the spring force. With the diaphram pressed down, rotate it about 90 degrees. Then release the diaphram to unhook the push rod.

### Electric fuel pump

2   On 1977 through 1979 model vehicles electric fuel pumps were installed on trucks with air conditioning. The pump is installed on a bracket adjacent to the fuel tank on the right-hand side.
**Removal**
3   Remove the inlet and outlet hoses from the fuel pump. Plug the hose ends so gasoline won't leak out.
4   Disconnect the electrical harness at the connecter.
5   Remove the bolts holding the pump to the bracket.
6   Installation is the reverse order of the removal.
**Inspection**
7   Disconnect the outlet hose from the fuel pump.
8   Connect a suitable hose (approximately 6 mm or 1/4 in inner diameter) to the pump outlet.
9   With the hose held higher than the pump outlet in a suitable container, operate the pump by turning the ignition switch "on" after disconnecting either the "L" alternator terminal or the oil pressure switch connector.
10   The capacity should be 1400cc s (48 fl oz) in under a minute, If not, replace the pump.

### Carburetor

**Note:** *Only minor differences occur in the 1977 — 1979 carburetors. The procedures appearing in Chapter 3 can be used for most operations. Figs. 13.2 and 13.3 show late-model carburetors.*

**Automatic choke heater circuit check**
11   With the engine off, check the continuity between A and B (Fig. 13.6). If continuity exists, the heater is functioning properly. If there is no continuity, check for a disconnected connector or an open in the P.T.C. heater circuit.
**CAUTION:** *Do not attach test leads from the circuit tester anywhere other than where it is designated.*
12   With the engine idling, check for the presence of voltage across A and B as shown (Fig. 13.6). If the voltmeter reading is 12 volts, the heater is functioning properly. If the voltmeter is zero, check for a disconnected connector, open circuit or a faulty automatic choke relay. Replace the faulty parts.
**Automatic choke heater test**
13   Measure the resistance of the choke heater. It should be between 3.7 and 8.9 ohms. If the value is not in this range replace the bi-metal cover of the auto-choke heater.
**Automatic choke relay**
14   Remove the choke relay from the relay bracket (Fig. 13.8).
15   Check for continuity between 4 and 5. It should exist. Check for continuity bteween 1 and 2. It should exist. Check for continuity between 1 and 3. It should not exist (Fig. 13.9).
16   Apply a 12 volt DC across 4 and 5 to ensure that continuity exists between 1 and 3 and that none exists between 1 and 2. If your test results do not satisfy these conditions replace the automatic choke relay.

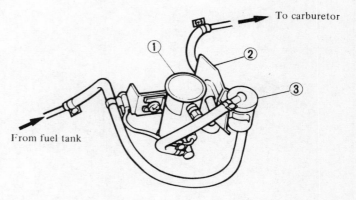

Fig. 13.1 Electric fuel pump

*1   Electric fuel pump*
*2   Mounting bracket*
*3   Fuel filter*

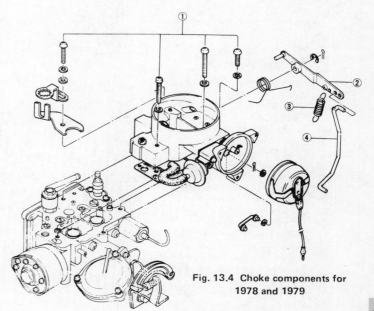

Fig. 13.4  Choke components for 1978 and 1979

*1   Securing screws*
*2   Accelerator pump lever*
*3   Throttle return spring*
*4   Accelerator pump rod*

**Fuel shut-off system**
17   The 1978 and 1979 California models are equipped with a fuel shut-off system on the carburetor. This is a switch which monitors manifold vacuum so during decceleration, fuel is shut off to the carburetor.

**13**

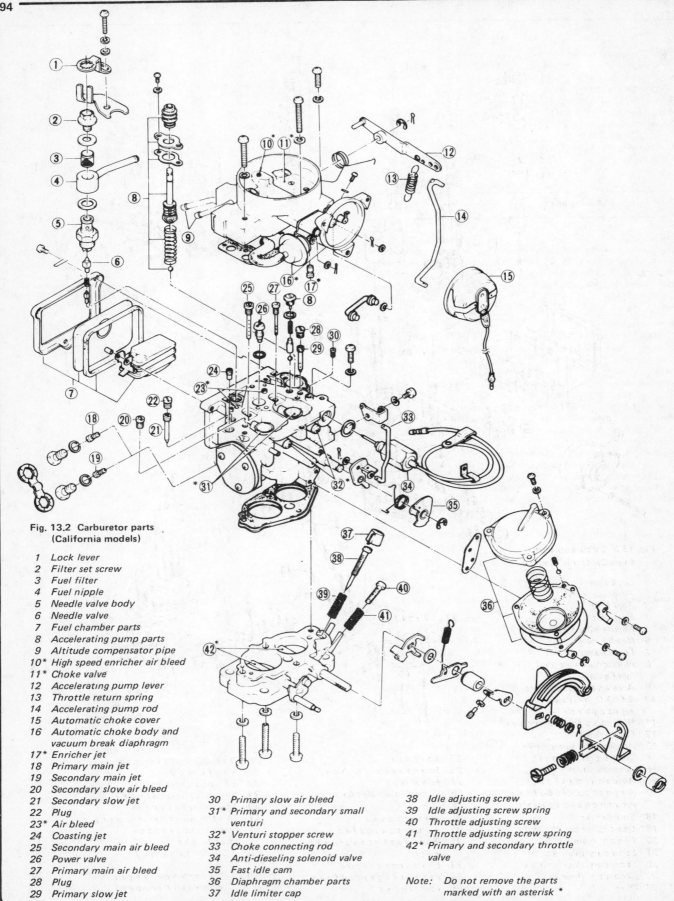

**Fig. 13.2 Carburetor parts (California models)**

 1  Lock lever
 2  Filter set screw
 3  Fuel filter
 4  Fuel nipple
 5  Needle valve body
 6  Needle valve
 7  Fuel chamber parts
 8  Accelerating pump parts
 9  Altitude compensator pipe
10* High speed enricher air bleed
11* Choke valve
12  Accelerating pump lever
13  Throttle return spring
14  Accelerating pump rod
15  Automatic choke cover
16  Automatic choke body and
    vacuum break diaphragm
17* Enricher jet
18  Primary main jet
19  Secondary main jet
20  Secondary slow air bleed
21  Secondary slow jet
22  Plug
23* Air bleed
24  Coasting jet
25  Secondary main air bleed
26  Power valve
27  Primary main air bleed
28  Plug
29  Primary slow jet

30  Primary slow air bleed
31* Primary and secondary small
    venturi
32* Venturi stopper screw
33  Choke connecting rod
34  Anti-dieseling solenoid valve
35  Fast idle cam
36  Diaphragm chamber parts
37  Idle limiter cap

38  Idle adjusting screw
39  Idle adjusting screw spring
40  Throttle adjusting screw
41  Throttle adjusting screw spring
42* Primary and secondary throttle
    valve

Note:  Do not remove the parts
       marked with an asterisk *

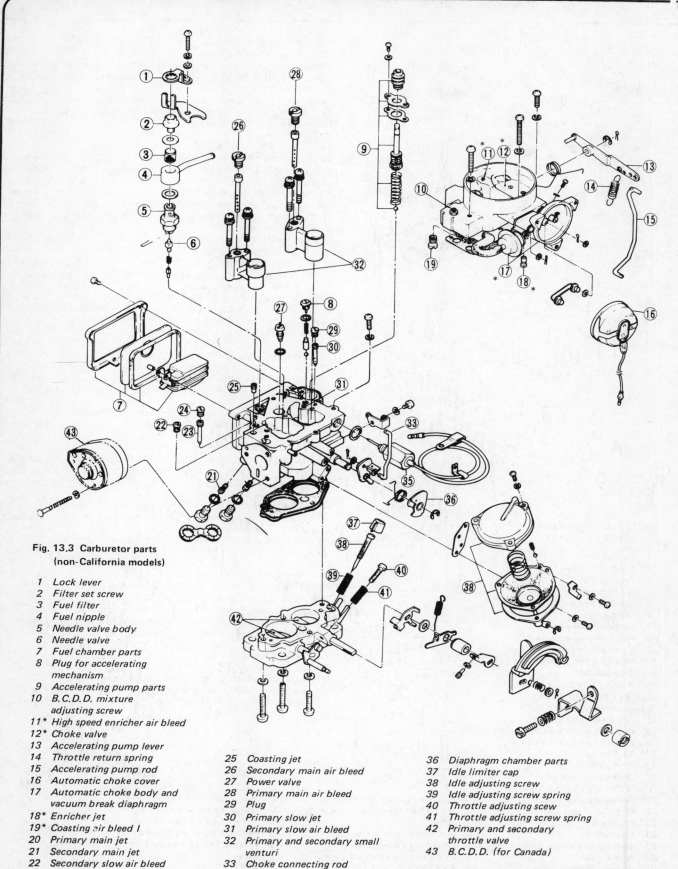

**Fig. 13.3 Carburetor parts
(non-California models)**

1  Lock lever
2  Filter set screw
3  Fuel filter
4  Fuel nipple
5  Needle valve body
6  Needle valve
7  Fuel chamber parts
8  Plug for accelerating
   mechanism
9  Accelerating pump parts
10  B.C.D.D. mixture
    adjusting screw
11* High speed enricher air bleed
12* Choke valve
13  Accelerating pump lever
14  Throttle return spring
15  Accelerating pump rod
16  Automatic choke cover
17  Automatic choke body and
    vacuum break diaphragm
18* Enricher jet
19* Coasting air bleed I
20  Primary main jet
21  Secondary main jet
22  Secondary slow air bleed
23  Secondary slow jet
24  Plug

25  Coasting jet
26  Secondary main air bleed
27  Power valve
28  Primary main air bleed
29  Plug
30  Primary slow jet
31  Primary slow air bleed
32  Primary and secondary small
    venturi
33  Choke connecting rod
34  Anti-dieseling solenoid valve
35  Fast idle cam

36  Diaphragm chamber parts
37  Idle limiter cap
38  Idle adjusting screw
39  Idle adjusting screw spring
40  Throttle adjusting scew
41  Throttle adjusting screw spring
42  Primary and secondary
    throttle valve
43  B.C.D.D. (for Canada)

Note:  Do not remove the parts
       marked with an asterisk *

**13**

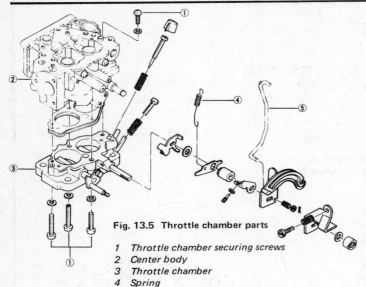

**Fig. 13.5 Throttle chamber parts**

1  *Throttle chamber securing screws*
2  *Center body*
3  *Throttle chamber*
4  *Spring*
5  *Accelerator pump rod*

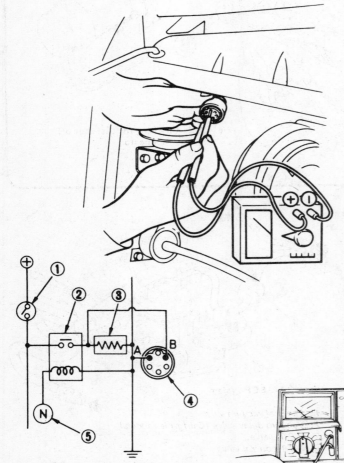

**Fig. 13.6 Checking the automatic choke**
**heater circuit**

1  *Ignition key*
2  *Automatic choke relay*
   *Engine stop : OFF*
   *Engine start : ON*
3  *Automatic choke heater*
4  *Function test connector*
5  *Alternator*

### Manual transmission model testing

18 Run the engine at an idle.
19 Disconnect the anti-dieseling solenoid valve connector. The engine should stop. If it doesn't, replace the anti-dieseling solenoid valve assembly (Fig. 13.10).
20 Connect a voltmeter to ground and to the harness side.
21 Connect the wire from the anti-dieseling solenoid valve directly to the (+) side of the battery.
22 Run the engine.
23 Disconnect the clutch pedal switch.
24 Push in the clutch pedal, shift to 4th gear and race the engine with no load. Keep the engine running at between 2500 and 3000 rpm, then quickly close the throttle valve. If the wiring is in good order the voltmeter should drop from 12V to 0V instantly. If it doesn't, either the neutral switch or the fuel-vacuum shut-off switch is out of order.
25 Reconnect the clutch pedal switch and disconnect the fuel shut-off vacuum switch connector.
26 Connect an ohmmeter as shown in Fig. 13.13. Increase the engine speed to between 2500 and 3000 rpm, then quickly shut the throttle valve. Check the continuity between terminals A and B and between A and C. If "ON–OFF" operation is normal, the fuel shut-off vacuum switch is in good working order.
**Note:** *Polarity between A and B should be reversed from that of A and C. Reconnect the fuel shut-off vacuum switch connector and repeat step 24. If the voltmeter doesn't deflect immediately from 12V to 0V, replace the neutral switch.*

### Automatic transmission model testing

27 Run the engine at an idle.
28 Disconnect the anti-dieseling solenoid valve connector. The engine should stop. If it doesn't, replace the anti-dieseling solenoid valve assembly.
29 Connect a voltmeter to ground and to the harness side.
30 Connect the wire from the anti-diesel solenoid valve directly to the (+) side of the battery.
31 Put the shifter into the "P" or "N" position.
32 Run the engine between 2500 and 3000 rpm, then shut off the throttle valve quickly. If the voltmeter doesn't drop from 12V to 0V instantly, either the inhibitor switch or the fuel shut-off vacuum switch needs replacing.
33 Reconnect the harness to the anti-dieseling solenoid valve.
34 Disconnect the fuel shut-off vacuum switch connector and connect an ohmmeter as shown in Fig. 13.13.
35 Run the engine between 2500 and 3000 rpm and quickly close the throttle valve. This time check the continuity between A and B and between A and C. If the "ON–OFF" operation is normal, the fuel shut-off vacuum switch is in good working order.
**Note:** *The polarity between A and B should be reversed from the polarity between A and C.*
*Reconnect the fuel shut-off vacuum switch connector and repeat step 26. If the voltmeter needle doesn't deflect immediately from 12V to 0V, replace the inhibitor switch.*

### Emission control systems
**Exhaust gas recirculation (EGR) system**
36 Introduced in 1978, and continuing through 1979 were some changes in the EGR system. A BPT valve was added to the system to monitor the exhaust pressure introduced to the intake manifold.

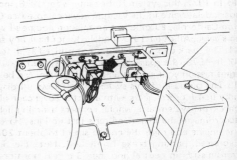

**Fig. 13.7 Automatic choke heater check**

**Fig. 13.8 Location of the automatic**
**choke relay**

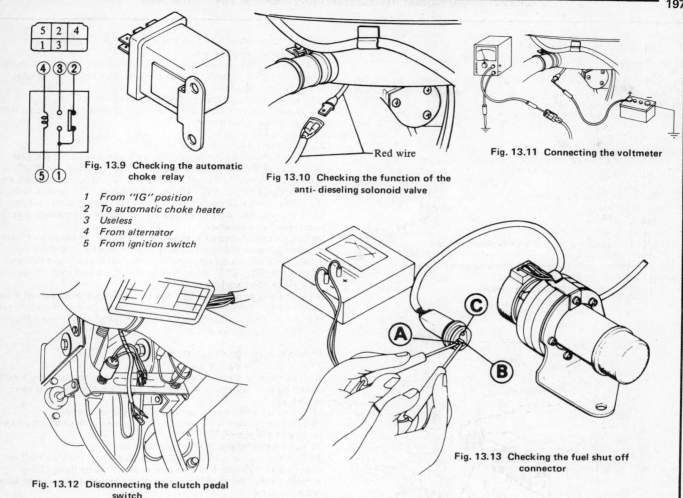

Fig. 13.9 Checking the automatic choke relay

1 From "IG" position
2 To automatic choke heater
3 Useless
4 From alternator
5 From ignition switch

Fig 13.10 Checking the function of the anti- dieseling solonoid valve

— Red wire

Fig. 13.11 Connecting the voltmeter

Fig. 13.12 Disconnecting the clutch pedal switch

Fig. 13.13 Checking the fuel shut off connector

A small vacuum delay valve was also added, its purpose to prevent a rapid vacuum drop in the control hose. Lastly, the thermal vacuum valve opening temperature was changed to $104 - 127^{\circ}F$ (40 to $53^{\circ}C$). To check the new components, proceed as follows:

37 BPT valve: Referring to the accompanying Figure, disconnect the two vacuum hoses on the valve. Plug one of the ports and then use a vacuum gauge to apply pressure above 50 mm $H_2O$ (1.97 in $H_2O$) to the valve. Orally suck back on the other port and check for any leakage. If a leak is detected, replace the valve.

38 Vacuum delay valve: Remove the valve, noting its installed direction. Blow through the valve from the EGR valve side. Air should flow freely through the valve. Now blow through the other side. The flow should be restricted. If this is not the case, replace the valve.

39 All other component checks are the same as for 1975/76 models as shown in Chapter 3, except for the modified temperature range as stated above.

### Spark timing control system

40 In 1977, this system is the same as for 1976, incorporating only a spark delay valve in the vacuum advance hose (see Chapter 3). Only non-California, automatic transmission equipped vehicles incorporate this valve. All other 1977 models do not have any spark control system.

41 The spark control system is not utilized at all for 1978.

42 In 1979, the spark timing control system re-surfaced on manual transmission equipped vehicles. This system can be checked as follows:

43 The purpose of this system is to allow full distributor advance only in 4th or 5th gears, with a partial advance in all other gears. To check the system as a whole, connect a timing light to the engine according to the manufacturer's instructions. Have an assistant start the engine and raise the engine speed to about 2000 rpm (clutch depressed, parking brake firmly set). Note the timing mark with transmission in neutral and then 3rd gear positions. Now have the assistant shift into 4th and 5th gear positions (clutch still depressed) and note the timing mark. The timing mark should change as the

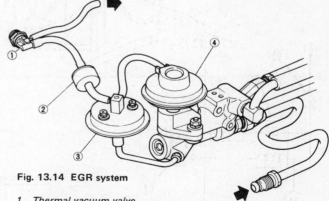

Fig. 13.14 EGR system

1 Thermal vacuum valve
2 Vacuum delay valve (California models)
3 B.P.T. valve
4 EGR control valve

**13**

shifter is moved into 4th or 5th.

44 If the transmission gear switch is suspected of being at fault, connect an ohmmeter to the electrical leads of the switch and have an assistant shift through the various gears. The ohmmeter should detect proper action of the switch.

45 If the transmission switch is working properly, yet the system is still not functioning, it must be assumed that either a fault exists in the electrical wiring (including fuse) or in the vacuum hoses themselves. As a last resort, the vacuum switching valve should be replaced with a new one to eliminate the problem.

### 4   Ignition

1  In 1977 both the mechanical and transistorized distributors are the same as described in Chapter 4. In 1978 the mechanical distributor was discontinued in favor of the transistorized distributor.

2  In 1977 model vehicles so equipped and all 1978 vehicles the transistorized ignition unit is mounted under the right-hand side of the dashboard.

3  In 1979 the transistorized ignition unit was replaced with an IC ignition unit. This unit is mounted on the side surface of the distributor and utilizes a semi-conductor IC device.

#### IC ignition unit removal and installation

4  Disconnect the battery ground cable.

5  Detach the distributor cap and remove the rotor head.

6  Disconnect the harness connector.

7  Remove the IC ignition unit mounting screws.

8  Disconnect the pick-up coil wire from the IC ignition unit.

9  Before installing the IC ignition unit, be sure both mating surfaces are free of dirt, sand, grease and moisture.

10  Install the IC ignition unit in the reverse order of the removal.

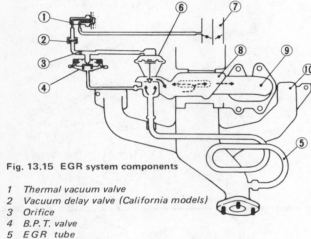

Fig. 13.15  EGR system components

1   Thermal vacuum valve
2   Vacuum delay valve (California models)
3   Orifice
4   B.P.T. valve
5   EGR tube
6   EGR control valve
7   Carburetor
8   E.G.R. passage
9   Intake manifold
10  Exhaust manifold

Fig. 13.17  Exploded view of a
             transistorized distributor

1   Cap assembly
2   Rotor head assembly
3   Roll pin
4   Reluctor
5   Stator
6   Magnet assembly
7   Pick-up coil assembly
8   Breaker plate assembly
9   Rotor shaft assembly
10  Governor spring
11  Governor weight
12  Shaft assembly
13  Housing assembly
14  Grommet
15  IC ignition unit
16  Vacuum controller
17  Fixing plate
18  Collar

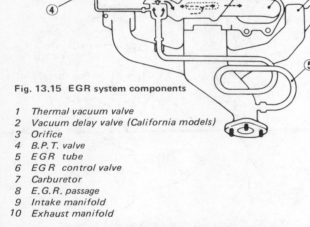

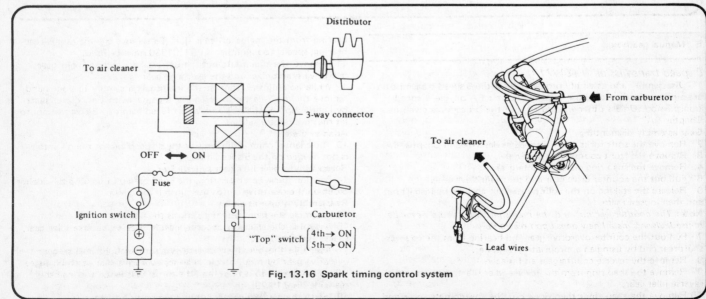

Fig. 13.16  Spark timing control system

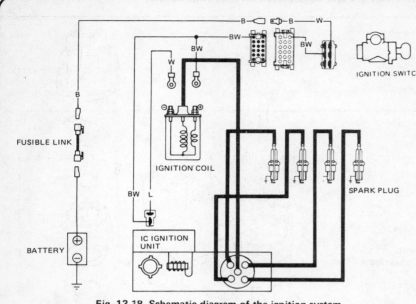

Fig. 13.18 Schematic diagram of the ignition system

Color code
B  = Black
BW= Black with white stripe
W  = White
L  = Blue

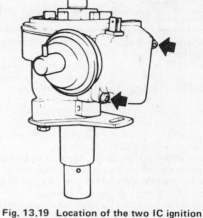

Fig. 13.19 Location of the two IC ignition unit mounting screws

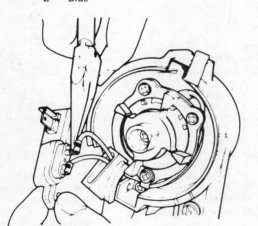

Fig. 13.20 Disconnecting the pick-up coil terminal

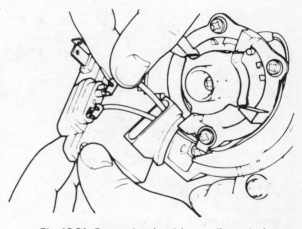

Fig. 13.21 Connecting the pick-up coil terminal

## 5  Manual gearbox

### 5 speed transmission (FS5W71B)

1  Disassembly and assembly procedures for the 5 speed transmission are almost identical to those used in Chapter 6A on the 4 speed transmission. Unless otherwise stated, use the procedures given in Chapter 6A.

**Gear assembly dismantling**

2  Remove the shift forks and fork rods as described in Chapter 6A.
3  Remove the front countergear bearing.
4  Remove the snap ring on the countergear.
5  Pull out the counter drive gear and the main drive gear.
6  Release the staking on the countergear nut and the mainshaft nut and then loosen them.

**Note:** *The countergear nut and the mainshaft nut should never be re-used; always install new ones upon reassembly.*

7  Pull out the counter overdrive gear and bearing from the counter-shaft rear end by using an appropriate gear puller.
8  Remove the reverse countergear and spacer.
9  Remove the snap ring from the reverse idler shaft, then remove the reverse idler gear.
10  Remove the snap rings then draw out the speedometer gear and

bearing from the mainshaft rear side. To remove the mainshaft rear bearing, special tool number KV32101330 must be used.
11  Remove the mainshaft nut, thrust washer, reverse main gear, overdrive syncronizer and the overdrive gear.
12  While holding the front of the mainshaft assembly in your hand, remove the mainshaft gear assembly together with the countershaft by lightly tapping the rear with a soft faced hammer. Be careful not to let the countergear fall off.

**Adapter plate**

13  The adapter plate is the same as the 4 speed except the oil gutter is not needed on the 5 speed model.

**Reassembly — overdrive gear syncronizer**

14  Position the syncronizer ring, the band brake, thrust and the anchor block on the overdrive clutch gear; install the circlip.

**Reassembly — gear assembly**

15  Assemble the front side the same as the 4 speed.
16  Assemble the snap ring, spacer, needle bearing, reverse idler gear, spacer and snap ring.
17  Assemble the overdrive reverse syncronizer hub, reverse gear overdrive gear bushing, needle bearing, overdrive gear assembly, steel ball (apply grease to it first), and the thrust washer on the mainshaft rear side (Fig. 13.28).
18  Install the new mainshaft nut and temporarily tighten it.

**13**

19 Assemble the spacer, reverse countergear, overdrive countergear, bearing and the new countergear lock nut.
20 With the gears doubly engaged, tighten the mainshaft lock nut. Stake the mainshaft and countergear nuts to the groove of the mainshaft and countergear with a punch.
21 Install the mainshaft rear bearing using special tool number

ST22350000 or an appropriate sized pipe. Install the proper size snap ring to the rear side of the bearing to eliminate end play (see Specifications).
22 Install the snap ring to the front of the speedometer drive gear.
23 Install the steel ball, speedometer drive gear and the rear snap ring.
24 Finish reassembly as described in Chapter 6A, 4 speed transmission.

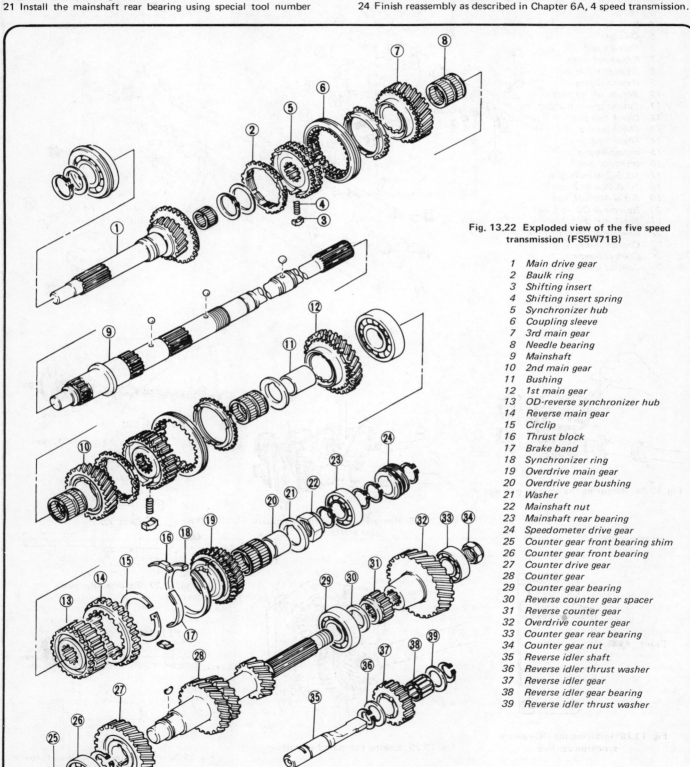

**Fig. 13.22 Exploded view of the five speed transmission (FS5W71B)**

1   Main drive gear
2   Baulk ring
3   Shifting insert
4   Shifting insert spring
5   Synchronizer hub
6   Coupling sleeve
7   3rd main gear
8   Needle bearing
9   Mainshaft
10  2nd main gear
11  Bushing
12  1st main gear
13  OD-reverse synchronizer hub
14  Reverse main gear
15  Circlip
16  Thrust block
17  Brake band
18  Synchronizer ring
19  Overdrive main gear
20  Overdrive gear bushing
21  Washer
22  Mainshaft nut
23  Mainshaft rear bearing
24  Speedometer drive gear
25  Counter gear front bearing shim
26  Counter gear front bearing
27  Counter drive gear
28  Counter gear
29  Counter gear bearing
30  Reverse counter gear spacer
31  Reverse counter gear
32  Overdrive counter gear
33  Counter gear rear bearing
34  Counter gear nut
35  Reverse idler shaft
36  Reverse idler thrust washer
37  Reverse idler gear
38  Reverse idler gear bearing
39  Reverse idler thrust washer

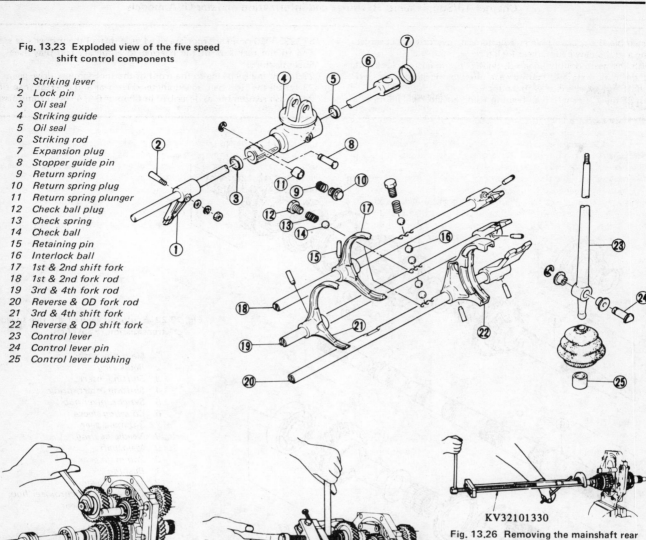

Fig. 13.23 Exploded view of the five speed
shift control components

1 Striking lever
2 Lock pin
3 Oil seal
4 Striking guide
5 Oil seal
6 Striking rod
7 Expansion plug
8 Stopper guide pin
9 Return spring
10 Return spring plug
11 Return spring plunger
12 Check ball plug
13 Check spring
14 Check ball
15 Retaining pin
16 Interlock ball
17 1st & 2nd shift fork
18 1st & 2nd fork rod
19 3rd & 4th fork rod
20 Reverse & OD fork rod
21 3rd & 4th shift fork
22 Reverse & OD shift fork
23 Control lever
24 Control lever pin
25 Control lever bushing

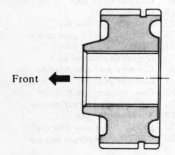

Fig. 13.24 Removing the counter gear nut

Front

Fig. 13.28 Installing the OD-reverse
synchronizer hub

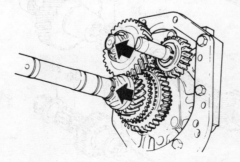

Fig. 13.25 Removing the counter overdrive
gear and bearing

Fig. 13.29 Staking the mainshaft nuts

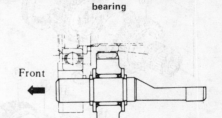

KV32101330

Fig. 13.26 Removing the mainshaft rear
bearing

Front

Fig. 13.27 Reverse idler gear

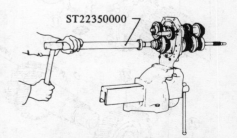

ST22350000

Fig. 13.30 Assembling the mainshaft rear
bearing

13

**6   Braking system**

## General information

1   The braking system is a split system design. It incorporates two separate circuits; one for the front brakes and one for the rear brakes. With this system if one circuit fails, the other circuit will still function.

2   The master cylinder is designed for the split system and incorporates a primary piston for one circuit and a secondary system for the other.

3   A vacuum servo unit is used which draws vacuum from the intake manifold to add power assistance to the normal brake pressure.

4   An NLSV valve regulates the fluid pressure in the brake lines so that all wheels receive equal pressure.

5   The front wheels are equipped with disc brakes. These consist of a flat, disc-like rotor which is attached to the axle and wheel. Around one section of the rotor is mounted a stationary caliper assembly which houses two hydraulically-operated disc brake pads. The inner pad is mounted to a piston facing the inner surface of the rotor, while the outer pad is mounted to a yoke and faces the outer

surface of the rotor. When the brake pedal is applied, brake fluid pressure forces the piston with the inner pad against the rotor. At the same time a second piston moves the yoke inward and forces the outer pad against the rotor. The pressure and resultant friction on the rotor is what slows the wheel.

6   The rear brakes are also equipped with cable-operated parking brake mechanisms, which activate the brake shoes against the brake drums.

7   The front disc brakes adjust automatically to lining wear.

8   After completing any operation involving the dismantling of any part of the brake system, always test drive the car to check for proper braking performance before resuming normal driving. When testing the brakes, perform the tests on a clean, dry, flat surface. Conditions other than these can lead to inaccurate test results. Test the brakes at various speeds with both light and heavy pedal pressure. The car should brake evenly without pulling to one side or the other. Avoid locking the brakes, as this slides the tires and diminishes braking efficiency and control.

9   Tires, car load and front end alignment are factors which also affect braking performance.

6.11 Removing the front brake pad pin retaining clip

6.12a Pliers can be used to remove the pad pins

6.12b Pad pins and springs removed from the caliper

6.13a Pliers can be used to remove the pads from the caliper

6.13b Using a vernier caliper to measure the thickness of the brake pad lining

6.18 The yoke must be levered outward to install the outer pad

6.25 Plug the brake line openings immediately after disconnecting the line

6.26a The caliper mounting bolts are located on the rear side

6.26b Lifting the caliper off of the rotor

## Front disc brake — pad replacement

10 Remove the wheel and tire.

11 Remove the pad clip (photo).

12 While holding the springs in position, remove the 2 pad pins. Lift off the springs (photos).

13 Remove both the inner and outer pads (photo). Measure the depth of the lining, and compare it with the specs to see if the pads need replacement (photo).

14 Place a piece of hose over the bleeder valve and place the end of the hose into a jar or other container.

15 Open the bleeder valve. Then push the outer piston in until the piston's dust seal is even with the outside edge of the dust seal retaining ring. **Caution:** *Do not push the piston in beyond this point. If the piston is pushed beyond the inside of the piston seal, the disc caliper must be removed and disassembled to remove the piston without damaging the seal.*

16 Prior to installation apply a light coat of an aerosol Teflon coating (disc brake anti-squeak coating) to the back of both pads.

17 Install the inner pad.

18 Using a large screwdriver or similar lever slide the yoke outward and install the outer pad (photo).

19 Apply a light coat of grease to the pad pins.

20 While holding the springs in place, install the pad pins. Be careful you do not get grease on the friction sides of the pads.

21 Install the pad clip.

22 Reinstall the wheel and tire.

23 Bleed the brakes as described in Section 3 of Chapter 9.

## Front disc caliper — removal and installation

24 Remove the brake pads.

25 Remove the brake tube and immediately plug the opening to prevent leakage of fluid and to keep foreign matter from entering the line (photo).

26 Remove the 2 caliper mounting bolts and lift the caliper off from the rotor (photos).

27 Installation is the reverse of the removal procedure.

28 Bleed the brakes as described in Section 3 of Chapter 9.

## Front disc caliper — overhaul

29 Clean the outside of the caliper thoroughly.

30 Prior to disassembling the caliper, purchase a front disc brake caliper overhaul kit.

31 Remove the two bolts that attach the caliper to the yoke (photo). Use a flathead screwdriver to pry the caliper toward the outside of the yoke (photo). This disengages the piston from the yoke.

32 Remove the caliper from the yoke (photo).

33 Remove the yoke holder from the inner piston, then remove the dust seal retaining rings located on each side of the caliper (photo).

34 Remove the dust seals (photo).

35 Push the pistons out of the caliper from the pad side (photo).

36 Using a wooden or plastic dowel, remove the piston seals from the inside of the caliper bore (photo).

37 Clean all of the metal parts in brake fluid or denatured alcohol. **Note:** *Never use mineral-based solvents as this can cause the rubber seals to swell and possibly fail.*

38 Check the inside surface of the cylinder bore for any scoring, rust, nicks or other damage. If light scoring or rust is present, it can be removed by polishing the bore with a fine 600 grade emery cloth. If the damage is deep the entire body will have to be replaced.

39 Check the yoke for cracks, excessive wear or other damage and replace it if necessary.

40 Inspect the piston for scoring, rust, nicks or other damage. The sliding surface of the piston is plated and cannot be polished with emery paper. If any defects are found, the piston must be replaced. If rubber grease is supplied with the overhaul kit use it to lubricate the cylinder bore. Brake fluid can also be used for this purpose.

41 Install the 2 rubber seals into the grooves in the caliper bore. Lubricate the seals with rubber grease or brake fluid.

42 Lubricate the outer surfaces of both the pistons with either the rubber grease supplied with the overhaul kit or brake fluid.

43 Carefully insert each piston into its respective end of the bore. Be careful not to disturb the rubber seals inside the bore.

44 Press the outer piston into the bore so that the inner edge of the piston seal groove is in line with the inner edge of the caliper seal grooves.

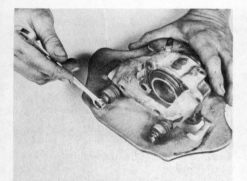

6.31a Removing the yoke-to-caliper bolts

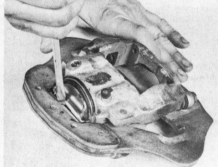

6.31b Using a screwdriver to pry the yoke holder off the yoke

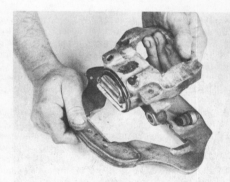

6.32 Separating the caliper from the yoke

6.33a Removing the retaining ring from the inner piston dust seal

6.33b Removing the retaining ring from the outer piston dust seal

6.34 Removing the outer piston dust seal

**13**

6.35 Both pistons are removed from the caliper by pushing on the outer piston

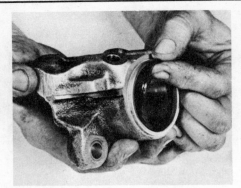

6.36 Do not use a metal tool to pry the piston seals from the caliper bore

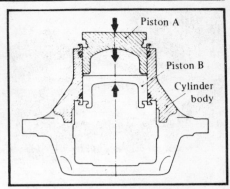

Fig. 13.31 Position of the pistons when installing caliper dust seals

6.45 Apply grease to the inside of the dust seals prior to installation

6.46 Installing the outer piston dust seal

6.47 Installing the retaining ring on the outer piston dust seal

45 If an orange grease is supplied with the overhaul kit use it to fill the inner sealing surface of the outer dust seal (photo.). If no orange grease is supplied, use an approved silicone-base grease.

46 Install the dust seal so that it fits correctly into both the piston seal groove and the caliper seal groove (photo).

47 Install the retaining ring securely around the dust seal (photo).

48 Repeat the same procedure with the inner piston and inner dust seal.

49 Press the yoke holder into its groove on the inner piston face (photo).

50 Insert the caliper into position inside the yoke making sure that the outer piston with yoke holder is properly aligned with the yoke. Place this assembly on a flat surface so that the outer piston is facing downward and apply pressure to the inner piston to press the yoke holder onto the yoke (photo). This can also be done with a hydraulic press if one is available.

51 Once the yoke holder is pressed onto the yoke, install the 2 mounting bolts that retain the yoke to the caliper housing. **Note:** *Before installing these bolts check the condition of the rubber boots and bushings, and if they are worn or otherwise damaged, replace them (photo).* Torque these bolts to 12 to 15 ft-lb.

### Front disc rotor — removal and installation

52 Remove the caliper assembly as described previously.

53 Use a screwdriver to pry off the hub dust cap (photo).

54 Remove the cotter pin.

55 Remove the adjusting cap.

56 Remove the wheel bearing nut and washer.

57 Remove the outer wheel bearing.

58 Remove the hub and rotor assembly (photo).

59 If the rotor needs machining, remove the inner wheel bearing and grease seal.

60 If the rotor needs replacing it must be separated from the hub. First, remove the bolts that secure the rotor to the hub (photo). Then use a plastic hammer to tap along the outer edge of the hub until the hub can be removed from the rotor. Once the hub has been separated slightly, two flathead screwdrivers (one on each side) can be used to pry the

two pieces apart. If the hub and rotor do not separate easily, apply penetrating oil where the two meet.

61 When installing the rotor to the hub fit it into position on the hub and loosely install the bolts.

62 Tighten the bolts in a criss-cross pattern a little at a time until they are torqued to 3.9 to 5.3 kg-m (28 to 38 ft lbs).

63 On the rear side of the hub, use a screwdriver to pry out the inner bearing grease seal. As this is done, note the direction of the installation.

64 The inner bearing can now be removed, again noting how it's installed.

65 Use clean parts solvent to remove old grease from the bearings, hub and spindle. Allow the parts to air dry.

66 Carefully inspect the bearings for cracks, heat discoloration, bent rollers, etc. Check the bearing races inside the hub for cracks, scoring or uneven surfaces. If the bearing races are in need of replacement, this job is best left to a repair shop which can press the new races into position.

67 Use an approved high temperature front wheel bearing grease to pack the bearings. Work the grease fully into the bearings, forcing the grease between the rollers, cone and cage.

68 Apply a thin coat of grease to the spindle at the outer bearing seat, inner bearing seat, shoulder and seal seat.

69 Put a small quantity of grease inboard of each bearing race inside the hub. Using your finger, form a dam at these points to provide extra grease availability and to keep thinned grease from flowing out of the bearing.

70 Place the grease-packed inner bearing into the rear of the hub and put a little more grease outboard of the bearing.

71 Place a new seal over the inner bearing and tap the seal with a flat plate and a hammer until it is flush with the hub.

72 Carefully place the hub assembly onto the spindle and push the grease-packed outer bearing into position.

73 Install the washer and spindle nut. Tighten the nut to 3.5 to 4.0 kg-m (25 to 29 ft lbs) torque. Spin the rotor and hub assembly to seat the bearings.

74 Re-torque, then loosen the nut 45 degrees.

75 Install the adjusting cap and tighten until any of its grooves align

6.49 Placing the yoke holder into position on the inner piston

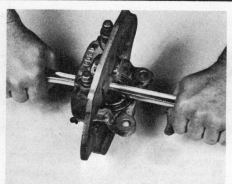

6.50 To seat the yoke holder on the yoke, downward pressure must be applied to the inner piston

6.51 Before installing the yoke-to-caliper bolts, inspect bushings and rubber boots

6.53 Use a screwdriver to pry off the hub dust cap

6.58 Lifting off the hub and rotor assembly

6.60 The rotor need be removed from the hub only if it is being replaced

with the hole in the spindle. Do not tighten the nut any more than 15 degrees.

76 Install a cotter pin through the hole, bend the ends over until they are flat against the nut. Cut any of the excess which could interfere with the dust cap.

77 Install the dust cap, tapping it into place with a rubber mallet.

### Master cylinder — overhaul

78 Clean away external dirt and then remove the reservoir caps and filters and empty out the fluid.

79 From the end of the master cylinder pry out the snap-ring, extract the stop washer, the primary piston and the spring.

80 Insert a rod to depress the secondary piston and then unscrew the stop screw from the base of the master cylinder. Release the rod and withdraw the secondary piston.

81 At this stage, inspect the surfaces of the pistons and cylinder bores for scoring or 'bright' wear areas. If these are evident, renew the complete master cylinder.

82 If the components are in good condition, discard the seals and obtain a repair kit which will contain all the necessary renewable items. Make sure that the kit is for the Tokico or Nabco master cylinder. These are different master cylinders and the parts ARE NOT interchangeable.

83 Wash all components in clean hydraulic fluid or alcohol — nothing else.

84 Do not detach the reservoirs. If they are removed, new ones must be installed. Do not remove the check valves unless absolutely essential.

85 Commence reassembly by manipulating the new seals into position using the fingers only to do it.

86 Dip all internal components in clean brake fluid before reassembly.

87 Install the secondary spring and piston assembly. Hold it depressed and screw in the stop screw.

88 Install the primary spring and the primary piston assembly. Fit the stop washer and the snap ring.

89 Bleed the system.

### Vacuum servo (booster) unit — general information and testing

90 A vacuum servo unit is fitted into the brake hydraulic circuit in series with the master cylinder, to provide assistance to the driver when the brake pedal is depressed. This reduces the effort required by the driver to operate the brakes under all braking conditions.

91 The unit operates by vacuum obtained from the induction manifold and comprises basically a booster diaphram and check valve. The servo unit and hydraulic master cylinder are connected together so that the servo unit piston rod acts as the master cylinder pushrod. The driver's braking effort is transmitted through another pushrod to the servo unit piston and its built-in control system. The servo unit piston does not fit tightly into the cylinder, but has a strong diaphram to keep its edges in constant contact with the cylinder wall, so assuring an air tight seal between the two parts. The forward chamber is held under vacuum conditions created in the inlet manifold of the engine and, during periods when the brake pedal is not in use, the controls open a passage to the rear chamber so placing it under vacuum conditions as well. When the brake pedal is depressed, the vacuum passage to the rear chamber is cut off and the chamber opened to atmospheric pressure. The consequent rush of air pushes the servo piston forward in the vacuum chamber and operates the main pushrod to the master cylinder.

92 The controls are designed so that assistance is given under all conditions and, when the brakes are not required, vacuum in the rear chamber is established when the brake pedal is released. All air from the atmosphere entering the rear chamber is passed through a small air filter.

93 Under normal operating conditions the vacuum servo unit is very reliable and does not require overhaul except at very high mileage. In this case it is far better to obtain a service exchange unit, rather than repair the original unit.

94 It is emphasised that the servo unit assists in reducing the braking effort required at the foot pedal and in the event of its failure, the hydraulic braking system is in no way affected except that the need for higher pedal pressures will be noticed.

95 To check for a satisfactory vacuum servo unit, depress the brake

**13**

pedal several times. The distance which the pedal travels on each depression should not vary.

96 Now hold the pedal fully depressed and start the engine. The pedal should be felt to move down slightly when the engine starts.

97 Depress the brake pedal, switch off the engine holding the pedal down for about 30 seconds. The position of the pedal should not alter.

98 Restart the engine, run it for a minute or two and then turn it off. Depress the brake pedal firmly several times. The pedal travel should decrease with each application.

99 If the unit does not perform as indicated locate the source of the problem by performing the following tests:

a) *First, carefully inspect the condition of the vacuum hoses connecting the servo unit with the check valve, the check valve with the intake manifold, and the check valve with its other connections. If any holes, cracking or other damage is found replace the defective hoses.*

b) *Next, remove the check valve from the vacuum line. If a vacuum pump is available, apply 7.87 inHg (26.7 kPa) of vacuum pressure to the valve opening that leads to the servo unit. If a vacuum pump is not available, put your mouth to the opening and attempt to suck air through the valve. If the pressure on the pump drops more that 0.39 inHg (1.3 kPa) in 15 seconds, or if you are able to suck air through the valve, the valve is defective and should be replaced.*

c) *Now blow air into the valve through the same opening as before. If the valve does not allow you to blow air into it, it is defective and should be replaced.*

d) *To test the servo unit, connect a vacuum gauge between the unit and the check valve. Start the engine and slowly increase the engine speed. Shut off the engine when the vacuum reading reaches 19.69 inHg (66.7 kPa) and observe the gauge. If the reading drops more than 0.98 inHg (3.3 kPa) within 15 seconds after the engine has been shut off, the servo unit is defective and should be replaced.*

e) *One final test is to repeat the previous test with the brake pedal fully depressed. Again, if the vacuum leakage is greater than specified, replace the servo unit.*

*Vacuum servo (booster) unit — removal and installation*
100 Remove the master cylinder (Chapter 9).

101 Disconnect the servo pushrod from the arm of the brake pedal by removing the snap pin and clevis pin.

102 Disconnect the vacuum line from the servo unit.

103 Remove the 4 retaining nuts from the servo unit's mounting studs, and withdraw the unit from the engine compartment.

104 Installation is the reverse of the removal procedure.

105 Bleed the entire brake system as described in Chapter 9.

106 Check the brake pedal height and adjust if necessary (Chapter 9).

## 7  Electrical system

1  The alternator and regulator used in the 1977 model are basically the same as used in 1975/76. In 1978 however, an IC voltage regulator was built into the alternator. Aside from the IC circuit, the only difference between 1978/79 alternators and the earlier ones is an addition of three sub diodes.

*Dismantling — alternator with IC regulator*
2  This procedure is the same as what is described in Chapter 10, Section 10 except, after the rear bearing is removed, Step 8, the IC regulator must be removed as follows:

3  Disconnect the wire connecting the diode set plate to the brush at the brush terminal by heating it with a soldering iron.

4  Disconnect the diode set plate from the side face of the rear cover.

5  Remove the nut securing the battery terminal bolt.

6  Partially lift the diode set plate together with the stator coil from the rear cover. Remove the screw that connects the diode set plate to the brush.

7  Separate the rear cover together with the stator coil and diode, and remove the brush and IC regulator.

## 8  Suspension and steering

1  Steering stayed the same up through 1979 but the suspension varied slightly. In 1978 upper and lower balljoints were installed instead of king pins.

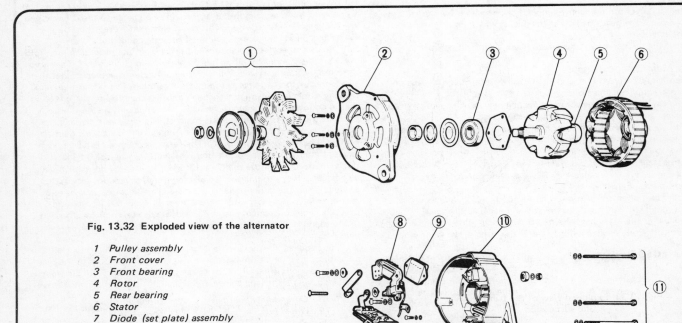

**Fig. 13.32 Exploded view of the alternator**

1  *Pulley assembly*
2  *Front cover*
3  *Front bearing*
4  *Rotor*
5  *Rear bearing*
6  *Stator*
7  *Diode (set plate) assembly*
8  *Brush assembly*
9  *IC voltage regulator*
10  *Rear cover*
11  *Through bolt*

## Upper link and balljoint

**Removal**

2   Lift and support the vehicle on jack stands safely on the frame.
3   Remove the front tires and wheels.
4   Loosen the spring anchor lock on the torsion bar and the adjusting nuts to counter the spring on the torsion bar.
5   Remove the cotter pin and nut from the upper balljoint stud.
6   Separate the balljoint from the knuckle spindle using a balljoint remover or pickle fork.
7   Loosen the nuts and remove the upper balljoint.
8   Remove the bolts holding the upper link spindle.
9   Remove the upper link with the camber adjusting shims from the body bracket. Pay close attention to the number and position of all shims.
10  Remove the washers and nuts at both ends of the upper link spindle.
11  Press the upper link spindle on both ends, one after the other.
12  Remove the upper link spindle and the rubber bushing.
13  The balljoint is a complete unit. Check for cracks, distortion, wear or damage on the dust cover, dust cover retainer and the clip. Replace if necessary.
14  Check the upper link spindle and the rubber bushing for damage and replace if necessary.

**Installation**

15  Liberally apply soapsuds to one of the rubber bushings and force fit it from the outside of the link. Position the guide on the end surface of the inside of the outer collar and press the inner collar of the bushing until dimension "C" exceeds 4.5 mm (0.177 in) (Fig. 13.35).

16  Insert the upper link spindle and upper link washer from a position where the bushing is not inserted. **Note**: *Be sure to install the washer in the designated direction. (Fig. 13.35).*
17  Press fit the other bushing in the same manner used for the first bushing.
18  Check dimensions C, D and E after installation to be sure that the bushing is fitted properly.
19  Set the upper link spindle, then tighten the bushing to between 7.7 and 10.5 kg-m (56 to 76 ft-lb). (Fig. 13.36).
20  Install the upper link and upper link spindle as an assembly to the frame. **Note**: *Be sure to install the alignment shims that were removed.* Torque to between 11.1 to 11.5 kg-m (80 to 108 ft-lb).
21  Install the upper balljoint to the upper link.
22  Guide the upper ball stud into the knuckle spindle and install the nut and cotter pin. Be sure that the tapered areas of the balljoint are clean and free of grease. Torque to between 8 and 10 kg-m (58 to 72 ft-lb).
23  Install the wheels and tires.
24  Immediately take the vehicle to a qualified shop to have the front wheels checked and/or aligned as necessary.

## Lower link and balljoint

**Removal**

25  Lift and support the vehicle on jack stands safely on the frame.
26  Remove the front tires and wheels.
27  Remove the lower shock absorber bolt.
28  Loosen the torsion bar spring anchor lock and adjusting nuts.

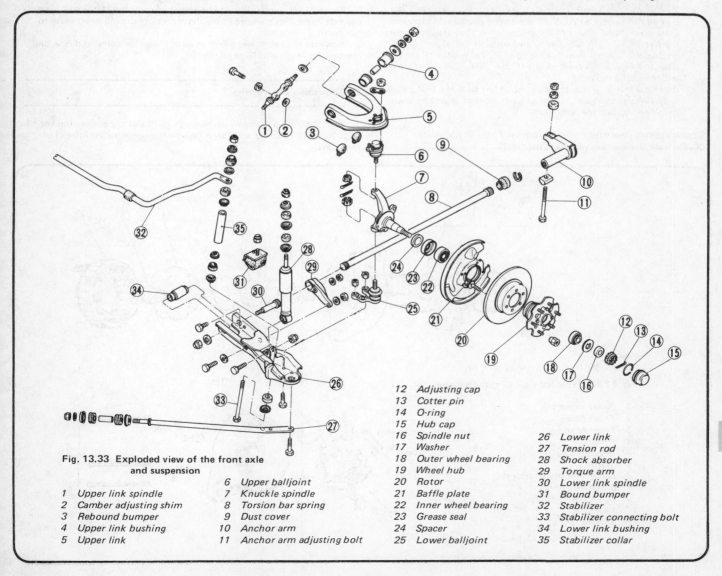

Fig. 13.33 Exploded view of the front axle
and suspension

| | | | |
|---|---|---|---|
| 1 | Upper link spindle | 6 | Upper balljoint |
| 2 | Camber adjusting shim | 7 | Knuckle spindle |
| 3 | Rebound bumper | 8 | Torsion bar spring |
| 4 | Upper link bushing | 9 | Dust cover |
| 5 | Upper link | 10 | Anchor arm |
| | | 11 | Anchor arm adjusting bolt |

| | | | |
|---|---|---|---|
| 12 | Adjusting cap | | |
| 13 | Cotter pin | | |
| 14 | O-ring | | |
| 15 | Hub cap | | |
| 16 | Spindle nut | 26 | Lower link |
| 17 | Washer | 27 | Tension rod |
| 18 | Outer wheel bearing | 28 | Shock absorber |
| 19 | Wheel hub | 29 | Torque arm |
| 20 | Rotor | 30 | Lower link spindle |
| 21 | Baffle plate | 31 | Bound bumper |
| 22 | Inner wheel bearing | 32 | Stabilizer |
| 23 | Grease seal | 33 | Stabilizer connecting bolt |
| 24 | Spacer | 34 | Lower link bushing |
| 25 | Lower balljoint | 35 | Stabilizer collar |

**13**

Separate the anchor arm bolt from the anchor arm.

29 Remove the snap ring and move the anchor arm and torsion bar spring fully rearward.

30 Disconnect the stabilizer connecting rod from the lower link.

31 Disconnect the tension rod from the lower link.

32 Remove the cotter pin and nut from the lower balljoint stud. Disconnect the lower balljoint from the knuckle spindle using a balljoint remover or pickle fork.

33 Remove the nut and washer at the lower link spindle front end.

34 Lightly tap on the front end of the lower link spindle and while pushing down on the torsion bar spring, remove the lower link spindle and the lower link.

35 Separate the lower link balljoint from the lower link by removing the attaching bolts.

36 Remove the lower link spindle bushing, using an appropriate sized socket and hammer (Fig. 13.37).

37 Check the dust cover, retainer and clip for damage, wear, distortion and cracks. Replace if necessary.

38 Check the lower link, lower link spindle and torque arm for cracks or distortion. Replace if necessary.

39 Check the lower link rubber bushing for damage or distortion. Replace if necessary.

**Installation**

40 Assemble the lower balljoint to the lower link. Torque at between 3.9 to 5.3 kg-m (28 to 38 ft-lb).

41 Assemble the torque arm to the lower link. Torque the outer nut at between 2.7 to 3.7 kg-m (20 to 27 ft-lb).

42 Torque the inner nut at between 3.6 to 4.6 kg-m (22 to 33 ft-lb).

43 Install the rubber bushing to the frame using an appropriate sized socket and hammer.

44 Insert the lower link spindle to install the lower arm to the frame.

45 Tighten the lower spindle nut to 11.1 to 15.0 kg-m (80 to 108 ft-lb).

46 Guide the lower ball stud into the knuckle spindle and install the nut. Be sure that the tapered areas of the balljoint and knuckle spindle and the threads of the balljoint are free of dirt or grease. Torque at between 17.5 to 19.5 kg-m (127 to 141 ft-lb).

47 Install the torsion bar spring to the torque arm.

48 Install the wheels and tires.

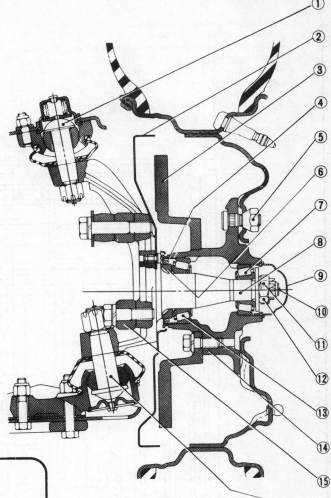

Fig. 13.34 Front axle cross section

| 1 Upper balljoint | 9 Hub cap |
|---|---|
| 2 Baffle plate | 10 Cotter pin |
| 3 Rotor | 11 Adjusting cap |
| 4 Grease seal | 12 Spindle nut |
| 5 Wheel nut | 13 Inner bearing |
| 6 Spacer | 14 Wheel hub |
| 7 Outer bearing | 15 Knuckle arm |
| 8 Knuckle spindle | 16 Lower balljoint |

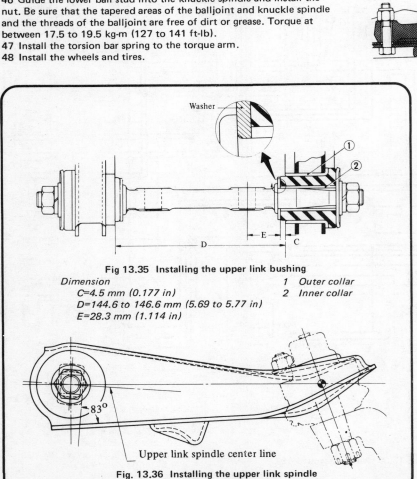

Fig 13.35 Installing the upper link bushing

*Dimension*
*C=4.5 mm (0.177 in)*        1 Outer collar
*D=144.6 to 146.6 mm (5.69 to 5.77 in)*        2 Inner collar
*E=28.3 mm (1.114 in)*

Upper link spindle center line

Fig. 13.36 Installing the upper link spindle

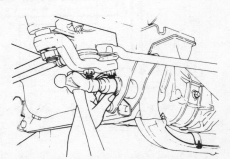

Fig. 13.37 Removing the lower link spindle bushing

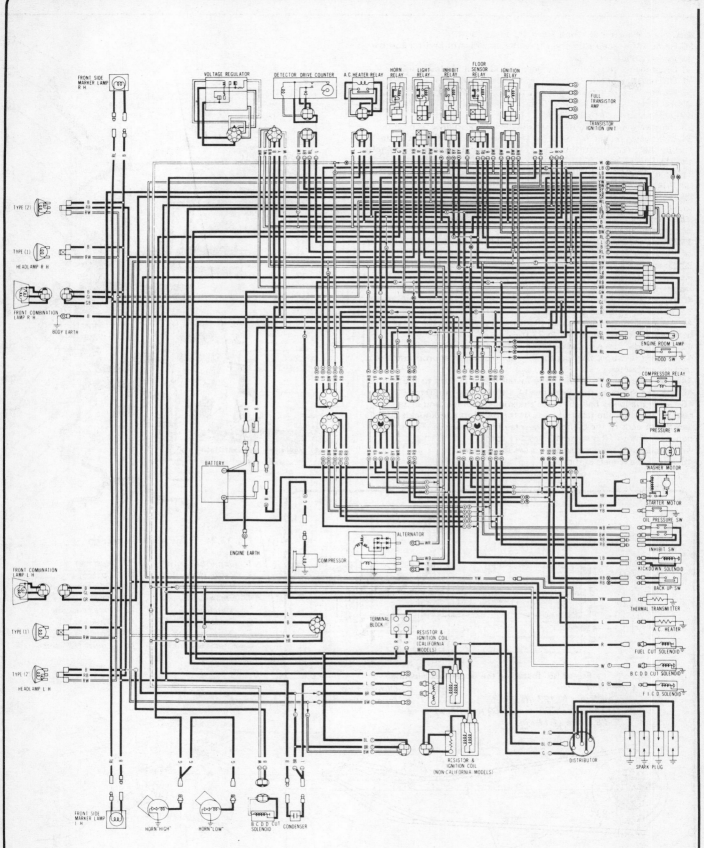

**Fig. 13.38 Wiring diagram - 1977**

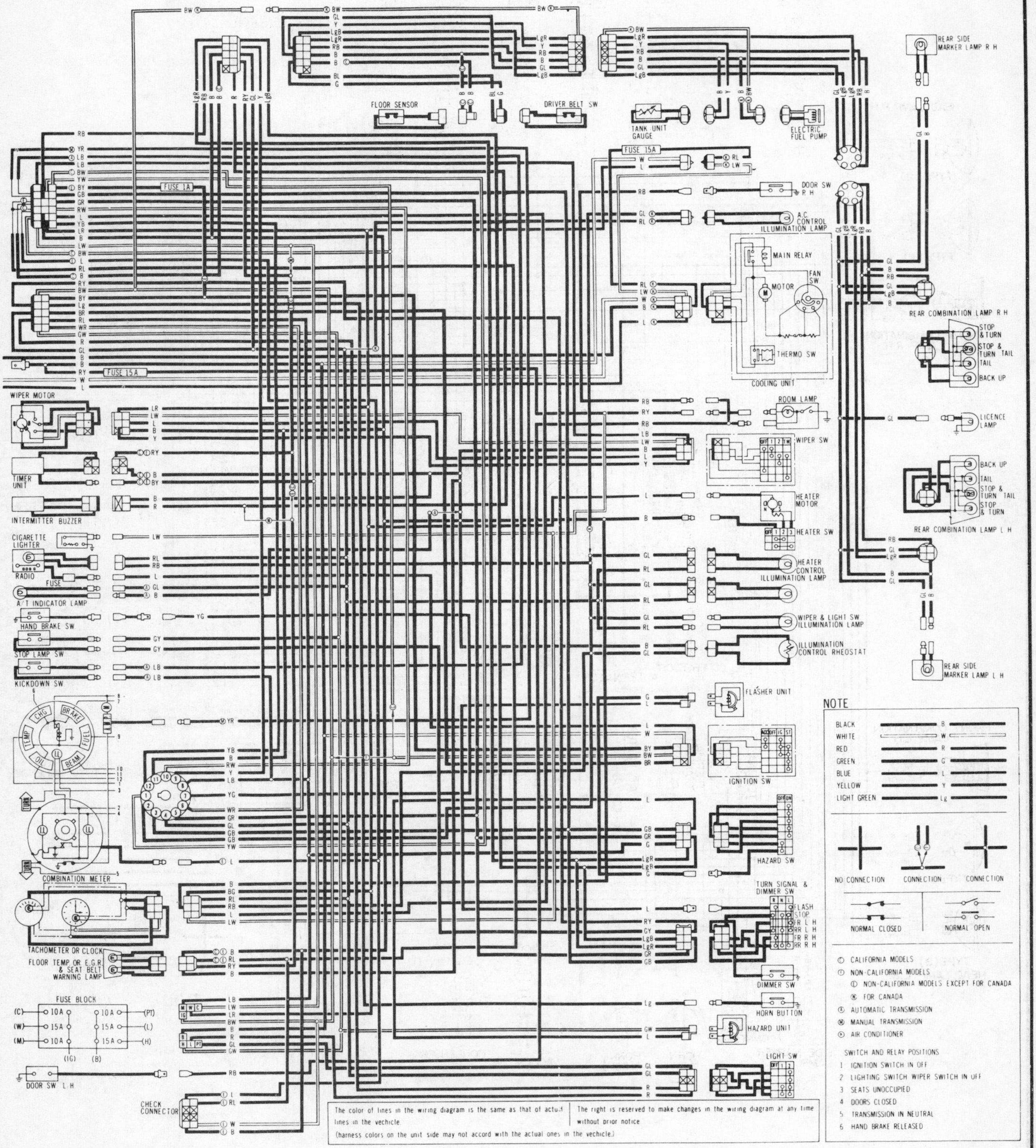

**Fig. 13.39 Wiring diagram - 1977 continued**

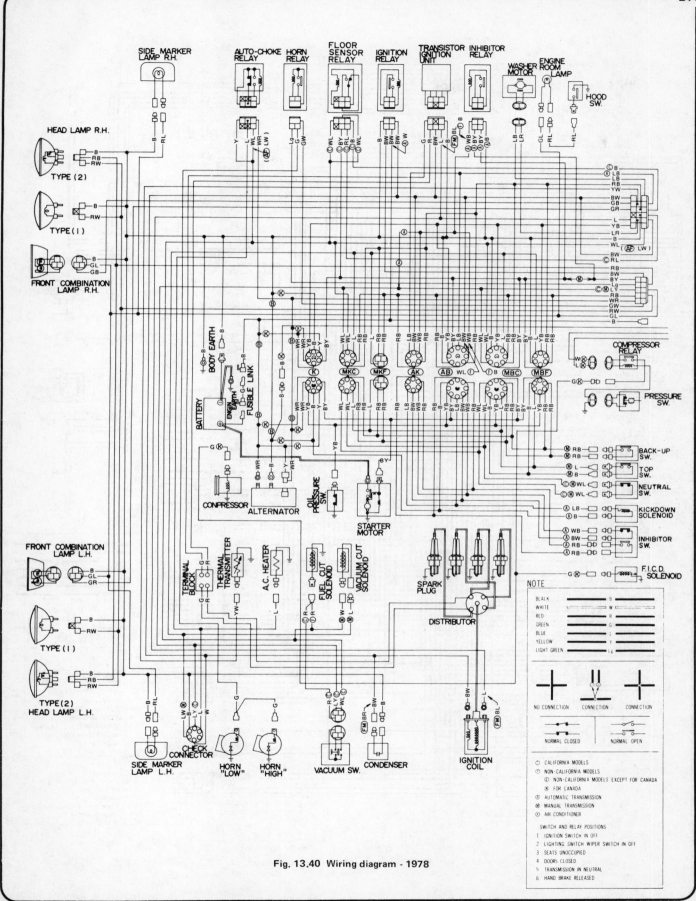

Fig. 13.40 Wiring diagram - 1978

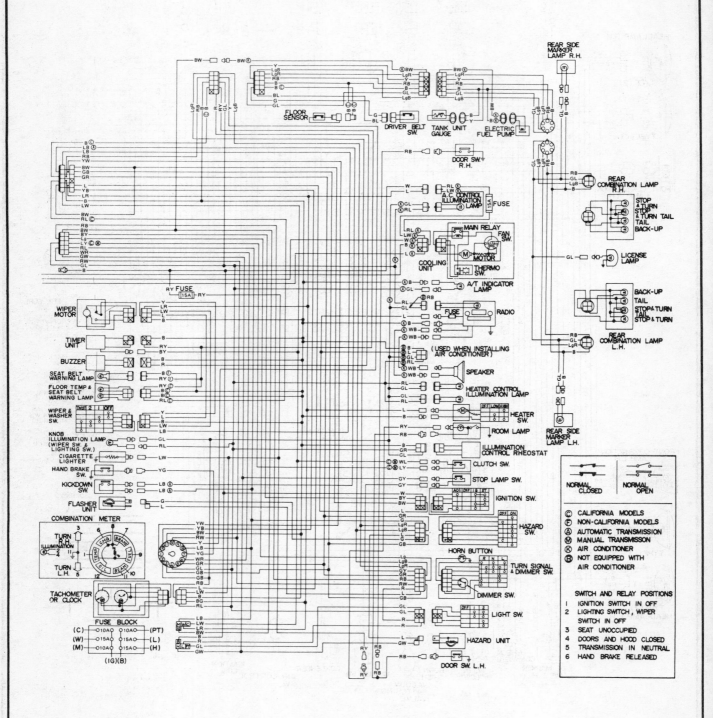

**Fig. 13.41 Wiring diagram - 1978 continued**

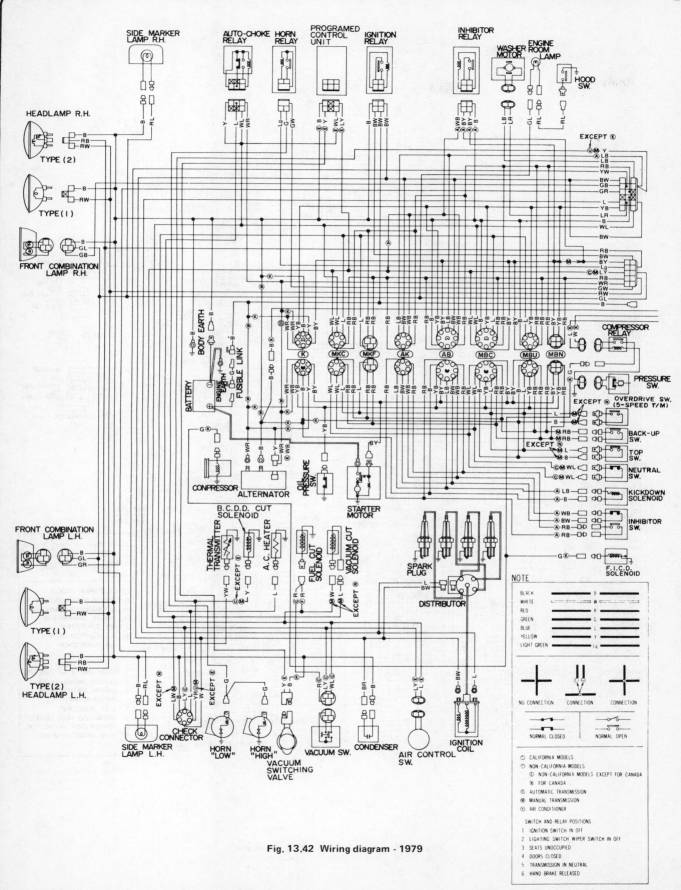

**Fig. 13.42 Wiring diagram - 1979**

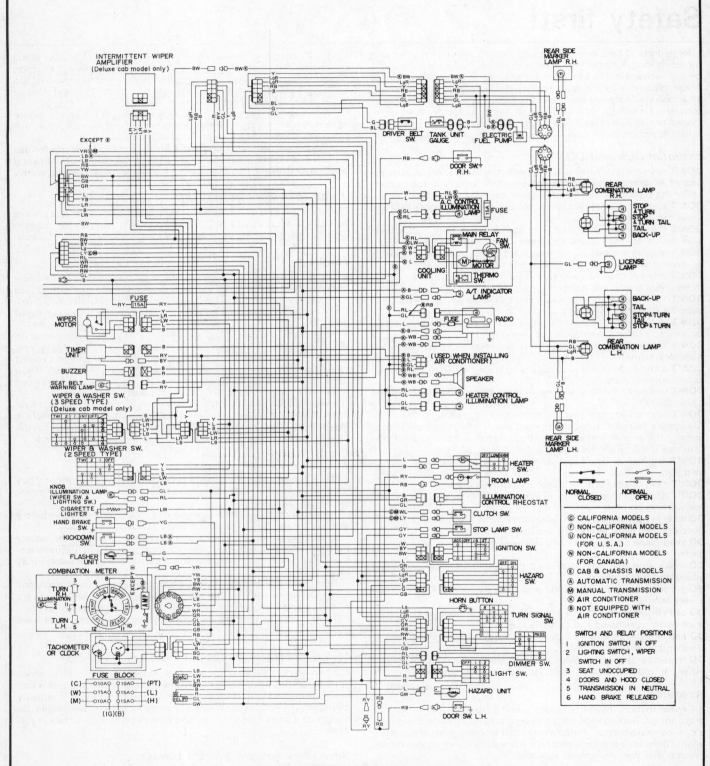

Fig. 13.43 Wiring diagram - 1979 continued

# Safety first!

Regardless of how enthusiastic you may be about getting on with the job at hand, take the time to ensure that your safety is not jeopardized. A moment's lack of attention can result in an accident, as can failure to observe certain simple safety precautions. The possibility of an accident will always exist, and the following points should not be considered a comprehensive list of all dangers. Rather, they are intended to make you aware of the risks and to encourage a safety conscious approach to all work you carry out on your vehicle.

## Essential DOs and DON'Ts

**DON'T** rely on a jack when working under the vehicle. Always use approved jackstands to support the weight of the vehicle and place them under the recommended lift or support points.

**DON'T** attempt to loosen extremely tight fasteners (i.e. wheel lug nuts) while the vehicle is on a jack — it may fall.

**DON'T** start the engine without first making sure that the transmission is in Neutral (or Park where applicable) and the parking brake is set.

**DON'T** remove the radiator cap from a hot cooling system — let it cool or cover it with a cloth and release the pressure gradually.

**DON'T** attempt to drain the engine oil until you are sure it has cooled to the point that it will not burn you.

**DON'T** touch any part of the engine or exhaust system until it has cooled sufficiently to avoid burns.

**DON'T** siphon toxic liquids such as gasoline, antifreeze and brake fluid by mouth, or allow them to remain on your skin.

**DON'T** inhale brake lining dust — it is potentially hazardous (see *Asbestos* below)

**DON'T** allow spilled oil or grease to remain on the floor — wipe it up before someone slips on it.

**DON'T** use loose fitting wrenches or other tools which may slip and cause injury.

**DON'T** push on wrenches when loosening or tightening nuts or bolts. Always try to pull the wrench toward you. If the situation calls for pushing the wrench away, push with an open hand to avoid scraped knuckles if the wrench should slip.

**DON'T** attempt to lift a heavy component alone — get someone to help you.

**DON'T** rush or take unsafe shortcuts to finish a job.

**DON'T** allow children or animals in or around the vehicle while you are working on it.

**DO** wear eye protection when using power tools such as a drill, sander, bench grinder, etc. and when working under a vehicle.

**DO** keep loose clothing and long hair well out of the way of moving parts.

**DO** make sure that any hoist used has a safe working load rating adequate for the job.

**DO** get someone to check on you periodically when working alone on a vehicle.

**DO** carry out work in a logical sequence and make sure that everything is correctly assembled and tightened.

**DO** keep chemicals and fluids tightly capped and out of the reach of children and pets.

**DO** remember that your vehicle's safety affects that of yourself and others. If in doubt on any point, get professional advice.

## Asbestos

Certain friction, insulating, sealing, and other products — such as brake linings, brake bands, clutch linings, torque converters, gaskets, etc. — contain asbestos. *Extreme care must be taken to avoid inhalation of dust from such products since it is hazardous to health.* If in doubt, assume that they *do* contain asbestos.

## Fire

Remember at all times that gasoline is highly flammable. Never smoke or have any kind of open flame around when working on a vehicle. But the risk does not end there. A spark caused by an electrical short circuit, by two metal surfaces contacting each other, or even by static electricity built up in your body under certain conditions, can ignite gasoline vapors, which in a confined space are highly explosive. Do not, under any circumstances, use gasoline for cleaning parts. Use an approved safety solvent.

Always disconnect the battery ground (−) cable *at the battery* before working on any part of the fuel system or electrical system. Never risk spilling fuel on a hot engine or exhaust component.

It is strongly recommended that a fire extinguisher suitable for use on fuel and electrical fires be kept handy in the garage or workshop at all times. Never try to extinguish a fuel or electrical fire with water.

## Torch (flashlight in the US)

Any reference to a "torch" appearing in this manual should always be taken to mean a hand-held, battery-operated electric light or flashlight. It DOES NOT mean a welding or propane torch or blowtorch.

## Fumes

Certain fumes are highly toxic and can quickly cause unconsciousness and even death if inhaled to any extent. Gasoline vapor falls into this category, as do the vapors from some cleaning solvents. Any draining or pouring of such volatile fluids should be done in a well ventilated area.

When using cleaning fluids and solvents, read the instructions on the container carefully. Never use materials from unmarked containers.

Never run the engine in an enclosed space, such as a garage. Exhaust fumes contain carbon monoxide, which is extremely poisonous. If you need to run the engine, always do so in the open air, or at least have the rear of the vehicle outside the work area.

If you are fortunate enough to have the use of an inspection pit, never drain or pour gasoline and never run the engine while the vehicle is over the pit. The fumes, being heavier than air, will concentrate in the pit with possibly lethal results.

## The battery

Never create a spark or allow a bare light bulb near a battery. They normally give off a certain amount of hydrogen gas, which is highly explosive.

Always disconnect the battery ground (−) cable *at the battery* before working on the fuel or electrical systems.

If possible, loosen the filler caps or cover when charging the battery from an external source (this does not apply to sealed or maintenance-free batteries). Do not charge at an excessive rate or the battery may burst.

Take care when adding water to a non maintenance-free battery and when carrying a battery. The electrolyte, even when diluted, is very corrosive and should not be allowed to contact clothing or skin.

Always wear eye protection when cleaning the battery to prevent the caustic deposits from entering your eyes.

## Mains electricity (household current in the US)

When using an electric power tool, inspection light, etc., which operates on household current, always make sure that the tool is correctly connected to its plug and that, where necessary, it is properly grounded. Do not use such items in damp conditions and, again, do not create a spark or apply excessive heat in the vicinity of fuel or fuel vapor.

## Secondary ignition system voltage

A severe electric shock can result from touching certain parts of the ignition system (such as the spark plug wires) when the engine is running or being cranked, particularly if components are damp or the insulation is defective. In the case of an electronic ignition system, the secondary system voltage is much higher and could prove fatal.

# Conversion factors

**Length (distance)**

| | | | | | |
|---|---|---|---|---|---|
| Inches (in) | X | 25.4 | = Millimetres (mm) | X 0.0394 | = Inches (in) |
| Feet (ft) | X | 0.305 | = Metres (m) | X 3.281 | = Feet (ft) |
| Miles | X | 1.609 | = Kilometres (km) | X 0.621 | = Miles |

**Volume (capacity)**

| | | | | | |
|---|---|---|---|---|---|
| Cubic inches (cu in; in³) | X | 16.387 | = Cubic centimetres (cc; cm³) | X 0.061 | = Cubic inches (cu in; in³) |
| Imperial pints (Imp pt) | X | 0.568 | = Litres (l) | X 1.76 | = Imperial pints (Imp pt) |
| Imperial quarts (Imp qt) | X | 1.137 | = Litres (l) | X 0.88 | = Imperial quarts (Imp qt) |
| Imperial quarts (Imp qt) | X | 1.201 | = US quarts (US qt) | X 0.833 | = Imperial quarts (Imp qt) |
| US quarts (US qt) | X | 0.946 | = Litres (l) | X 1.057 | = US quarts (US qt) |
| Imperial gallons (Imp gal) | X | 4.546 | = Litres (l) | X 0.22 | = Imperial gallons (Imp gal) |
| Imperial gallons (Imp gal) | X | 1.201 | = US gallons (US gal) | X 0.833 | = Imperial gallons (Imp gal) |
| US gallons (US gal) | X | 3.785 | = Litres (l) | X 0.264 | = US gallons (US gal) |

**Mass (weight)**

| | | | | | |
|---|---|---|---|---|---|
| Ounces (oz) | X | 28.35 | = Grams (g) | X 0.035 | = Ounces (oz) |
| Pounds (lb) | X | 0.454 | = Kilograms (kg) | X 2.205 | = Pounds (lb) |

**Force**

| | | | | | |
|---|---|---|---|---|---|
| Ounces-force (ozf; oz) | X | 0.278 | = Newtons (N) | X 3.6 | = Ounces-force (ozf; oz) |
| Pounds-force (lbf; lb) | X | 4.448 | = Newtons (N) | X 0.225 | = Pounds-force (lbf; lb) |
| Newtons (N) | X | 0.1 | = Kilograms-force (kgf; kg) | X 9.81 | = Newtons (N) |

**Pressure**

| | | | | | |
|---|---|---|---|---|---|
| Pounds-force per square inch (psi; lbf/in²; lb/in²) | X | 0.070 | = Kilograms-force per square centimetre (kgf/cm²; kg/cm²) | X 14.223 | = Pounds-force per square inch (psi; lbf/in²; lb/in²) |
| Pounds-force per square inch (psi; lbf/in²; lb/in²) | X | 0.068 | = Atmospheres (atm) | X 14.696 | = Pounds-force per square inch (psi; lbf/in²; lb/in²) |
| Pounds-force per square inch (psi; lbf/in²; lb/in²) | X | 0.069 | = Bars | X 14.5 | = Pounds-force per square inch (psi; lbf/in²; lb/in²) |
| Pounds-force per square inch (psi; lbf/in²; lb/in²) | X | 6.895 | = Kilopascals (kPa) | X 0.145 | = Pounds-force per square inch (psi; lbf/in²; lb/in²) |
| Kilopascals (kPa) | X | 0.01 | = Kilograms-force per square centimetre (kgf/cm²; kg/cm²) | X 98.1 | = Kilopascals (kPa) |
| Millibar (mbar) | X | 100 | = Pascals (Pa) | X 0.01 | = Millibar (mbar) |
| Millibar (mbar) | X | 0.0145 | = Pounds-force per square inch (psi; lbf/in²; lb/in²) | X 68.947 | = Millibar (mbar) |
| Millibar (mbar) | X | 0.75 | = Millimetres of mercury (mmHg) | X 1.333 | = Millibar (mbar) |
| Millibar (mbar) | X | 0.401 | = Inches of water (inH₂O) | X 2.491 | = Millibar (mbar) |
| Millimetres of mercury (mmHg) | X | 0.535 | = Inches of water (inH₂O) | X 1.868 | = Millimetres of mercury (mmHg) |
| Inches of water (inH₂O) | X | 0.036 | = Pounds-force per square inch (psi; lbf/in²; lb/in²) | X 27.68 | = Inches of water (inH₂O) |

**Torque (moment of force)**

| | | | | | |
|---|---|---|---|---|---|
| Pounds-force inches (lbf in; lb in) | X | 1.152 | = Kilograms-force centimetre (kgf cm; kg cm) | X 0.868 | = Pounds-force inches (lbf in; lb in) |
| Pounds-force inches (lbf in; lb in) | X | 0.113 | = Newton metres (Nm) | X 8.85 | = Pounds-force inches (lbf in; lb in) |
| Pounds-force inches (lbf in; lb in) | X | 0.083 | = Pounds-force feet (lbf ft; lb ft) | X 12 | = Pounds-force inches (lbf in; lb in) |
| Pounds-force feet (lbf ft; lb ft) | X | 0.138 | = Kilograms-force metres (kgf m; kg m) | X 7.233 | = Pounds-force feet (lbf ft; lb ft) |
| Pounds-force feet (lbf ft; lb ft) | X | 1.356 | = Newton metres (Nm) | X 0.738 | = Pounds-force feet (lbf ft; lb ft) |
| Newton metres (Nm) | X | 0.102 | = Kilograms-force metres (kgf m; kg m) | X 9.804 | = Newton metres (Nm) |

**Power**

| | | | | | |
|---|---|---|---|---|---|
| Horsepower (hp) | X | 745.7 | = Watts (W) | X 0.0013 | = Horsepower (hp) |

**Velocity (speed)**

| | | | | | |
|---|---|---|---|---|---|
| Miles per hour (miles/hr; mph) | X | 1.609 | = Kilometres per hour (km/hr; kph) | X 0.621 | = Miles per hour (miles/hr; mph) |

**Fuel consumption***

| | | | | | |
|---|---|---|---|---|---|
| Miles per gallon, Imperial (mpg) | X | 0.354 | = Kilometres per litre (km/l) | X 2.825 | = Miles per gallon, Imperial (mpg) |
| Miles per gallon, US (mpg) | X | 0.425 | = Kilometres per litre (km/l) | X 2.352 | = Miles per gallon, US (mpg) |

**Temperature**

Degrees Fahrenheit = (°C x 1.8) + 32        Degrees Celsius (Degrees Centigrade; °C) = (°F - 32) x 0.56

*It is common practice to convert from miles per gallon (mpg) to litres/100 kilometres (l/100km), where mpg (Imperial) x l/100 km = 282 and mpg (US) x l/100 km = 235

# Index

# Haynes Automotive Manuals

*NOTE: New manuals are added to this list on a periodic basis. If you do not see a listing for your vehicle, consult your local Haynes dealer for the latest product information.*

## ACURA
*12020 **Integra** '86 thru '89 & **Legend** '86 thru '90

## AMC
**Jeep CJ** - see JEEP (50020)
14020 **Mid-size models,** Concord, Hornet, Gremlin & Spirit '70 thru '83
14025 **(Renault) Alliance & Encore** '83 thru '87

## AUDI
15020 **4000** all models '80 thru '87
15025 **5000** all models '77 thru '83
15026 **5000** all models '84 thru '88

## AUSTIN-HEALEY
**Sprite** - see MG Midget (66015)

## BMW
*18020 **3/5 Series** not including diesel or all-wheel drive models '82 thru '92
*18021 **3 Series** except 325iX models '92 thru '97
18025 **320i** all 4 cyl models '75 thru '83
18035 **528i & 530i** all models '75 thru '80
18050 **1500 thru 2002** except Turbo '59 thru '77

## BUICK
**Century (front wheel drive)** - see GM (829)
*19020 **Buick, Oldsmobile & Pontiac Full-size (Front wheel drive)** all models '85 thru '98
**Buick** Electra, LeSabre and Park Avenue; **Oldsmobile** Delta 88 Royale, Ninety Eight and Regency; **Pontiac** Bonneville
19025 **Buick Oldsmobile & Pontiac Full-size (Rear wheel drive)**
**Buick** Estate '70 thru '90, Electra'70 thru '84, LeSabre '70 thru '85, Limited '74 thru '79
**Oldsmobile** Custom Cruiser '70 thru '90, Delta 88 '70 thru '85,Ninety-eight '70 thru '84
**Pontiac** Bonneville '70 thru '81, Catalina '70 thru '81, Grandville '70 thru '75, Parisienne '83 thru '86
19030 **Mid-size Regal & Century** all rear-drive models with V6, V8 and Turbo '74 thru '87
**Regal** - see GENERAL MOTORS (38010)
**Riviera** - see GENERAL MOTORS (38030)
**Roadmaster** - see CHEVROLET (24046)
**Skyhawk** - see GENERAL MOTORS (38015)
**Skylark** '80 thru '85 - see GM (38020)
**Skylark** '86 on - see GM (38025)
**Somerset** - see GENERAL MOTORS (38025)

## CADILLAC
*21030 **Cadillac Rear Wheel Drive** all gasoline models '70 thru '93
**Cimarron** - see GENERAL MOTORS (38015)
**Eldorado** - see GENERAL MOTORS (38030)
**Seville** '80 thru '85 - see GM (38030)

## CHEVROLET
*24010 **Astro & GMC Safari Mini-vans** '85 thru '93
24015 **Camaro V8** all models '70 thru '81
24016 **Camaro** all models '82 thru '92
**Cavalier** - see GENERAL MOTORS (38015)
**Celebrity** - see GENERAL MOTORS (38005)
24017 **Camaro & Firebird** '93 thru '97
24020 **Chevelle, Malibu & El Camino** '69 thru '87
24024 **Chevette & Pontiac T1000** '76 thru '87
**Citation** - see GENERAL MOTORS (38020)
*24032 **Corsica/Beretta** all models '87 thru '96
24040 **Corvette** all V8 models '68 thru '82
*24041 **Corvette** all models '84 thru '96
10305 **Chevrolet Engine Overhaul Manual**
24045 **Full-size Sedans** Caprice, Impala, Biscayne, Bel Air & Wagons '69 thru '90
24046 **Impala SS & Caprice and Buick Roadmaster** '91 thru '96
**Lumina** - see GENERAL MOTORS (38010)

---

24048 **Lumina & Monte Carlo** '95 thru '98
**Lumina APV** - see GM (38035)
24050 **Luv Pick-up** all 2WD & 4WD '72 thru '82
*24055 **Monte Carlo** all models '70 thru '88
**Monte Carlo** '95 thru '98 - see LUMINA (24048)
24059 **Nova** all V8 models '69 thru '79
*24060 **Nova and Geo Prizm** '85 thru '92
24064 **Pick-ups '67 thru '87** - Chevrolet & GMC, all V8 & in-line 6 cyl, 2WD & 4WD '67 thru '87; Suburbans, Blazers & Jimmys '67 thru '91
*24065 **Pick-ups '88 thru '98** - Chevrolet & GMC, all full-size pick-ups, '88 thru '98; Blazer & Jimmy '92 thru '94; Suburban '92 thru '98; Tahoe & Yukon '98
24070 **S-10 & S-15 Pick-ups** '82 thru '93, **Blazer & Jimmy** '83 thru '94,
*24071 **S-10 & S-15 Pick-ups** '94 thru '96 **Blazer & Jimmy** '95 thru '96
*24075 **Sprint & Geo Metro** '85 thru '94
*24080 **Vans - Chevrolet & GMC,** V8 & in-line 6 cylinder models '68 thru '96

## CHRYSLER
25015 **Chrysler Cirrus, Dodge Stratus, Plymouth Breeze** '95 thru '98
25025 **Chrysler Concorde, New Yorker & LHS, Dodge** Intrepid, **Eagle** Vision, '93 thru '97
10310 **Chrysler Engine Overhaul Manual**
*25020 **Full-size Front-Wheel Drive** '88 thru '93
**K-Cars** - see DODGE Aries (30008)
**Laser** - see DODGE Daytona (30030)
*25030 **Chrysler & Plymouth Mid-size** front wheel drive '82 thru '95
**Rear-wheel Drive** - see Dodge (30050)

## DATSUN
28005 **200SX** all models '80 thru '83
28007 **B-210** all models '73 thru '78
28009 **210** all models '79 thru '82
28012 **240Z, 260Z & 280Z** Coupe '70 thru '78
28014 **280ZX** Coupe & 2+2 '79 thru '83
**300ZX** - see NISSAN (72010)
28016 **310** all models '78 thru '82
28018 **510 & PL521 Pick-up** '68 thru '73
28020 **510** all models '78 thru '81
28022 **620 Series Pick-up** all models '73 thru '79
**720 Series Pick-up** - see NISSAN (72030)
28025 **810/Maxima** all gasoline models, '77 thru '84

## DODGE
**400 & 600** - see CHRYSLER (25030)
*30008 **Aries & Plymouth Reliant** '81 thru '89
30010 **Caravan & Plymouth Voyager Mini-Vans** all models '84 thru '95
*30011 **Caravan & Plymouth Voyager Mini-Vans** all models '96 thru '98
30012 **Challenger/Plymouth Saporro** '78 thru '83
30016 **Colt & Plymouth Champ** (front wheel drive) all models '78 thru '87
*30020 **Dakota Pick-ups** all models '87 thru '96
30025 **Dart, Demon, Plymouth Barracuda, Duster & Valiant** 6 cyl models '67 thru '76
*30030 **Daytona & Chrysler Laser** '84 thru '89
**Intrepid** - see CHRYSLER (25025)
*30034 **Neon** all models '95 thru '97
*30035 **Omni & Plymouth Horizon** '78 thru '90
*30040 **Pick-ups** all full-size models '74 thru '93
*30041 **Pick-ups** all full-size models '94 thru '96
*30045 **Ram 50/D50 Pick-ups & Raider and Plymouth Arrow Pick-ups** '79 thru '93
30050 **Dodge/Plymouth/Chrysler** rear wheel drive '71 thru '89
*30055 **Shadow & Plymouth Sundance** '87 thru '94
*30060 **Spirit & Plymouth Acclaim** '89 thru '95
*30065 **Vans - Dodge & Plymouth** '71 thru '96

## EAGLE
**Talon** - see Mitsubishi Eclipse (68030)
**Vision** - see CHRYSLER (25025)

## FIAT
34010 **124 Sport Coupe & Spider** '68 thru '78
34025 **X1/9** all models '74 thru '80

---

## FORD
10355 **Ford Automatic Transmission Overhaul**
*36004 **Aerostar Mini-vans** all models '86 thru '96
*36006 **Contour & Mercury Mystique** '95 thru '98
36008 **Courier Pick-up** all models '72 thru '82
36012 **Crown Victoria & Mercury Grand Marquis** '88 thru '96
10320 **Ford Engine Overhaul Manual**
36016 **Escort/Mercury Lynx** all models '81 thru '90
*36020 **Escort/Mercury Tracer** '91 thru '96
*36024 **Explorer & Mazda Navajo** '91 thru '95
36028 **Fairmont & Mercury Zephyr** '78 thru '83
36030 **Festiva & Aspire** '88 thru '97
36032 **Fiesta** all models '77 thru '80
36036 **Ford & Mercury Full-size,** Ford LTD & Mercury Marquis, ('75 thru '82); Ford Custom 500,Country Squire, Crown Victoria & Mercury Colony Park ('75 thru '87); Ford LTD Crown Victoria & Mercury Gran Marquis ('83 thru '87)
36040 **Granada & Mercury Monarch** '75 thru '80
36044 **Ford & Mercury Mid-size,** Ford Thunderbird & Mercury Cougar ('75 thru '82); Ford LTD & Mercury Marquis ('83 thru '86); Ford Torino,Gran Torino, Elite, Ranchero pick-up, LTD II, Mercury Montego, Comet, XR-7 & Lincoln Versailles ('75 thru '86)
36048 **Mustang V8** all models '64-1/2 thru '73
36049 **Mustang II** 4 cyl, V6 & V8 models '74 thru '78
36050 **Mustang & Mercury Capri** all models Mustang, '79 thru '93; Capri, '79 thru '86
*36051 **Mustang** all models '94 thru '97
36054 **Pick-ups & Bronco** '73 thru '79
36058 **Pick-ups & Bronco** '80 thru '96
36059 **Pick-ups, Expedition & Mercury Navigator** '97 thru '98
36062 **Pinto & Mercury Bobcat** '75 thru '80
36066 **Probe** all models '89 thru '92
36070 **Ranger/Bronco II** gasoline models '83 thru '92
*36071 **Ranger** '93 thru '97 & **Mazda Pick-ups** '94 thru '97
36074 **Taurus & Mercury Sable** '86 thru '95
*36075 **Taurus & Mercury Sable** '96 thru '98
*36078 **Tempo & Mercury Topaz** '84 thru '94
36082 **Thunderbird/Mercury Cougar** '83 thru '88
*36086 **Thunderbird/Mercury Cougar** '89 and '97
36090 **Vans** all V8 Econoline models '69 thru '91
*36094 **Vans** full size '92-'95
*36097 **Windstar Mini-van** '95-'98

## GENERAL MOTORS
*10360 **GM Automatic Transmission Overhaul**
*38005 **Buick Century, Chevrolet Celebrity, Oldsmobile Cutlass Ciera & Pontiac 6000** all models '82 thru '96
*38010 **Buick Regal, Chevrolet Lumina, Oldsmobile Cutlass Supreme & Pontiac Grand Prix** front-wheel drive models '88 thru '95
*38015 **Buick Skyhawk, Cadillac Cimarron, Chevrolet Cavalier, Oldsmobile Firenza & Pontiac J-2000 & Sunbird** '82 thru '94
*38016 **Chevrolet Cavalier & Pontiac Sunfire** '95 thru '98
38020 **Buick Skylark, Chevrolet Citation, Olds Omega, Pontiac Phoenix** '80 thru '85
38025 **Buick Skylark & Somerset, Oldsmobile Achieva & Calais and Pontiac Grand Am** all models '85 thru '95
38030 **Cadillac Eldorado** '71 thru '85, **Seville** '80 thru '85, **Oldsmobile Toronado** '71 thru '85 & **Buick Riviera** '79 thru '85
*38035 **Chevrolet Lumina APV, Olds Silhouette & Pontiac Trans Sport** all models '90 thru '95
**General Motors Full-size Rear-wheel Drive** - see BUICK (19025)

*(Continued on other side)*

---

*\* Listings shown with an asterisk (\*) indicate model coverage as of this printing. These titles will be periodically updated to include later model years - consult your Haynes dealer for more information.*

**Haynes North America, Inc., 861 Lawrence Drive, Newbury Park, CA 91320-1514 • (805) 498-6703**

# Haynes Automotive Manuals (continued)

*NOTE: New manuals are added to this list on a periodic basis. If you do not see a listing for your vehicle, consult your local Haynes dealer for the latest product information.*

## GEO

**Metro** - *see CHEVROLET Sprint (24075)*
**Prizm** - *'85 thru '92 see CHEVY (24060), '93 thru '96 see TOYOTA Corolla (92036)*
*40030 **Storm** all models '90 thru '93
**Tracker** - *see SUZUKI Samurai (90010)*

## GMC

**Safari** - *see CHEVROLET ASTRO (24010)*
**Vans & Pick-ups** - *see CHEVROLET*

## HONDA

42010 **Accord CVCC** all models '76 thru '83
42011 **Accord** all models '84 thru '89
42012 **Accord** all models '90 thru '93
42013 **Accord** all models '94 thru '95
42020 **Civic 1200** all models '73 thru '79
42021 **Civic 1300 & 1500 CVCC** '80 thru '83
42022 **Civic 1500 CVCC** all models '75 thru '79
42023 **Civic** all models '84 thru '91
*42024 **Civic & del Sol** '92 thru '95
*42040 **Prelude CVCC** all models '79 thru '89

## HYUNDAI

*43015 **Excel** all models '86 thru '94

## ISUZU

**Hombre** - *see CHEVROLET S-10 (24071)*
*47017 **Rodeo** '91 thru '97; **Amigo** '89 thru '94; **Honda Passport** '95 thru '97
*47020 **Trooper & Pick-up**, all gasoline models Pick-up, '81 thru '93; Trooper, '84 thru '91

## JAGUAR

*49010 **XJ6** all 6 cyl models '68 thru '86
*49011 **XJ6** all models '88 thru '94
*49015 **XJ12 & XJS** all 12 cyl models '72 thru '85

## JEEP

*50010 **Cherokee, Comanche & Wagoneer Limited** all models '84 thru '96
50020 **CJ** all models '49 thru '86
*50025 **Grand Cherokee** all models '93 thru '98
50029 **Grand Wagoneer & Pick-up** '72 thru '91 Grand Wagoneer '84 thru '91, Cherokee & Wagoneer '72 thru '83, Pick-up '72 thru '88
*50030 **Wrangler** all models '87 thru '95

## LINCOLN

**Navigator** - *see FORD Pick-up (36059)*
59010 **Rear Wheel Drive** all models '70 thru '96

## MAZDA

61010 **GLC Hatchback (rear wheel drive)** '77 thru '83
61011 **GLC (front wheel drive)** '81 thru '85
*61015 **323 & Protogé** '90 thru '97
*61016 **MX-5 Miata** '90 thru '97
*61020 **MPV** all models '89 thru '94
**Navajo** - *see Ford Explorer (36024)*
61030 **Pick-ups** '72 thru '93
**Pick-ups** '94 thru '96 - *see Ford Ranger (36071)*
61035 **RX-7** all models '79 thru '85
*61036 **RX-7** all models '86 thru '91
61040 **626 (rear wheel drive)** all models '79 thru '82
*61041 **626/MX-6 (front wheel drive)** '83 thru '91

## MERCEDES-BENZ

63012 **123 Series Diesel** '76 thru '85
*63015 **190 Series** four-cyl gas models, '84 thru '88
63020 **230/250/280** 6 cyl sohc models '68 thru '72
63025 **280 123 Series** gasoline models '77 thru '81
63030 **350 & 450** all models '71 thru '80

## MERCURY

**See FORD Listing.**

## MG

66010 **MGB** Roadster & GT Coupe '62 thru '80
66015 **MG Midget, Austin Healey Sprite** '58 thru '80

## MITSUBISHI

*68020 **Cordia, Tredia, Galant, Precis & Mirage** '83 thru '93
*68030 **Eclipse, Eagle Talon & Ply. Laser** '90 thru '94
*68040 **Pick-up** '83 thru '96 & **Montero** '83 thru '93

## NISSAN

72010 **300ZX** all models including Turbo '84 thru '89
*72015 **Altima** all models '93 thru '97
*72020 **Maxima** all models '85 thru '91
*72030 **Pick-ups** '80 thru '96 **Pathfinder** '87 thru '95
72040 **Pulsar** all models '83 thru '86
72050 **Sentra** all models '82 thru '94
72051 **Sentra & 200SX** all models '95 thru '98
*72060 **Stanza** all models '82 thru '90

## OLDSMOBILE

*73015 **Cutlass** V6 & V8 gas models '74 thru '88
**For other OLDSMOBILE titles, see BUICK, CHEVROLET or GENERAL MOTORS listing.**

## PLYMOUTH

**For PLYMOUTH titles, see DODGE listing.**

## PONTIAC

79008 **Fiero** all models '84 thru '88
79018 **Firebird** V8 models except Turbo '70 thru '81
79019 **Firebird** all models '82 thru '92
**For other PONTIAC titles, see BUICK, CHEVROLET or GENERAL MOTORS listing.**

## PORSCHE

*80020 **911** except Turbo & Carrera 4 '65 thru '89
80025 **914** all 4 cyl models '69 thru '76
80030 **924** all models including Turbo '76 thru '82
*80035 **944** all models including Turbo '83 thru '89

## RENAULT

**Alliance & Encore** - *see AMC (14020)*

## SAAB

*84010 **900** all models including Turbo '79 thru '88

## SATURN

87010 **Saturn** all models '91 thru '96

## SUBARU

89002 **1100, 1300, 1400 & 1600** '71 thru '79
*89003 **1600 & 1800** 2WD & 4WD '80 thru '94

## SUZUKI

*90010 **Samurai/Sidekick & Geo Tracker** '86 thru '96

## TOYOTA

92005 **Camry** all models '83 thru '91
92006 **Camry** all models '92 thru '96
92015 **Celica Rear Wheel Drive** '71 thru '85
*92020 **Celica Front Wheel Drive** '86 thru '93
92025 **Celica Supra** all models '79 thru '92
92030 **Corolla** all models '75 thru '79
92032 **Corolla** all rear wheel drive models '80 thru '87
92035 **Corolla** all front wheel drive models '84 thru '92
*92036 **Corolla & Geo Prizm** '93 thru '97
92040 **Corolla Tercel** all models '80 thru '82
92045 **Corona** all models '74 thru '82
92050 **Cressida** all models '78 thru '82
92055 **Land Cruiser** FJ40, 43, 45, 55 '68 thru '82
92056 **Land Cruiser** FJ60, 62, 80, FZJ80 '80 thru '96
*92065 **MR2** all models '85 thru '87
92070 **Pick-up** all models '69 thru '78
*92075 **Pick-up** all models '79 thru '95
*92076 **Tacoma** '95 thru '98, **4Runner** '96 thru '98, **& T100** '93 thru '98
*92080 **Previa** all models '91 thru '95
92085 **Tercel** all models '87 thru '94

## TRIUMPH

94007 **Spitfire** all models '62 thru '81
94010 **TR7** all models '75 thru '81

## VW

96008 **Beetle & Karmann Ghia** '54 thru '79
96012 **Dasher** all gasoline models '74 thru '81
*96016 **Rabbit, Jetta, Scirocco, & Pick-up** gas models '74 thru '91 & Convertible '80 thru '92
96017 **Golf & Jetta** all models '93 thru '97
96020 **Rabbit, Jetta & Pick-up** diesel '77 thru '84
96030 **Transporter 1600** all models '68 thru '79
96035 **Transporter 1700, 1800 & 2000** '72 thru '79
96040 **Type 3 1500 & 1600** all models '63 thru '73
96045 **Vanagon** all air-cooled models '80 thru '83

## VOLVO

97010 **120, 130 Series & 1800 Sports** '61 thru '73
97015 **140 Series** all models '66 thru '74
*97020 **240 Series** all models '76 thru '93
97025 **260 Series** all models '75 thru '82
*97040 **740 & 760 Series** all models '82 thru '88

## TECHBOOK MANUALS

10205 **Automotive Computer Codes**
10210 **Automotive Emissions Control Manual**
10215 **Fuel Injection Manual, 1978 thru 1985**
10220 **Fuel Injection Manual, 1986 thru 1996**
10225 **Holley Carburetor Manual**
10230 **Rochester Carburetor Manual**
10240 **Weber/Zenith/Stromberg/SU Carburetors**
10305 **Chevrolet Engine Overhaul Manual**
10310 **Chrysler Engine Overhaul Manual**
10320 **Ford Engine Overhaul Manual**
10330 **GM and Ford Diesel Engine Repair Manual**
10340 **Small Engine Repair Manual**
10345 **Suspension, Steering & Driveline Manual**
10355 **Ford Automatic Transmission Overhaul**
10360 **GM Automatic Transmission Overhaul**
10405 **Automotive Body Repair & Painting**
10410 **Automotive Brake Manual**
10415 **Automotive Detaiing Manual**
10420 **Automotive Eelectrical Manual**
10425 **Automotive Heating & Air Conditioning**
10430 **Automotive Reference Manual & Dictionary**
10435 **Automotive Tools Manual**
10440 **Used Car Buying Guide**
10445 **Welding Manual**
10450 **ATV Basics**

## SPANISH MANUALS

98903 **Reparación de Carrocería & Pintura**
98905 **Códigos Automotrices de la Computadora**
98910 **Frenos Automotriz**
98915 **Inyección de Combustible 1986 al 1994**
99040 **Chevrolet & GMC Camionetas** '67 al '87 Incluye Suburban, Blazer & Jimmy '67 al '91
99041 **Chevrolet & GMC Camionetas** '88 al '95 Incluye Suburban '92 al '95, Blazer & Jimmy '92 al '94, Tahoe y Yukon '95
99042 **Chevrolet & GMC Camionetas Cerradas** '68 al '95
99055 **Dodge Caravan & Plymouth Voyager** '84 al '95
99075 **Ford Camionetas y Bronco** '80 al '94
99077 **Ford Camionetas Cerradas** '69 al '91
99083 **Ford Modelos de Tamaño Grande** '75 al '87
99088 **Ford Modelos de Tamaño Mediano** '75 al '86
99091 **Ford Taurus & Mercury Sable** '86 al '95
99095 **GM Modelos de Tamaño Grande** '70 al '90
99100 **GM Modelos de Tamaño Mediano** '70 al '88
99110 **Nissan Camionetas** '80 al '96, **Pathfinder** '87 al '95
99118 **Nissan Sentra** '82 al '94
99125 **Toyota Camionetas y 4Runner** '79 al '95

---

Over 100 Haynes motorcycle manuals also available

5-98

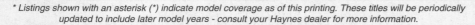

**Haynes North America, Inc., 861 Lawrence Drive, Newbury Park, CA 91320-1514 • (805) 498-6703**